CICS for the COBOL Programmer

Part 1: An Introductory Course

CICS for the COBOL Programmer

Part 1: An Introductory Course

Second Edition

Doug Lowe

Mike Murach & Associates, Inc.

2560 West Shaw Lane, Suite 101, Fresno, California 93711-2765 • (209) 275-3335

Acknowledgements

Thanks to Marjorie Robertson and Mike Fidel of Micro Focus Inc. and Kathy Magenheim of XDB Systems, Inc. for providing technical assistance and the software used to develop the application programs in this book.

Editorial team:	Steve Eckols
	Anne Prince
Production/Design:	Steve Ehlers

Related books

CICS for the COBOL Programmer, Part 2: An Advanced Course, Doug Lowe
The CICS Programmer's Desk Reference, Doug Lowe

Structured ANS COBOL, Part 1: A Course for Novices, Mike Murach & Paul Noll
Structured ANS COBOL, Part 2: An Advanced Course, Mike Murach & Paul Noll
Structured COBOL Methods, Paul Noll

VS COBOL II: A Guide for Programmers and Managers, Anne Prince

VSAM: Access Method Services and Application Programming, Doug Lowe

MVS TSO, Part 1: Concepts and ISPF, Doug Lowe
MVS TSO, Part 2: Commands and Procedures, Doug Lowe

20 19 18 17 16 15 14 13 12 11 10 9 8 7 6

ISBN: 0-911625-60-7

Library of Congress Cataloging-in-Publication Data

Lowe, Doug.
  CICS for the COBOL programmer / Doug Lowe. -- 2nd ed.
    p. cm.
  Includes index.
  Contents: Pt. 1. An introductory course
  ISBN 0-911625-60-7 (pbk. : v. 1 : alk. paper)
    1. COBOL (Computer program language) 2. CICS (Computer system)
I. Title.
QA76.73.C25L67   1992
005.13'3--dc20   92-17814
                                                  CIP

Contents

■   **V**

Preface

Does it make sense to learn CICS in the 1990's?

That's a good question. It certainly made sense to learn CICS in the 1980's. When the first edition of this book was published in 1984, IBM totally dominated the computer industry, and CICS was IBM's flagship product for supporting on-line applications. At 15 years old, CICS was already a mature product, with more than 10,000 licenses sold worldwide.

The computer industry has changed dramatically since 1984. But, as they say, the more things change, the more they stay the same. Whether or not IBM continues to dominate the computer industry is debatable. But the role of CICS is not. CICS clearly dominates the world of on-line applications. In fact, 490 of the Fortune 500 support their critical transaction-processing applications with CICS. IBM estimates that there are almost a million CICS programmers. And more than a billion lines of production CICS code support nearly 15 million CICS terminals.

CICS is not just for today's on-line applications, either. It is the ideal platform for the truly cooperative applications of the future. Versions of CICS are available, or will be soon, for a wide variety of operating systems besides mainframe MVS and VSE: OS/2, DOS, Windows, OS/400 (for AS/400 systems), and AIX (IBM's version of Unix).

So yes, it does make sense to learn CICS in the 1990's. And this book will help you do it.

What this book does

This book, the first in a two-part series, teaches you a basic subset of CICS command-level programming in COBOL. It shows you how to program for 3270 terminals using basic mapping support, how to process VSAM files using file control commands, and many other programming techniques. The second book in this series covers advanced CICS programming features like alternate indexing, browsing, accessing IMS and DB2 databases, and more.

If you take a quick look at the contents, you'll see that I've organized the chapters of this book into four sections. The three chapters in section 1 provide the background information you need to fully understand CICS programming. Here, you'll learn the basics of on-line applications, terminal networks, and CICS facilities. Then, the chapters in section 2 present a subset of CICS programming. Here, you'll learn how all of the elements of CICS programming work together to create a functioning program. Then, the chapters in section 3 present three model programs from a typical application. These programs will help you see the programming techniques presented in section 2 in a variety of realistic situations. Finally, the chapters in section 4 present techniques for testing and debugging a CICS program.

Why this book is effective

Learning CICS is a challenge because it requires you to grasp a number of difficult concepts all at once. I carefully planned this book in a way that integrates the presentation of those concepts, always showing how each element relates to the whole. In contrast, most books and courses present individual CICS elements separately, without integration. No wonder so many people are baffled by CICS.

In addition, there are three other reasons this book is effective. First, I spent much time selecting the content of this book. In doing so, I kept my sights on a usable—and teachable—subset of CICS. Many CICS books and courses fail at this point. They present just about every element of CICS, without regard for what's important and what isn't. In this book, you won't learn every feature of CICS. But you will learn the most useful elements. And you'll be well prepared to learn the advanced CICS elements presented in the second book of this series.

Second, I emphasize the use of coding models in this book. The programming examples not only illustrate CICS language elements, but also serve as models for similar programs you'll write on the job. In addition, I've included models for common COBOL routines and BMS map definitions. I think your productivity will increase significantly if you use these models.

Third, I stress careful program design. Although design is critical to the success of any programming project, few courses or books deal adequately with how to design a CICS program. In fact, most don't say anything about design at all, except maybe to advise against the use of PERFORM statements for the sake of efficiency. Unfortunately, you just can't design a CICS program using the same mindset that works for designing batch programs. As a result, this book teaches an altogether different approach to design, one that takes into account the considerations unique to CICS.

Who this book is for

This book is for anyone who wants to learn how to write application COBOL programs in a CICS environment. Although it does not assume any prior CICS experience, it *does* assume an understanding of elementary COBOL. If you work as a COBOL programmer or have taken a COBOL course, you probably have all the background you need. If not, you can learn the COBOL you need to know from *Structured ANS COBOL, Part 1* and *Part 2*, by Mike Murach and Paul Noll. You can order these books from Mike Murach & Associates using the order form at the back of this book.

If you're using the VS COBOL II compiler, you may want to pick up some additional background from *VS COBOL II: A Guide for Programmers and Managers*, by Anne Prince. And if you'd like some VSAM background, you can use my book, *VSAM: Access Method Services and Application Programming*. These titles are also available from Mike Murach & Associates and can be ordered using the form at the back of the book.

A note about CICS versions

As I write this book, IBM supports five versions of CICS for MVS users: 1.7, 2.1, 3.1.1, 3.2.1, and 3.3. For VSE users, two versions are supported: 1.7 and 2.1. (Service for CICS 1.7 under MVS will be discontinued in December of 1992, but support for CICS 1.7 under VSE will continue.) For OS/2 users, the current version is 1.2. (Don't be confused by the version number used for CICS OS/2; it's unrelated to the version numbers used for mainframe CICS.)

The CICS elements presented in this book will work for any of these CICS versions. With each new CICS release, IBM adds new application programming features. However, these new features are usually minor. The last major overhaul of the application programming interface came with version 1.7, which introduced a new method of condition checking that has a dramatic effect on the overall structure of a CICS program. All of the programs in this book use the new condition handling technique, but the older technique (which is still allowable) is presented in chapter 8.

A note about COBOL versions

IBM also currently supports three COBOL compilers: OS/VS COBOL, VS COBOL II, and COBOL/370. OS/VS COBOL (and its VSE equivalent DOS/VS COBOL) is maintained mostly because of the huge inventory of OS/VS COBOL programs in production. VS COBOL II implements the additions to the COBOL language that were standardized by ANSI in 1985. IBM's newest COBOL compiler, COBOL/370, is meant to replace VS COBOL II. It introduces a few new COBOL features (such as intrinsic functions) as well as a new run-time library and debugger. Otherwise, COBOL/370 differs little from VS COBOL II.

The sample programs presented in the body of this book were developed for Release 3 of VS COBOL II. Because so many shops still use OS/VS COBOL, however, I've included OS/VS COBOL versions of the programs in appendix D. I considered restricting my use of VS COBOL II features (such as the EVALUATE statement and scope terminators like END-IF) to make the programs compatible with either compiler, but in the end decided against that option. So the VS COBOL II programs fully utilize the features of VS COBOL II.

Conclusion

I'm confident that this book will help you learn CICS as efficiently and as effectively as possible. But I'd love to hear any comments or suggestions you might have. Please feel free to use the postage-paid comment form at the back of this book. I look forward to hearing from you.

Doug Lowe
Fresno, California
May, 1992

Section 1

Preliminary concepts

Before you can start learning the details of CICS command-level COBOL programming, you need to understand some basic concepts. As a result, this section presents the minimum background you need before you can learn how to write a command-level program.

Chapter 1 introduces you to on-line systems. Here, you'll learn about the basic types of on-line programs you'll develop under CICS. And you'll learn about four basic problems you need to recognize as you develop CICS applications.

Chapters 2 and 3 describe what makes up the CICS environment. Chapter 2 introduces you to the components of a terminal network that supports CICS. Then, chapter 3 describes what CICS is and how it relates to the operating system and your application programs.

If you've had some experience with on-line programming in general or with CICS in particular, you may already know some of the material in this section. If so, you can use these chapters as a review.

An introduction to on-line systems

An *on-line system* (sometimes called an *interactive system*) is a collection of computer programs that lets end users access mainframe computers via terminal devices. In the early days of computing, on-line systems were rare. Instead, most computer applications used *batch processing*. In a batch processing system, transactions are accumulated into groups, or batches, before they are processed. For example, a full day's orders might be manually collected and transferred to machine-readable media such as punched cards or magnetic tape before being processed by the batch system.

Today, on-line systems are the norm. In an on-line system, transactions are not batched before they are processed. Instead, users enter transactions one at a time into the on-line system through terminals. As each transaction is entered, it is immediately edited, errors are corrected, and files are updated.

On-line systems have many advantages over batch systems, but the biggest advantage of on-line systems is their responsiveness. In a batch system, turn-around time is usually measured in days. For example, a user might submit a batch of transactions on Monday. Those transactions would be keypunched on Tuesday and scheduled to run on Wednesday. The results of the run might be returned on Thursday. Then, the user must check the output and resubmit any transactions that were keypunched incorrectly.

In contrast, response time for an on-line system is measured in seconds. The intermediate step of keypunching the data is eliminated. Scheduling isn't necessary because the on-line system is available throughout the day. And if the user enters incorrect data, the on-line system displays an error message, and the user can immediately correct the error.

Most on-line systems on IBM mainframe computers rely on the software product *CICS* (*Customer Information Control System*). This book introduces you to CICS and teaches you how to develop effective CICS programs in COBOL. But first, you need to understand the different types of programs that make up a typical on-line system, as well as some of the unique considerations that on-line application designers must deal with.

A sample on-line application

To help you understand on-line applications, figures 1-1 through 1-4 present screens displayed by four on-line application programs that run under CICS: a menu program, an inquiry program, a file maintenance program, and a data entry program. These four programs represent the most common types of on-line programs. Later in this book, you'll see the source code for each of them.

The menu program

A *menu program* displays a list of functions that are available and lets the user pick which one he or she wishes to perform. The menu program then invokes the appropriate application program to perform the selected function. When the selected program has completed its processing, it invokes the menu program so the list of functions is displayed again.

Figure 1-1 shows the screen displayed by the menu program for the sample application. As you can see, it presents three choices: display customer information, maintain customer information, and enter orders. The user selects one of these functions by entering the number 1, 2, or 3 in the Action field and pressing the Enter key. Or, the user can leave the menu by pressing the F3 key or the F12 key.

Of course, a menu program in an actual production system would probably include more than three selections. In addition, some menu

The menu program displays a list of choices. The user selects one by typing the appropriate number in the Action field, then pressing the Enter key.

```
MENMAP1              Master Menu

Select an action.  Then press Enter.

Action . . . . _  1.  Display customer information
                  2.  Maintain customer information
                  3.  Enter orders












F3=Exit    F12=Cancel
```

Figure 1-1   The screen displayed by a typical menu program

selections may lead to other menu programs rather than directly to application programs. In other words, menus can be nested to organize functions into a hierarchy. Nevertheless, the simple menu program in figure 1-1 illustrates the basic functions of a typical menu program.

The inquiry program

An *inquiry program* provides a response to a user's inquiry. Figure 1-2 shows three screens from an inquiry program that displays information for a selected customer. In the first screen, the program is waiting for the user to enter a customer number. In part 2 of figure 1-2, you can see the customer number the user typed. When the user presses the Enter key, the program retrieves and displays the data for customer 400001, as shown in the part 3 of figure 1-2.

Inquiry programs can be simple, retrieving one record from a master file and displaying it on a single screen, or quite complex, retrieving several records from several files. The program in figure 1-2 retrieves data from just one file. The most complicated inquiry program I've written retrieves data from 13 files and displays it with 29 different screen formats. Fortunately, most inquiry programs aren't that complex.

Part 1

The inquiry program displays its initial screen.

```
INQMAP1              Customer Inquiry

Type a customer number.   Then press Enter.

Customer number. . . . . _____

Name and address . . . :













F3=Exit    F12=Cancel
```

Part 2

The user enters customer number 400001 and presses the Enter key.

```
INQMAP1              Customer Inquiry

Type a customer number.   Then press Enter.

Customer number. . . . . 400001

Name and address . . . :













F3=Exit    F12=Cancel
```

Figure 1-2   The operation of a typical inquiry program

Part 3

The program retrieves
the data for customer
400001 and displays it
on the screen.

```
  INQMAP1               Customer Inquiry

  Type a customer number.   Then press Enter.

  Customer number. . . . .  400001

  Name and address . . . :  MCDONALD
                            KEITH
                            4501 W MOCKINGBIRD
                            DALLAS                TX 75209










  F3=Exit    F12=Cancel
```

Figure 1-2   The operation of a typical inquiry program (continued)

The file maintenance program

A *file maintenance program* updates a file by adding, changing, or deleting
records. Figure 1-3 illustrates the operation of a file maintenance
program that lets the user maintain a customer master file. Part 1 shows
the first screen displayed by the program. It asks the user to type a
customer number, then select which action to perform (add a new
customer, change an existing customer, or delete an existing customer).
In part 2, you can see that the user entered customer number 400002 and
selected action 2 to change an existing customer.

In part 3, the program has retrieved the record for customer 400002
and displayed it on the screen so the user can make any necessary
changes. Part 4 shows the change made by the user. When the user
pressed the Enter key, the program updated the customer record and
redisplayed its initial screen, as part 5 shows. Here, the message
"Customer record updated" appears near the bottom of the screen to
confirm that the change was made.

Part 1

The file maintenance
program displays its
initial screen.

```
MNTMAP1             Customer Maintenance

Type a customer number.  Then select an action and press Enter.

Customer number. . . . .  _____

Action . . . . . . . . . _ 1. Add a new customer
                           2. Change an existing customer
                           3. Delete an existing customer

















F3=Exit    F12=Cancel
```

Part 2

The user types
customer number
400002 and selects
action 2 to change an
existing customer, then
presses the Enter key.

```
MNTMAP1             Customer Maintenance

Type a customer number.  Then select an action and press Enter.

Customer number. . . . . 400002

Action . . . . . . . . . 2 1. Add a new customer
                           2. Change an existing customer
                           3. Delete an existing customer

















F3=Exit    F12=Cancel
```

Figure 1-3   The operation of a typical file maintenance program

Part 3

The file maintenance program retrieves the data for customer 400002 and displays it so the user can make any necessary corrections.

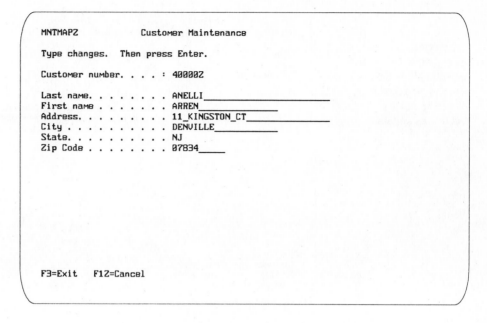

```
MNTMAP2          Customer Maintenance

Type changes.  Then press Enter.

Customer number. . . . : 400002

Last name. . . . . . . . ANELLI_____
First name . . . . . . . ARREN_____
Address. . . . . . . . . 11_KINGSTON_CT_____
City . . . . . . . . . . DENVILLE_____
State. . . . . . . . . . NJ
Zip Code . . . . . . . . 07834_____




F3=Exit    F12=Cancel
```

Part 4

The user types the address change for customer 400002, then presses the Enter key.

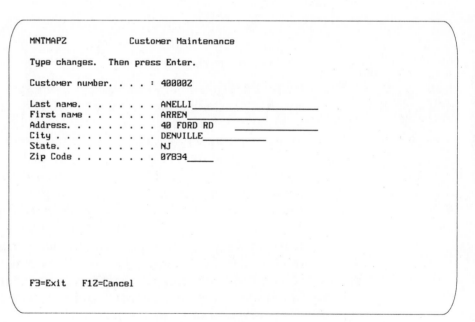

```
MNTMAP2          Customer Maintenance

Type changes.  Then press Enter.

Customer number. . . . : 400002

Last name. . . . . . . . ANELLI_____
First name . . . . . . . ARREN_____
Address. . . . . . . . . 40 FORD RD       _____
City . . . . . . . . . . DENVILLE_____
State. . . . . . . . . . NJ
Zip Code . . . . . . . . 07834_____




F3=Exit    F12=Cancel
```

Figure 1-3   The operation of a typical file maintenance program (continued)

Part 5

The program updates the customer record and redisplays its initial screen with a message indicating that the record was updated.

```
MNTMAP1              Customer Maintenance

Type a customer number.  Then select an action and press Enter.

Customer number. . . . . _____

Action . . . . . . . . . _ 1. Add a new customer
                           2. Change an existing customer
                           3. Delete an existing customer




Customer record updated.
F3=Exit    F12=Cancel
```

Figure 1-3 The operation of a typical file maintenance program (continued)

The data entry program

Figure 1-4 shows several screens from a program that accepts orders and writes them to a file of order transactions. This is an example of a *data entry program*. Data entry programs are often the most critical and the most complicated programs in an on-line system.

Part 1 of figure 1-4 shows the screen initially displayed by the program. It asks the user to enter the details for an order: the customer number, purchase order number, and the product code and quantity for each item ordered. In part 2, you can see that the user entered an order from customer 400001 with three line items. When the user pressed the Enter key, the program retrieved information from the customer and product files and displayed the screen shown in part 3. Here, the user can verify that he or she entered the correct customer and product codes by examining the customer name and address and the product descriptions. In addition, the program has extended each line item by multiplying the net price by the quantity ordered, and it has calculated the total for the invoice.

The user was satisfied with the order in part 3 and pressed the Enter key without making any corrections. As a result, the program posted the order and redisplayed its initial screen as shown in part 4. Here, the message "Order posted" appears near the bottom of the screen to confirm that the order was posted.

Part 1

The data entry program displays its initial screen.

```
ORDMAP1              Order Entry

Type order details.  Then press Enter.

Customer number . . . _____        Customer:
P.O. number . . . . . _____


Prod code     Qty  Description              List        Net       Amount
_____      ____                          _____
_____      ____                          _____
_____      ____                          _____
_____      ____                          _____
_____      ____                          _____
_____      ____                          _____
_____      ____                          _____
_____      ____                          _____

                                         Invoice total:

F3=Exit    F12=Cancel
```

Part 2

The user types the information for an order for customer 400001, then presses the Enter key.

```
ORDMAP1              Order Entry

Type order details.  Then press Enter.

Customer number . . . 400001        Customer:
P.O. number . . . . . AB-3945___


Prod code     Qty  Description              List        Net       Amount
3000-002__    1___                          _____
3100-001__    4___                          _____
3100-002__    2___                          _____
_____      ____                          _____
_____      ____                          _____
_____      ____                          _____
_____      ____                          _____
_____      ____                          _____
_____      ____                          _____

                                         Invoice total:

F3=Exit    F12=Cancel
```

Figure 1-4   The operation of a typical data entry program

Part 3

The program retrieves
the data from the
customer and product
files, calculates the
amount for each line
item and the invoice
total, and displays the
results so the user can
confirm the order.

```
ORDMAP1             Order Entry

Press Enter to post this order.   Or press F4 to enter corrections.

Customer number . . . 400001       Customer: MCDONALD
P.O. number . . . . . AB-3945                KEITH
                                             4501 W MOCKINGBIRD
                                             DALLAS           TX 75209

Prod code      Qty  Description          List      Net       Amount
3000-002        1   ETHERNET CARD PLUS   599.00    599.00    599.00
3100-001        4   2400 BAUD MODEM      229.00    229.00    916.00
3100-002        2   2400 MNP-5 MODEM     249.00    249.00    498.00




                                        Invoice total:       2,013.00


F3=Exit    F4=Change    F12=Cancel
```

Part 4

The program redisplays
its initial screen along
with a message
indicating that the order
was posted.

```
ORDMAP1             Order Entry

Type order details.   Then press Enter.

Customer number . . . _____       Customer:
P.O. number . . . . . _____


Prod code      Qty  Description          List      Net       Amount
_____       ____                                _____
_____       ____                                _____
_____       ____                                _____
_____       ____                                _____
_____       ____                                _____
_____       ____                                _____
_____       ____                                _____
_____       ____                                _____
_____       ____                                _____

                                        Invoice total:
Order posted.
F3=Exit    F12=Cancel
```

Figure 1-4   The operation of a typical data entry program (continued)

Part 5

The user enters an
order for customer
512003.

```
ORDMAP1              Order Entry

Type order details.  Then press Enter.

Customer number . . . 512003     Customer:
P.O. number . . . . .  _____


Prod code    Qty  Description                    List         Net        Amount
3200-001__   4___                                          _____
_____   ____                                           _____
_____   ____                                           _____
_____   ____                                           _____
_____   ____                                           _____
_____   ____                                           _____
_____   ____                                           _____
_____   ____                                           _____
_____   ____                                           _____

                                           Invoice total:

Order posted.
F3=Exit   F12=Cancel
```

Part 6

The program displays
an error message
indicating that customer
512003 doesn't exist.

```
ORDMAP1              Order Entry

Type corrections.  Then press Enter.

Customer number . . . 512003     Customer:
P.O. number . . . . .  _____


Prod code    Qty  Description                    List         Net        Amount
3200-001      4   4 PORT PASSIVE HUB            35.99        35.99       143.96
_____   ____                                           _____
_____   ____                                           _____
_____   ____                                           _____
_____   ____                                           _____
_____   ____                                           _____
_____   ____                                           _____
_____   ____                                           _____
_____   ____                                           _____

                                           Invoice total:                143.96

That customer does not exist
F3=Exit   F12=Cancel
```

Figure 1-4   The operation of a typical data entry program (continued)

What if the user enters incorrect data? For example, what happens if the user enters an incorrect customer number? Look at parts 5 and 6 of figure 1-4. In part 5, the user entered an order for customer 512003, which doesn't exist. In part 6, you can see that the program responded by displaying an error message near the bottom of the screen and instructing the user to correct the error. Validating input data and displaying appropriate error messages are essential functions of any data entry program.

On-line system considerations

Now that you understand the types of programs found in an on-line system, you should be aware of some of the special considerations you must contend with when you design and develop these programs. In this section, I'll cover four of these considerations: ease of use, performance, file integrity, and security.

Ease of use

Because the users of on-line programs have a variety of skill and experience levels, those programs must be designed and implemented with ease of use in mind. One of the best ways to achieve that is to adopt a consistent approach to the way programs interact with users. At the minimum, all of the programs in a particular application should have a consistent user interface. Ideally, all of the applications within an installation should follow the same interface guidelines as well.

IBM promotes a user interface standard called *CUA*, which stands for *Common User Access*. CUA provides three distinct user interface models. All of the programs in this book follow CUA's *Entry Model*, which is designed specifically for non-programmable terminals like the ones most often used for CICS applications. The most advanced CUA standard, called the *Graphical Model*, is designed for programmable workstations such as personal computers. The Presentation Manager component of IBM's advanced operating system for PCs, called *OS/2*, uses the Graphical Model. It includes features such as pull-down menus, pop-up dialog boxes, and scroll bars. The intermediate model, called the *Text Subset of the Graphical Model,* provides a standard way of implementing these elements of the Graphical Model using non- programmable terminals.

CUA's Entry Model is not difficult to learn. If you'll look at the screens in figures 1-1 through 1-4, you can see many elements of the CUA Entry Model. For example, the use of leading periods to identify data entry fields is a part of the CUA Entry Model. And the Action field in part 1 of figure 1-3 is what CUA calls a "Single Choice Selection Field." The exact layout of the choices that are allowed for this field is dictated by the CUA Entry Model standard.

Performance

Performance is a critical consideration for on-line programs. Performance for on-line systems is measured in terms of *response time,* which is simply the amount of time a user must wait while a transaction is being processed. Most on-line applications should provide a response time of just a few seconds. Unfortunately, that's often a difficult goal to reach.

Many factors affect response time. Among the most critical factors are the total number of programs running within the CICS system, the amount of data sent over the communications network between the terminals and the host computer, and the amount of disk I/O required. Some of these factors are beyond your control as an application programmer, but some of them are your direct responsibility. In this book, I'll teach you how to use a few basic programming techniques that can have a dramatic effect on program efficiency.

File integrity

A batch program typically has complete control of the files it uses, so there's no chance of another program interfering with its processing. In an on-line system, however, many terminal users use the system simultaneously, and all must have access to the files they require. As a result, when an on-line system lets users share files, it must coordinate all file updates to insure *file integrity.* In other words, the on-line system must insure that two users aren't allowed to update the same record at the same time.

On-line systems do this by locking records that are in the process of being updated so other users can't access them. Unfortunately, the locking mechanisms CICS provides are often inadequate to insure complete file integrity. So as a programmer, you often have to consider file integrity issues when you develop programs that update files. You'll learn the programming techniques needed to provide file integrity later in this book.

Security

In a batch system, computer *security* is relatively easy to maintain because the only access to the computer is the computer room. However, in an on-line system, terminals are located in many places, and security is a problem.

The main security technique used in today's on-line systems is the *logon procedure.* Unless a terminal user completes the logon procedure, the system prevents him from using the computer. To complete the logon procedure, the user must enter his name and a *password* known only to him. If the name doesn't appear in the list of authorized users, or if he enters the password incorrectly, he can't access the system.

In addition to the logon procedure, most on-line systems have a multi-level security system that lets some users access certain files and programs, while other users have access to other files and programs. In other words, each user is allowed to access only those files and programs he's authorized to use. For example, an order entry clerk must have access to order processing files but probably doesn't need to have access to payroll files.

CICS provides rudimentary security features, and many CICS installations use other security management systems that provide even tighter control. In any event, although security is an important consideration in any on-line system, it doesn't affect the way you develop application programs. So I won't discuss CICS security features in this book, other than to show you how to use the CICS logon procedure.

Discussion   If your programming experience has been limited to batch systems, I think you can now appreciate the complexities on-line systems present. Obviously, to develop programs for an on-line system, you need to know how they differ from the traditional edit, update, and report programs of a batch system. But, just as important, you need to know how the hardware components of an on-line system differ from those of a batch system. So, in the next chapter, I'll give you the hardware background you need to develop CICS programs.

Terms

on-line system
interactive system
batch processing
CICS
Customer Information Control System
menu program
inquiry program
file maintenance program
data entry program
CUA
Common User Access
Entry Model
Graphical Model
Text Subset of the Graphical Model
performance
response time
file integrity
security
logon procedure
password

Objectives

1. Describe the basic differences between batch and on-line systems and discuss the advantages on-line systems have over batch systems.

2. Describe the four major types of on-line programs.

3. Describe the following considerations for on-line systems:
    ease of use
    performance
    file integrity
    security

Chapter 2

An introduction to terminal networks for CICS

A *network* allows users at *terminals* to access a *host computer*. The terminals themselves can be *local terminals* (that is, terminals that are near the host computer, usually in the same building). Or, they can be *remote terminals* (terminals that are some distance from the host computer, usually not in the same building and perhaps not in the same city). Either way, the terminals used most often for CICS applications are members of IBM's 3270 family of terminals.

In this chapter, I'll begin by presenting the components of the 3270 Information Display System. Then, I'll describe how 3270 terminals can be connected to a local host computer. Finally, I'll explain how remote 3270 terminals are connected to a host computer. When you complete this chapter, you won't know everything there is to know about terminal networks. But you'll know enough about the basic components of a network to develop CICS applications.

The 3270 Information Display System
The 3270 family of terminal devices has been the standard for IBM mainframe computers since its introduction in 1971. Although other types of terminals can be used with CICS, 3270 devices are by far the

most popular. So odds are you'll be developing CICS applications that are designed to work with 3270 terminals.

The *3270 Information Display System* is not a single terminal, but rather a system of terminals (officially called *display stations*), printers, and controllers. Figure 2-1 illustrates these components. As you can see, several display stations and printers can be connected to a single controller. The controller, in turn, is connected to the host computer system, either by a direct cable connection or by a remote communication link.

3270 display stations   A 3270 display station consists of a CRT monitor, a keyboard, and an electronics unit. For many years, the standard 3270 terminal was the 3278, which had a monitor capable of displaying 24 lines of 80 characters each. In the 1980's, IBM phased out this terminal and replaced it with smaller, lighter, and more reliable models. These terminals have the same basic display characteristics (24 lines of 80 characters each), but have better designed keyboard layouts.

3278-compatible terminals have monochrome displays. In other words, they display characters in a single color (usually green, white, or amber) against a dark background. In contrast, a 3279 display station can display characters in seven different colors. Like the 3278, IBM phased out the original 3279 color terminal, replacing it with newer models that have similar characteristics.

In addition to color, 3270 display stations can be configured with many different options. For example, you can configure a 3270 with a specialized keyboard for special applications or foreign languages. Other options include a light pen, extended highlighting that lets the terminal display underlined, blinking, or reversed characters, and graphics capabilities. Although these options are useful for specialized purposes, most CICS application programs are developed to operate on 24x80 monochrome or color terminals. So in this book, we'll concentrate on writing applications for these terminals.

3270 printers   In addition to display stations, printers can be attached to a 3270 controller. IBM offers a variety of 3270 printers, including dot-matrix printers that print up to 400 characters per second, line printers that print up to 2,000 lines per minute, and high-speed laser printers.

You should be aware that there's little distinction between a display station and a printer as far as CICS is concerned. When output is directed to a terminal, it's displayed at the screen if the terminal is a display station. If the terminal is a printer, the output is printed. The major difference is, of course, that printers cannot accept input data, while display stations can.

Since programming for 3270 printers can be complicated, I won't cover it in this book. You'll learn how to develop programs that direct output to a 3270 printer in *Part 2: An Advanced Course.*

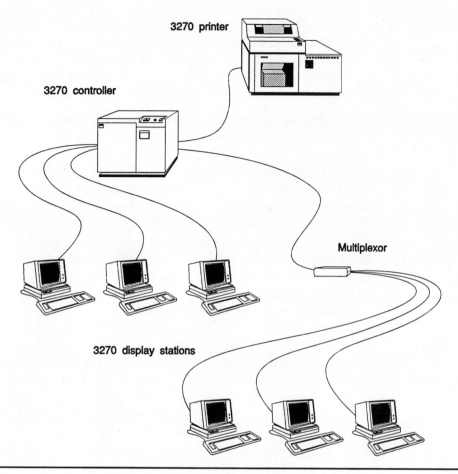

3270 printer

3270 controller

Multiplexor

3270 display stations

Figure 2-1   Components of a 3270 Information Display System

3270 controllers   As I mentioned earlier, several 3270 display stations and printers can be connected to a *3270 controller*, which in turn is connected to the host computer. For many years, the standard 3270 controller was the 3274. Although many 3274 controllers are still in use, IBM has replaced it with newer control units. Depending on the controller model, as many as 32 display stations and printers can be connected to the controller.

Display stations and printers are connected to controllers via standard coaxial cables. In many cases, the controller is in the same room as the terminals that are connected to it. In that case, it's convenient to route a separate cable from the controller to each terminal. However, terminals can also be located as far as 1,000 feet from the controller. In that case, it's not uncommon to use a *multiplexor* to connect as many as eight display stations or printers to the controller via a single coaxial cable. Three of the six display stations in figure 2-1 are connected to the controller via a multiplexor.

From a CICS programmer's standpoint, it doesn't matter what kind of controller or cabling arrangement is used to connect a user's terminal to the controller and host computer. As long as the connection is properly made, CICS allows your application programs to access the terminal.

3270-compatible devices and emulators   Because of the enormous popularity of the 3270 system, many manufacturers besides IBM offer compatible terminals, printers, and controllers. And most minicomputers and microcomputers can run *emulator programs* that allow them to behave as if they were 3270 devices. Because of cost advantages and additional benefits, it's becoming more and more common to see such products in use in 3270 networks.

One common type of emulation lets an IBM-compatible PC running under DOS or OS/2 emulate 3270 terminals. To do this, you must install a special card in the PC that lets you connect the PC to a 3270 controller. And you must run special software that provides for the terminal emulation. Once the hardware and software is in place, however, you have all of the benefits of a personal computer coupled with the benefits of terminal access to the mainframe host. In addition, you can *download* data files from the mainframe to the PC, and you can *upload* files from the PC to the mainframe.

Another common type of emulation allows ASCII terminals to emulate 3270 terminals. *ASCII terminals* are the most popular terminal types for non-IBM mainframe computers and minicomputers, such as DEC VAX systems and UNIX systems. The most common ASCII terminals are the DEC VT-100 and the IBM 3101.

There are two main differences between ASCII terminals and 3270 terminals. First, they use the ASCII character code rather than the EBCDIC code used by 3270s. So data must be converted between the two formats. Second, ASCII terminals are character-oriented devices that normally display data one line at a time, scrolling the display when necessary as each new line is displayed. In contrast, 3270 terminals are full-screen oriented. In other words, they generally format and display an entire screen full of data at once. Fortunately, IBM's newer 3270 control units can be equipped with options that allow them to support ASCII terminals as if they were 3270 terminals. So your application programs don't need to deal with these differences.

Local host connections   The way 3270 terminals are connected to a host computer depends on whether the host computer is local or remote. A *local host* is generally in the same building as the terminal controller. Usually, the controller must be located within 200 feet of the host computer's CPU. If fiber-optic cables are used, the control unit can be as far as five miles away from the CPU.

Local host processor

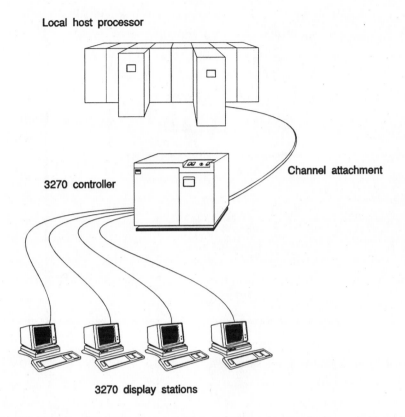

Channel attachment

3270 controller

3270 display stations

Figure 2-2   How 3270 devices are connected to a local host

Figure 2-2 shows a local terminal attachment. Here, you can see that the 3270 controller is attached by cable to one of the CPU's channels. (A *channel* is the primary I/O path for IBM mainframe processors.) Each channel on the CPU can be connected to as many as eight 3270 controllers. With a maximum of 32 terminals per controller, this means that each CPU channel can serve as many as 256 local 3270 terminals.

Software requirements for local terminal connection   While the hardware required to attach local terminals is simple enough, the software required to support those terminals is anything but simple. Figure 2-3 shows that three types of software are required to support local terminals. First, the host computer requires an *operating system* to manage its jobs and resources. For CICS users, the operating system can be MVS (including MVS/XA and MVS/ESA), VSE, or VM.

These operating systems do not directly support application programs that use 3270 terminals. Instead, a *host subsystem* is required to control the execution of terminal-based application programs. This book, of course, deals with CICS. Other host subsystems that let you execute terminal-based application programs are IMS/DC, TSO, and VM/CMS.

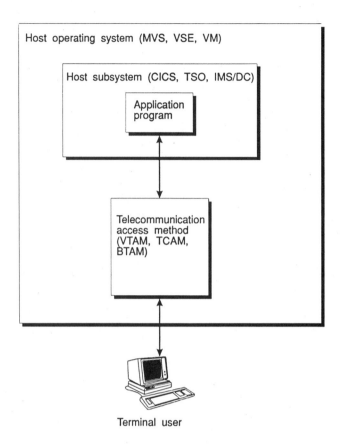

Figure 2-3   Host software required to support a network of 3270 terminals

CICS is the only one of these subsystems that can be run under any of the three main operating systems (MVS, VSE, and VM).

Host subsystems, in turn, communicate with terminals via a *telecommunication access method*, which handles the details required to manage the terminal network. The most sophisticated and most commonly used access method is *ACF/VTAM*. *BTAM* is the simplest and oldest of the access methods and is rarely used today except for very small terminal networks. *TCAM* isn't as sophisticated as VTAM, but can be more efficient for extremely large terminal networks. So it is occasionally used. Some installations use TCAM and VTAM together.

Remote host connections   When 3270 terminals are connected to a remote host, additional hardware and software components are required. Figure 2-4 shows a typical remote terminal connection. Here, as before, 3270 display stations are connected to a 3270 controller via direct cable connection. In this case, the 3270 controller is a small desktop unit rather than the larger

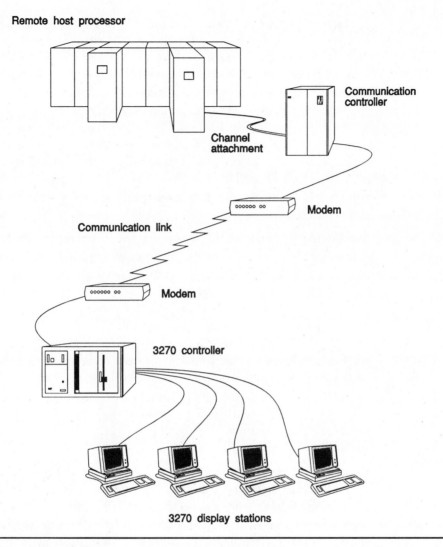

Remote host processor

Communication controller

Channel attachment

Modem

Communication link

Modem

3270 controller

3270 display stations

Figure 2-4   How 3270 devices are connected to a remote host

freestanding units illustrated in figures 2-1 and 2-2. Instead of being connected directly to a host processor channel, the 3270 controller is connected to the remote host using three types of components: (1) a communication link; (2) modems; and (3) a communication controller.

Communication link   The first major component of a remote connection is the *communication link* (or *communication line*). Simply put, the communication link is the connection that spans the distance between the terminal controller and the remote host. The other two components—the modems and the communication controller—are required primarily as interfaces to the communication link. The communication link is usually supplied by a *common carrier* such as AT&T, MCI, or US Sprint.

Several types of communication links are commonly used to support remote 3270s. A communication link can be switched or non-switched. A *switched line*, also called a *dial-up line*, is a simple telephone connection. In a switched line, the connection is established when you dial a phone number. When you hang up, the connection is broken.

In a *non-switched line*, often called a *leased line*, the communication link is permanently established. So dialing is not required. Non-switched lines have less interference than switched lines, and, as a result, can transmit data accurately at higher speeds. Transmission speed is measured in units called *baud*. For switched lines, transmission speed is generally 2,400 or 9,600 baud. Leased lines can support substantially faster transmission rates.

Modems   The second critical component in a remote terminal connection is a pair of *modems*. As you can see in figure 2-4, a modem is required at each end of the communication line. A modem's function is to convert digital signals to analog signals that can be sent over the phone line and to convert analog signals it receives to digital signals that can be processed by the computer system.

Modems use precisely defined *communication protocols* to ensure that they transmit data reliably and efficiently. The simplest of these protocols is called *asynchronous communication*, or *async* for short. 3270 devices do not support asynchronous communications. Instead, they rely on one of two *synchronous communication* protocols: *SDLC* and *BSC*. Because SDLC is a more advanced protocol, it is more commonly used than BSC.

Communication controllers   The third critical component in a remote terminal connection is the *communication controller*. In figure 2-4, you can see that the modem on the host side of the communication line is connected to a communication controller. The communication controller is then connected to the host system via a channel.

Don't confuse the function of the 3270 controller with the function of the communication controller. The function of the 3270 controller is to support multiple 3270 display stations. The communication controller's function is to support multiple communication links, each of which might be attached to a remote 3270 controller.

The communication controller performs a variety of critical communication functions. Its most important function is to remove the burden of managing communication lines from the host system's CPU. IBM's largest communication controllers can manage hundreds of communication lines at once. The communication controller constantly polls each of these lines, stores data in buffers as it is received, detects and corrects transmission errors, and performs many other vital functions. To accomplish this, of course, the communication controller is itself a powerful computer, with its own CPU and memory. The software that runs in the communication controller is called *NCP* (*Network Control Program*).

Discussion Although this chapter has presented many terms and acronyms you may not be familiar with, it has only scratched the surface of telecommunications capabilities. Fortunately, the network is managed by system software products: the operating system (MVS, VSE, or VM), the telecommunication access method (VTAM or TCAM), and, of course, CICS. Maintaining this software so it manages the network properly is the responsibility of systems programmers. As an application programmer, all you need to know is how to invoke the CICS functions that use the network. So the next chapter explains at a conceptual level what CICS is and how it operates.

Terms

network	TCAM
terminal	communication link
host computer	communication line
local terminal	common carrier
remote terminal	switched line
3270 Information Display System	dial-up line
display station	non-switched line
3270 controller	leased line
multiplexor	baud
emulator program	modem
download	communication protocol
upload	asynchronous communication
ASCII terminal	async
local host	synchronous communication
channel	SDLC
operating system	BSC
host subsystem	communication controller
telecommunication access method	NCP
ACF/VTAM	Network Control Program
BTAM	

Objectives

1. Describe the basic components of the 3270 Information Display System.

2. Describe the basic components required to connect a 3270 system to a local or remote host computer.

Chapter 3

An introduction to CICS: Concepts and terms

In this chapter, you'll learn about what CICS is and how it works. You don't need a detailed understanding of CICS internals to develop application programs in COBOL. However, you do need a general understanding of the basic concepts I'll present here.

What is CICS? *CICS* stands for *Customer Information Control System*. And that's just what CICS is: a system designed to control information in a modern on-line environment. Since CICS provides database functions as well as data-communication functions, it's often called a *database/ data-communication system*, or just a *DB/DC system*.

CICS runs on all of IBM's mainframe computer operating systems: MVS (both XA and ESA), VSE, and VM/CMS. There's a version of CICS that runs on microcomputers under the OS/2 operating system. And, as I write this, IBM has announced, but not delivered, a version of CICS that will run on AS/400 minicomputers under the OS/400 operating system. Regardless of the operating system in use, however, CICS programming is the same. As a result, the information in this book applies to any CICS system.

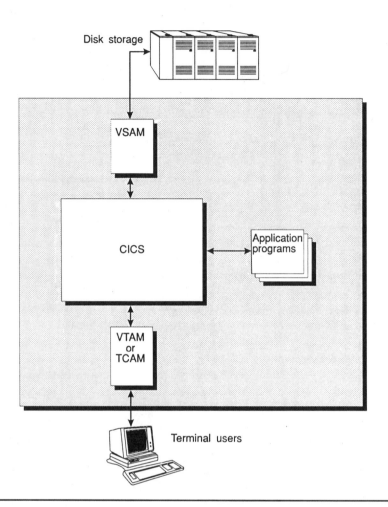

Figure 3-1   How CICS acts as an interface between application programs and the host operating system's access methods

Just what does CICS do? Quite simply, CICS lets operating systems such as MVS and VSE, which were designed to run batch-oriented applications, efficiently handle on-line applications. Batch operating systems work best when a small number of jobs is running at the same time and when each of these jobs has exclusive use of the data files it requires. In contrast, an efficient on-line system must allow for hundreds of concurrent users, many of whom share the same files.

That's where CICS comes in. It acts as an interface between application programs and the operating system's services, as shown in figure 3-1. As you can see, when the application program wants to access a terminal or a disk device, it doesn't communicate directly with the device. Instead, it communicates with CICS, which communicates with one of the operating system's access methods. Then, the access method communicates directly with the device. One of the benefits of CICS is that it shelters your application programs from the device dependent

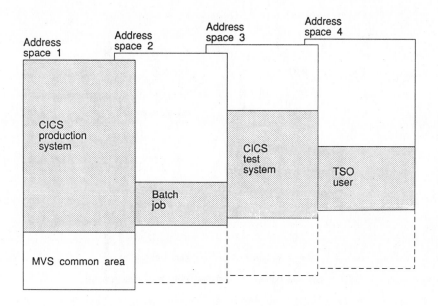

Figure 3-2   CICS in an MVS address space

and operating-system dependent details of using terminal and disk devices.

But CICS is more than an interface between application programs and operating systems. In a way, CICS is itself an operating system, because it provides many of the functions normally associated with an operating system. For example, CICS manages its own processor storage, provides its own file management functions, and includes a task manager that handles the concurrent execution of multiple programs. So you can think of CICS as an operating system within an operating system.

I must make an important point before I go on: As far as the operating system is concerned, CICS is an application program. Under MVS, for example, CICS runs as a batch job in its own address space. That means it has its own JCL with an EXEC statement that starts CICS and DD statements that allocate data sets and other resources. Unlike most batch jobs, however, CICS does not perform a specific function and then stop. Instead, CICS runs throughout the day. In fact, at many installations, CICS runs 24 hours a day.

Figure 3-2 illustrates how CICS executes in an address space under MVS. As you can see, CICS must compete for system resources with batch jobs and TSO users running in other address spaces. The system resource that CICS depends on most is virtual storage. Most batch jobs and TSO users require only a small amount of virtual storage. CICS, however, uses a substantial amount of it. (Of course, figure 3-2 presents a simplified view of the jobs running on a typical MVS system. For

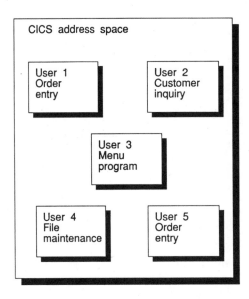

Figure 3-3   How CICS uses its address space to support multitasking

example, it doesn't show separate address spaces required by VTAM, DB2, IMS, JES, and so on.)

Figure 3-2 also shows that more than one CICS system can be running on the same computer. Here, the CICS production system handles all CICS production application programs, while the CICS test system is used by the programming staff to test new CICS programs. As a result, the production programs are protected from failures caused by programs that are still being tested.

Multitasking and multithreading
In CICS, a *task* is the execution of an application program for a specific user. For example, if User 1 is running an application program under CICS, then User 1 has created a task.

One of the basic features of CICS is *multitasking*. Multitasking simply means that CICS allows more than one task to be executing at the same time. For example, figure 3-3 shows a CICS address space that has five running tasks, one for each of five users.

All of the operating systems that support CICS provide multitasking on their own. But CICS provides for multitasking *within* the single address space or partition provided by the operating system. So it ignores the multitasking capabilities of the operating system and provides its own multitasking capabilities instead. As a result, multitasking works the same under CICS regardless of which operating system you use.

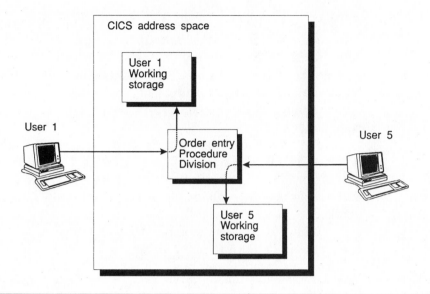

Figure 3-4 CICS provides a separate copy of working storage for each user

Notice in figure 3-3 that two of the users, User 1 and User 5, are running the order entry application program. This would waste valuable processor storage if the same program were loaded into storage at two different locations. Under CICS, however, a concept called *multithreading* is used so only one copy of each program is loaded into storage. With multithreading, the area of storage containing a program is not allocated to a specific user. Instead, all users running the program have access to the same storage locations.

For multithreading to work, the program must be *reentrant*. A program that's completely reentrant doesn't change itself in any way. In other words, a true reentrant program cannot modify data in working storage. Obviously, application programs that can't use working storage are difficult to write. So CICS provides a separate copy of working storage for each user running a program. Figure 3-4 shows how this works. As you can see, the users share the same copy of the program's executable code, but each is given a separate working storage area.

Transactions and task initiation

Under CICS, a user cannot directly invoke a program. Instead, the user invokes a *transaction*, which in turn specifies the program to be run. When a user invokes a transaction, CICS locates the application program associated with the transaction, loads it into storage (if it isn't in storage already), and starts a task. The difference between a task and a transaction is that while several users may invoke the same transaction, each is given a separate task.

Each transaction is identified by a unique four-character code called a *transaction identifier*, or just *trans-id*. A user initiates a transaction by entering the transaction identifier into the terminal. For example, if the operator keys the characters ORD1 and presses the Enter key, the transaction named ORD1 is invoked. This is the most common way to invoke a transaction, but there are others. I'll explain them later in this book.

Every transaction must be defined in a special CICS table called the *Program Control Table*, or *PCT*. Basically, the PCT is a list of valid transaction identifiers. Each trans-id in the PCT is paired with the name of the program CICS will load and execute when the transaction is invoked.

Another CICS table, called the *Processing Program Table*, or *PPT*, contains a list of all valid program names. The PPT keeps track of which programs are located in storage. CICS uses it to determine whether a new copy of a program needs to be loaded into storage when a transaction is invoked.

CICS creates these internal control tables based on *resource definitions* created by systems programmers. There are two ways a systems programmer can create these resource definitions: by using special macro instructions that must be processed by the assembler, or by using *Resource Definition On-Line*, or *RDO*. RDO lets the systems programmer define resources such as transactions and programs from a CICS terminal. By the way, RDO is sometimes called *CEDA*, because that's the trans-id that starts it.

Figure 3-5 shows how a task is initiated under CICS. Here, a user enters the trans-id ORD1. Then, CICS searches the Program Control Table to find the program to be executed. As you can see, the program for transaction ORD1 is ORDPGM1. Next, CICS searches the Processing Program Table to determine if the program is currently in main storage. In this case, it isn't. So CICS locates the program on disk, loads it into storage, updates the PPT, and initiates a new task.

On the other hand, suppose the operator enters the trans-id DM01. The entry for DM01 in the PCT indicates that the program to be executed is DMPGM01. Since the PPT entry for DMPGM01 shows the program is already in storage, the program doesn't have to be retrieved from disk, and the task is started immediately.

CICS services

CICS is a complicated software product that provides many services that are available to application programs. Figure 3-6 shows most of those services. As you can see, I've divided these services into three categories: data communication services, which let your program access terminals; data management services, which let your program access VSAM files and databases; and CICS management services, which let your program access unique features of CICS.

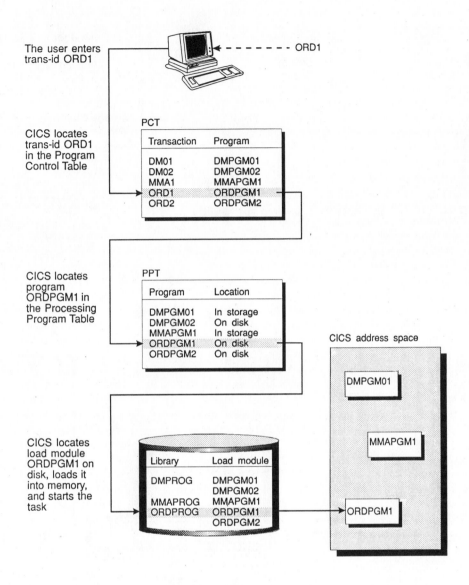

The user enters trans-id ORD1

CICS locates trans-id ORD1 in the Program Control Table

CICS locates program ORDPGM1 in the Processing Program Table

CICS locates load module ORDPGM1 on disk, loads it into memory, and starts the task

Figure 3-5   How a task is started under CICS

Much of the challenge of learning CICS is learning how to use the commands that access these services. All of these services are accessed through a common interface called the *Application Programming Interface*, or *API*. Figure 3-7 shows how an application program communicates with the API, which in turn communicates with the individual CICS services. The API insures that all of the CICS services are invoked in a consistent manner, and it provides a consistent way to test response codes.

Data communication services	Data management services	CICS management services
Terminal control Basic mapping support	File control DL/I access SQL access	Program control Transient data control Temporary storage control Interval control Storage control Task control Dump control Trace control Journal control

Figure 3-6   CICS services available to application programs

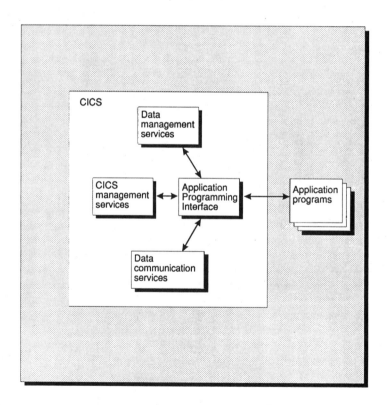

Figure 3-7   Application programs access CICS functions through the Application Programming Interface

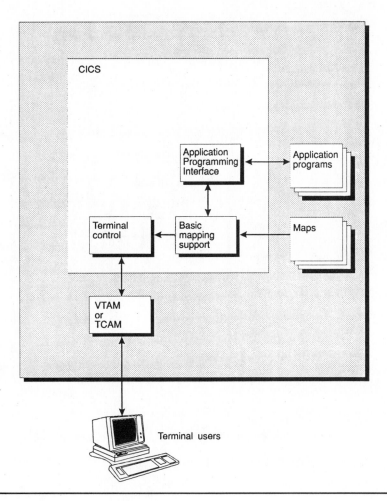

Figure 3-8   Terminal control

Data communication services   Data communication services let a CICS application program communicate with terminal devices. As you can see in figure 3-6, terminal control and basic mapping support are the two CICS services in this group.

Terminal control is CICS's interface with the operating system's telecommunication access method (VTAM, TCAM, or BTAM), as shown in figure 3-8. Terminal control lets you send text to or receive text from the terminal that initiated the task. Although terminal control handles most of the details of working with the VTAM, TCAM, or BTAM, it is still difficult to use directly. An application program that uses terminal control directly must process complicated strings of control characters and data sent to and received from the terminal.

To relieve you of the task of building and decoding complicated strings of control characters and data, *basic mapping support*, or *BMS*, was developed. As figure 3-9 shows, BMS is an interface between application

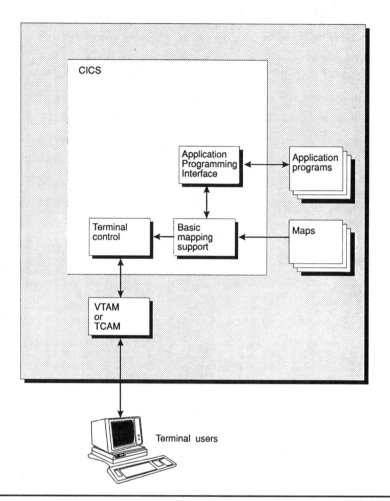

Figure 3-9 Basic mapping support

programs and terminal control. BMS lets you create a *map* that specifies the format of data as it appears on the terminal display. To receive data from or send data to a terminal, an application program issues a BMS request. After BMS retrieves the specified map, it creates a terminal control request that will process the data according to the format specified by the map. In chapter 5, you'll learn how to create BMS maps.

A special CICS table called the *Terminal Control Table* (or *TCT*) is required to define each terminal (whether a display station or printer) to the CICS system. In the TCT, each terminal is given a unique four-character *terminal identifier*, or *term-id*. Fortunately, creating and maintaining the TCT is the responsibility of CICS systems programmers. However, as a CICS programer, you should be aware of the use of term-ids, and you should know your own terminal's term-id.

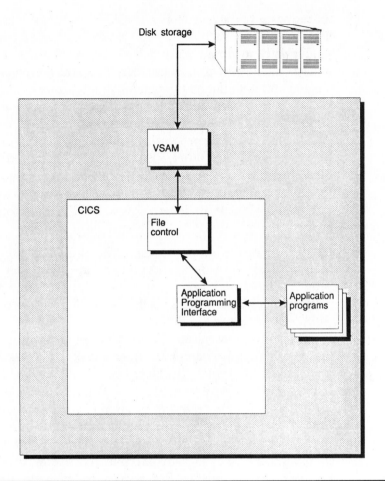

Figure 3-10 File control

Data management services   The data management services in figure 3-6 consist of three CICS services: *file control*, *DL/I*, and *SQL*. DL/I and SQL are interfaces to IBM's hierarchical and relational database managers (IMS and DB2 under MVS; DL/I and SQL/DS under VSE). In this book, you'll learn how to use file control to access standard VSAM files. I'll cover DL/I and SQL in *Part 2: An Advanced Course*.

Figure 3-10 shows how file control works. Here, you can see that when an application program issues a file control request, file control passes it on to VSAM. VSAM, in turn, manages the data stored on direct access devices. One of the major responsibilities of the file control module is managing shared access to files. Thus, while an application program is updating a record in a file, file control locks the record so other programs can't access it until the update is complete.

To keep track of which files are available to application programs, CICS maintains a table called the *File Control Table*, or *FCT*. In addition to the name and type of each file, the FCT lists the file control operations that are valid for each file. It lists whether existing records can be read sequentially, read randomly, deleted, or modified, and whether new records can be added. Like the PPT, PCT, and TCT, entries in the FCT are created and maintained by systems programmers.

CICS file control simplifies the file processing code in your application programs. In a CICS program, you don't use any of the standard COBOL file processing statements. Instead of using standard I/O statements like OPEN, READ, and CLOSE in your program's Procedure Division, you use CICS file control commands. And because the FCT keeps track of file characteristics, you don't use SELECT and FD statements, either. You'll learn how to use CICS file control commands in chapter 8.

CICS management services   The nine CICS management services in figure 3-6 provide functions you probably won't use in every CICS program, but you'll need them on occasion. Only one of these services, program control, is covered in this book. The rest are covered in *Part 2: An Advanced Course.*

The *program control* service manages programs executing within a task. Earlier in this chapter, I defined a task as the execution of an application program on behalf of a particular user. Although that's true in the simplest case, a task may execute more than one application program. For example, the application program invoked when a task is started might be a menu program that accepts the menu selection made by the user and transfers control to another program. That program may invoke yet another program, or it may return control to the menu program when it finishes. Program control provides the commands that let you invoke other programs, and it manages the flow of control from one program to the next. I'll describe program control commands in chapter 8.

Transient data control provides a convenient way to use simple sequential files called *destinations*. Whenever a record is written to a destination, it is added to the end of the destination. Whenever a record is read, it is read from the front of the destination and deleted. As a result, you can read each record in the destination only once.

Temporary storage control provides a simple method for storing data outside your program's working storage area. Temporary storage data is stored in simple files called *temporary storage queues*. If the amount of data is small, it can be stored in main storage. If it is large, it can reside on disk.

The *interval control* service lets you implement time-dependent applications. Interval control provides a method of starting a task that's an alternative to entering a trans-id. You can use interval control to specify that a task start at a specific time or after a specific time interval has passed.

The *storage control* service allocates storage space to application programs. Since most programs keep all of their data in working storage, which is allocated automatically, you won't use storage control commands very often.

The *task control* service lets you control the execution of your task. You can use task control to suspend your task temporarily to prevent it from monopolizing CICS resources. You can also use task control to gain exclusive control of a resource, such as temporary storage, that isn't automatically protected from other users.

When a CICS application program encounters an unrecoverable error, the *dump control* service produces a *transaction dump* that shows the contents of main storage used by the program. You can also use dump control to force a transaction dump at specific points in your program without terminating the program. In chapter 12, I'll show you how to interpret a transaction dump. And in *Part 2: An Advanced Course*, I'll show you how to produce a transaction dump without terminating your program.

As an aid to program debugging, the *trace control* module maintains a *trace table* that indicates the sequence of CICS operations performed within a task. In chapter 12, I'll show you how to interpret a trace table.

The *journal control* module provides a standardized method of creating output files, called *journals*, that are used to restore files in the event of a system failure.

Discussion

Some of the concepts this chapter presents aren't essential to the COBOL programmer writing CICS applications. I've presented them here, however, because (1) they'll help you understand how CICS works, and (2) the IBM manuals are filled with this type of terminology.

If you're having trouble understanding some of these concepts, take heart. I think you'll better understand the concepts and terms after you've seen them in context. So read on. As you do, you can return to this chapter to review the points that are still unclear to you.

Terms

CICS	transaction identifier
Customer Information	trans-id
Control System	Program Control Table
database/data-communication	PCT
system	Processing Program Table
DB/DC system	PPT
task	resource definition
multitasking	Resource Definition On-Line
multithreading	RDO
reentrant	CEDA
transaction	Application Programming Interface

API
terminal control
basic mapping support
BMS
map
Terminal Control Table
TCT
terminal identifier
term-id
file control
DL/I
SQL
File Control Table
FCT

program control
transient data control
destination
temporary storage control
temporary storage queue
interval control
storage control
task control
dump control
transaction dump
trace control
trace table
journal control
journal

Objectives

1. Describe the most common way a task is started under CICS.

2. Distinguish between multitasking and multithreading.

3. Briefly describe the function of each of the following CICS modules:
   a. terminal control
   b. basic mapping support
   c. file control
   d. program control
   e. transient data control
   f. temporary storage control
   g. interval control
   h. storage control
   i. task control
   j. dump control
   k. trace control
   l. journal control

4. Briefly describe the function of each of the following CICS tables:
   a. Program Control Table
   b. Processing Program Table
   c. File Control Table

Section 2

CICS command-level programming

This section presents the critical material of your CICS training. If you master it, you'll be able to design and code complete CICS programs in a professional style. What's more, you'll find it relatively easy to build on this base of knowledge by learning how to use additional CICS features. As a result, you should be prepared to put maximum effort into mastering the material in this section.

Chapter 4

The eight steps of CICS program development

In this chapter, I'm going to describe eight steps you must complete to develop a CICS command-level program. Figure 4-1 lists these steps. As you can see, most of them are not unique to CICS. For example, the first two (developing specifications and designing the program) must be done for any type of programming project. Some of the steps, however, are unique to CICS.

Keep in mind that this chapter presents just an overview of the CICS program development steps. In later chapters, I'll cover critical steps such as designing, coding, and testing the program in greater detail.

Step 1: Develop a complete set of program specifications

The first step in CICS program development is developing a complete set of program specifications. After all, you can't (or at least you *shouldn't*) begin to design or code a program until you know exactly what the program is supposed to do. If you forge ahead with design and coding while the specifications are incomplete, you'll pay for it later by having to redo your work.

Before you start coding	1. Develop a complete set of program specifications.
	2. Design the program.
Coding the program	3. Create the necessary CICS table entries.
	4. Prepare the BMS mapset.
	5. Code the program.
	6. Compile the program.
After you code the program	7. Test the program under CICS.
	8. Document the program.

Figure 4-1   The CICS program development process

In some cases, you may be given a detailed set of program specifications developed by an analyst. In other cases, the specifications you're given may be quite sketchy. If that's the case, you'll have to fill in the missing details yourself.

At the minimum, your program specifications should include (1) a program overview, (2) a screen layout for each map used by the program, and (3) a listing of the COPY member for each file used by the program. In addition, your specifications may include decision tables, editing rules, and so on. Try to look beyond the obvious to make sure you have all of the information you need to develop a program.

Figure 4-2 shows a simple *program overview* for an inquiry program that displays data retrieved from a customer master file. As you can see, the overview begins with a brief description of the program's function. Then, it lists the I/O requirements for the program. Finally, it contains a detailed list of processing specifications. These specifications state what the program is to do in response to various input actions. For example, if the user presses PF3, the program is to return to the menu that invoked it.

Figure 4-3 presents the *screen layout* for the inquiry program. This document shows the positions of headings, labels, and data on the screen. For example, you can see that the label "Customer number" begins in column 2 of line 5. The user will enter the customer number in the entry field at column 27 on line 5. And the program will display the customer's name and address in the fields on lines 7, 8, 9, and 10. (By the way, F3 in the instructions on the screen layout and PF3 in the program overview refer to the same key: program function key 3. Similarly, F12 and PF12 refer to the same key.)

Program	CUSTINQ1
Overview	Displays customer information from the customer master file based on customer numbers entered by the user.
Input/output specifications	CUSTMAS Customer master file INQMAP1 Customer inquiry map
Processing specifications	1. Control is transferred to this program via XCTL from the menu program INVMENU with no communication area. The user can also start the program by entering the trans-id INQ1. In either case, the program should respond by displaying the customer inquiry map. 2. If the user enters a customer number, read the customer record from CUSTMAS and display it. If the record doesn't exist, display an error message instead. 3. If the user presses PF3 or PF12, return to the menu program INVMENU by issuing an XCTL command.

Figure 4-2   Specifications for the inquiry program

Step 2: Design the program

Design is a critical stage in program development. With good design, you can code and test a program efficiently. With poor design, coding is likely to be inefficient, and testing can be a nightmare.

If you're an experienced COBOL programmer but you're not experienced with CICS, I think you'll find design the most difficult aspect of CICS programming to learn. That's because most CICS programs must use an unusual programming technique called *pseudo-conversational programming*. Most standard COBOL programs are designed around a basic looping structure that controls the overall execution of the program. In a pseudo-conversational CICS program, there is no basic looping structure. Instead, CICS invokes your program whenever an interaction with the user occurs. Your CICS program must be designed to respond appropriately to each type of user action that might occur. I'll describe pseudo-conversational programming in detail in chapter 6.

The key to successfully designing a pseudo-conversational program is good program specifications. If the specifications carefully document how the program is to respond to each user action, the program will be easy to design. All you need to do is develop a program design that will implement the specified response for each user action.

Map name	INQMAP1	Date	10/31/91
Program name	CUSTINQ1	Designer	Doug Lowe

```
         1         2         3         4         5         6         7         8
1234567890123456789012345678901234567890123456789012345678901234567890123456789 0
 1  INQMAP1              Customer Inquiry
 2
 3  Type a customer number.  Then press Enter.
 4
 5  Customer number. . . . .  XXXXXX
 6
 7  Name and address . . . :  XXXXXXXXXXXXXXXXXXXXXXXXXXXXXXXXXX
 8                            XXXXXXXXXXXXXXXXXXXXX
 9                            XXXXXXXXXXXXXXXXXXXXXXXXXXXXXX
10                            XXXXXXXXXXXXXXXXXXXX XX XXXXXXXXXXX
11
12
13
14
15
16
17
18
19
20
21
22
23  XXXXXXXXXXXXXXXXXXXXXXXXXXXXXXXXXXXXXXXXXXXXXXXXXXXXXXXXXXXXXXXXXXXXXXXXXXXXXXX
24  F3=Exit    F12=Cancel                                                       X
```

Figure 4-3   Screen layout for the inquiry program

The best way to do that is to prepare a simple summary of the processing required in response to every possible user action. Figure 4-4 shows the processing summary for the inquiry program. This summary is not written in rigorous COBOL code. Instead, I wrote it in simple English. You can see that the processing summary is derived from the program overview in figure 4-2 and is similar to it. However, it clarifies the processing that must be done to retrieve and display a customer record, and it provides for several input actions that were omitted from the specifications.

To specify the overall program structure, I use the techniques of *top-down design*. Basically, the idea of top-down program design is to design a program by dividing it into major functional modules, then dividing these modules into their functional component modules, and so forth. Each module is then implemented as a COBOL paragraph. The resulting structure is documented using a structure chart like the one in

Event	Response
Start the program	Display the customer map.

Enter key	Receive the customer map.
	Edit the customer number.
	If valid
	    read the record.
	If the record exists
	    display it.
	If the number isn't valid or the record doesn't exist
	    display an error message.

PF3 or PF12	Return to the menu program.
Clear key	Redisplay the customer map.
Any PA key	Ignore the key.
Any other key	Display an error message.

Figure 4-4   Processing summary for the inquiry program

figure 4-5. I'll show you how to design a CICS program in chapter 7. So if you're confused about CICS program design now, don't be concerned.

Step 3: Create the necessary CICS table entries

Before you can test a CICS program, you need to make sure that all of the CICS table entries required to support the program are in place. For most programs, this means that entries need to be made in three tables: the Processing Program Table (PPT), the Program Control Table (PCT), and the File Control Table (FCT). In the PCT, an entry is required to define the trans-id that's used to start the program. In the PPT, two entries are required: one for the program, the other for the program's mapset. If the program uses any files, appropriate entries are required in the FCT. If the program uses other CICS facilities, additional table entries may be required as well.

At most installations, application programmers are not authorized to create CICS table entries. Instead, that responsibility is assigned to a CICS system administrator. If that's the case, you'll need to discuss the required CICS table entries with the administrator.

Step 4: Prepare the BMS mapset

The next step is to prepare the basic mapping support (BMS) definition for each map your program will use. As you should remember from the last chapter, BMS controls formatted input for terminal devices. To

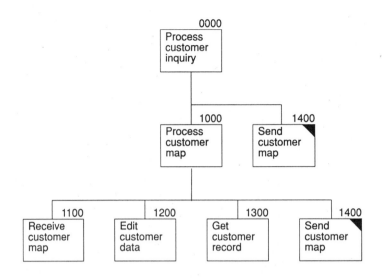

Figure 4-5   Structure chart for the inquiry program

define the format of the BMS maps, you code an assembler language program called a *mapset*. Figure 4-6 is a portion of a typical BMS mapset. For now, don't worry about the details of creating mapsets. You'll learn how to do it in the next chapter.

Incidentally, many shops use a *mapset generator* to create mapsets. With a mapset generator, you describe the final appearance of a map at your terminal by keying in data at the correct screen locations. Then, the mapset generator converts that description into appropriate BMS instructions. Since BMS mapsets can be complicated, a good mapset generator can be a tremendous time-saver.

Step 5: Code the program

Coding a CICS program involves writing a mixture of standard COBOL code and special *CICS commands* to invoke CICS services. The main purpose of this book, of course, is to teach you how to code CICS programs.

Figure 4-7 shows one paragraph of a CICS command-level program. This paragraph reads a record from a customer file named CUSTMAS, then formats data so it can be sent to the terminal. You don't need to worry about the details of how this COBOL paragraph works for now. I just want you to notice how you can mix CICS commands with standard COBOL statements. If you wish, you can think of CICS commands as extensions to standard COBOL. In effect, though, CICS commands transform COBOL into a language with an entirely different flavor.

```
          PRINT NOGEN
INQSET1   DFHMSD TYPE=&SYSPARM,                                        X
                 LANG=COBOL,                                           X
                 MODE=INOUT,                                           X
                 TERM=3270-2,                                          X
                 CTRL=FREEKB,                                          X
                 STORAGE=AUTO,                                         X
                 TIOAPFX=YES
*******************************************************************
INQMAP1   DFHMDI SIZE=(24,80),                                         X
                 LINE=1,                                               X
                 COLUMN=1
*******************************************************************
          DFHMDF POS=(1,1),                                           X
                 LENGTH=8,                                             X
                 ATTRB=(NORM,PROT),                                    X
                 COLOR=BLUE,                                           X
                 INITIAL='MMINQ01'
          DFHMDF POS=(1,20),                                          X
                 LENGTH=16,                                            X
                 ATTRB=(NORM,PROT),                                    X
                 COLOR=BLUE,                                           X
                 INITIAL='Customer Inquiry'
*******************************************************************
          DFHMDF POS=(3,1),                                           X
                 LENGTH=42,                                            X
                 ATTRB=(NORM,PROT),                                    X
                 COLOR=GREEN,                                          X
                 INITIAL='Type a customer number.  Then press Enter.'
          DFHMDF POS=(5,1),                                           X
                 LENGTH=24,                                            X
                 ATTRB=(NORM,PROT),                                    X
                 COLOR=GREEN,                                          X
                 INITIAL='Customer number. . . . .'
CUSTNO    DFHMDF POS=(5,26),                                          X
                 LENGTH=6,                                             X
                 ATTRB=(NORM,UNPROT,IC),                               X
                 COLOR=TURQUOISE,                                      X
                 INITIAL='_____'
          DFHMDF POS=(5,33),                                          X
                 LENGTH=1,                                             X
                 ATTRB=ASKIP
*******************************************************************
          DFHMDF POS=(7,1),                                           X
                 LENGTH=24,                                            X
                 ATTRB=(NORM,PROT),                                    X
                 COLOR=GREEN,                                          X
                 INITIAL='Name and address . . . :'
LNAME     DFHMDF POS=(7,26),                                          X
                 LENGTH=30,                                            X
                 COLOR=TURQUOISE,                                      X
                 ATTRB=(NORM,PROT)
```

Figure 4-6   A portion of a BMS mapset

```
    1300-GET-CUSTOMER-RECORD.
*
        EXEC CICS
            READ DATASET('CUSTMAS')
                 INTO(CUSTOMER-MASTER-RECORD)
                 RIDFLD(CUSTNOI)
                 RESP(RESPONSE-CODE)
        END-EXEC.
        IF RESPONSE-CODE = DFHRESP(NORMAL)
            MOVE SPACE          TO MESSAGEO
            MOVE CM-LAST-NAME   TO LNAMEO
            MOVE CM-FIRST-NAME  TO FNAMEO
            MOVE CM-ADDRESS     TO ADDRO
            MOVE CM-CITY        TO CITYO
            MOVE CM-STATE       TO STATEO
            MOVE CM-ZIP-CODE    TO ZIPCODEO
        ELSE IF RESPONSE-CODE = DFHRESP(NOTFND)
            MOVE 'N' TO VALID-DATA-SW
            MOVE 'That customer does not exist.' TO MESSAGEO
            MOVE SPACE TO LNAMEO
                          FNAMEO
                          ADDRO
                          CITYO
                          STATEO
                          ZIPCODEO
        ELSE
            EXEC CICS
                ABEND
            END-EXEC.
*
```

Figure 4-7   One paragraph of a CICS program

Beginning in chapter 6, and continuing through the rest of this book, I'll explain the forms and functions of the CICS commands you'll use most often.

Step 6: Compile the program

After you've coded a CICS program, you must compile it. The compilation process, shown in figure 4-8, is similar to the compilation process for standard COBOL programs. However, before the usual steps of compiling and link-editing the program, there is a preliminary step: The program must be processed by the *CICS command-level translator*. The translator converts each CICS command into appropriate COBOL statements that invoke the CICS services specified by the command. The result is a translated source program that's used as input to the COBOL compiler.

Figure 4-9 shows how the CICS translator converts CICS commands into standard COBOL statements. Here, the top part of the figure shows a typical CICS command as you would code it in your program. The bottom part of the figure shows how this command would appear in the translated source program. As you can see, the command itself has been

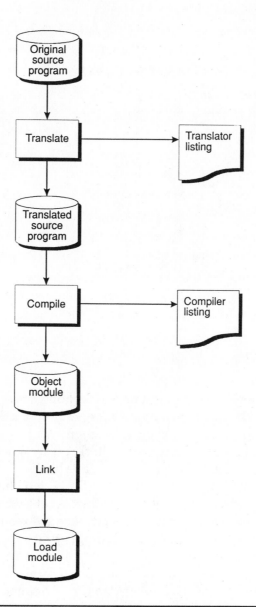

Figure 4-8   Translating and compiling a CICS program

converted to comments. Therefore, the compiler will ignore these lines. After the original CICS command, the translator inserted a series of MOVE statements followed by a CALL statement. The MOVE statements assign values to the fields that are used as arguments of the CALL statement. The CALL statement invokes the command-level interface to invoke the required CICS services.

In addition to translating CICS commands, the translator also inserts other code into your program. It consists mostly of fields defined in the

Original source code

```
EXEC CICS
    READ DATASET('CUSTMAS')
        INTO(CUSTOMER-MASTER-RECORD)
        RIDFLD(CUSTNOI)
        RESP(RESPONSE-CODE)
END-EXEC.
```

Translated source code

```
*     EXEC CICS
*         READ DATASET('CUSTMAS')
*             INTO(CUSTOMER-MASTER-RECORD)
*             RIDFLD(CUSTNOI)
*             RESP(RESPONSE-CODE)
*     END-EXEC.
          MOVE '..0......00061   ' TO DFHEIVO
          MOVE 'CUSTMAS' TO DFHC0080
          MOVE LENGTH OF CUSTOMER-MASTER-RECORD TO DFHB0020
          CALL 'DFHEI1' USING DFHEIVO DFHC0080 CUSTOMER-MASTER-RECORD
      DFHB0020 CUSTNOI
          MOVE EIBRESP TO RESPONSE-CODE.
```

Figure 4-9   How the CICS translator converts CICS commands to standard COBOL statements

Working-Storage and Linkage Sections. This code is required for your COBOL program to operate properly under CICS. Most of it is of little concern to you. However, one segment of code in the Linkage Section, called the Execute Interface Block, is important. You'll see how to use the Execute Interface Block later in this book.

After the program has been translated, the COBOL compiler is invoked to compile it and produce an object module. Then, the linkage-editor is invoked to produce an executable program.

Since the translator and compiler execute as separate job steps, you get two sets of source listings and diagnostics. The translator output contains a listing of the source program as you wrote it, plus any diagnostic messages related to CICS commands. The compiler output contains a listing of the translated program, plus any diagnostics related to standard COBOL statements. As a result, you must review both listings to determine if your program compiled without errors.

If you're developing CICS programs under OS/2, the procedure for compiling your program is a little different. When you use the Micro Focus Workbench, the translate-compile-link process is integrated into a single function, called the *checker*. When the checker detects an error, either in a CICS command or in the COBOL source code, it returns you to the editor. There, you can view the diagnostic messages alongside the related source statements, correct the problems, and recheck the program. So although you can print a compiler listing if you wish, you rarely will.

Trans-id	Function	Examples
C E S N	Sign on	`C E S N` `C E S N   U S E R = H O R A C E , P W = J A S P E R`
C E S F	Sign off	`C E S F` `C E S F   L O G O F F`
C E M T	Master terminal	`C E M T   S E T   P R O G R A M = O R D P G M 1 , N E W C O P Y`
C E D F	Execution Diagnostics Facility	`C E D F`
C E C I	Command-Level Interpreter	`C E C I`

Figure 4-10 CICS service transactions

Step 7: Test the program under CICS

As a programmer, you are responsible for ensuring that your programs perform according to their specifications. To test a CICS program, you must create test data designed to validate every combination of user input against expected results. When the actual results vary from the expected results, you must locate the problem, correct it, and test the program again.

Like a batch program, a CICS program can encounter unrecoverable conditions that can cause it to abend. When this happens, a cryptic message is displayed at the terminal, and a storage dump is produced. In many cases, the terminal message is sufficient to isolate the problem, so the dump isn't needed. Otherwise, you need to print the dump or view it on-line to determine the cause of the error. Alternatively, you can use an on-line debugging tool to debug your program.

In some cases, a program bug may bring the entire CICS system down. When this happens, the problem is more difficult to isolate. Because it's surprisingly easy to bring down a CICS system, most installations run separate CICS systems for production and testing. That way, you can test your programs without putting the production system at risk.

To test a program under CICS, you need to know how to connect your terminal to CICS. The procedures to do that vary from shop to shop, so you'll have to check with your supervisor to find out how. In addition, you need to know how to use a few IBM-supplied *service transactions* to perform common CICS functions. Figure 4-10 lists the service transactions you'll use most often.

The first two service transactions in figure 4-10 are the sign-on and sign-off transactions. Depending on how the systems programmers have set up CICS, you may or may not need to use the CESN transaction to sign on to CICS before you test your programs. You can use the USER and PW parameters on the CESN transaction to supply your user-id and password, or you can just type CESN without parameters. Then, CICS will display a sign-on screen where you can enter your user-id and password. If you use the CESN transaction to sign on to CICS, you should also use the CESF transaction to sign off when you are finished working.

The next service transaction listed in figure 4-10 is the master terminal transaction, CEMT. This transaction lets you perform a variety of supervisory CICS functions. For example, CEMT can be used to cancel a task that's running at another terminal. Whenever you recompile a program while CICS is running, you must use CEMT with the NEWCOPY parameter to update the Processing Program Table so you can access the new version of the program. As a programmer, this is the master terminal function you'll use most often. You'll learn about other CEMT functions in chapter 11.

A special service transaction, CEDF, invokes a debugging aid called *Execution Diagnostics Facility*, or just *EDF*. When EDF is activated, you can run a program step-by-step, checking the completion of each CICS command and examining the contents of working storage as necessary. I'll show you how to use EDF in chapter 12.

Another CICS service transaction that's useful for program development is the *Command-Level Interpreter*. It is invoked with the trans-id CECI. The Command-Level Interpreter interactively executes CICS commands. With it, you can perform almost any CICS operation interactively. You'll use it often to display maps, read or write VSAM file records, and so on. Like CEDF, I'll show you how to use CECI in chapter 11.

Step 8: Document the program

Nobody likes to put together program documentation. It's tedious, time consuming, and a bit anti-climactic. However, it is a must. Without proper documentation, your program will be difficult to use and maintain.

There are two primary audiences for program documentation: programmers and users. Naturally, the documentation you assemble must be appropriate for its audience. For programmers, your documentation should include copies of the program's specifications, your design documents, the program code, and test data. Your shop undoubtedly has standards for how this information should be gathered and stored.

For users, documentation often includes a user's guide that explains all aspects of the program's operation. This user's guide may include both a tutorial and a reference section. Although some form of written documentation is almost always appropriate, the best form of documentation is a well-designed and well-implemented program with built-in helps.

Discussion

In this chapter, I've described the CICS program development process in general terms. The particulars of CICS program development, of course, vary from shop to shop. The exact procedures you use to prepare a BMS mapset and to translate and compile a CICS program depend on which operating system you're using. In appendix C, you'll find an overview of the program development procedures for MVS and VSE. Still, you'll need to learn additional requirements for your own shop.

Fortunately, whether you're developing CICS applications under MVS, VSE, VM, or OS/2, the CICS programming techniques the rest of this book presents are identical. So once you've learned the program development procedures used at your shop, you can get on with the task of learning how to develop CICS programs.

Terms

program overview	CICS command-level translator
screen layout	checker
pseudo-conversational programming	service transaction
top-down design	Execution Diagnostics Facility
mapset	EDF
mapset generator	Command-Level Interpreter
CICS command	

Objectives

1. Describe the eight steps of CICS program development.

2. Explain the translation and compilation process used for a CICS command-level program.

3. Explain the purpose of each of the following CICS transactions:
    CESN
    CESF
    CEMT
    CEDF
    CECI

Chapter 5

How to create
a BMS
mapset

Before you can code an interactive CICS program, you need to define the screen it will display. In this chapter, I'll show you how to use basic mapping support (BMS) to do that. This chapter has two topics. The first describes how the 3270 display station's screen operates. The second explains how to create a BMS map definition.

Characteristics of the 3270 display screen

Before you can use BMS to define a screen layout, you need to understand the functional characteristics of the 3270 display station's screen. In this topic, I'll explain those characteristics.

Fields

The 3270 screen is a *field oriented display*. In other words, the screen is logically divided into a number of user-defined *fields*. Simply put, a screen field is a specified area that contains a particular category of information. Some screen fields allow the user to key data into them, while others are protected from data entry.

The location and characteristics of screen fields are determined by special characters called *attribute bytes*. The beginning of each field is indicated by the presence of an attribute byte. The attribute byte takes up one position on the screen (the position immediately to the left of the field it defines), but it's displayed on the screen as a space.

A screen field starts at the position immediately following its attribute byte and ends at the position immediately before the next field's attribute byte. Thus, the length of a screen field depends on the position of the next attribute byte. If there's no subsequent attribute byte, the field continues to the end of the screen.

Figure 5-1 shows how attribute bytes precede fields in a 3270 display. Here, the small shaded boxes represent attribute bytes. These boxes don't appear on the actual display. Instead, spaces appear in the attribute byte positions.

Most of the fields in the screen in figure 5-1 are used to display messages, labels, and data retrieved from the customer file. The user cannot enter data into these fields. However, the customer number field (the second field on line five) is a data entry field where the user types the customer number for the customer record to be retrieved.

Unlike display-only fields, data entry fields actually require *two* attribute bytes: one to mark the beginning of the field, the other to mark the field's end. You'll understand why this second attribute byte is required once you know about the various types of field attributes that are controlled by attribute bytes.

Field attributes

As its name implies, an attribute byte does more than just mark the beginning or end of a field. An attribute byte also determines a field's characteristics, called its *attributes*. The three attributes you use are:

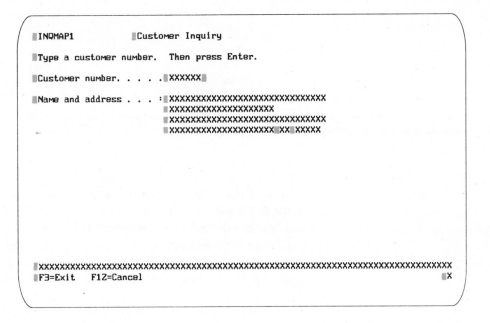

Figure 5-1   Attribute bytes in a 3270 display

(1) protection, (2) intensity, and (3) shift. Figure 5-2 shows the selections you can make for these attributes. Now, I'll explain the meaning of each.

The protection attribute   The *protection attribute* indicates whether or not the user can key data into a field. If a field is protected, the user can't key data into it. On the other hand, if a field is unprotected, the user is free to key data into it. As a result, data entry fields are often called *unprotected fields*, while display-only fields are also called *protected fields*.

A third protection attribute option, *auto-skip*, defines a *skip field*. As with a protected field, a user cannot enter data into a skip field. The difference between a protected field and a skip field is that when the *cursor* (a marker that indicates where the next character the user types will appear on the screen) is moved to a skip field, it automatically advances to the first position of the next unprotected field on the screen. In contrast, when the cursor moves to a protected field without auto-skip, it stops, even though the user cannot enter data there. Because of this characteristic, protected fields without auto-skip are sometimes called *stop fields*.

Skip fields are usually used to mark the ends of data entry fields. That way, when the user enters enough characters to fill the unprotected field, the cursor automatically moves on to the next data entry field, and the user can continue entering data. If a stop field is used to mark the end of an unprotected field, the user has to press the tab key to advance to the next data entry field.

Protection	Intensity	Shift
Protected Unprotected Auto-skip	Normal Bright No-display	Alphanumeric Numeric

Figure 5-2   Basic attributes for 3270 fields

Either way, though, an attribute byte is required to mark the end of an unprotected field. If you omit the ending attribute byte, the screen will be unprotected beyond the intended data entry field until the beginning attribute byte of the next field. For example, suppose I had omitted the ending attribute byte for the customer number field in figure 5-1. In that case, the unprotected attribute would extend beyond the six screen positions I had intended for the customer number field through the rest of the line and all of the following line as well. The unprotected attribute would be in effect until the attribute byte that precedes the label "Name and address."

The intensity attribute   The *intensity attribute* indicates how the data in the field is displayed. Normal means just what it says: The data is displayed with normal intensity. If you specify bright, the data is displayed with brighter than normal intensity. And if you specify no-display, the field isn't displayed at all. If no-display is specified for an unprotected field, spaces are displayed no matter what characters the user keys into the field.

The shift attribute   The *shift attribute* indicates whether the keyboard is in *alphanumeric shift* or *numeric shift*. On older 3270 models, the numerals are located on the same keys as some of the letters, so the user has to shift the keyboard to enter numeric data. However, if a field's attribute byte indicates numeric shift, the keyboard is automatically put into numeric shift so the user doesn't have to press the numeric shift key.

Newer 3270 display stations have a *numeric lock* feature that allows the user to enter *only* numeric data (numerals, a sign, and a decimal point) into a field. On these newer terminals, the numeric shift attribute in the attribute byte activates the numeric lock feature. As a result, you'll usually specify the numeric shift attribute for numeric data entry fields. Bear in mind, however, that even when the numeric shift attribute is on, the user can still enter invalid numeric data. For example, the user can enter data with two decimal points or two minus signs. So, your programs must still edit all numeric data entry fields to be sure they're valid.

Attribute byte bit positions

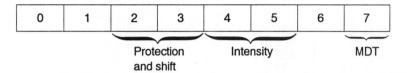

| 0 | 1 | 2 | 3 | 4 | 5 | 6 | 7 |

Protection and shift (bits 2–3)

Intensity (bits 4–5)

MDT (bit 7)

Explanation

Positions	Functions	Bit settings
0-1		Contents of bits 2 through 7 determine settings
2-3	Protection and shift	00 = Unprotected alphanumeric 01 = Unprotected numeric 10 = Protected stop 11 = Protected skip
4-5	Intensity	00 = Normal 01 = Normal 10 = Bright 11 = No-display
6		Must be 0
7	MDT	0 = Field has not been modified 1 = Field has been modified

Figure 5-3   Format of the attribute byte

The format of the attribute byte

A field's attributes are determined by the bit settings in the attribute byte, as figure 5-3 shows. (The bit positions within a byte are always numbered from zero.) Although you don't need to memorize the meaning of each bit position in the attribute byte, you do need to understand in general terms how the attribute byte functions.

The last bit in the attribute byte, the *MDT* (*Modified Data Tag*) indicates whether or not the user has modified the data in a field. If the user keys any data into the field, the terminal turns the MDT on to indicate that the data has been modified. To save transmission time, the 3270 sends a field over the TC line only if its MDT is on. Otherwise, the field is not transmitted.

Extended attributes

In addition to the standard attributes I've described so far, some 3270 terminal models provide additional features that are controlled with *extended attributes*. Extended attributes are similar to standard attributes,

Extended color	Extended highlighting	Validation	Programmed symbols
Blue Red Pink Green Turquoise Yellow White	Blinking Reverse video Underline	Must fill Must enter Trigger	Up to six alternate user-definable character sets

Figure 5-4   Extended attributes for 3270 fields

with one important exception: An extended attribute doesn't take up a position on the screen.

Figure 5-4 lists the optional 3270 features that are controlled by extended attributes. As you can see, these features fall into four categories: extended color, extended highlighting, validation, and programmed symbols. Since you're unlikely to use validation and programmed symbols, I won't mention them again. Instead, I'll concentrate on extended color and extended highlighting.

Extended color   Terminals that support *extended color* can display fields in any of seven colors: blue, red, pink, green, turquoise, yellow, or white. Typically, you use extended color to draw attention to specific fields. For example, the CUA Entry Model specifies that the screen title should be blue, instructions and field prompts should be green, and data entry fields should be turquoise.

To control the color of a field, you specify an extended color attribute in the field's mapset definition. I'll show you how to do that in the next topic.

Extended highlighting   *Extended highlighting* lets you draw attention to a field by *underlining* it, causing it to *blink*, or displaying it in *reverse video* (that is, dark characters against a light background, instead of the other way around). These forms of highlighting, along with color and the standard intensity attribute, are used most commonly to draw attention to a field. For example, the CUA Entry Model specifies that when a user enters incorrect data, the program should highlight the error using reverse video.

CUA also specifies that data entry fields can be identified with the underline attribute to make them easy to locate. Alternatively, the program can fill data entry fields with underscore characters. For the sample programs in this book, I'll use the second technique.

Like extended color, extended highlighting can be specified for a field in its map definition. I'll show you how to do that in the next topic.

Discussion   Actually, the programming required to operate a 3270 display station is much more complicated than you might guess from the information I've presented here. Fortunately, basic mapping support handles most of this programming for you. So, on now to topic 2, where you'll learn how to use BMS to define a 3270 screen.

Terms

field oriented display	shift attribute
field	alphanumeric shift
attribute byte	numeric shift
attribute	numeric lock
protection attribute	MDT
unprotected field	Modified Data Tag
protected field	extended attribute
auto-skip	extended color
skip field	extended highlighting
cursor	underline
stop field	blink
intensity attribute	reverse video

Objectives

1. Describe the two primary functions of attribute bytes in a 3270 display.

2. List the three attributes controlled by standard attribute bytes.

3. Explain why two attribute bytes are required for an unprotected field.

4. Explain the function of the Modified Data Tag.

5. List the three extended highlighting attributes.

Topic 2

How to code BMS macro instructions

This topic shows you how to create a BMS map. As you know, you must code a *mapset*, a special kind of assembler language program, to define the format of each screen your programs display. After you've completed this topic, you'll be able to create mapsets for most of the screens you'll ever use.

Incidentally, if your shop uses a map generator to create BMS maps, you may feel you don't need to learn the material this topic presents. Still, I think it's important to know how to create maps of your own. So I suggest you read this topic even if you have access to a map generator.

Once you've created a map, you must assemble it. A job to assemble a map requires two steps. The first transforms your map into a physical map. The second creates a symbolic map from your map. Though both the physical and symbolic maps are required for BMS to operate properly, you only need to create one version of your map since both types of maps are derived from it.

A *physical map* is a load module that contains a table BMS uses to determine the screen locations of data transmitted to and received from the display station. For example, a physical map might indicate that a particular field is displayed on the screen at column 16 of line 4. A physical map also indicates the attributes of each field, such as protection and intensity.

A *symbolic map* is a COPY library member that contains the COBOL definitions of data sent to and received from the terminal screen. When an application program requests that a map be sent to a terminal, BMS takes data from the symbolic map, formats (or *maps*) it according to the physical map, and transmits it to the terminal. Likewise, when an application program requests that data be retrieved from a terminal, BMS uses the physical map to map the data from the screen into the symbolic map.

The term mapset refers to a collection of one or more maps. For efficiency, most mapsets contain only one map definition. As a result, the terms *map* and *mapset* are often used to mean the same thing.

This topic is divided into three sections. First, I'll show you how to code a BMS mapset. Second, I'll give you some models you can follow for most of the BMS field definitions you'll ever need to code. And third, I'll describe the symbolic map.

Map name _____ INQMAP1 _____ Date _____ 10/31/91 _____

Program name __ CUSTINQ2 _____ Designer __ Doug Lowe _____

```
     1234567890123456789012345678901234567890123456789012345678901234567890123456789 0
 1   INQMAP1            Customer Inquiry
 2
 3   Type a customer number.  Then press Enter.
 4
 5   Customer number. . . . . XXXXXX
 6
 7   Name and address . . . : XXXXXXXXXXXXXXXXXXXXXXXXXXXXXXXX
 8                            XXXXXXXXXXXXXXXXXXXXXX
 9                            XXXXXXXXXXXXXXXXXXXXXXXXXXXXXX
10                            XXXXXXXXXXXXXXXXXXX XX XXXXXXXXXXX
11
12
13
14
15
16
17
18
19
20
21
22
23   XXXXXXXXXXXXXXXXXXXXXXXXXXXXXXXXXXXXXXXXXXXXXXXXXXXXXXXXXXXXXXXXXXXXXXXXXXXXXXXXX
24   F3=Exit   F12=Cancel                                                          X
```

Figure 5-5 Screen layout for the inquiry program

How to code a mapset

Figure 5-5 shows the screen used by an application that retrieves data from a file of customer records based on a customer number entered by the user. This screen has just one input field, beginning in column 27 on line 5. It has a total of seven output fields: six on lines 7-10 for customer information, and one on line 23 for user messages. In addition, the screen has a number of constants that identify screen fields and provide instructions. The next chapter presents the COBOL program for this application. For now, I want to discuss how to define the screen it displays.

The mapset in figure 5-6 defines this screen. As you can see, a BMS mapset is an assembler language program. Don't let that scare you, though. Although some mapsets can be long, they're all simple assembler language programs. Moreover, one mapset is about the same as another. As a result, once you've coded one, you've mastered the skills you need to code almost any other you'll ever be called upon to create.

```
          PRINT NOGEN
INQSET1   DFHMSD TYPE=&SYSPARM,                                        X
                 LANG=COBOL,                                           X
                 MODE=INOUT,                                           X
                 TERM=3270-2,                                          X
                 CTRL=FREEKB,                                          X
                 STORAGE=AUTO,                                         X
                 DSATTS=(COLOR,HIGHLIGHT),                             X
                 MAPATTS=(COLOR,HIGHLIGHT),                            X
                 TIOAPFX=YES
************************************************************************
INQMAP1   DFHMDI SIZE=(24,80),                                         X
                 LINE=1,                                               X
                 COLUMN=1
************************************************************************
          DFHMDF POS=(1,1),                                           X
                 LENGTH=8,                                            X
                 ATTRB=(NORM,PROT),                                   X
                 COLOR=BLUE,                                          X
                 INITIAL='INQMAP1'
          DFHMDF POS=(1,20),                                          X
                 LENGTH=16,                                           X
                 ATTRB=(NORM,PROT),                                   X
                 COLOR=BLUE,                                          X
                 INITIAL='Customer Inquiry'
************************************************************************
          DFHMDF POS=(3,1),                                           X
                 LENGTH=42,                                           X
                 ATTRB=(NORM,PROT),                                   X
                 COLOR=GREEN,                                         X
                 INITIAL='Type a customer number.  Then press Enter.'
          DFHMDF POS=(5,1),                                           X
                 LENGTH=24,                                           X
                 ATTRB=(NORM,PROT),                                   X
                 COLOR=GREEN,                                         X
                 INITIAL='Customer number. . . . .'
CUSTNO    DFHMDF POS=(5,26),                                          X
                 LENGTH=6,                                            X
                 ATTRB=(NORM,UNPROT,IC),                              X
                 COLOR=TURQUOISE,                                     X
                 INITIAL='_____'
          DFHMDF POS=(5,33),                                          X
                 LENGTH=1,                                            X
                 ATTRB=ASKIP
```

Figure 5-6   BMS mapset for the inquiry program (part 1 of 2)

To create a mapset, you only need to know the two assembler commands and three BMS macro instructions that are summarized in figure 5-7. A *macro instruction*, or just *macro*, is a single instruction that's replaced by two or more other instructions. The first and last lines of the mapset are the assembler commands; the other lines make up the macro instructions.

The PRINT NOGEN assembler command causes the assembler not to print instructions generated by the BMS macro instructions. If you don't include a PRINT NOGEN command, your assembler listing will contain hundreds of lines that aren't important to you. So always start your mapsets with PRINT NOGEN.

```
*************************************************************************
          DFHMDF POS=(7,1),                                            X
                 LENGTH=24,                                            X
                 ATTRB=(NORM,PROT),                                    X
                 COLOR=GREEN,                                          X
                 INITIAL='Name and address . . . :'
LNAME     DFHMDF POS=(7,26),                                           X
                 LENGTH=30,                                            X
                 COLOR=TURQUOISE,                                      X
                 ATTRB=(NORM,PROT)
FNAME     DFHMDF POS=(8,26),                                           X
                 LENGTH=20,                                            X
                 COLOR=TURQUOISE,                                      X
                 ATTRB=(NORM,PROT)
ADDR      DFHMDF POS=(9,26),                                           X
                 LENGTH=30,                                            X
                 COLOR=TURQUOISE,                                      X
                 ATTRB=(NORM,PROT)
CITY      DFHMDF POS=(10,26),                                          X
                 LENGTH=20,                                            X
                 COLOR=TURQUOISE,                                      X
                 ATTRB=(NORM,PROT)
STATE     DFHMDF POS=(10,47),                                          X
                 LENGTH=2,                                             X
                 COLOR=TURQUOISE,                                      X
                 ATTRB=(NORM,PROT)
ZIPCODE   DFHMDF POS=(10,50),                                          X
                 LENGTH=10,                                            X
                 COLOR=TURQUOISE,                                      X
                 ATTRB=(NORM,PROT)
*************************************************************************
MESSAGE   DFHMDF POS=(23,1),                                           X
                 LENGTH=79,                                            X
                 ATTRB=(BRT,PROT),                                     X
                 COLOR=YELLOW
          DFHMDF POS=(24,1),                                           X
                 LENGTH=20,                                            X
                 ATTRB=(NORM,PROT),                                    X
                 COLOR=BLUE,                                           X
                 INITIAL='F3=Exit    F12=Cancel'
DUMMY     DFHMDF POS=(24,79),                                          X
                 LENGTH=1,                                             X
                 ATTRB=(DRK,PROT,FSET),                                X
                 INITIAL=' '
*************************************************************************
          DFHMSD TYPE=FINAL
          END
```

Figure 5-6   BMS mapset for the inquiry program (part 2 of 2)

The END assembler command tells the assembler that there are no more source statements in the mapset program. It must be the last line in the mapset.

The three kinds of BMS macros you code in a mapset are DFHMSD, DFHMDI, and DFHMDF. First, a DFHMSD macro marks the beginning of the mapset. Then, a DFHMDI macro marks the beginning of each map in the mapset. (Remember that most mapsets contain only one map.) Next, each field on the screen is defined by one or more DFHMDF

Macro or command	Usage
PRINT NOGEN	Coded once at the beginning of the mapset; tells the assembler not to print the statements generated as a result of expanding the BMS macro instructions that follow.
DFHMSD	Coded once; supplies values that apply to the entire mapset.
DFHMDI	Coded once for each map within the mapset; supplies values that apply to a single map.
DFHMDF	Coded once for each field (or attribute byte) within the map; specifies the position, length, and attributes of a map field.
DFHMSD TYPE=FINAL	Coded after the last map in the mapset; tells BMS that the mapset is complete.
END	Must be the last statement in the input stream; tells the assembler that there are no more source statements.

Figure 5-7   Assembler commands and macro instructions used in BMS mapsets

macros. Finally, you code the DFHMSD macro with TYPE = FINAL to mark the end of the mapset. In a moment, I'll describe each of these assembler language macros in detail. But first, I want to give you the rules for coding them.

How to code an assembler language statement

When you code an assembler language statement (including a BMS macro), you have to follow a few rules. All assembler language statements follow this general pattern:

```
label           op-code          parameters...
```

Now, I'll explain the meaning of each part of an assembler language statement.

Label   The *label* supplies a symbolic name for the statement and begins in column 1. For a BMS macro, the label must begin with a letter and can be up to seven characters long. (This is in contrast to a standard assembler language label that can be up to eight characters long; that's because CICS adds a one-character suffix to some of the labels you code.) The label field is optional in some instances, so you may omit it if it isn't required. When I present the details of coding BMS macro instructions, I'll point out when labels are required.

Op-code   The *op-code* specifies the instruction to be executed (in a mapset, usually one of the BMS macros). It begins in column 10. For a BMS macro instruction, the op-code is DFHMSD, DFHMDI, or

DFHMDF. The op-codes for the two assembler commands you use in a mapset are PRINT and END.

Parameters   The *parameters* (sometimes called *operands*) provide information the instruction requires to work properly. They're separated from one another by commas with no intervening spaces. The first parameter should follow the op-code after one space. Although parameters usually begin in column 16, the first parameter following a BMS macro op-code begins in column 17 because the BMS macro op-codes are all six characters long and start in column 10.

To specify a parameter's value, use an equal sign, like this:

```
LENGTH=16
```

If a parameter requires more than one value, separate the values with commas, and enclose them in parentheses, as follows:

```
POS=(1,20)
```

If a value contains special characters or spaces, enclose it in single quotes, like this:

```
INITIAL='Customer Inquiry'
```

You can include an apostrophe in a parameter's value by coding two consecutive apostrophes, as in this example:

```
INITIAL='Customer''s name'
```

Here, the parameter's value is Customer's name.

When I code BMS macro instructions, I code only one parameter per line. Although this results in a longer listing, it makes the mapset easier to read. To code only one parameter per line, you need to use continuation lines.

Continuation lines   To continue a statement on the next line, code a comma after a parameter and place any non-blank character in column 72. I use an X. Then, begin the next parameter in column 16 of the following line. The following line is called a *continuation line*. I think you'll find that if you code BMS macros with only one parameter per line, your mapsets will be far easier to read than if you code several parameters on a single line.

Comment lines   You can also improve the readability of a mapset by using comment lines to separate groups of related macros from one another. A *comment line* is any line with an asterisk in column 1. For clarity, I separate groups of related DFHMDF macros from one another with lines of asterisks.

Now, I'll explain the format and function of each of the BMS macro instructions.

How to use the DFHMSD macro to define a mapset

The format of the DFHMSD macro is shown in figure 5-8. As you can see, you code the DFHMSD macro in one of two formats. You use format 1 at the beginning of a mapset, and you use format 2 just before the END command at the end of a mapset. Since format 2 is so simple, I won't discuss it any further.

In format 1 (at the beginning of a mapset), you must specify the name of the mapset in the label field. In figure 5-6, the mapset name is INQSET1. This name will appear in the Processing Program Table (PPT) and in the COPY statement for the symbolic map in your COBOL application program. Since the mapset name must be unique within a CICS system, most installations have naming standards for mapsets. Remember that the maximum length of a mapset name (and of any label you code for a BMS macro) is seven characters.

The TYPE parameter   The TYPE parameter indicates whether a physical map (TYPE=MAP) or a symbolic map (TYPE=DSECT) is being generated. Usually, you'll want to generate both. To do that, you can code TYPE=&SYSPARM. Then, you can process the mapset using a JCL procedure that has two steps. In the first step, the procedure substitutes MAP for &SYSPARM, assembles the mapset, and saves the physical map in a load library. In the second step, it substitutes DSECT for &SYSPARM, generates the symbolic map, and saves it in a source statement library.

The LANG parameter   The LANG parameter specifies the language to be used for the symbolic map. The default is assembler (ASM). If you specify COBOL, the symbolic map will be an 01-level group item that can be copied into a COBOL program. If you specify PLI, the symbolic map will be a structure variable that can be included in a PL/I program. If you specify ASM, the symbolic map will be a dummy section (DSECT) that can be included in an assembler language program. (Incidentally, you'll sometimes hear programmers refer to a symbolic map as a *DSECT* even if it isn't assembler language code.)

The MODE parameter   The MODE parameter specifies whether the map is used for input (IN), output (OUT), or both (INOUT). The default is OUT, so if you need the map for input and output, you must code MODE=INOUT. Since coding IN or OUT isn't any more efficient than coding INOUT, there's no reason you can't code MODE=INOUT for all mapsets.

The TERM parameter   The TERM parameter specifies what type of terminal the map can be used with. If you code ALL or 3270, the map can be used with any type of terminal (even non-3270 devices). Although it's a bit less flexible, it's more efficient to specify the exact terminal type if you know it. Figure 5-8 shows the values you can code for 40-column

The DFHMSD macro

Format 1

```
name      DFHMSD    TYPE=   {&SYSPARM}
                            {DSECT   } ,
                            {MAP     }

                    LANG=   {COBOL}
                            {ASM  } ,
                            {PLI  }

                    MODE=   {IN   }
                            {OUT  } ,
                            {INOUT}

                    TERM=terminal-type,

                    CTRL=(option,option...),

                    STORAGE=AUTO,

                    MAPATTS=(COLOR,HILIGHT),

                    DSATTS=(COLOR,HILIGHT),

                    EXTATT=  {YES    }
                             {NO     } ,
                             {MAPONLY}

                    TIOAPFX= {YES}
                             {NO }
```

Format 2

```
          DFHMSD    TYPE=FINAL
```

Explanation

name	Specifies the one- to seven-character name of the mapset.
TYPE	For format 1, specifies whether a physical map (TYPE=MAP), symbolic map (TYPE=DSECT), or both (TYPE=&SYSPARM) will be generated. TYPE=&SYSPARM is usually coded. For format 2, marks the end of a mapset (TYPE=FINAL).
LANG	Specifies the programming language: ASM (assembler), COBOL, or PLI (PL/I). LANG=COBOL is usually coded.
MODE	Specifies whether the mapset is used for input (IN), output (OUT), or both (INOUT). MODE=INOUT is usually coded.

Figure 5-8   The DFHMSD macro (part 1 of 2)

Explanation *(continued)*

TERM	Specifies the type of terminal that will be supported by the physical map generated from this mapset. Common values are:

         ALL   The physical map will support any terminal.

         3270   Same as ALL.

         3270-1   The physical map will support a 3270 model 1 terminal (40-character lines).

         3270-2   The physical map will support a 3270 model 2 terminal (80-character lines).

         The IBM manual documents other values you can code for more obscure terminal types. Usually, you'll code TERMINAL=3270-2.

CTRL	Specifies a list of control options in effect for each map in the mapset. Two common options are:

         FREEKB   Free the keyboard after each output operation.

         ALARM   Sound the audio alarm at the terminal during each output operation.

STORAGE	If STORAGE=AUTO is coded, the symbolic maps for the maps in the mapset will occupy separate storage locations. Otherwise, they will occupy the same storage locations.
MAPATTS	Specifies which extended attributes should be supported by the physical map. Although other attributes can be coded, COLOR and HILIGHT are the most common and are usually coded together.
DSATTS	Specifies which extended attributes should be supported by the symbolic map. Although other attributes can be coded, COLOR and HILIGHT are the most common and are usually coded together.
EXTATT	Specifies whether support for extended attributes should be provided. EXTATT=YES means support for all extended attributes should be provided in both the physical and symbolic maps; EXTATT=MAPONLY generates support only in the physical map.

         Note: The EXTATT parameter is provided only for compatibility with CICS releases prior to 1.7. If you're using CICS 1.7 or later, you should use MAPATTS and DSATTS instead.

TIOAPFX	YES generates a 12-byte FILLER item at the beginning of the symbolic map and should always be specified for COBOL maps. NO, the default, should not be specified for COBOL maps.

Figure 5-8   The DFHMSD macro (part 2 of 2)

and 80-column 3270 terminals. Since nearly all 3270s have 24x80 screens, you'll probably always code TERM=3270-2.

The value you specify for the TERM parameter affects the name CICS creates for the physical map. CICS adds a one-character suffix to the mapset name you code on the label of the DFHMSD macro. The exact character used depends on the terminal type selected. For example, the mapset definition in figure 5-6 generates a symbolic map named INQSET1 and a physical map named INQSET1M, since M is the suffix for 3270 model 2 terminals.

This naming convention lets you use several different physical maps with a single symbolic map. For example, if you want to use the mapset in figure 5-6 on a 3270 model 1 terminal, all you need to do is change the TERM parameter to 3270-1 and reassemble the map. Then, BMS generates a physical mapset named INQSET1L, since L is the suffix for 3270 model 1 terminals.

When you refer to the mapset in an application program, you use the seven-character name without the suffix. CICS automatically retrieves the physical map that's appropriate for the terminal the program is running on by appending the correct suffix. For example, if you run the program at a 3270 model 1 terminal, CICS retrieves the physical map named INQSET1L; if you run the program at a 3270 model 2 terminal, CICS retrieves the physical map named INQSET1M.

If CICS can't locate the appropriate physical map, it looks for one that has the same name as the mapset, but without a suffix. An unsuffixed name is generated when you code TERM=ALL or TERM=3270; such a physical map can be used for any type of terminal. To accommodate any terminal type, however, CICS requires considerable run-time overhead. That's why it's better to specify the terminal type in the mapset.

The CTRL parameter   The CTRL parameter specifies the *control options* used by the maps a mapset defines. Alternatively, you can specify control options individually for each map on the DFHMDI macro. Since the same control options usually apply to all maps in a mapset, I normally code the CTRL parameter on the DFHMSD macro.

The most common control option is FREEKB. If you specify FREEKB, the keyboard is unlocked whenever a map is sent to the terminal. If you don't specify FREEKB, the keyboard is locked, and the operator must press the Reset key to enter data. So always specify FREEKB in the CTRL parameter.

The ALARM option causes the audio alarm to sound whenever a map is sent to the terminal. In some installations, the audio alarm is used to warn the operator of an error condition. If you do need to use the alarm, you probably don't want it to sound on every output operation. Instead, you want it to sound only when there's an error. So rather than coding the ALARM option in the mapset, you usually use a different technique to request the audio alarm in a COBOL program. You'll see an example of that technique in the next chapter.

You can specify many other control options. Some apply to mapsets used for printer output, while others apply to special features that aren't commonly used. As a result, I'm not going to explain those options here.

The STORAGE parameter   You must use the STORAGE parameter when you define more than one map in a mapset. It indicates how storage will be allocated to the symbolic map. Each symbolic map will have its own storage area if you code STORAGE=AUTO. If you omit the STORAGE parameter, the symbolic maps will overlay the same storage locations. That is, a REDEFINES clause will be included in the 01-level items for the symbolic maps. I recommend you always code STORAGE=AUTO, even when a mapset defines just one map, as in figure 5-6. (Incidentally, the term AUTO comes from PL/I, where items with their own storage are said to have automatic storage.)

The MAPATTS, DSATTS, and EXTATT parameters   You use the next three parameters if your map needs to support extended attributes such as color or extended highlighting. The MAPATTS and DSATTS parameters were introduced with CICS release 1.7 and were designed to replace the older EXTATT parameter. Although EXTATT is supported by current releases of CICS, you should use it only if you're using a CICS release prior to 1.7.

The MAPATTS parameter tells BMS what type of extended attributes should be supported by the physical map. Similarly, the DSATTS parameter specifies which extended attributes should be provided, but for the symbolic map. Although both MAPATTS and DSATTS have options other than COLOR and HILIGHT, you won't use them often. So I've just shown the COLOR and HILIGHT options here.

If you omit the DSATTS parameter, the symbolic map BMS generates won't include any support for extended attributes. So if you want to change a field's color or extended highlighting under program control (for example, to highlight an error), you should include the DSATTS parameter.

You might think the MAPATTS parameter is unnecessay, since BMS can determine which extended attributes the physical map should support by the way you define individual fields. While that's true, you do need to code MAPATTS whenever you code DSATTS. When you code both MAPATTS and DSATTS, they should specify the same set of options (usually, COLOR and HILIGHT).

The older EXTATT parameter tells BMS whether you want to provide support for extended attributes in both the physical and the symbolic map (YES), just the physical map (MAPONLY), or not at all (NO). The main difference between EXTATT and MAPATTS/DSATTS is that EXTATT isn't selective. In other words, when you specify EXTATT, BMS generates support for all extended attributes, not just color and

The DFHMDI macro

```
name       DFHMDI   SIZE=(lines,columns),
                    LINE=line-number,
                    COLUMN=column-number,
                    CTRL=(option,option...)
```

Explanation

name	Specifies the one- to seven-character name of the map.
SIZE	Specifies the size of the map in lines and columns. Usually coded SIZE=(24,80) for a 24x80 screen.
LINE	Specifies the starting line number. Usually coded LINE=1.
COLUMN	Specifies the starting column number. Usually coded COLUMN=1.
CTRL	Same as the CTRL option for the DFHMSD macro.

Figure 5-9 The DFHMDI macro

highlighting. So you get support for features you probably won't need, like field validation and programmed symbols.

The TIOAPFX parameter   If you're going to process a map using a command-level COBOL program, you *must* specify TIOAPFX=YES on the DFHMSD macro. The TIOAPFX parameter generates a 12-byte FILLER item at the beginning of the symbolic map. The system uses those 12 bytes to maintain control information.

How to use the DFHMDI macro to define a map within a mapset

To define a map within a mapset, you use the DFHMDI macro. The format of the DFHMDI macro is shown in figure 5-9. Although you can specify many options on the DFHMDI macro other than those in figure 5-9, they're seldom used.

The label on the DFHMDI macro is the name of the map. In figure 5-6, the map name is INQMAP1. You'll use this name, along with the mapset name you specified on the DFHMSD macro, in your COBOL program. Recall that a mapset name must be unique within a CICS system. Similarly, a map name must be unique within a mapset. You'll see in the next chapter that to refer to a specific map in a CICS command, you specify both the mapset name and the map name. Of course, if your installation has standards for forming map names, be sure to follow them.

The SIZE parameter specifies the number of lines and columns in the map (*not* the screen). The map can be smaller than the screen, but usually the two are the same size. As a result, you'll usually code SIZE=(24,80) for a standard 24x80 screen.

The LINE and COLUMN parameters specify the starting position of the map on the screen. You'll usually code LINE=1 and COLUMN=1. In other words, most maps start at the first column of the first line on the screen.

If you didn't code the CTRL parameter for the entire mapset on the DFHMSD macro, you can still code it on the DFHMDI macro for an individual map. However, since you usually want control options to apply to all maps in a mapset, you should code the CTRL parameter on the DFHMSD macro.

How to use the DFHMDF macro to define a field within a map

To define a field on a screen, you use the DFHMDF macro. Actually, the DFHMDF macro defines an attribute byte. To define a protected field, you code one DFHMDF macro. To define an unprotected field, you must code *two* DFHMDF macros, since two attribute bytes are required for each unprotected field. The first specifies the field's attributes, while the second simply marks where it ends. Figure 5-10 gives the format of the DFHMDF macro.

If you code a label on a DFHMDF macro, items are generated in the symbolic map. As a result, each screen field your COBOL program processes must have a label on the DFHMDF macro that specifies its attributes. In other words, you should code a label for each data entry field and for each display-only field with a variable value. You don't need to code a label for a constant field. If you scan the label fields in figure 5-6, you can see the names of the fields that can be processed by the customer inquiry program: CUSTNO, LNAME, FNAME, ADDR, CITY, STATE, ZIPCODE, MESSAGE, and DUMMY.

The POS and LENGTH parameters The first parameter in figure 5-10, POS, specifies the line and column position of the attribute byte. Remember that the actual data field follows the attribute byte, so if you want a field to start in column 5 of line 10, you code POS=(10,4).

The next parameter, LENGTH, specifies the length of the data field, *not* including the attribute byte. As a result, if you specify LENGTH=5, you actually define six screen positions: five positions for the field itself and one position for its attribute byte.

As you create a BMS mapset, you often need to calculate the location of the first available screen position following a field. To do this, simply take the column position of the attribute byte (specified in the POS

The DFHMDF macro

```
name       DFHMDF   POS=(line,column),

                    LENGTH=field-length,

                           (BRT  )  (PROT  )
                    ATTRB=( {NORM },  {ASKIP },NUM,IC,FSET),
                           (DRK  )  (UNPROT)

                    INITIAL='literal',

                    COLOR=color,

                    HILIGHT=highlight,

                    PICIN='picture-string',

                    PICOUT='picture-string'
```

Explanation

name	Specifies a one- to seven-character name for the field. If omitted, the field is not included in the symbolic map.
POS	Specifies the line and column position of the attribute byte.
LENGTH	Specifies the length of the field, *not* including the attribute byte.
ATTRB	Specifies one or more attribute byte settings for the field:

	BRT	The field is displayed with high intensity.
	NORM	The field is displayed with regular intensity.
	DRK	The field is *not* displayed on the screen.
	PROT	The field is protected; data may not be keyed into it.
	ASKIP	The field is protected, and the cursor will automatically skip over it.
	UNPROT	The field is unprotected; data may be keyed into it.
	NUM	The field is assumed to be numeric and is right justified and zero filled. If omitted, the field is assumed to be alphanumeric and is left justified and space filled.
	IC	Specifies that the cursor should be located at the start of the data field.
	FSET	Specifies that the MDT bit in the attribute byte should be turned on before the map is sent to the terminal.

Figure 5-10 The DFHMDF macro (part 1 of 2)

Explanation (*continued*)

INITIAL   Specifies the initial value of the field. If omitted, the default is hexadecimal zeros (LOW-VALUE).

COLOR   Specifies the field's color. You may specify DEFAULT for the terminal's default color, or you may specify BLUE, RED, PINK, GREEN, TURQUOISE, YELLOW, or NEUTRAL (white). If omitted, DEFAULT is assumed.

HILIGHT   Specifies the field's extended highlighting. Valid highlighting options are BLINK, REVERSE, UNDERLINE, and OFF. If omitted, the default is OFF.

PICIN   Specifies a COBOL PICTURE string that defines the format of the data on input. Example: PICIN='999V99'. The length implied by PICIN must agree with the LENGTH parameter. If omitted, PICIN='X(*n*)' will be assumed, where *n* is the value specified for the LENGTH parameter.

PICOUT   Specifies a COBOL PICTURE string that defines the format of the data on output. Example: PICOUT='ZZZ,ZZ9.99'. The length implied by PICOUT must agree with the LENGTH parameter. If omitted, PICOUT='X(*n*)' will be assumed, where *n* is the value specified for the LENGTH parameter.

Figure 5-10 The DFHMDF macro (part 2 of 2)

parameter), and add the length plus 1 to it. For example, suppose you defined a field like this:

```
DFHMDF POS=(5,13),
       LENGTH=14
```

To calculate the next available position, add 14 plus 1 to the starting column, 13. In this example, the next available position is column 28 of line 5.

The ATTRB parameter   The next parameter in figure 5-10, ATTRB, specifies the characteristics of the attribute byte. The first set of options for the ATTRB parameter controls the intensity attribute. If you code NORM, the field displays at normal intensity. If you code BRT, the field displays at bright intensity. If you code DRK, the field won't be displayed at all. If you don't specify the display intensity, NORM is assumed.

The second set of options for the ATTRB parameter specifies a field's protection attribute. If you code PROT, the field is protected; the user cannot key data into the field. PROT is the normal attribute for captions and display-only fields. ASKIP has the same effect as PROT, except that the cursor automatically jumps over the field to the next unprotected field. You normally code ASKIP on the DFHMDF macro that defines the attribute byte that marks the end of the data entry field. That causes the cursor to skip automatically to the next data entry field. If you code UNPROT, the field is unprotected, so data can be keyed into the field.

The NUM option of the ATTRB parameter specifies a numeric unprotected field. The NUM option causes data to be automatically right-justified and zero-filled. In contrast, if the NUM option is omitted, data is left-justified and padded with blanks. In addition, the NUM option places the keyboard in numeric shift, and, if the terminal supports the numeric lock feature, it allows only numeric characters to be keyed into the field.

The IC option indicates that the cursor should be positioned at the beginning of the data field. Although you can use IC to control the cursor position, I don't recommend you do. In chapter 8, I'll explain a more flexible way to control the position of the cursor from your COBOL programs.

The last ATTRB option, FSET, causes the MDT bit to be turned on before the map is transmitted to the terminal. That way, the contents of the field will be transmitted back to the program, whether or not the user enters data in the field. Usually, you don't specify the FSET option, since the MDT bit is set automatically when a user keys data into an unprotected field. However, if you want a *protected* field to be transmitted to your program, you should specify the FSET option. (Don't worry if the FSET option confuses you. It will make more sense when you've seen the commands used to send and receive map data in the next chapter.)

Notice the last DFHMDF macro in figure 5-6. This field, named DUMMY, is one byte long and specifies these ATTRB options: DRK, PROT, and FSET. As a result, this field can't be seen or modified by the operator but is always transmitted to the program. I'll explain why this field is always required later in this book. For now, just remember that you should define a field like this on *all* your maps.

The INITIAL parameter　The INITIAL parameter assigns a value to a constant field. The value is enclosed in single quotes like this:

```
INITIAL='Customer Inquiry'
```

The number of characters you code in the literal should agree with the field length you specify in the LENGTH parameter. If you omit the initial parameter, the field is set to hexadecimal zeros (LOW-VALUE).

In the DUMMY field in figure 5-6, an INITIAL parameter assigns an initial value of one space to the field. If the INITIAL parameter is omitted from this field, the field is *not* transmitted to your program, even though FSET is specified. That's because hexadecimal zeros are *never* transmitted between your program and the terminal.

The COLOR parameter　The next parameter specifies the color for the field. If you omit it, the field is displayed in the terminal's default color. The use of color is generally governed by shop standards. In this book, I've followed IBM's Common User Access (CUA) guidelines for color usage. This means that screen titles are displayed in blue, instructions and captions are displayed in green, and entry fields and variable data are displayed in turquoise.

If you specify the COLOR parameter and the map is used for a terminal that doesn't support extended color, the color attribute is simply ignored. Since color terminals are becoming more and more common, it's a good idea to specify color attributes for all of your maps.

The HILIGHT parameter   The HILIGHT parameter specifies which extended highlighting option you wish to use for the field. You can specify BLINK, REVERSE, or UNDERLINE to enable extended highlighting. OFF means you don't want extended highlighting for the field. If you omit the HILIGHT parameter, OFF is assumed by default.

If you want to use reverse video to mark entry errors, you don't need to code the HILIGHT parameter here. Instead, you should make sure that support for extended highlighting is provided in the symbolic map (by coding DSATTS=HILIGHT in the DFHMSD macro). Then, you can activate reverse video whenever your program detects invalid data for the field.

On the other hand, you may want to use underlining to mark input fields. In that case, you'd specify HILIGHT=UNDERLINE for the field.

The PICIN and PICOUT parameters   The next two parameters, PICIN and PICOUT, describe the PICTURE clauses that will be generated in the symbolic map for input and output fields. The picture string must be a valid COBOL PICTURE clause and must agree in length with the LENGTH parameter.

If you omit PICIN or PICOUT, BMS assigns a default alphanumeric picture. For a six-byte field, the default picture is X(6), whether you want the field to be alphanumeric or numeric. In almost all cases, that's what you'd want the picture of a six-byte alphanumeric field to be. As a result, you seldom code PICIN or PICOUT for an alphanumeric field.

You might assume that you should specify a numeric PICIN for numeric input fields, but that's not the case. Instead, you should let BMS generate an alphanumeric picture. Then, your program can call a specialized numeric editing routine that determines whether the user has entered a valid number and formats the number using proper decimal alignment. You'll learn how to edit numeric input fields in chapter 8.

In contrast, you'll often use the PICOUT parameter for numeric output fields. You use it to control the format of numeric output data, by inserting commas and decimal points, suppressing lead zeros, and so on. For example, if you code PICOUT='ZZ,ZZ9.99' and move a numeric value of 1234.56 to the field, the data displays as 1,234.56 with a leading space.

Screen layout

Map definition

```
DFHMDF POS=(1,1),                                          X
       LENGTH=7,                                           X
       ATTRB=(NORM,PROT),                                  X
       COLOR=BLUE,                                          X
       INITIAL='INQMAP1'
DFHMDF POS=(1,20),                                         X
       LENGTH=16,                                          X
       ATTRB=(NORM,PROT),                                  X
       COLOR=BLUE,                                          X
       INITIAL='Customer Inquiry'
```

Figure 5-11   Model definition for constant fields

Although you need to understand the functions of the parameters I've just described, in practice you'll use only a few combinations of them. Fortunately, you can create almost all BMS mapsets by basing your coding on a few simple models of field definitions.

Model BMS field definitions   In my experience, I've found that the DFHMDF macros used to define screen fields almost always follow a few patterns. As a result, this section presents six models you can use to define your screen fields. These models should cover most BMS requirements you're likely to encounter.

As for the DFHMSD and DFHMDI macros, they're almost always coded just as they are in figure 5-6. So you can refer to that figure for models of those macro instructions.

In general, you need to know how to define five types of fields: (1) constant fields, whose values never change; (2) alphanumeric data entry fields; (3) numeric data entry fields; (4) alphanumeric display-only fields; and (5) numeric display-only fields. The five examples that follow are models for each of these five types of fields. The sixth example is a model for a standard message area that includes a field for displaying user messages and another with a description of the PF keys available.

Example 1: A constant field   Figure 5-11 shows two sample constant fields. Constant fields are typically used as headings to identify the screen or individual fields on the screen. In this case, the first constant field identifies the map (INQMAP1), and the second is a screen title

Screen layout

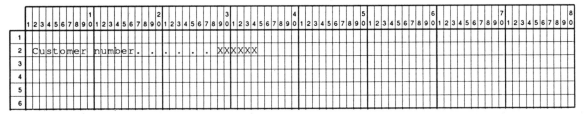

Map definition

```
          DFHMDF POS=(2,1),                              X
                 LENGTH=26,                              X
                 ATTRB=(NORM,PROT),                      X
                 COLOR=GREEN,                            X
                 INITIAL='Customer number. . . . . .'
CUSTNO    DFHMDF POS=(2,28),                             X
                 LENGTH=6,                               X
                 ATTRB=(NORM,UNPROT),                    X
                 COLOR=TURQUOISE,                        X
                 INITIAL='_____'
          DFHMDF POS=(2,35),                             X
                 LENGTH=1,                               X
                 ATTRB=ASKIP
```

Figure 5-12 Model definition for an alphanumeric data entry field

containing the words "Customer Inquiry." The map identification begins in column 2 of line 1, and the screen title begins in column 21 of line 1. (I could have defined this screen heading as a single 35-byte constant field, but it's slightly more efficient to define it as two fields.)

The two DFHMDF macros I used to define these fields are similar. The POS parameter locates the attribute byte, immediately to the left of the constant data. The LENGTH parameter specifies the number of characters in the constant field. The ATTRB parameter indicates that the field is protected and is to be displayed with normal intensity. And the COLOR parameter specifies that the constant field is to be displayed in blue, the CUA standard for screen titles. Depending on the purpose of the constant and your shop's standards, you may need to specify a different color here. The last parameter, INITIAL, supplies the value of the constant.

Example 2: An alphanumeric data entry field   Figure 5-12 is an example of a data entry field that accepts alphanumeric data. Typically, a data entry field contains two parts: a caption and the entry field itself. In this case, the caption is "Customer number. . . . . ." and the data entry field is 6 bytes long.

Three DFHMDF macros are required to define this entry field and its caption. The first one is for the caption, so it's similar to the examples in figure 5-11 except for its color. (CUA specifies green for field captions.)

Screen layout

```
        1         2         3         4         5         6         7         8
  1234567890123456789012345678901234567890123456789012345678901234567890123456789 0
1
2 Quantity . . . . . . . 99999
3
4
5
6
```

Map definition

```
          DFHMDF POS=(2,1),                                              X
                 LENGTH=24,                                              X
                 ATTRB=(NORM,PROT),                                      X
                 COLOR=GREEN,                                            X
                 INITIAL='Quantity . . . . . . . .'
QTY       DFHMDF POS=(2,26),                                             X
                 LENGTH=5,                                               X
                 ATTRB=(NORM,NUM),                                       X
                 COLOR=TURQUOISE,                                        X
                 INITIAL='_____'
          DFHMDF POS=(2,32),                                             X
                 LENGTH=1,                                               X
                 ATTRB=ASKIP
```

Figure 5-13   Model definition for a numeric data entry field

The next DFHMDF macro in figure 5-12 defines the entry field itself. Since you want this field to appear in the symbolic map, a label is assigned to it (in this case, CUSTNO). The POS parameter indicates that the attribute byte is in column 28 of line 2, and the LENGTH parameter indicates that the entry field is 6 bytes long. The ATTRB parameter says that the field is unprotected, so the user can enter data into it. The COLOR parameter specifies the standard CUA color for entry fields, turquoise. The INITIAL parameter specifies an initial value of underscores to help the user locate the entry field. Because the use of underscores is specified in the CUA standard for entry fields, I'll use them in the examples in this book.

The last DFHMDF macro marks the end of the entry field. As you know, BMS doesn't automatically generate an attribute byte to mark the end of an unprotected field. So you have to do it yourself. If you don't, the rest of the line will be unprotected.

You mark the end of an entry field with an attribute byte that immediately follows it, in this case, in column 35 of line 2 (POS=(2,35)). The ATTRB parameter should specify ASKIP so if the operator keys to the end of the preceding field, the cursor will automatically skip to the next unprotected field.

Example 3: A numeric data entry field.   Figure 5-13 shows a typical numeric data entry field. Like the example in figure 5-12, this field consists of two parts: a caption and a data entry field. The main

Screen layout

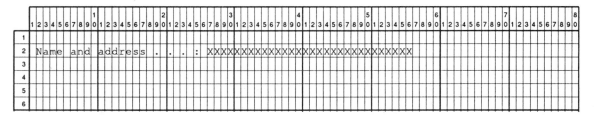

Map definition

```
           DFHMDF POS=(2,1),                                        X
                  LENGTH=24,                                        X
                  ATTRB=(NORM,PROT),                                X
                  COLOR=GREEN,                                      X
                  INITIAL='Name and address . . . :'
LNAME      DFHMDF POS=(2,26),                                       X
                  LENGTH=30,                                        X
                  COLOR=TURQUOISE,                                  X
                  ATTRB=(NORM,PROT)
```

Figure 5-14 Model definition for an alphanumeric variable output field

difference is that the entry field contains numeric data. Again, three
DFHMDF macros are required. The first one defines the caption, the
second defines the entry field using the NUM attribute, and the third
marks the end of the entry field.

Example 4: An alphanumeric display-only field   Figure 5-14
shows a typical alphanumeric display-only field. The data to be
displayed in the field is supplied by a COBOL program.

Two DFHMDF macros define this field. The first defines the field
caption. The second defines the display field. The attribute for this
display-only field is protected, so data can't be keyed into it. Since the
field is protected, you don't have to code a third DFHMDF macro to
mark its end.

Notice that the field's caption ends with a colon rather than a period.
This is how CUA distinguishes entry fields from display-only fields.
Your shop may use some other way to distinguish data entry fields from
display-only fields, such as using different colors. If that's the case, you'll
have to adjust these macros to meet your shop standards.

Example 5: A numeric display-only field   Figure 5-15 shows a
typical numeric display-only field. This model is similar to figure 5-14
except that the PICOUT parameter indicates that the field should be
zero-suppressed with comma and decimal point insertion.

Screen layout

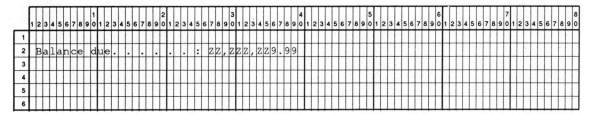

Map definition

```
          DFHMDF POS=(2,1),                             X
                 LENGTH=24,                             X
                 ATTRB=(NORM,PROT),                     X
                 COLOR=GREEN,                           X
                 INITIAL='Balance due. . . . . . :'
BALDUE    DFHMDF POS=(2,26),                            X
                 LENGTH=13,                             X
                 COLOR=TURQUOISE,                       X
                 ATTRB=(NORM,PROT),                     X
                 PICOUT='ZZ,ZZZ,ZZ9.99'
```

Figure 5-15 Model definition for a numeric variable output field

Example 6: User message area Figure 5-16 shows a set of DFHMDF macros that set up standard fields for displaying user messages and function key assignments. Here, a field named MESSAGE is displayed on line 23. And function key assignments are shown as a constant in line 24. Notice that I specified COLOR=YELLOW for the message field; yellow is CUA's standard color for warning messages.

As I've already mentioned, you should always include a one-byte protected field with the DRK and FSET options specified, like the field named DUMMY in figure 5-16. In chapter 8, I'll explain why this field is required. For now, just be sure to include this field in all your mapsets.

The symbolic map As you know, you use a symbolic map in a COBOL program to access data sent to and received from a terminal screen. When you assemble a mapset, a symbolic map is created and placed in a COBOL COPY library. Then, you use a COPY statement to include the symbolic map in a COBOL program.

Figure 5-17 is the symbolic map BMS generated from the mapset in figure 5-6. Frankly, I don't care for the symbolic maps BMS generates. As you can see, they're difficult to read because they follow no consistent rules of abbreviation or indentation. Data names are created that aren't needed. And the names generated by BMS are fine for assembler language but less than adequate for COBOL programming. However, understanding the structure of the symbolic map BMS creates is critical

Screen layout

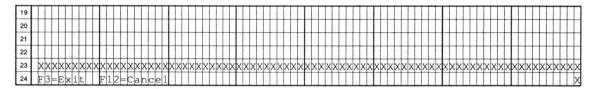

Map definition

```
MESSAGE    DFHMDF POS=(23,1),                                              X
                  LENGTH=79,                                               X
                  ATTRB=(BRT,PROT),                                        X
                  COLOR=YELLOW
           DFHMDF POS=(24,1),                                              X
                  LENGTH=19,                                               X
                  ATTRB=(NORM,PROT),                                       X
                  COLOR=BLUE,                                              X
                  INITIAL='F3=Exit   F12=Cancel'
DUMMY      DFHMDF POS=(24,79),                                             X
                  LENGTH=1,                                                X
                  ATTRB=(DRK,PROT,FSET),                                   X
                  INITIAL=' '
```

Figure 5-16 Model definition for a message area, function key area, and dummy FSET field

to your learning how to develop CICS programs. So you'll have to study it carefully.

The symbolic map in figure 5-17 has two 01-level items named INQMAP1I and INQMAP1O. Since the second 01-level item contains a REDEFINES clause, these items overlay each other. The fields in the first 01-level group are intended for use in input operations (hence the suffix I), while the fields in the second 01-level group are meant for output (suffix O).

Each of these 01-level groups begins with a 12-byte FILLER item generated because TIOAPFX=YES was specified in the mapset. Within these 01-level groups, five data names were created for each DFHMDF macro coded with a label. The data names for these fields were created by adding a one-character suffix to the label coded on the DFHMDF macro.

The shaded areas of figure 5-17 show the code generated for the data entry field labeled CUSTNO in figure 5-6. As you can see, five names have been created for this field: CUSTNOL, CUSTNOF, CUSTNOA, CUSTNOI, CUSTNOO. Figure 5-18 lists the suffixes used to create these names and briefly describes the function of each field. Figure 5-18 also shows two additional field suffixes—C and H—that aren't included in the symbolic map in figure 5-17. That's because the inquiry map didn't specify the DSATTS parameter.

```
01   INQMAP1I.
     02    FILLER      PIC X(12).
     02    CUSTNOL     PIC S9(4) COMP.
     02    CUSTNOF     PIC X.
     02    FILLER REDEFINES CUSTNOF.
      03   CUSTNOA     PIC X.
     02    CUSTNOI     PIC X(0006).
     02    LNAMEL      PIC S9(4) COMP.
     02    LNAMEF      PIC X.
     02    FILLER REDEFINES LNAMEF.
      03   LNAMEA      PIC X.
     02    LNAMEI      PIC X(0030).
     02    FNAMEL      PIC S9(4) COMP.
     02    FNAMEF      PIC X.
     02    FILLER REDEFINES FNAMEF.
      03   FNAMEA      PIC X.
     02    FNAMEI      PIC X(0020).
     02    ADDRL       PIC S9(4) COMP.
     02    ADDRF       PIC X.
     02    FILLER REDEFINES ADDRF.
      03   ADDRA       PIC X.
     02    ADDRI       PIC X(0030).
     02    CITYL       PIC S9(4) COMP.
     02    CITYF       PIC X.
     02    FILLER REDEFINES CITYF.
      03   CITYA       PIC X.
     02    CITYI       PIC X(0020).
     02    STATEL      PIC S9(4) COMP.
     02    STATEF      PIC X.
     02    FILLER REDEFINES STATEF.
      03   STATEA      PIC X.
     02    STATEI      PIC X(0002).
     02    ZIPCODEL    PIC S9(4) COMP.
     02    ZIPCODEF    PIC X.
     02    FILLER REDEFINES ZIPCODEF.
      03   ZIPCODEA    PIC X.
     02    ZIPCODEI    PIC X(0010).
     02    MESSAGEL    PIC S9(4) COMP.
     02    MESSAGEF    PIC X.
     02    FILLER REDEFINES MESSAGEF.
      03   MESSAGEA    PIC X.
     02    MESSAGEI    PIC X(0079).
     02    DUMMYL      PIC S9(4) COMP.
     02    DUMMYF      PIC X.
     02    FILLER REDEFINES DUMMYF.
      03   DUMMYA      PIC X.
     02    DUMMYI      PIC X(0001).
```

Figure 5-17 The symbolic map for the inquiry program (part 1 of 2)

The length field   The first data name generated for each screen field in the symbolic map is a two-byte binary field (COMP PIC S9(4)) that contains the length of the data sent to the program. BMS forms this name by adding the letter L to the end of the label on the DFHMDF macro. So the length field for CUSTNO is CUSTNOL. The value of this field is the actual number of characters sent, which may well be different from the length of the field specified in the LENGTH parameter on the DFHMDF macro.

```
01   INQMAP1O REDEFINES INQMAP1I.
     02    FILLER    PIC X(12).
     02    FILLER    PIC X(3).
     02    CUSTNOO   PIC X(0006).
     02    FILLER    PIC X(3).
     02    LNAMEO    PIC X(0030).
     02    FILLER    PIC X(3).
     02    FNAMEO    PIC X(0020).
     02    FILLER    PIC X(3).
     02    ADDRO     PIC X(0030).
     02    FILLER    PIC X(3).
     02    CITYO     PIC X(0020).
     02    FILLER    PIC X(3).
     02    STATEO    PIC X(0002).
     02    FILLER    PIC X(3).
     02    ZIPCODEO  PIC X(0010).
     02    FILLER    PIC X(3).
     02    MESSAGEO  PIC X(0079).
     02    FILLER    PIC X(3).
     02    DUMMYO    PIC X(0001).
```

Figure 5-17 The symbolic map for the inquiry program (part 2 of 2)

To illustrate, suppose the user enters ABCD into a field defined with LENGTH=20. The value of the length field will be four since the user entered four characters. Embedded spaces are included in the count, so if the user entered JOHN SMITH, the length would be ten.

If the user doesn't enter any data, the field's length value is set to zero. As a result, you can test the length field for a value of zero to see whether or not the user entered any data. You'll see examples of this common programming technique later in this book.

The attribute and flag fields   The next two fields generated in the symbolic map are redefinitions of a single byte of storage:

```
02    CUSTNOF    PICTURE X.
02    FILLER REDEFINES CUSTNOF.
  03  CUSTNOA    PICTURE X.
```

After an input operation, CUSTNOF contains a *flag byte* that is normally set to hexadecimal zero (LOW-VALUE). However, if the user modifies the field but does *not* enter data into it (for example, by using the delete key to erase data in the field), the flag byte is set to hexadecimal 80.

CUSTNOA is used for output operations to override the field attributes defined in the physical map. You'll learn how to use this field in chapter 8.

If you specified extended attributes with the DSATTS option, fields for those attributes would appear in the symbolic map following the attribute and flag fields. For example, if you specified

Suffix	Usage	Example
L	A binary halfword (PIC S9(4) COMP) that contains the length of the data returned in the input field.	CUSTNOL LNAMEL
F	A single-character field (PIC X) that contains hexadecimal 80 if the user made a change to the field, but no data was transmitted; otherwise, it contains LOW-VALUES.	CUSTNOF LNAMEF
A	A single-character field that contains the attribute byte for output operations. Occupies the same storage location as the F field.	CUSTNOA LNAMEA
C	A single-character field that contains the attribute for extended color. Generated only if DSATTS=COLOR is specified.	CUSTNOC LNAMEC
H	A single-character field that contains the attribute for extended highlighting. Generated only if DSATTS=HILIGHT is specified.	CUSTNOH LNAMEH
I	The input data field.	CUSTNOI LNAMEI
O	The output data field. Occupies the same storage location as the input field.	CUSTNOO LNAMEO

Figure 5-18 How suffixes are used to name fields in the symbolic map

DSATTS=(COLOR,HILIGHT) in the DFHMSD macro, these two fields would appear immediately after the CUSTNOA field:

```
02   CUSTNOC    PICTURE X.
02   CUSTNOH    PICTURE X.
```

Since I didn't specify a DSATTS parameter for the inquiry map, these fields don't appear in figure 5-17.

The data field   Two data names are generated in the symbolic map for the actual data field. In figure 5-17, the names are CUSTNOI and CUSTNOO. (If you look carefully at the number of bytes in INQMAPI and INQMAPO, you'll see that CUSTNOI and CUSTNOO occupy the same storage location.) CUSTNOI is used for input operations, while CUSTNOO is used for output. Two data names are provided to allow the PICTURE clauses to differ if you specify a PICIN or PICOUT parameter on the DFHMDF macro.

How to create your own symbolic map   Although I don't usually recommend it, sometimes you'll find it necessary to discard the symbolic map generated by BMS in favor of one you create yourself. The most likely reason for this is if the map contains two or more lines of repeated fields. BMS doesn't take advantage of the COBOL OCCURS clause to make this type of map easier to process. You'll see an example of this when I present the source code for an order entry program in chapter 10.

```
 01   INQMAP1.
*
      05   FILLER                        PIC X(12).
*
      05   INQ-L-CUSTNO                  PIC S9(4) COMP.
      05   INQ-A-CUSTNO                  PIC X.
      05   INQ-D-CUSTNO                  PIC X(6).
*
      05   INQ-L-LNAME                   PIC S9(4) COMP.
      05   INQ-A-LNAME                   PIC X.
      05   INQ-D-LNAME                   PIC X(30).
*
      05   INQ-L-FNAME                   PIC S9(4) COMP.
      05   INQ-A-FNAME                   PIC X.
      05   INQ-D-FNAME                   PIC X(20).
*
      05   INQ-L-ADDR                    PIC S9(4) COMP.
      05   INQ-A-ADDR                    PIC X.
      05   INQ-D-ADDR                    PIC X(30).
*
      05   INQ-L-CITY                    PIC S9(4) COMP.
      05   INQ-A-CITY                    PIC X.
      05   INQ-D-CITY                    PIC X(20).
*
      05   INQ-L-STATE                   PIC S9(4) COMP.
      05   INQ-A-STATE                   PIC X.
      05   INQ-D-STATE                   PIC XX.
*
      05   INQ-L-ZIPCODE                 PIC S9(4) COMP.
      05   INQ-A-ZIPCODE                 PIC X.
      05   INQ-D-ZIPCODE                 PIC X(10).
*
      05   INQ-L-MESSAGE                 PIC S9(4) COMP.
      05   INQ-A-MESSAGE                 PIC X.
      05   INQ-D-MESSAGE                 PIC X(79).
*
      05   INQ-L-DUMMY                   PIC S9(4) COMP.
      05   INQ-A-DUMMY                   PIC X.
      05   INQ-D-DUMMY                   PIC X.
*
```

Figure 5-19 Programmer-generated symbolic map for the inquiry program

The map for that program has 10 lines of line item data, each of which has six fields. By creating my own symbolic map, I was able to process these line item fields as a simple table.

Figure 5-19 shows a symbolic map I created for the inquiry map. To create a symbolic map like this one, work from the mapset definition using the procedure summarized in figure 5-20. If you follow these guidelines, the resulting symbolic map will be easy to read and understand.

Whenever you substitute your own symbolic map for the one generated by BMS, be aware of the possibility of error. When you use the BMS-generated symbolic map, you can make a change to the mapset, reassemble it, and then recompile your program with confidence that the physical map and the symbolic map agree. When you create your own

1. Code only one 01-level item, rather than separate 01-level items that redefine one another for input and output purposes.

2. Code a 12-byte FILLER item for the TIOAPFX at the beginning of the map.

3. For each labeled map field, code a group of 05-level items, following these rules to create the data names:

    a. Start each name with a two- or three-character prefix that relates the data name to the group item. In figure 5-19, I started each name with INQ.

    b. Include one character to identify the field's function: L for the length field, A for the attribute field, and D for the data field.

    c. If you need different pictures for input and output, create a fourth data name that redefines the data field. Then, identify the input and output data fields with the characters I and O.

    d. If you specified extended attributes with the DSATTS parameter, insert fields for them between the attribute field and the data field. Use the characters C and H to identify extended color and extended highlighting attributes.

4. Separate each set of data names with a blank comment line.

5. Align the elements of the symbolic map so it's easy to read.

Figure 5-20   Rules for creating your own symbolic map

symbolic map, it's up to you to make sure that any changes to the mapset are reflected in your symbolic map.

Discussion   Right now, you're probably thinking that the process of BMS map definition is overly complicated. Quite frankly, you're right. That's why many shops use map generators to ease the burden of creating mapsets. When you use a map generator, you create an image of the screen on a terminal, using special codes for unprotected fields, numeric fields, and so forth. Next, you assign names to the fields that you want in the symbolic map. Then, the map generator analyzes the screen image and creates a BMS mapset you can assemble in the usual way. At the same time, many map generators produce screen documentation that's more useful than a BMS assembler listing. The map generator may also allow you to save your screen image so you can recall it later to make modifications without having to reenter it. Obviously, a map generator can be a tremendous time-saver. If one is available, by all means use it.

Still, it's important to know how to create BMS mapsets. Since map generators cannot handle all situations, you may need to create your own mapsets for complicated screen layouts. Also, you may need to modify the output produced by the map generator.

Terms

mapset
physical map
symbolic map
map
macro instruction
macro
label
op-code
parameter
operand
continuation line
comment line
DSECT
control option
flag byte

Objectives

1. Given a sample screen layout, code the BMS mapset for it.

2. Describe the function of the fields generated in the symbolic map for each named map field.

Chapter 6

A basic subset of command-level CICS

In the last chapter, I showed you how to create a BMS mapset for the screen a simple inquiry program uses. In this chapter, I'll use the inquiry program to present a basic subset of CICS command-level programming in COBOL. The subset includes the programming techniques and CICS commands you'll use in a wide variety of CICS applications. Because this chapter presents the most difficult CICS programming concepts, you can expect to work hard to master the information it presents.

This chapter has three topics. The first presents a programming technique you'll have to use in almost every CICS program you write: pseudo-conversational programming. The second presents the inquiry program and explains its operation step by step. And the third shows you the formats of the CICS commands the inquiry program uses. When you finish these three topics, you should be able to code simple command-level inquiry programs of your own.

Pseudo-conversational programming

Before you can write a command-level program, you need to understand a fundamental CICS programming technique called *pseudo-conversational programming*. Most CICS shops require that all application programs be developed using this technique. Simply put, a *pseudo-conversational program* is an on-line program that has actually ended while it appears to be waiting for an operator to enter data. To illustrate, let me show you how the customer inquiry program works.

Operation of the inquiry program

The seven parts of figure 6-1 represent a terminal session where a user executes the customer inquiry program. You'll recall from chapter 3 that a user can start a program by entering a transaction identifier. To begin the customer inquiry program, the user enters the trans-id INQ1, as shown in part 1 of figure 6-1. When the user presses the Enter key, CICS searches the Program Control Table (PCT) to determine which program is associated with INQ1. Then, it starts that program.

Once the program is started, it displays the screen in part 2 of figure 6-1. The user types a customer number, as shown in part 3, and presses the Enter key. In response, the program retrieves the correct record from the customer file and displays the appropriate customer information in part 4. In part 5, the user types another customer number and presses Enter again. This time, the inquiry program can't locate the record specified by the user, so it displays an appropriate error message, as shown in part 6. Then, the user presses the PF3 key to end the program. As a result, the menu shown in part 7 of figure 6-1 is displayed.

The menu screen in part 7 of figure 6-1 is *not* displayed by the customer inquiry program. Instead, the inquiry program transfers control directly to a menu program, which in turn displays the menu map. In the next topic, you'll learn how this transfer of control takes place. And later in this book, you'll see the source code for the menu program itself. So you don't need to worry about how the menu program works for now.

Conversational vs. pseudo-conversational programs

In parts 2 through 6 of figure 6-1, the customer inquiry program appears to be sitting idle, waiting for the user to enter data. An on-line program that *does* sit idle while it waits for data is called a *conversational program.* That's because it carries on a conversation with the user.

You can easily imagine that a conversational program spends almost all of its time doing nothing but waiting. On a single-user system, forcing

Part 1

The user enters the
transaction identifier
INQ1 and presses the
Enter key.

```
INQ1
```

Part 2

The program displays
the inquiry map.

```
INQMAP1              Customer Inquiry

Type a customer number.   Then press Enter.

Customer number. . . . . _____

Name and address . . . :
```

```
F3=Exit   F12=Cancel
```

Figure 6-1   Operation of the inquiry program

Part 3

The user types a
customer number and
presses the Enter key.

```
INQMAP1            Customer Inquiry

Type a customer number.   Then press Enter.

Customer number. . . . .  400001

Name and address . . . :




F3=Exit  F12=Cancel
```

Part 4

The program retrieves
the customer record and
displays it.

```
INQMAP1            Customer Inquiry

Type a customer number.   Then press Enter.

Customer number. . . . .  400001

Name and address . . . :  MCDONALD
                          KEITH
                          4501 W MOCKINGBIRD
                          DALLAS            TX 75209




F3=Exit  F12=Cancel
```

Figure 6-1 Operation of the inquiry program (continued)

Part 5

The user types another customer number and presses the Enter key.

```
INQMAP1              Customer Inquiry

Type a customer number.  Then press Enter.

Customer number. . . . . 520000

Name and address . . . : MCDONALD
                         KEITH
                         4501 W MOCKINGBIRD
                         DALLAS              TX 75209










F3=Exit  F12=Cancel
```

Part 6

The program displays a message indicating that the record doesn't exist. The user presses PF3 to end the program.

```
INQMAP1              Customer Inquiry

Type a customer number.  Then press Enter.

Customer number. . . . . 520000

Name and address . . . :










That customer does not exist
F3=Exit  F12=Cancel
```

Figure 6-1   Operation of the inquiry program (continued)

Part 7

The inquiry program
transfers control to a
menu program, which
displays a menu.

```
MNUMAP1              MASTER MENU

Select one of the following.  Then press Enter.

Action . . . . _ 1.  Display customer information
                 2.  Maintain customer information
                 3.  Enter orders













F3=Exit  F12=Cancel
```

Figure 6-1   Operation of the inquiry program (continued)

the computer to wait for user input isn't a problem because there's
nothing else for the computer to do. But in a system such as CICS, with
many users, it *is* a problem.

To illustrate, figure 6-2 shows the time utilization for a typical
terminal interaction from the perspective of the user, a conversational
program, and a pseudo-conversational program. In this example, the
entire terminal interaction takes 18 seconds, including the time it takes
the user to key in the data and the time it takes CICS to process it. The
top bar shows the timing from the user's perspective. Here, you can see
that the user spends 15 seconds entering data and 3 seconds waiting for
CICS to process the data. The middle bar shows that from the
conversational program's perspective, 15 seconds are spent waiting for
the user's input and 3 seconds are spent processing the data.

I exaggerated the timings shown in figure 6-2 to make the figure
easier to understand. In a more realistic terminal interaction, the user
might spend as much as a minute entering data or reviewing the results
of an inquiry, while CICS might process the transaction in less than one
second. So although figure 6-2 shows a program whose ratio of waiting
time to working time is 5 to 1, a more realistic ratio might be 50 to 1.

During the time that the conversational program is idle while it waits
for terminal input, CICS is free to dispatch other programs for execution.
However, the conversational program itself must remain in main
storage. In addition, all of the CICS control blocks that are required to

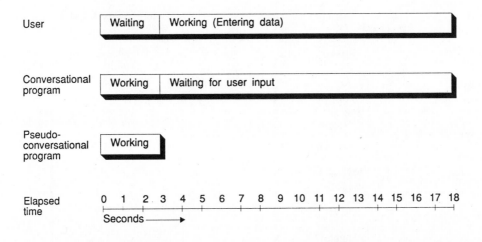

Figure 6-2   Time usage for a typical terminal interaction from the perspective of the user, a conversational program and a pseudo-conversational program

keep track of the program's execution must be kept in main storage, too. The left side of figure 6-3 shows how virtual storage might be allocated to five conversational programs. As you can see, all five of the programs occupy virtual storage, even though only two of them are actually working.

Clearly, conversational programs can be inefficient when it comes to virtual storage usage. And virtual storage is one of the most critical resources under CICS. In fact, one of the most common CICS problems is a condition known as *Short On Storage*, or, appropriately, *SOS*. When CICS goes short on storage, it suspends all work and begins terminating tasks in an effort to free up storage. As you can imagine, the result of an SOS condition can be disruptive as CICS grinds to a halt. And conversational programs are often a major cause of SOS conditions.

The solution to this efficiency problem is to remove a program from storage while it's waiting for terminal input. And that's just what happens with a pseudo-conversational program. While the inquiry map in parts 2 through 6 of figure 6-1 is displayed on the terminal, the inquiry program itself has terminated and is no longer in storage. When the user enters another customer number and presses the Enter key, the inquiry program is restarted. The result is that the program is in storage only when it needs to be: when it's processing data.

The bottom bar in figure 6-2 shows that a pseudo-conversational program has no waiting time. Rather than work for 3 seconds and wait for 15 as the conversational program does, the pseudo-conversational program simply works for 3 seconds and stops. When it stops, it releases its virtual storage. Thus, the right-hand side of figure 6-3 shows that only working pseudo-conversational programs occupy virtual storage. As you can see, this frees storage for other uses.

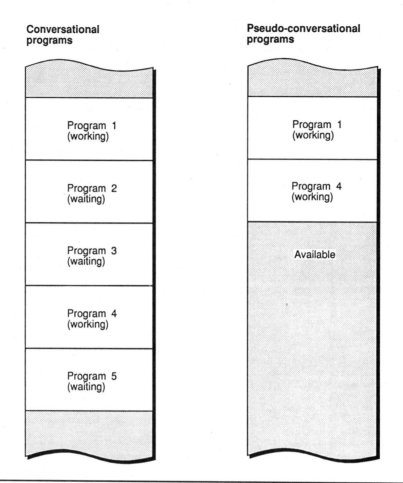

Figure 6-3   Virtual storage usage for conversational and pseudo-conversational programs

Because pseudo-conversational programs use main storage and other CICS resources far more efficiently than conversational programs, almost all CICS installations require that programs be pseudo-conversational.

How a pseudo-conversational program works

Remember that when the screens in parts 2 through 6 of figure 6-1 are displayed, the customer inquiry program is not executing. As the user types a customer number, it is displayed on the screen. That's a function of the terminal, though, and not of the program. After the user has filled in the required data, the program needs to be reloaded so it can process that data. But just how does CICS know when to restart a pseudo-conversational program?

Basically, the user signals CICS to restart a pseudo-conversational program by pressing one of the terminal's attention keys: the Enter key, a

PF key, a PA key, or the Clear key. Of course, the user doesn't think in terms of restarting the program when he or she presses an attention key. Instead, the user just knows that pressing a specific attention key causes the program to perform a specific function. On the other hand, as a CICS programmer, you do need to think of an attention key as causing a program to be loaded and executed.

In part 3 of figure 6-1, the user types a customer number and presses the Enter key (the attention key used most). Then, CICS reloads the inquiry program. The program in turn retrieves the customer number the user entered from the terminal, reads the corresponding customer record, displays the result on the terminal, and ends. That's the typical processing sequence for most CICS programs.

The two parts of figure 6-4 show this processing sequence in the form of flowcharts so you can compare conversational and pseudo-conversational programming. Once started, a conversational program sends its initial map. Then, it enters into a loop where it waits for input, retrieves the input data from the terminal, processes it, sends its output, and waits again.

In contrast, look at what the pseudo-conversational program does when it is first started: It sends its first map and ends. When the user presses an attention key, the pseudo-conversational program starts up, retrieves the input data, processes it, sends its output data, and ends again. The dashed lines in the pseudo-conversational flowchart indicate the portion of the processing loop that occurs while the program is not executing.

In figure 6-4, the function that retrieves input data from the terminal is called "Receive map." That's because the program uses a CICS command called RECEIVE MAP to accomplish this. For now, don't worry about the format or complexities of this command. I just want you to realize that the command transfers the data entered by the user to the symbolic map in your program's working storage. If you'd like, you can think of RECEIVE MAP as a READ statement that retrieves data from a terminal instead of a file.

After the program retrieves the data the user entered, it processes it. In the inquiry program, the processing is done by a CICS READ command that retrieves the appropriate record from the customer file. Although the CICS READ command performs the same function as a COBOL READ statement, you can't use standard COBOL facilities for file I/O. You must use CICS file-control commands instead.

Next, the program issues a CICS SEND MAP command to display the results of the inquiry on the screen. If the CICS RECEIVE MAP command is like a COBOL READ statement, then SEND MAP is like a WRITE statement.

After the program issues the SEND MAP command, it ends. It does this by issuing a CICS RETURN command. RETURN is the key to understanding how pseudo-conversational programming works,

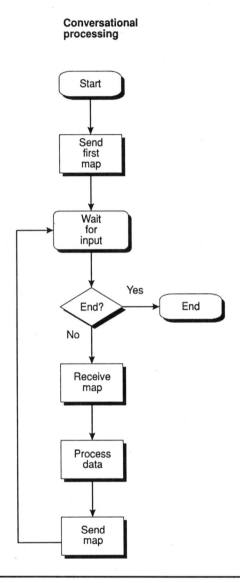

Conversational processing

Start

Send first map

Wait for input

End? — Yes → End

No

Receive map

Process data

Send map

Figure 6-4 Conversational and pseudo-conversational processing (part 1 of 2)

because it does more than end the program. It also lets you specify what trans-id CICS should invoke the next time the user presses an attention key. In this example, the trans-id specified in the RETURN command is INQ1, the same as the one the user supplied to start the program in part 1 of figure 6-1. As a result, when the user presses the Enter key or any other attention key, CICS will automatically invoke transaction INQ1, which will in turn restart the inquiry program.

How do you truly end a CICS program, so that it does *not* restart itself automatically? Simply by issuing a RETURN command *without* a

**Pseudo-conversational
processing**

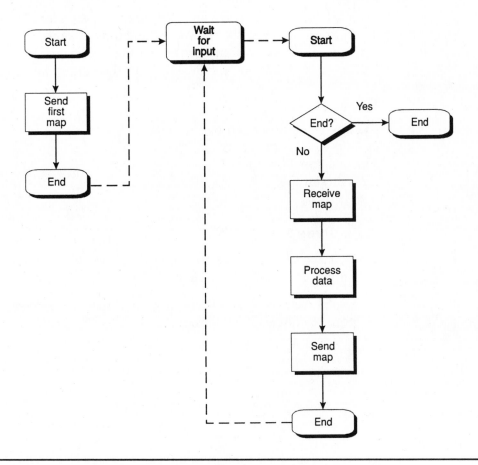

Figure 6-4   Conversational and pseudo-conversational processing (part 2 of 2)

trans-id. That causes the program to return control to CICS. Then, the
user can type in another trans-id to run another program.

Alternatively, a program can end by transferring control directly to
another CICS program, such as a menu program that lets the user pick
the next program without having to remember its trans-id. That's how
the customer inquiry program works. In the next topic, you'll see that
this function is performed by a CICS command called XCTL. And in
chapter 8, you'll learn more about using the RETURN and XCTL
commands in applications that involve more than one program.

Discussion   Unfortunately, pseudo-conversational programming complicates the
logic of your COBOL programs and, as a result, makes your job harder.
However, as I've already mentioned, almost all CICS programs are

pseudo-conversational because conversational programs are so inefficient.

Now that you've seen a sample terminal session for the customer inquiry program, you should understand how this program works and what pseudo-conversational programming is. The next topic presents and describes the COBOL source code for the inquiry program in detail.

Terms

pseudo-conversational programming
pseudo-conversational program
conversational program
short on storage
SOS

Objectives

1. Describe the difference between the operation of a conversational program and the operation of a pseudo-conversational program.

2. Explain why conversational programs are not as efficient as pseudo-conversational programs.

A command-level CICS program: An overview

Now that you've learned about the pseudo-conversational programming technique, you have the background you need to understand a command-level CICS program. Figure 6-5 presents the source listing for a simple command-level program: the customer inquiry program I presented in topic 1. If you study this figure, you'll see many similarities to a standard batch COBOL program. However, you'll also see many differences. This topic describes those differences in detail. In addition, it introduces you to several basic CICS commands using the customer inquiry program as an example.

As you read this topic, try to understand how this CICS program works in general terms. In topic 3, I'll explain each of the CICS commands it uses in detail. You'll better understand those commands after you're familiar with the COBOL source code for the customer inquiry program.

Identification Division
There's no difference between the Identification Division of a CICS program and a batch COBOL program. As you can see in figure 6-5, the PROGRAM-ID paragraph supplies the program name (CUSTINQ1). Many shops have standards for what other information should be included here, such as the author, date, and notes. If yours does, be sure to find out what they are and follow them.

Environment Division
The Environment Division in a CICS COBOL program must be empty. Environment Division entries, such as SELECT statements, aren't used in CICS programs. Instead, files are defined in the CICS File Control Table (FCT). Beginning with Release 3 of the VS COBOL II compiler, you can omit the Environment Division header altogether.

Data Division
The first thing you may notice about the Data Division in figure 6-5 is that it doesn't have a File Section. It's omitted for the same reason the Environment Division is left empty: All files are defined in the File Control Table and are processed with CICS commands, not with standard COBOL file-handling statements. What's left in the Data Division, then, is the Working-Storage Section and the Linkage Section.

Working-Storage Section In a CICS program, you use the Working-Storage Section to define program variables just as you do in a

```
         IDENTIFICATION DIVISION.
       *
         PROGRAM-ID.  CUSTINQ1.
       *
         ENVIRONMENT DIVISION.
       *
         DATA DIVISION.
       *
         WORKING-STORAGE SECTION.
       *
         01   SWITCHES.
       *
             05   VALID-DATA-SW              PIC X      VALUE 'Y'.
                  88 VALID-DATA                         VALUE 'Y'.
       *
         01   FLAGS.
       *
             05   SEND-FLAG                  PIC X.
                  88   SEND-ERASE                        VALUE '1'.
                  88   SEND-DATAONLY                     VALUE '2'.
                  88   SEND-DATAONLY-ALARM               VALUE '3'.
       *
         01   COMMUNICATION-AREA             PIC X.
       *
         01   RESPONSE-CODE                  PIC S9(8)   COMP.
       *
         COPY CUSTMAS.
       *
         COPY INQSET1.
       *
         COPY DFHAID.
       *
         LINKAGE SECTION.
       *
         01   DFHCOMMAREA                    PIC X.
       *
```

Figure 6-5 Source listing for the customer inquiry program (part 1 of 3)

batch program. Let me briefly explain each of the Working-Storage Section entries in figure 6-5.

The first two 01-level items in this program's Working-Storage Section contain fields I use to control the program's executions. This program uses one *switch* and one *flag*. A switch is a control field that can have one of two possible values: on or off. A flag is similar, except that it has more than two possible values.

Although you can set up program switches in many ways, I code a one-byte alphanumeric data field (PIC X) whose value will be Y if the switch is on or N if the switch is off. Then, I use a condition name (88-level item) to make the Procedure Division statements that test the switch easier to understand. The name of the switch field is the condition name followed by -SW. Thus, the switch for the condition name VALID-DATA is named VALID-DATA-SW. You'll see how I use this switch when I describe the inquiry program's Procedure Division.

```
     PROCEDURE DIVISION.
*
 0000-PROCESS-CUSTOMER-INQUIRY.
*
     EVALUATE TRUE

         WHEN EIBCALEN = ZERO
             MOVE LOW-VALUE TO INQMAP1O
             SET SEND-ERASE TO TRUE
             PERFORM 1400-SEND-CUSTOMER-MAP

         WHEN EIBAID = DFHCLEAR
             MOVE LOW-VALUE TO INQMAP1O
             SET SEND-ERASE TO TRUE
             PERFORM 1400-SEND-CUSTOMER-MAP

         WHEN EIBAID = DFHPA1 OR DFHPA2 OR DFHPA3
             CONTINUE

         WHEN EIBAID = DFHPF3 OR DFHPF12
             EXEC CICS
                 XCTL PROGRAM('INVMENU')
             END-EXEC

         WHEN EIBAID = DFHENTER
             PERFORM 1000-PROCESS-CUSTOMER-MAP

         WHEN OTHER
             MOVE LOW-VALUE TO INQMAP1O
             MOVE 'Invalid key pressed.' TO MESSAGEO
             SET SEND-DATAONLY-ALARM TO TRUE
             PERFORM 1400-SEND-CUSTOMER-MAP

     END-EVALUATE.

     EXEC CICS
         RETURN TRANSID('INQ1')
                 COMMAREA(COMMUNICATION-AREA)
     END-EXEC.
*
 1000-PROCESS-CUSTOMER-MAP.
*
     PERFORM 1100-RECEIVE-CUSTOMER-MAP.
     PERFORM 1200-EDIT-CUSTOMER-DATA.
     IF VALID-DATA
         PERFORM 1300-GET-CUSTOMER-RECORD.
     IF VALID-DATA
         SET SEND-DATAONLY TO TRUE
         PERFORM 1400-SEND-CUSTOMER-MAP
     ELSE
         SET SEND-DATAONLY-ALARM TO TRUE
         PERFORM 1400-SEND-CUSTOMER-MAP.
*
 1100-RECEIVE-CUSTOMER-MAP.
*
     EXEC CICS
         RECEIVE MAP('INQMAP1')
                 MAPSET('INQSET1')
                 INTO(INQMAP1I)
     END-EXEC.
*
```

Figure 6-5   Source listing for the customer inquiry program (part 2 of 3)

```
 1200-EDIT-CUSTOMER-DATA.
*
     IF        CUSTNOL = ZERO
         OR CUSTNOI = SPACE
        MOVE 'N' TO VALID-DATA-SW
        MOVE 'You must enter a customer number.' TO MESSAGEO.
*
 1300-GET-CUSTOMER-RECORD.
*
     EXEC CICS
         READ DATASET('CUSTMAS')
              INTO(CUSTOMER-MASTER-RECORD)
              RIDFLD(CUSTNOI)
              RESP(RESPONSE-CODE)
     END-EXEC.
     IF RESPONSE-CODE = DFHRESP(NORMAL)
        MOVE SPACE          TO MESSAGEO
        MOVE CM-LAST-NAME   TO LNAMEO
        MOVE CM-FIRST-NAME  TO FNAMEO
        MOVE CM-ADDRESS     TO ADDRO
        MOVE CM-CITY        TO CITYO
        MOVE CM-STATE       TO STATEO
        MOVE CM-ZIP-CODE    TO ZIPCODEO
     ELSE IF RESPONSE-CODE = DFHRESP(NOTFND)
        MOVE 'N' TO VALID-DATA-SW
        MOVE 'That customer does not exist.' TO MESSAGEO
        MOVE SPACE TO LNAMEO
                      FNAMEO
                      ADDRO
                      CITYO
                      STATEO
                      ZIPCODEO
     ELSE
        EXEC CICS
            ABEND
        END-EXEC.
*
 1400-SEND-CUSTOMER-MAP.
*
     IF SEND-ERASE
        EXEC CICS
            SEND MAP('INQMAP1')
                 MAPSET('INQSET1')
                 FROM(INQMAP1O)
                 ERASE
        END-EXEC
     ELSE IF SEND-DATAONLY
        EXEC CICS
            SEND MAP('INQMAP1')
                 MAPSET('INQSET1')
                 FROM(INQMAP1O)
                 DATAONLY
        END-EXEC
     ELSE IF SEND-DATAONLY-ALARM
        EXEC CICS
            SEND MAP('INQMAP1')
                 MAPSET('INQSET1')
                 FROM(INQMAP1O)
                 DATAONLY
                 ALARM
        END-EXEC.
```

Figure 6-5   Source listing for the customer inquiry program (part 3 of 3)

```
 01   CUSTOMER-MASTER-RECORD.
 *
      05   CM-CUSTOMER-NUMBER        PIC X(6).
      05   CM-FIRST-NAME             PIC X(20).
      05   CM-LAST-NAME              PIC X(30).
      05   CM-ADDRESS                PIC X(30).
      05   CM-CITY                   PIC X(20).
      05   CM-STATE                  PIC X(2).
      05   CM-ZIP-CODE               PIC X(10).
```

Figure 6-6   The CUSTMAS copy member used in the customer inquiry program

I set up flags in much the same way as I set up switches, except that I code one 88-level condition name for each valid setting of the flag. For the customer inquiry program, I defined one flag, named SEND-FLAG. The inquiry program uses this flag field to specify which of three forms of the SEND MAP command to use when it sends the customer map to the terminal. You'll see how I use this flag when I describe the inquiry program's Procedure Division, and you'll learn the specifics of the SEND MAP command's options in the next topic.

The next entry in the Working-Storage Section is an 01-level item named COMMUNICATION-AREA. The *communication area* is a special field used to pass data from one program execution to the next. In a more complicated program, the communication area can contain many fields. In this program, however, the communication area is a simple one-byte field (PIC X).

The next working storage entry is a binary fullword item (PIC S9(8) COMP) named RESPONSE-CODE. This field is used to test the completion status of the CICS READ command that retrieves records from the customer master file. You'll see how this field is used in a few moments.

After the RESPONSE-CODE field are three COPY statements that copy data structures into the inquiry program. The first COPY statement copies the record description for the customer master file (CUSTMAS), shown in figure 6-6. This data structure is used to hold data read from the customer file.

The second COPY statement copies the symbolic map for the inquiry program's mapset (INQSET1), shown in figure 6-7. This is the symbolic map BMS produced for the mapset I presented in the last chapter. The program uses this data structure to process data sent to and received from the terminal. In figure 6-7, I've shaded the individual fields that are used in the inquiry program.

The third COPY statement copies DFHAID, an IBM-supplied copy member that contains standard definitions for BMS attribute bytes and AID keys. Figure 6-8 shows the DFHAID copy member. The program

```
01  INQMAP1I.
    02    FILLER     PIC X(12).
    02    CUSTNOL    PIC S9(4) COMP.
    02    CUSTNOF    PIC X.
    02    FILLER REDEFINES CUSTNOF.
     03   CUSTNOA    PIC X.
    02    CUSTNOI    PIC X(0006).
    02    LNAMEL     PIC S9(4) COMP.
    02    LNAMEF     PIC X.
    02    FILLER REDEFINES LNAMEF.
     03   LNAMEA     PIC X.
    02    LNAMEI     PIC X(0030).
    02    FNAMEL     PIC S9(4) COMP.
    02    FNAMEF     PIC X.
    02    FILLER REDEFINES FNAMEF.
     03   FNAMEA     PIC X.
    02    FNAMEI     PIC X(0020).
    02    ADDRL      PIC S9(4) COMP.
    02    ADDRF      PIC X.
    02    FILLER REDEFINES ADDRF.
     03   ADDRA      PIC X.
    02    ADDRI      PIC X(0030).
    02    CITYL      PIC S9(4) COMP.
    02    CITYF      PIC X.
    02    FILLER REDEFINES CITYF.
     03   CITYA      PIC X.
    02    CITYI      PIC X(0020).
    02    STATEL     PIC S9(4) COMP.
    02    STATEF     PIC X.
    02    FILLER REDEFINES STATEF.
     03   STATEA     PIC X.
    02    STATEI     PIC X(0002).
    02    ZIPCODEL   PIC S9(4) COMP.
    02    ZIPCODEF   PIC X.
    02    FILLER REDEFINES ZIPCODEF.
     03   ZIPCODEA   PIC X.
    02    ZIPCODEI   PIC X(0010).
    02    MESSAGEL   PIC S9(4) COMP.
    02    MESSAGEF   PIC X.
    02    FILLER REDEFINES MESSAGEF.
     03   MESSAGEA   PIC X.
    02    MESSAGEI   PIC X(0079).
    02    DUMMYL     PIC S9(4) COMP.
    02    DUMMYF     PIC X.
    02    FILLER REDEFINES DUMMYF.
     03   DUMMYA     PIC X.
    02    DUMMYI     PIC X(0001).
```

Figure 6-7   Symbolic map for the customer inquiry program (part 1 of 2)

uses the fields I've shaded in this copy member to detect the use of AID keys.

Before I go on, I want to point out that each time a program is executed, a fresh copy of working storage is obtained. As a result, changes you make to the contents of working storage fields are *not* saved between executions of a pseudo-conversational program, and any initial values established by VALUE clauses are restored. If you need to preserve data from one program execution to the next, you can pass the

```
01  INQMAP1O REDEFINES INQMAP1I.
    02   FILLER     PIC X(12).
    02   FILLER     PIC X(3).
    02   CUSTNOO    PIC X(0006).
    02   FILLER     PIC X(3).
    02   LNAMEO     PIC X(0030).
    02   FILLER     PIC X(3).
    02   FNAMEO     PIC X(0020).
    02   FILLER     PIC X(3).
    02   ADDRO      PIC X(0030).
    02   FILLER     PIC X(3).
    02   CITYO      PIC X(0020).
    02   FILLER     PIC X(3).
    02   STATEO     PIC X(0002).
    02   FILLER     PIC X(3).
    02   ZIPCODEO   PIC X(0010).
    02   FILLER     PIC X(3).
    02   MESSAGEO   PIC X(0079).
    02   FILLER     PIC X(3).
    02   DUMMYO     PIC X(0001).
```

Figure 6-7   Symbolic map for the customer inquiry program (part 2 of 2)

data between executions using the communication area. That's why the communication area in a more complicated program can contain many fields. I'll explain how to pass data from one program execution to the next in chapter 8.

Linkage Section   All CICS programs must have a Linkage Section. At the minimum, you need to code a Linkage Section definition for the communication area with the special name DFHCOMMAREA. In figure 6-5, DFHCOMMAREA is one byte long, the same as the working storage field COMMUNICATION-AREA.

Why define the communication area in both the Working-Storage Section and the Linkage Section? Because, as figure 6-9 illustrates, the Working-Storage Section definition of the communication area is the source of the data passed on to the next execution of the program, while the Linkage Section definition is used to access the data passed by the previous execution.

Incidentally, if you don't include an entry for DFHCOMMAREA, the CICS command translator will insert a one-byte DFHCOMMAREA field automatically. Even so, I recommend you always code your own definition for DFHCOMMAREA.

Although you can't see it in the source listing in figure 6-5, the CICS command translator also inserts another special field called the *Execute Interface Block* (or *EIB*) in all CICS programs before the DFHCOMMAREA entry. Unlike DFHCOMMAREA, you don't code your own definitions for the EIB because its fields are the same in all CICS programs. The Execute Interface Block contains several useful items of system

```
01      DFHAID.                                          02000000
    02    DFHNULL    PIC  X  VALUE IS '.'.               04000000
    02    DFHENTER   PIC  X  VALUE IS QUOTE.             06000000
    02    DFHCLEAR   PIC  X  VALUE IS '_'.               08000000
    02    DFHCLRP    PIC  X  VALUE IS '|'.               09000000
    02    DFHPEN     PIC  X  VALUE IS '='.               10000000
    02    DFHOPID    PIC  X  VALUE IS 'W'.               12000000
    02    DFHMSRE    PIC  X  VALUE IS 'X'.               14000000
    02    DFHSTRF    PIC  X  VALUE IS 'h'.               16000000
    02    DFHTRIG    PIC  X  VALUE IS '"'.               18000000
    02    DFHPA1     PIC  X  VALUE IS '%'.               20000000
    02    DFHPA2     PIC  X  VALUE IS '>'.               22000000
    02    DFHPA3     PIC  X  VALUE IS ','.               25000000
    02    DFHPF1     PIC  X  VALUE IS '1'.               28000000
    02    DFHPF2     PIC  X  VALUE IS '2'.               31000000
    02    DFHPF3     PIC  X  VALUE IS '3'.               34000000
    02    DFHPF4     PIC  X  VALUE IS '4'.               37000000
    02    DFHPF5     PIC  X  VALUE IS '5'.               40000000
    02    DFHPF6     PIC  X  VALUE IS '6'.               43000000
    02    DFHPF7     PIC  X  VALUE IS '7'.               46000000
    02    DFHPF8     PIC  X  VALUE IS '8'.               49000000
    02    DFHPF9     PIC  X  VALUE IS '9'.               52000000
    02    DFHPF10    PIC  X  VALUE IS ':'.               55000000
    02    DFHPF11    PIC  X  VALUE IS '#'.               58000000
    02    DFHPF12    PIC  X  VALUE IS '@'.               61000000
    02    DFHPF13    PIC  X  VALUE IS 'A'.               64000000
    02    DFHPF14    PIC  X  VALUE IS 'B'.               67000000
    02    DFHPF15    PIC  X  VALUE IS 'C'.               70000000
    02    DFHPF16    PIC  X  VALUE IS 'D'.               73000000
    02    DFHPF17    PIC  X  VALUE IS 'E'.               76000000
    02    DFHPF18    PIC  X  VALUE IS 'F'.               79000000
    02    DFHPF19    PIC  X  VALUE IS 'G'.               82000000
    02    DFHPF20    PIC  X  VALUE IS 'H'.               85000000
    02    DFHPF21    PIC  X  VALUE IS 'I'.               88000000
    02    DFHPF22    PIC  X  VALUE IS '\'.               91000000
    02    DFHPF23    PIC  X  VALUE IS '.'.               94000000
    02    DFHPF24    PIC  X  VALUE IS '<'.               97000000
*
```

Figure 6-8   The DFHAID copy member

information I'll show you how to use in chapter 8. For now, you need to know about only two of them: EIBCALEN and EIBAID.

When your program starts, EIBCALEN contains a value that represents the length of the communication area passed to your program. If no communication area is passed to your program, EIBCALEN is set to zero. Since no communication area is passed if you start a program by entering a transaction identifier at a terminal, you can evaluate EIBCALEN to detect the first-time condition in a pseudo-conversational program. You'll see in a moment why a program needs to be able to distinguish its first execution in a terminal session from subsequent executions.

The only reason the customer inquiry program uses a communication area at all is so its next execution can determine that it's not the first execution of the program. On all program executions after the first, the program will check the length of the communication area (by evaluating

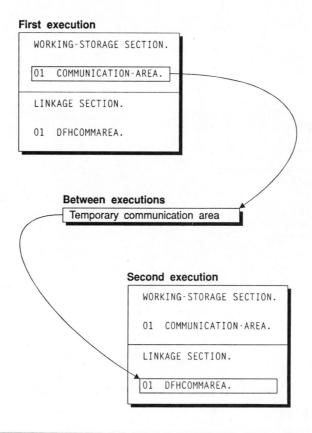

First execution

```
WORKING-STORAGE SECTION.

01   COMMUNICATION-AREA.

LINKAGE SECTION.

01   DFHCOMMAREA.
```

Between executions
Temporary communication area

Second execution

```
WORKING-STORAGE SECTION.

01   COMMUNICATION-AREA.

LINKAGE SECTION.

01   DFHCOMMAREA.
```

Figure 6-9   How the communication area is passed from one program execution to the next

EIBCALEN) and find that it did indeed receive a communication area. But it doesn't do anything with the one byte of data it received. In contrast, more complicated programs often process the data passed to them through the communication area.

The other EIB field you need to know about is EIBAID. When CICS starts (or restarts) a program, it sets the EIBAID field to a value that represents the attention key the user just pressed. For example, if the user presses the Enter key to start a program, the EIBAID field will be set to indicate that the Enter key was pressed. You'll see in a moment how to test EIBAID to determine which attention key was pressed.

Procedure Division   In the Procedure Division, you code a mixture of standard COBOL statements (like MOVE, ADD, and so on) and special *CICS commands* that invoke CICS functions. Before I go on, I want to point out that many of the COBOL statements you use in batch programs aren't allowed in CICS programs. Specifically, you can't use any of the standard COBOL features in figure 6-10. CICS commands handle most of the functions

COBOL features not allowed under any compiler

Operator communication statements	ACCEPT DISPLAY
File I/O statements	OPEN CLOSE READ WRITE REWRITE DELETE START
Sort statements	SORT RELEASE RETURN
Debugging statements	EXHIBIT TRACE
Segmentation feature	
Report Writer feature	

COBOL features not allowed under OS/VS COBOL

Program termination statements	STOP RUN GOBACK
String handling statements	EXAMINE INSPECT STRING UNSTRING

Figure 6-10   COBOL features that aren't supported under CICS

performed by these COBOL elements. Other functions, such as the Report Writer feature or the SORT statement, simply aren't available under CICS.

Notice that if you are using the older OS/VS COBOL (or DOS/VS COBOL) compiler, you cannot use the STOP RUN or GOBACK statements or string manipulation statements. These statements are allowed with the VS COBOL II compiler. In addition to the difference in these restrictions, there are other differences between OS/VS COBOL and VS COBOL II when used for CICS programming. I developed all of the programs in this book under VS COBOL II and made full use of its features. Whenever differences for OS/VS COBOL come up, I'll be sure to point them out. And you'll find OS/VS COBOL versions of all the

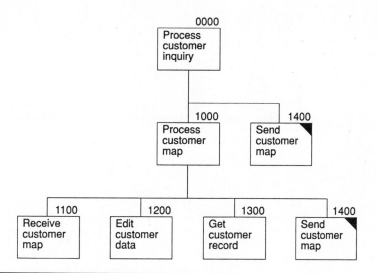

Figure 6-11 Structure chart for the customer inquiry program

programs in this book in appendix D. So if you're an OS/VS COBOL user, you may want to look at the customer inquiry program there.

Figure 6-11 shows the structure chart I used to develop the customer inquiry program. Each of the boxes (or *modules*) in figure 6-11 represents a major function of the program. In the next chapter, I'll show you how I developed the chart in figure 6-11. For now, I just want you to recognize that each module in the structure chart is implemented as a paragraph in the program in figure 6-5, and PERFORM statements are used to invoke those paragraphs as necessary. The two boxes whose corners are shaded represent a single program module that is invoked at two locations. Now, I'll describe the function of each paragraph of the inquiry program's Procedure Division.

Module 0000: Process customer inquiry   The key to understanding how the customer inquiry program works is understanding how its high-level module works. It contains the code necessary to implement pseudo-conversational programming.

If you'll look at the code for module 0000 in figure 6-5, you'll see that most of it is actually a single COBOL EVALUATE statement. The purpose of this EVALUATE statement is to determine the state of the program during a particular execution and perform whatever processing is appropriate. After the EVALUATE statement is a CICS statement (RETURN) that terminates the program, specifies a trans-id to be invoked when the user presses an attention key, and passes a communication area to the next execution of the program.

In case you're not familiar with the EVALUATE statement, figure 6-12 shows its general format as I've used it in the inquiry program. The

```
EVALUATE TRUE

    WHEN condition-1
        statements
            .
            .

    WHEN condition-2
        statements
            .
            .

        .
        .

    WHEN OTHER
        statements
            .
            .

END-EVALUATE.
```

Figure 6-12   General format of the EVALUATE statement

conditions listed in the WHEN clauses are evaluated one at a time. The statements in the first WHEN clause whose condition evaluates to *true* are executed. If none of the WHEN conditions is true, the statements following WHEN OTHER are executed. It's important to realize that for a given execution of the EVALUATE statement, the statements for only one of the WHEN clauses will be executed.

Notice the use of CONTINUE in the EVALUATE statement in figure 6-5. The CONTINUE statement simply means that no action should be taken when it is executed. I used it here because the EVALUATE statement requires at least one statement in each WHEN clause.

If you're not using VS COBOL II, you can't use the EVALUATE statement. Instead, you must simulate its processing by using a series of nested IF statements, as figure 6-13 shows. If you are using VS COBOL II, however, I strongly recommend you use the EVALUATE statement. It not only presents a clearer picture of the program's execution, but it's easier to code and considerably less error-prone.

Another VS COBOL II statement I use frequently in the programs in this book is the SET *condition-name* statement. To understand how it works, look back to the SEND-FLAG field in the Working-Storage Section. It has three condition names associated with it. To set the SEND-ERASE condition to true using OS/VS COBOL, you would use a MOVE statement, like this:

```
MOVE '1' TO SEND-FLAG
```

```
0000-PROCESS-CUSTOMER-INQUIRY.
*
    IF EIBCALEN = ZERO
        MOVE LOW-VALUE TO INQMAP1O
        MOVE '1' TO SEND-FLAG
        PERFORM 1400-SEND-CUSTOMER-MAP

    ELSE IF EIBAID = DFHCLEAR
        MOVE LOW-VALUE TO INQMAP1O
        MOVE '1' TO SEND-FLAG
        PERFORM 1400-SEND-CUSTOMER-MAP

    ELSE IF EIBAID = DFHPA1 OR DFHPA2 OR DFHPA3
        NEXT SENTENCE

    ELSE IF EIBAID = DFHPF3 OR DFHPF12
        EXEC CICS
            XCTL PROGRAM('INVMENU')
        END-EXEC

    ELSE IF EIBAID = DFHENTER
        PERFORM 1000-PROCESS-CUSTOMER-MAP

    ELSE
        MOVE LOW-VALUE TO INQMAP1O
        MOVE 'Invalid key pressed.' TO MESSAGEO
        MOVE '3' TO SEND-FLAG
        PERFORM 1400-SEND-CUSTOMER-MAP.

    EXEC CICS
        RETURN TRANSID('INQ1')
               COMMAREA(COMMUNICATION-AREA)
               LENGTH(1)
    END-EXEC.
```

Figure 6-13 Module 0000 of the customer inquiry program under OS/VS COBOL

Unfortunately, this technique is error-prone because it forces you to double-check the working-storage definition of SEND-FLAG to make sure 1 is the correct code for the SEND-ERASE condition.

In contrast, you can accomplish the same thing with the VS COBOL II compiler using the SET statement, like this:

```
SET SEND-ERASE TO TRUE
```

This statement has the same effect as the MOVE statement, but doesn't force you to remember that 1 is the code for the SEND-ERASE condition. Because this coding is clearer and less error-prone, I recommend you use it. (To set simple switches whose values can be Y or N, I still prefer to use the MOVE statement rather than the SET statement.)

Take a look now at the six WHEN clauses in the EVALUATE statement in module 0000. The first condition is this:

```
WHEN EIBCALEN = ZERO
```

This condition will be true whenever the inquiry program is invoked without a communication area. And that will happen only when the terminal user invokes the inquiry program for the first time in a particular terminal session. In response to this condition, the program initializes the output map (INQMAP1O) by moving LOW-VALUE to it, sets SEND-ERASE to true, and performs module 1400 to send the output map to the terminal. (With SEND-ERASE set, module 1400 will erase the previous contents of the screen.) Then, the remaining WHEN clauses in the EVALUATE statement are skipped (remember, only the statements in the first WHEN clause that evaluates to true are executed), and the CICS RETURN command at the end of module 0000 is executed.

Notice that the RETURN command specifies two options: TRANSID and COMMAREA. The TRANSID option specifies that the transaction INQ1 should be started when the user next presses an attention key. This is the same trans-id that the user entered at the terminal to start the program. As a result, the program will be started again. This time, however, a communication area is passed forward to the next execution of the program via the COMMAREA option. So on subsequent executions, EIBCALEN will *not* be equal to zero.

The next four WHEN clauses in the EVALUATE statement deal with specific attention keys the user might press. Each tests the value of EIBAID. Remember that EIBAID is set to a value that indicates which attention key the user pressed, and the copy member DFHAID contains definitions for those values. If you'll look at the DFHAID copy member in figure 6-8, you'll see that I've highlighted the entries for the AID keys the inquiry program uses.

The second WHEN clause deals with the Clear key:

```
WHEN EIBAID = DFHCLEAR
```

When the user presses the Clear key, the terminal does two things: It erases the screen, and it sends an attention identifier, but no data, to CICS. CICS responds by restarting the INQ1 transaction. Then, the inquiry program handles the Clear key by displaying the inquiry map as if the program were being started for the first time. The effect to the user is that the Clear key simply causes the inquiry map to be redisplayed.

The third WHEN clause deals with the three PA keys (PA1, PA2, and PA3) by ignoring them. The CONTINUE statement causes control to fall out of the EVALUATE statement, so the program immediately issues the RETURN statement at the end of module 0000.

The fourth WHEN clause deals with two PF keys, PF3 and PF12:

```
WHEN EIBAID = DFHPF3 OR DFHPF12
```

The bottom line of the inquiry map indicates that these two keys perform the End and Cancel functions. For this program, both of these keys end the inquiry program by transferring control to another program. To do this, another CICS command is used: XCTL.

The XCTL command immediately terminates the inquiry program and passes control directly to another program, named INVMENU. For the purposes of understanding this program, you don't have to know what the INVMENU program does when it receives control. What you do need to know is that this breaks the pseudo-conversational cycle for the inquiry program.

The fifth WHEN clause is executed when the user presses the Enter key:

```
WHEN EIBAID = DFHENTER
    PERFORM 1000-PROCESS-CUSTOMER-MAP
```

Module 1000 will then perform the functions necessary to process a customer inquiry.

The last WHEN clause in the EVALUATE statement in module 0000 is this:

```
WHEN OTHER
    MOVE LOW-VALUE TO INQMAP1O
    MOVE 'Invalid key pressed.' TO MESSAGEO
    SET SEND-DATAONLY-ALARM TO TRUE
    PERFORM 1400-SEND-CUSTOMER-MAP
```

This WHEN clause is executed if none of the other WHEN clauses test true. In other words, it is executed if: (1) it is not the first execution; (2) the user didn't press the Clear key; (3) the user didn't press one of the PA keys; (4) the user didn't press PF3 or PF12; and (5) the user didn't press the Enter key. First, it moves LOW-VALUE to the output map. Then, it moves an error message to MESSAGEO, the message output field in the symbolic map. Finally, it sets SEND-DATAONLY-ALARM to true and performs module 1400 to send the error message to the terminal.

Module 1000: Process customer map Besides module 0000, which implements the basic pseudo-conversational processing cycle for the inquiry program, module 1000 is the inquiry program's main processing module. Its structure is straightforward. First, it invokes module 1100 to retrieve input data from the terminal. Then, it invokes module 1200 to edit that data. For the inquiry program, there isn't much data to edit: just the customer number. The only editing requirement is that the user must enter something in the field. Module 1200 sets VALID-DATA-SW to indicate whether or not the data is valid.

If the data is valid, module 1300 is invoked to read a customer record from the customer master file. This module will set VALID-DATA-SW to N if the record could not be found. Then, module 1400 is invoked to send data back to the terminal, with either SEND-DATAONLY or SEND-DATAONLY-ALARM set to true depending on the setting of VALID-DATA-SW. The only difference here is that with SEND-DATAONLY-ALARM, module 1400 will cause the terminal to beep, while with SEND-DATAONLY, it will not.

Module 1100: Receive customer map   This module consists of a single CICS RECEIVE MAP command that receives data from the terminal and formats it according to the symbolic input map (INQMAP1I). You'll learn about the details of the RECEIVE MAP command in the next topic.

Module 1200: Edit customer data   This module consists of a single IF statement that edits the input data. For this program, the only editing requirement is to make sure that the user entered a customer number. The IF statement in module 1200 checks for this condition in two ways. First, it checks the length of the customer number that was entered. If the value of the CUSTNOL field from the symbolic map is zero, it means the user did not enter anything. Second, the IF statement checks to make sure the entered customer number is not equal to spaces. If either of these conditions is true, module 1200 sets VALID-DATA-SW to N and moves an error message to the MESSAGEO field.

Module 1300: Get customer record   This module retrieves a record from the customer master file and formats data in the output symbolic map. It starts by issuing a CICS READ command, which tells CICS to read a record from the CUSTMAS file (indicated by the DATASET option) into the working-storage field CUSTOMER-MASTER-RECORD (indicated by the INTO option). And the RIDFLD option specifies that the key value for the record to be retrieved is in CUSTNOI (the customer number input field in the symbolic map).

The READ command also specifies the RESP option, which tells CICS to place a response code in the RESPONSE-CODE field to indicate whether or not the READ command was successful. To understand why this option is required, you need to know about CICS error handling. Whenever a CICS command encounters an unusual situation, CICS responds by raising an *exceptional condition.* Each exceptional condition has a descriptive name. For example, if you try to send a map that's too big for the terminal, CICS raises the INVMPSZ (invalid map size) condition. If you try to read a record using a key that doesn't exist, CICS raises the NOTFND condition.

CICS provides several ways to deal with exceptional conditions. The easiest, and often the most appropriate, is to let CICS deal with exceptional conditions using its default action. For all but a few exceptional conditions, the default action is to terminate your program abnormally. All of the CICS commands in the inquiry program except the READ command in module 1300 allow CICS to deal with exceptional conditions using this default action. That's because all of the possible exceptional conditions for those commands represent serious errors from which the inquiry program cannot recover.

It would be unacceptable, however, to allow the program to abend if the READ command results in a NOTFND condition. After all, in an inquiry program, you should expect that the user will occasionally enter a key value that doesn't exist in the file. The program should respond not by abending, but by displaying an appropriate error message. That's why the READ command in module 1300 includes the RESP option. This option tells CICS not to take its default action if this command raises an exceptional condition. Instead, CICS returns a *response code* in the field specified in the RESP option (in this case, RESPONSE-CODE). The program can then test the response code to determine what action should be taken based on the status of the command.

To test the CICS response code, you use a somewhat peculiar condition syntax: You list the condition name in parentheses after the special keyword DFHRESP. For example, to test for the NOTFND condition, you would code an IF statement like this:

```
IF RESPONSE-CODE = DFHRESP(NOTFND)
```

You can also use the special condition name NORMAL to determine if a command completed without error.

The nested IF statements that follow the READ command in module 1300 evaluate RESPONSE-CODE to handle any exceptional conditions that may have been raised. If the response code indicates the command completed normally (the NORMAL condition), the program moves data from the customer record to the corresponding fields in the output map. If the response code indicates that the NOTFND condition occurred, the program sets VALID-DATA-SW to N, moves an appropriate error message to MESSAGEO, and moves spaces to the output fields in the symbolic map.

If RESPONSE-CODE indicates any condition other than NORMAL or NOTFND, a serious error occurred when the READ statement was executed. For example, the data set may not be available or an I/O error may have occurred. In any event, the program handles the error by issuing a CICS ABEND command to terminate the program abnormally. Although this is a crude way to handle serious errors, it is effective.

In chapter 8, I'll present more sophisticated ways of dealing with serious errors. And I'll present an alternative method of dealing with exceptional conditions: the HANDLE CONDITION command.

Module 1400: Send customer map   If you think about the terminal output requirements of the inquiry program, you'll see that there are three distinct situations where the program needs to send data to the terminal. The first is when the current contents of the terminal screen are unknown, such as when the program first starts. In this situation, the program needs to erase the current contents of the screen and format the screen with the customer inquiry map.

The second situation is when the user has typed a valid customer number and the program needs to send that customer's data to the screen. In this situation, it isn't necessary to format the terminal screen again. Instead, the program should simply update the screen with the results of the inquiry.

The third situation is when a user error has occurred. Here again, the program doesn't need to reformat the terminal screen. Instead, it needs to send just the error message and cause the terminal to beep so the user's attention is drawn to the message.

Each of these terminal output situations requires a different form of the SEND MAP command, and module 1400 provides all of them. Thus, module 1400 serves as a general-purpose send module, which the program can invoke at any time to send data to the terminal. Module 1400 uses SEND-FLAG to determine which form of the SEND MAP command to issue, so the program should set one of its associated condition names before invoking module 1400.

Before I point out the differences in the three SEND MAP commands in module 1400, I want to point out the similarities. Each specifies the MAP option to indicate which map to send (INQMAP1) and the MAPSET option to indicate which mapset contains the map (INQSET1). Each also specifies the FROM option to identify the symbolic output map (INQMAP1O). Keep in mind that hexadecimal zeros (LOW-VALUES) are never sent to the terminal screen. So if module 1400 is invoked immediately after the program has moved LOW-VALUE to INQMAP1O, no symbolic map data is sent to the terminal.

The first SEND MAP command in module 1400 uses the ERASE option to cause the previous contents of the screen to be erased. It then combines data from the physical map (headings and legends as well as formatting information) with variable data from the symbolic map and sends the information to the terminal. This form of the SEND MAP command is used to format the terminal screen when the user invokes the program for the first time and to reformat the screen if the user inadvertently erases the screen by pressing the Clear key.

The second SEND MAP command updates the terminal screen by sending customer information to the terminal. It is invoked by module 1000 if VALID-DATA-SW is Y after module 1300 reads the customer record. The DATAONLY option means that only data in the symbolic map is actually sent to the terminal. The screen headings and formatting information specified in the physical map are already displayed (they were sent to the terminal by the first SEND MAP command), so they don't have to be sent again.

The third SEND MAP command is used to display an error message. It is similar to the second SEND MAP command, but adds the ALARM option to cause the terminal to beep.

Discussion   At this point, you should understand how the customer inquiry program works. Still, you lack a complete understanding of each of the

CICS commands the program uses. So, in the next topic, I'll describe each of those commands in detail.

Terms

switch
flag
communication area
Execute Interface Block
EIB
CICS command
module
exceptional condition
response code

Objectives

1. Explain the COBOL code used to detect the first execution of a program in a pseudo-conversational session.

2. Explain the COBOL code required to pass a communication area from one program execution to the next.

3. Explain the COBOL code used to test CICS response codes.

CICS commands of the basic subset

Now that you've seen several CICS commands within the context of the customer inquiry program, you're ready to learn about them in more detail. First, this topic describes how to code a CICS command. Then, it presents the specific options you can code for the CICS commands in the inquiry program.

How to code a CICS command

When you code a CICS command, you must follow a few rules. To begin with, all CICS commands follow this general pattern:

```
EXEC CICS
    command option(value)...
END-EXEC.
```

The words EXEC CICS and END-EXEC are required. The command specifies the operation to be performed, and the *options* (or *parameters*) provide information CICS needs to perform the specified operation.

When a CICS command requires more than one option, use spaces to separate them, not commas. To make your program listings easier to read, I recommend you code each option on a separate line. No special coding is necessary to continue a CICS command from one line to the next.

Before I describe the details of specific CICS commands, I want to point out that with CICS version 1.7 and later, you can code the RESP option on any CICS command to check the command's response code. The RESP option has a simple syntax:

```
[RESP(data-name)]
```

The data name should be defined in working storage as a binary fullword field (PIC S9(8) COMP).

Note that RESP is optional. Whether or not you should code RESP on all your CICS commands depends on your shop's standards for error processing. For most CICS commands, the exceptional conditions that can occur represent serious errors from which the program cannot recover. For these commands, it's often best to omit the RESP option and let CICS abend the program. But for some CICS commands, such as READ, response code checking is a must. In any event, I won't show the RESP option when I present the formats of CICS commands. Just be aware that you can code RESP on any CICS command.

In the customer inquiry program in topic 2 (figure 6-5), I used six CICS commands: RETURN, XCTL, SEND MAP, RECEIVE MAP, READ,

The RETURN command

```
EXEC CICS
    RETURN  [ TRANSID(name) ]
            [ COMMAREA(data-area) ]
            [ LENGTH(data-value) ]
END-EXEC
```

Options

TRANSID   Specifies the one- to four-character name of the transaction to be invoked when the
                       user presses an attention key. The trans-id must be defined in the Program Control
                       Table (PCT).

COMMAREA   Specifies a data area that's passed to the next execution of a pseudo-conversational
                       program. The next program execution accesses the communication area via its
                       DFHCOMMAREA field.

LENGTH   Specifies a binary halfword (PIC S9(4) COMP) or numeric literal that indicates the
                       length of the data area specified in the COMMAREA option. Under OS/VS COBOL,
                       LENGTH is required if you code COMMAREA.

Figure 6-14 The RETURN command

and ABEND. I've already explained the basic operation of each of these commands. Now, I'll present the details of how you use them.

The RETURN command

The RETURN command, shown in figure 6-14, returns control to CICS. If you code the RETURN command with no options, control simply returns to CICS, and the terminal session ends. On the other hand, if you code the TRANSID option, CICS invokes the trans-id you specify the next time the operator presses an attention key.

The COMMAREA and LENGTH options are used to pass a communication area to the next program execution. COMMAREA specifies the name of the field in working storage that contains the data to be passed, and LENGTH specifies the number of bytes to be passed. The LENGTH option is required only if you're using the older OS/VS COBOL compiler. If you omit LENGTH under VS COBOL II, CICS will use the actual length of the field you specify in the COMMAREA option.

When the next program execution begins, the data passed via the communication area is available in the DFHCOMMAREA field in the Linkage Section, and the length of the received data is available in the Execute Interface Block field EIBCALEN.

The XCTL command

The XCTL command, shown in figure 6-15, transfers control from the current program to the program specified in the PROGRAM option. No

The XCTL command

```
EXEC CICS
    XCTL  [ PROGRAM(name) ]
          [ COMMAREA(data-area) ]
          [ LENGTH(data-value) ]
END-EXEC
```

Options

PROGRAM   Specifies the one- to eight-character name of the program to be invoked. This name
                       must be defined in the Processing Program Table (PPT).

COMMAREA   Specifies a data area that's passed to the invoked program as a communication area.
                       The invoked program accesses the communication area via its DFHCOMMAREA field.

LENGTH   Specifies a binary halfword (PIC S9(4) COMP) or numeric literal that indicates the
                       length of the data area specified in the COMMAREA option. Under OS/VS COBOL,
                       LENGTH is required if you code COMMAREA.

Figure 6-15 The XCTL command

return mechanism is set up, so control doesn't return automatically to a program that issues an XCTL command. When a program issues an XCTL command, that program is terminated and its working storage is discarded before the program specified in the PROGRAM option is started.

If you wish, you may pass a communication area to the program by coding the COMMAREA and LENGTH options. (LENGTH is not required under VS COBOL II.) The invoked program receives the data in DFHCOMMAREA and the length of the data in EIBCALEN.

In chapter 8, you'll learn more about the RETURN and XCTL commands. In addition, you'll learn about a third command that can invoke another program: LINK.

The SEND MAP command

The SEND MAP command, shown in figure 6-16, sends data from your program to the terminal screen. The MAP and MAPSET options indicate, respectively, the map and mapset names for the physical map. The FROM option names the symbolic map definition in the program's Working-Storage Section.

If you specify the MAPONLY option on a SEND MAP command, only the data in the physical map is sent to the screen. As a result, only the screen's headings will be displayed. In contrast, if you specify the DATAONLY option, only the data from the symbolic map is sent to the screen. So, only the actual data values are sent to the screen; the headings are not. If you omit the MAPONLY and DATAONLY options, the data in

The SEND MAP command

```
EXEC CICS
    SEND   MAP(name)
        [ MAPSET(name) ]
        [ FROM(data-area) ]
        [ MAPONLY | DATAONLY ]
        [ ERASE | ERASEAUP ]
        [ CURSOR [(data-value)] ]
END-EXEC
```

Options

MAP	Specifies the one- to seven-character name of the map to be used to map the output data.
MAPSET	Specifies the one- to eight-character name of the mapset that contains the map. If omitted, the map name is used. This name must be defined in the Processing Program Table (PPT).
FROM	Specifies the data area from which the data to be mapped is obtained (that is, the symbolic map).
MAPONLY	Specifies that only constant data from the BMS physical map is to be sent; no FROM area is used.
DATAONLY	Specifies that data from the FROM area is to be mapped; constant data from the physical map is not to be sent.
ERASE	Specifies that the entire display screen is to be erased before data is displayed.
ERASEAUP	Specifies that all of the unprotected fields on the screen are to be erased.
CURSOR	Specifies cursor positioning. For details, see chapter 8.

Figure 6-16   The SEND MAP command

the symbolic map is combined with the data in the physical map, and both are sent to the screen.

The first SEND MAP command executed in a terminal session usually sends both headings and initial data to the screen. As a result, you'll code the first SEND MAP with neither the MAPONLY nor the DATAONLY option. Subsequent SEND MAP commands generally use the DATAONLY option so the headings aren't transmitted again. Using the DATAONLY option improves transmission time. I'll have more to say about this efficiency technique in chapter 8.

The ERASE option causes CICS to erase the contents of the screen before any data is displayed. If ERASE is not specified, the screen isn't erased, so any characters that aren't overlaid by new data remain on the screen. ERASE is usually specified for the first SEND MAP issued by a

The RECEIVE MAP command

```
EXEC CICS
    RECEIVE MAP(name)
            MAPSET(name)
            INTO(data-area)
END-EXEC
```

Explanation

MAP   Specifies the one- to seven-character name of the map used to map the input data.

MAPSET   Specifies the one- to eight-character name of the mapset that contains the map. If
                         omitted, the map name is used. This name must be defined in the Processing Program
                         Table (PPT).

INTO   Specifies the data area into which the mapped data is to be placed.

Figure 6-17 The RECEIVE MAP command

program. That way, whatever was on the screen before the SEND MAP command is executed is erased. On subsequent SEND MAP commands, however, you generally do not code the ERASE option, particularly if you code the DATAONLY option.

The ERASEAUP option is similar to the ERASE option. The difference is that the ERASEAUP option specifies that only unprotected fields are erased, while ERASE completely clears the screen. In other words, ERASEAUP causes only data entry fields to be erased. Whether you use the ERASEAUP option depends on whether you want to erase all data entry fields between transactions. In some applications, you do, so you code a SEND MAP with the DATAONLY and ERASEAUP options. In other applications, you want to leave the previous transaction's data on the screen so the operator can enter only the fields that are changed. In this case you do not code the ERASEAUP option.

Bear in mind that the ERASEAUP option erases only unprotected fields. So if you want to erase protected fields in your symbolic map—such as the error-message field—you must move SPACE to them. Moving LOW-VALUE to protected fields does not cause them to be erased because CICS doesn't transmit LOW-VALUE to the terminal.

The last SEND MAP option in figure 6-16, the CURSOR option, is used for cursor positioning. I'll explain cursor-positioning techniques in chapter 8.

The RECEIVE MAP command

The RECEIVE MAP command, shown in figure 6-17, receives input data from the terminal. The MAP and MAPSET options indicate the map and

The READ command

```
EXEC CICS
    READ   DATASET(filename)
           INTO(data-area)
           RIDFLD(data-area)
        [ RRN | RBA ]
        [ UPDATE]
END-EXEC
```

Explanation

DATASET	Specifies the name of the data set to be read. This name must be defined in the File Control Table (FCT).
INTO	Specifies the data area into which data is to be read.
RIDFLD	For a keyed file, specifies the key of the record to be read. If RRN or RBA is specified, this field is interpreted as a relative record number or a relative byte address.
UPDATE	Specifies that you intend to update the record with a subsequent REWRITE or DELETE command.

Figure 6-18 The READ command

the mapset that contains it. The INTO option names the symbolic map in the Working-Storage Section of your program.

When the operator enters data at the terminal and presses an attention key, the data is transferred to a CICS buffer. Then, when your program executes a RECEIVE MAP command, the data in the buffer is mapped into your symbolic map. As a result, your program must not do a RECEIVE MAP before the operator has sent data from the terminal. This is only a problem in conversational programs. As long as your program is pseudo-conversational, data will always be available in the buffer because your program won't be executed until the operator presses an attention key.

The READ command   The READ command, shown in figure 6-18, retrieves a record from a VSAM keyed file. The DATASET option specifies the name of the file to be read, and the INTO option names the working-storage field that will receive the data. The RIDFLD option supplies the key value for the record to be retrieved. So, if the variable named in the RIDFLD option has a value of 400001, the record with key 400001 is read. Naturally, the format of the field you specify in the RIDFLD option should correspond to the format of the file's key.

If the record doesn't exist, CICS raises the NOTFND condition which, by default, causes your program to abend. To prevent this, you

The ABEND command

```
EXEC CICS
    ABEND [ ABCODE(name) ]
END-EXEC
```

Explanation

ABCODE   Specifies that a storage dump should be produced and the one- to four-character value
                                supplied should be used as the abend code. If you omit ABCODE, a storage dump is
                                not produced.

Figure 6-19   The ABEND command

will almost certainly want to code the RESP option. Then, the READ command will return a response code in the field you specify, which should be defined in working storage as a binary fullword (PIC S9(8) COMP). Immediately after the READ command, you should code IF statements to test the value of the response code field, as I described in the last topic.

The READ command can also be used to read records from relative record or entry-sequenced data sets. To do that, you just specify the RRN option for relative record files or the RBA option for entry-sequenced files. These options cause CICS to interpret the contents of the RIDFLD field differently. If you specify RRN, CICS interprets the RIDFLD field as a relative record number that identifies a record in a relative record file. And if you specify RBA, the RIDFLD is interpreted as a relative byte address to identify a record in an entry-sequenced file. In both cases, the field you specify in the RIDFLD option should be defined in working storage as a binary fullword field (PIC S9(8) COMP).

You use the last option in figure 6-18, UPDATE, when you intend to change the retrieved record using a CICS REWRITE command or delete it using a DELETE command. I'll describe these commands and other CICS file control commands in detail in chapter 8.

The ABEND command The ABEND command, shown in figure 6-19, terminates your program abnormally. It causes a message to be displayed at the terminal. To continue after an abend, the user must clear the screen by pressing the Clear key. Then, the user must type a trans-id and press the Enter key.

If you specify the ABCODE option on the ABEND command, CICS will produce a storage dump for your program. The value you supply in the ABCODE option will be used to identify the storage dump. You'll learn more about storage dumps in chapter 12.

Discussion The CICS commands in this topic are among the most commonly used. As a result, you should be sure you understand the material this topic presents. You'll need to learn other commands as your CICS training progresses, but they'll seem easy after you've mastered the ones presented in this topic.

Terms

option
parameter

Objectives

1. Describe the basic format and coding rules for any CICS command.

2. Describe the function of each of the CICS commands in this topic: RETURN, XCTL, SEND MAP, RECEIVE MAP, READ, and ABEND.

3. Explain when it is and isn't appropriate to code the DATAONLY, MAPONLY, ERASE, and ERASEAUP options on the SEND MAP command.

Chapter 7

How to design a structured CICS program

You're now familiar with BMS and the complexities of coding a simple command-level CICS program in COBOL. Although you've learned what you need to know to code a simple program, you're still not ready to take on a realistic CICS programming assignment. Before you can do that, you need to know how to design a command-level CICS program. In this chapter, I'll show you how to do that.

Frankly, CICS presents many unique program design challenges. The most obvious of these challenges is the need for pseudo-conversational programming. Pseudo-conversational programming makes it difficult, if not impossible, to design programs using the same mindset that works for designing batch COBOL programs. As a result, CICS programming calls for an altogether different approach to design, one that takes into account the considerations unique to CICS.

This chapter begins by describing an overall approach to CICS design called *event-driven design*. Event-driven design forces you to think in terms of the events that can trigger the execution of a pseudo-conversational program and the program's response to each event. Once you understand this design technique, I think you'll discover that most CICS programs are actually quite easy to design.

Then, this chapter will show you how to develop a program structure chart. Although you don't hear much talk about structured program design anymore, I still believe that drawing a structure chart helps you design better programs because it forces you to consider functions. When you draw a structure chart, you work from the top down, focusing first on broad functions rather than the kinds of trivial details that can bog you down.

To illustrate these CICS program design techniques, I'll present the design for a typical CICS program that lets the user maintain a file of customer records. Figure 7-1 presents the specifications for this program. As you can see, the program uses two BMS maps. In the first map (MNTMAP1), the user enters a customer number and an action code that indicates whether he or she wishes to add, change, or delete a customer. For an addition or change, the user enters appropriate data in the second map (MNTMAP2). For a deletion, the second map allows the user to verify that the correct customer record is to be deleted.

Event-driven program design

Simply put, the idea of event-driven program design is to identify the various events that can cause a pseudo-conversational CICS program to be invoked and to design an appropriate response to each event. An *event* is any action that causes a pseudo-conversational program to be started. The *response* is the processing that the program does for a particular event. For example, if the user presses the PF3 key, the program should exit to the menu by issuing an XCTL command that invokes the menu program. In this case, the event that triggered the execution of the menu program is the user pressing the PF3 key. The program's response is to issue the XCTL command.

As I see it, the primary benefit of event-driven design is that it lets you focus on the most challenging aspect of CICS programming: managing interactions with the user. All other aspects of a CICS program's operation, such as managing VSAM files, are straightforward and predictable. But a program's interactions with its user—or, more appropriately, a user's interactions with a program—are often convoluted and anything but predictable. In a CICS program, the user controls the path of execution through the pseudo-conversation, not the program. Event-driven design recognizes this at the outset and uses this fact as the basis of the program's design.

In fact, I think that as you work with this design approach, you will find that it actually makes pseudo-conversational programming easier than conversational programming. Conversational programming does not lend itself well to the event-driven design model. As a result, the most significant aspects of a conversational program's user interactions are often buried deeply within the program's structure. In contrast, the design of an event-driven pseudo-conversational program is based on its user interactions.

Program	CUSTMNT1

Overview   Maintains customer information in the customer master file by allowing the user to enter new customers, change existing customers, or delete existing customers.

Input/output specifications

CUSTMAS	Customer master file
MNTMAP1	Customer maintenance key map
MNTMAP2	Customer maintenance data map

Processing specifications

1. Control is transferred to this program via XCTL from the menu program INVMENU with no communication area. The user can also start the program by entering the trans-id MNT1. In either case, the program should respond by displaying the customer maintenance key map.

2. On the key map, the user selects a processing action (Add, Change, or Delete) and enters a customer number. Both the action field and the customer number field must be entered. If the user selects Add, the customer number entered must not exist in the file. For Change or Delete, the customer number must exist in the file.

3. If the user enters a valid combination of action and customer number, the program displays the customer maintenance data map. For an addition or a change request, all data fields must be entered. For a delete request, all fields should be set to protected so the user cannot enter changes.

4. If the user presses PF3 from either the key map or the data map, return to the menu program INVMENU by issuing an XCTL command. If the user presses PF12 from the key map, return to the menu program. However, if the user presses PF12 from the data map, redisplay the key map without processing any data that was entered.

5. For an addition or change, maintain an image of the customer record in the communication area between program executions. If the record is changed in any way between program executions, notify the user and do not complete the change or delete operation.

Figure 7-1   Specifications for a maintenance program (part 1 of 2)

To design a CICS program using the event-driven approach, you begin by identifying each event that can cause your program to be invoked. Then, you must carefully identify the context where each event can occur. And finally, you plan the program's response to each event in its context.

Identifying user input events

The first step in event-driven design is to identify the events. To do that, you begin by listing all of the potential user actions that can cause the program to be invoked along with a brief description of the program's appropriate response to each. Figure 7-2 shows such a list for the customer maintenance program.

The first event listed in figure 7-2 is "Start the program." This event occurs when the user initiates this program for the first time by selecting it from a menu or typing its trans-id at the terminal. The program's

Map name ___ MNTMAP1 _____ Date ___ 2-26-92 _____
Program name _CUSTMNT1 _____ Designer _Doug Lowe _____

```
    1234567890 1234567890 1234567890 1234567890 1234567890 1234567890 1234567890 1234567890
 1  MNTMAP1                Customer Maintenance
 2
 3  XXXXXXXXXXXXXXXXXXXXXXXXXXXXXXXXXXXXXXXXXXXXXXXXXXXXXXXXXXXXXXXXXXXXXXXXXXXXXXXXXX
 4
 5  Customer number. . . . . XXXXXX
 6
 7  Action . . . . . . . . . X 1.  Add a new customer
 8                             2.  Change an existing customer
 9                             3.  Delete an existing customer
10
11
12
13
14
15
16
17
18
19
20
21
22
23  XXXXXXXXXXXXXXXXXXXXXXXXXXXXXXXXXXXXXXXXXXXXXXXXXXXXXXXXXXXXXXXXXXXXXXXXXXXXXXXXXX
24  PF3=Exit    F12=Cancel                                                          X
```

Map name ___ MNTMAP2 _____ Date ___ 2-26-92 _____
Program name _CUSTMNT1 _____ Designer _Doug Lowe _____

```
    1234567890 1234567890 1234567890 1234567890 1234567890 1234567890 1234567890 1234567890
 1  MNTMAP2                Customer Maintenance
 2
 3  XXXXXXXXXXXXXXXXXXXXXXXXXXXXXXXXXXXXXXXXXXXXXXXXXXXXXXXXXXXXXXXXXXXXXXXXXXXXXXXXXX
 4
 5  Customer number. . . . . XXXXXX
 6
 7  Name and address . . . : XXXXXXXXXXXXXXXXXXXXXXXXXXXXXXX
 8                           XXXXXXXXXXXXXXXXXXXXXXX
 9                           XXXXXXXXXXXXXXXXXXXXXXXXXXXXX
10                           XXXXXXXXXXXXXXXXXXX XX XXXXXXXXXX
11
12
13
14
15
16
17
18
19
20
21
22
23  XXXXXXXXXXXXXXXXXXXXXXXXXXXXXXXXXXXXXXXXXXXXXXXXXXXXXXXXXXXXXXXXXXXXXXXXXXXXXXXXXX
24  PF3=Exit    F12=Cancel                                                          X
```

Figure 7-1   Specifications for a maintenance program (part 2 of 2)

Event	Response
Start the program	Display the key map.
PF3	Transfer control to the menu program.
PF12	If the key map is displayed, transfer control to the menu program. If the data map is displayed, cancel the operation and display the key map.
Enter	If the key map is displayed, prepare the data map according to the requested action and display it. If the data map is displayed, add, change, or delete the customer as appropriate.
Clear	Redisplay the current map.
PA1, PA2, or PA3	Ignore the key.
Any other key	Display an appropriate error message.

Figure 7-2 User input events for the maintenance program and appropriate program responses

appropriate response is to display the key map and return. For this event and all the other events listed in figure 7-2, I didn't include "return" in the description of the appropriate response to the event. That's because returning with the TRANSID and COMMAREA options is an assumed final step in the response to all events unless the response implies otherwise (such as transferring control to another program).

The other events listed in figure 7-2 are all triggered by the use of attention keys. If the user presses PF3, the program should end. If the user presses PF12, the program's response depends on whether the key map or the data map is currently displayed. If the key map is currently displayed, the program should exit to the menu as if PF3 were pressed. But if the data map is displayed, the program should cancel the operation and display the key map.

In the same way, the program's response to the Enter key depends on the map currently displayed. If it's the key map, the program should prepare the data map appropriately, depending on the action selected by the user (add, change, or delete), then display the data map. If it's the data map that's displayed, the program should edit the data and complete the action (add, change, or delete) if the data is valid.

The other events listed in figure 7-2 are straightforward. For the Clear key, the program simply redisplays the map that was on the screen. The program ignores the PA keys. And for any other key, the program displays an error message.

Managing the context of user input events

In figure 7-2, the program's response to some of the events depends on the context of the event. This *context* is determined by a combination of factors, such as the map that's currently displayed at the terminal and the selections the user has made.

For example, the program's response to the PF12 key depends on whether the key map or the data map is displayed. If the key map is displayed, the program should exit to a menu program. But if the data map is displayed, the program should simply redisplay the key map.

Similarly, the program's response to the Enter key depends on whether the key map or the data map is currently displayed. And if the data map is displayed, the response depends on the action the user requested on the key map: Add, Change, or Delete. In a moment, we'll refine the design for the maintenance program by planning exactly how the program should add, change, or delete customer data. But first, I want to focus on how your program can determine the context of user input events.

It's easy to determine which event occurred because CICS provides AID key information in the Execute Interface Block via the EIBAID field. Determining the context of the event is more difficult, however. CICS does not provide you with information about which map is currently displayed, nor can it tell you what information the user entered on a previous map. So it's up to you to manage the event context.

Although there are several methods available to do that, the easiest is to store context information in the communication area. Then, each execution of the program can pass the current context forward to the next program execution. When the context changes, you can update the information in the communication area to indicate the new context for the next execution of the program.

Figure 7-3 shows the event contexts for the maintenance program. Here, you can see that I've identified four distinct contexts for the program. The "Get key" context means that the key map is currently displayed on the screen, so the Enter key should be interpreted as a request to process an action code and customer number, and the PF12 key should be interpreted as a request to exit to the menu program. The "Add customer" context means that the data map has been displayed in response to an "Add" action, so the Enter key should be interpreted as a request to edit new customer data and write a new customer record if the data is valid; the PF12 key should be interpreted as a request to cancel the add operation and redisplay the key map. The "Change customer" and "Delete customer" contexts have similar meanings.

The names I used for these contexts are descriptive, but not rigorous. If you want, you can adopt a more formal naming convention. For example, you might name each context using the name of the map that's currently displayed, followed by other conditions that indicate context.

Context	Explanation
Get key	The key map is displayed, awaiting input of a valid combination of action code and customer number.
Add customer	The data map is displayed in response to a request to add a customer.
Change customer	The data map is displayed in response to a request to change a customer.
Delete customer	The data map is displayed in response to a request to delete a customer.

Figure 7-3 Event contexts for the maintenance program

Then, the four contexts for the maintenance program would be "MNTMAP1," "MNTMAP2-add," MNTMAP2-change," and "MNTMAP2-delete."

To keep track of which context is current, I created an entry in the communication area like the one shown in figure 7-4. To determine the current context, the program uses the 88-level condition names. For example, the statement

```
IF CA-GET-KEY
```

could be used to determine if the current context is "Get key." To set the context for the next program execution, the program must move an appropriate value to CA-CONTEXT-FLAG.

Identifying the various event contexts that affect your program's operation and planning how you'll keep track of the current context is an essential part of designing your program. As a result, I don't think it's premature to code this portion of your program's communication area at this stage of development. As you continue to plan and code your program, you may find that you need additional items in the communication area. But the earlier you decide how you'll manage the program's context, the better.

Designing the program's response to each event

So far, I've described the program's response to each event only in sketchy terms. Once you've identified all of the user input events, identified the possible contexts of each event, and planned how your program will keep track of those contexts, it's time to refine the program's response to each event in its context. To do that, I suggest you prepare a summary of the program's event processing such as the one in figure 7-5. As you can see, this summary specifies the response to each event with a substantial amount of detail.

The left column in figure 7-5 lists each input event that the maintenance program must respond to. Then, the second column lists

```
01  COMMUNICATION-AREA.
*
    05  CA-CONTEXT-FLAG        PIC X.
        88  CA-GET-KEY              VALUE '1'.
        88  CA-ADD-CUSTOMER         VALUE '2'.
        88  CA-CHANGE-CUSTOMER      VALUE '3'.
        88  CA-DELETE-CUSTOMER      VALUE '4'.
```

Figure 7-4   A communication area field to manage the maintenance program's event contexts

the contexts that are significant for each event. For example, you can see that the program must respond differently to the Enter key for each context, but the context doesn't matter for the PF3 key. And since there is no established context for the "Start the program" event, the context doesn't matter.

Next, the third column summarizes the program's response to each event/context combination. Finally, the fourth column lists the new context that results from each response. For example, if the user presses PF12 when the context is "Add customer," the program will set the context for the next program execution to "Get key." And for the Enter key with the "Add customer" or "Change customer" context, the new context depends on whether or not the input data is valid.

Look now at the description of the program's response when the user presses the Enter key. As you can see, I've divided this response into four sections, depending on the context. For each context, the response is similar: receive the map, edit the data, then perform processing that's appropriate for the context. For the CA-ADD-CUSTOMER context, that means to write a new record to the customer file, send the key map with an appropriate message, and set the new context to CA-GET-KEY. If the entered data is invalid, however, no record is written. Instead, an error message is sent to the terminal, and the context is left at CA-ADD-CUSTOMER.

The summary in figure 7-5 is nothing more than a planning tool, so it can be as detailed or as general as necessary. As you gain experience developing CICS programs, you'll find it unnecessary to include the amount of detail I included in figure 7-5. Instead, you'll be able to just jot down the major processing functions and fill in the details later. Also, since this is a design tool and is not intended to document the final version of the program, I recommend against maintaining a summary like this as a part of the program's documentation. Instead, as you'll soon see, the program structure chart, which is derived from the processing summary, should be used as final program documentation instead.

Event	Context	Response	New context
Start the program	n/a	Display the key map.	Get key
PF3	All	Transfer control to the menu program.	n/a
PF12	Get key	Transfer control to the menu program.	n/a
	Add customer Change customer Delete customer	Cancel the operation and display the key map.	Get key
Enter	Get key	Edit input data. If valid read customer record display data map else display an error message.	Add customer, Change customer, or Delete customer Get key
	Add customer	Edit input data. If valid add the customer record display the key map else display an error message.	Get key Add customer
	Change customer	Edit input data. If valid change the customer record display the key map else display an error message.	Get key Change customer
	Delete customer	Delete the customer record. Display the key map.	Get key
Clear	All	Redisplay the current map.	Unchanged
PA1, PA2, or PA3	All	Ignore the key.	Unchanged
Any other key	All	Display an appropriate error message.	Unchanged

Figure 7-5   An event/response chart for the maintenance program

How to create a program structure chart

Once you've planned the event processing for your program, you can use it as the basis for a program structure chart. The structure chart, in turn, will serve as a basis for your program code. Each box on the structure chart represents one program module, which can be easily implemented as a single paragraph in your COBOL program. The

COBOL paragraph for a module invokes the modules subordinate to it by issuing PERFORM statements.

How to design the first two levels of the structure chart

To create a structure chart, start by drawing a box for the top-level module. This module represents the entire program, and it will contain the COBOL statements necessary to manage the event processing you designed for the program. As a result, it should be given a name that represents the overall function of the program. For the customer maintenance program, I'll use the name "Process customer maintenance."

Next, decide which portions of the event processing summary should be implemented as separate program modules and draw a box subordinate to the top-level module for each one. For the customer maintenance program, it seemed reasonable to isolate the processing required to respond to the Enter key in each of the program's four contexts. Thus, I created the four modules shown in figure 7-6: "Process key map," "Process add customer," "Process change customer," and "Process delete customer." Each of these modules represents a major function of the program. Because the processing required to respond to other program events is trivial, I didn't include separate modules for them.

Frankly, a certain amount of judgement is necessary to determine which modules should make up the second level of the structure chart. At one extreme, you could create a module to process every event to which the program must respond. At the other extreme, you could implement the entire program in one module, with no subordinate modules at all. In most cases, the best design is somewhere between these two extremes.

Although there are no hard and fast rules you should follow, there are a few general guidelines that can help you determine whether an event calls for a separate module. To begin, if the program's response to the event requires you to receive data from the terminal, process it, and send data back to the terminal, you should almost certainly create a separate module for it. Second, even if you don't need to receive data from the terminal, you should consider creating a separate module for events whose response requires more than a few COBOL statements to implement. And finally, if the COBOL statements required to implement the top-level module require more than a page or two, you should consider creating additional second-level modules to simplify the coding in the top-level module.

The design that will result from following these guidelines will vary from program to program. For some programs, such as the maintenance program, you'll end up with one second-level module for each context. For other programs, you'll end up with second-level modules associated

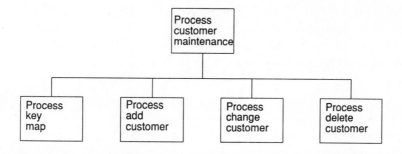

Figure 7-6   The first two levels of the structure chart for the maintenance program

with particular function keys. Still other programs will have a combination of the two. I think each of these approaches is useful, depending on the particulars of the program and as long as there's a clear relationship between the structure chart and the events and their contexts.

You might be tempted to spread the modules that process events and contexts across several levels of the structure chart. For example, look at the alternative structure for the customer maintenance program in figure 7-7. Here, instead of creating four second-level modules, I created only two: one to process the key map, the other to process the customer data map. The second module then has three subordinates to process add, change, and delete functions. Although this program structure will work, I prefer the one in figure 7-6 because it places all of the event context logic in the top-level module. With the design in figure 7-7, the logic for managing the event context is split between the top-level module and the process-customer-map module. Whenever practical, it's best to keep this type of logic together in the same module.

How to design the lower levels of the structure chart

When you've decided which modules to place at the second level of the structure chart, you can start dividing each of them into their component functions. To illustrate, figure 7-8 shows the functional breakdown of the process-key-map module. Here, you can see I've broken that module down into four subordinate modules: "Receive key map," "Edit key map," "Send customer map," and "Send key map." In addition, since editing the data from the key map requires that the customer master file be read (to make sure that the customer record for an addition does not exist or that the customer record for a change or deletion does), I added a read-customer-record module subordinate to the edit-key-map module.

The other three second-level modules of the customer maintenance program can be broken down in the same way. Figure 7-9 shows the resulting structure chart. Here, you can see that the second-level

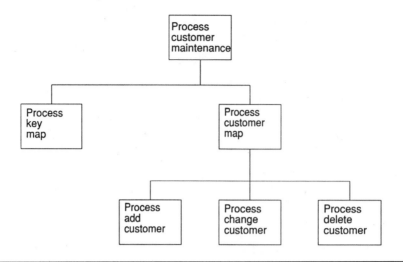

Figure 7-7   An alternative design for the maintenance program

modules to add and change a customer include similar subordinate modules to receive the customer map, edit the data, write or rewrite the customer record, and send a key map or a customer map. The subordinate modules for the process-delete-customer module are different. Since the user doesn't enter data into the customer screen for a deletion, the process-delete-customer module doesn't need to invoke a module to receive the customer map or edit data. Instead, it just deletes the customer record and redisplays the key map.

As you design the lower levels of your structure chart, there are three general guidelines you should follow. First, each module of the program should represent one and only one function. Avoid modules that perform a variety of unrelated functions or appear to have no definable function at all.

Second, the function of a called module must be logically contained in the function of its calling module. For example, does the read-customer-record module really belong subordinate to the edit-key-map module? I think it does, because to determine whether or not the action code and customer number entered on the key map are valid, the program has to read the customer record to determine whether or not it exists. Thus, reading the customer record is an integral part of editing the data from the key map.

And third, the modules must be manageable. If you expect that a module will require more than 50 or so lines of COBOL to implement, consider further subdividing the module into subordinate modules. Of course, this is not a hard and fast rule. If a module consists of 100 simple MOVE statements, you don't need to break it up just to make it shorter. On the other hand, a module that requires a deeply nested structure of IF statements may become overly complicated in just a few dozen lines.

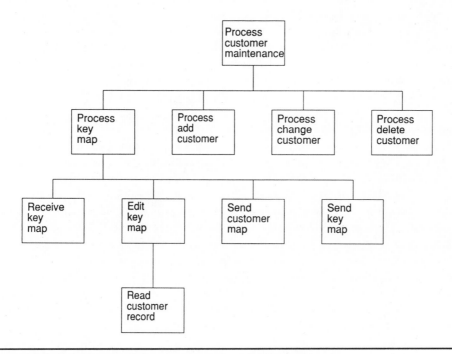

Figure 7-8   Functional breakdown for the process-key-map module

Why you should use a generalized send module for each map

To simplify your program design, I recommend you create a single, general-purpose send module for each map your program processes. This send module will contain one or more SEND MAP commands with various options (such as ERASE, DATAONLY, and ALARM). The send module decides which form of the SEND MAP command to use by evaluating a flag that's set by the calling module.

This approach has several advantages. First, it simplifies your structure charts by avoiding the need for separate modules with names like "Send customer map erase" and "Send customer map dataonly." Second, the send module will be nearly identical from one program to the next. All you'll need to change is the name you specify in the MAP, MAPSET, and FROM options. And finally, it places all of the SEND MAP commands for a particular map in the same program module. That way, the program will be easier to maintain if a change is made to the map or mapset.

Incidentally, you'll almost certainly need to add this generalized send module as a subordinate to the program's top-level module. That's because the top-level module will need to invoke it to send the map when the first-time event occurs and when the user presses the Clear key or an invalid PF key. When you design the first two levels of the

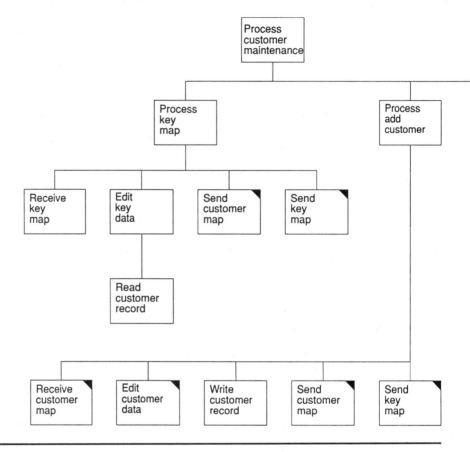

Figure 7-9   Structure chart for the maintenance program

program, you try to identify the main event-processing modules for the program. Since this isn't one of them, you needn't include the generalized send module at that time. Eventually, however, you'll need to add the send module alongside the main event-processing modules at the second level of the structure chart.

How to identify common modules

Because the send module in figure 7-9 appears more than once in the structure chart, it's called a *common module*. To indicate a common module, I shade the upper right-hand corner of the box. As you can see in figure 7-9, that makes the common modules easy to identify on the structure chart. If there are any modules subordinate to a common module, I draw them only once on the chart.

How to number the modules

Once you've decided your structure chart is complete, you should number the modules. When you code the program, you combine these

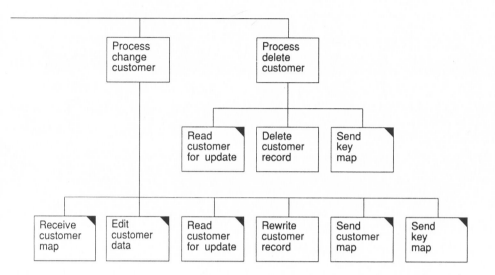

numbers with the module names to form the COBOL paragraph names. Then, you code the paragraphs in numeric sequence in your program.

Although you can adopt complicated numbering schemes, I recommend you avoid them. Instead, use a simple numbering scheme such as the one in figure 7-10. Here, I numbered the modules of the maintenance program using four-digit numbers. For the second-level modules, I used multiples of 1000. I used multiples of 100 for modules at lower levels. This numbering scheme leaves room for you to add modules later without forcing you to renumber existing modules.

Structure listings: an alternative to structure charts

Creating a structure chart such as the one in figure 7-10 has great value during the design stage of program development. However, keeping a structure chart current quickly becomes a burden as you begin to implement the program. Inevitably, you will discover weaknesses in your design that force you to adjust your program's structure by adding additional modules, removing modules, or combining modules. You'll

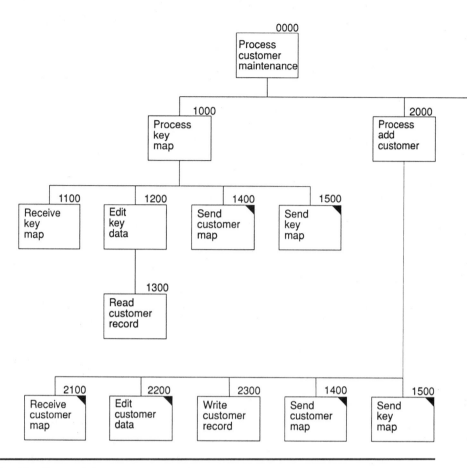

Figure 7-10 Final structure chart for the maintenance program

be reluctant to make such changes if you know you'll have to redraw a complicated structure chart.

In our shop, we use a program called LISTMODS that reads a COBOL source program as input, analyzes its paragraphs and PERFORM statements, and produces a listing of the program's structure as output. Figure 7-11 shows a LISTMODS listing for the customer maintenance program. Although it isn't as interesting graphically, in some respects, it presents the maintenance program's structure more clearly than a structure chart. It is certainly more concise.

The biggest benefit of the LISTMODS listing, of course, is that it is generated automatically. So when you make a change that affects the program's structure, you don't have to redraw a chart. You just have to run LISTMODS against the program to produce an updated listing. If you add LISTMODS to the procedure that translates and compiles your programs, you'll automatically get a current structure listing every time you compile your program. I think you'll agree that this benefit far outweighs the drawback of not being as graphic. So I recommend you

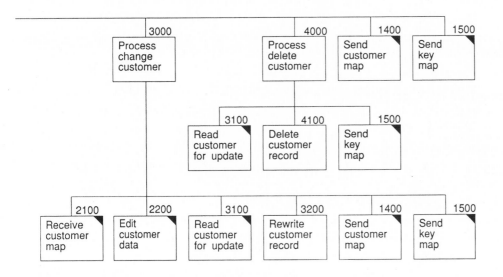

draw structure charts only for design purposes, and discard them when the program is completed.

Incidentally, if you're using CICS OS/2, you should realize that a component of the MicroFocus Workbench called *COBOL Source Information* (or just *CSI*) can produce a similar listing. You can access CSI directly from the Workbench editor, but you must first compile the program with the CSI compiler directive. Consult the *MicroFocus Workbench Reference* manual for more information.

Discussion   In summary, the approach to CICS program design I recommend is first to identify how your program should respond to the various events that can trigger its execution, then to develop a structure chart that identifies the program functions necessary to provide those responses. Once you've identified the proper response to each event and created an appropriate structure chart, coding the program is relatively easy. Each module on the structure chart becomes a paragraph in the program.

```
PROGRAM-ID:  CUSTMNT1.

0000-PROCESS-CUSTOMER-MAINT

    1000-PROCESS-KEY-MAP
        1100-RECEIVE-KEY-MAP
        1200-EDIT-KEY-MAP
            1300-READ-CUSTOMER-RECORD
        1400-SEND-CUSTOMER-MAP              *
        1500-SEND-KEY-MAP                   *

    2000-PROCESS-ADD-CUSTOMER
        2100-RECEIVE-CUSTOMER-MAP           *
        2200-EDIT-CUSTOMER-DATA             *
        2300-WRITE-CUSTOMER-RECORD
        1500-SEND-KEY-MAP                   *
        1400-SEND-CUSTOMER-MAP              *

    3000-PROCESS-CHANGE-CUSTOMER
        2100-RECEIVE-CUSTOMER-MAP           *
        2200-EDIT-CUSTOMER-DATA             *
        3100-REWRITE-CUSTOMER-RECORD
        1500-SEND-KEY-MAP                   *
        1400-SEND-CUSTOMER-MAP              *

    4000-PROCESS-DELETE-CUSTOMER
        4100-DELETE-CUSTOMER-RECORD
        1500-SEND-KEY-MAP                   *


*  =  COMMON MODULE
```

Figure 7-11   Structure listing for the customer maintenance program

I think you'll find that the majority of CICS programs you develop follow the patterns suggested by the programs in this book. If you're still uncertain about CICS program design, you'll gain more confidence as you study the model programs in section 3. Before you move on to those programs, however, you need to know about the CICS programming techniques the next chapter presents.

Terms

event-driven design
event
response
context
common module
COBOL Source Information
CSI

Objectives

1. Explain why event-driven program design is appropriate for pseudo-conversational CICS programs.

2. Given specifications for a CICS program, create a list of each user input event that can trigger execution of the program, identify the various contexts the program must manage, and create a summary of the program's response to each event.

3. Working from an event/response chart such as the one in figure 7-5, create a program structure chart that indicates the major event-processing modules and the major functional modules subordinate to each event-processing module.

Chapter 8

Expanding the basic subset of command-level CICS

In this chapter, I'll expand the basic CICS subset I presented in chapter 6. This chapter is divided into five topics. Topic 1 covers CICS file control commands, which let you perform basic file I/O operations with VSAM files. Topic 2 presents program control commands, which let you manage several programs as a part of a single task. Topic 3 describes a variety of programming techniques for working with terminal input and output. Topic 4 presents error handling techniques. And finally, topic 5 shows you how to access main storage via your program's Linkage Section.

File control commands

CICS provides file handling commands to perform all basic file manipulation operations, including random and sequential read, write, rewrite, and delete. You can use these commands on key-sequenced (indexed), relative record (direct), or entry-sequenced (sequential) VSAM files. (VSAM files are also called data sets, and you'll often see the abbreviations KSDS, RRDS, and ESDS for key-sequenced, relative record, and entry-sequenced data sets.) You don't have to have an in-depth understanding of VSAM to use the commands this topic presents, as long as you understand the basic differences between the three kinds of data sets. So I won't present details on VSAM file organization in this topic. If you desire this background, or if you need to learn how to use the VSAM utility program (IDCAMS), I recommend my book, *VSAM: Access Method Services and Application Programming*, available from Mike Murach & Associates.

The READ command
Because the inquiry program I presented in chapter 6 required a READ command, I introduced its format in chapter 6. Figure 8-1 presents the READ command again, but with more detail. In its simplest form, you code the READ command like this:

```
EXEC CICS
    READ DATASET('CUSTMAS')
         INTO(CUSTOMER-MASTER-RECORD)
         RIDFLD(CM-CUSTOMER-NUMBER)
         RESP(RESPONSE-CODE)
END-EXEC.
```

Here, a record is read from a VSAM key-sequenced file named CUSTMAS and placed in a working-storage field named CUSTOMER-MASTER-RECORD. The RIDFLD option supplies the key value for the record to be read. (In this example, the RIDFLD data area is part of the record. Although that's usually the case, the RIDFLD data area can also be a separate field defined in working storage.) The last option, RESP, names a working-storage field that will contain the command's response code.

Figure 8-2 shows typical coding for a program module that reads a file record. Immediately after the READ command, I coded an IF statement to test the response code. In this example, I move Y to RECORD-FOUND-SW if the response is NORMAL. If the NOTFND condition is detected, I move N to RECORD-FOUND-SW. For any other

The READ command

```
EXEC CICS
    READ  DATASET(filename)
          INTO(data-area)
          RIDFLD(data-area)
        [ RRN | RBA ]
        [ LENGTH(data-area) ]
        [ UPDATE ]
END-EXEC
```

Explanation

DATASET — Specifies the name of the data set from which the record is to be read. This name must be defined in the File Control Table (FCT).

INTO — Specifies the data area into which data is to be read.

RIDFLD — For a keyed file, specifies the key of the record to be read. If RRN or RBA is specified, this field is interpreted as a relative record number or a relative byte address.

RRN — Specifies that the file is a relative record file, and the RIDFLD option should be interpreted as a relative record number.

RBA — Specifies that the file is an entry-sequenced data set, and the RIDFLD option should be interpreted as a relative byte address.

LENGTH — Specifies a binary halfword field (PIC S9(4) COMP) that specifies the maximum record length the program can accept. When the READ command completes, CICS sets this field to the actual length of the record read. Not required for fixed-length records or under VS COBOL II.

UPDATE — Specifies that you intend to update the record with a subsequent REWRITE or DELETE command.

Figure 8-1   The READ command

type of error condition, I issue an ABEND command to terminate the program.

To read a record from a relative record file, you specify RRN on the READ command. Then, the RIDFLD value represents the number of the record you wish to retrieve. For example, if the RIDFLD value is 1, the first record in the file is read; it it's 2, the second record is read; and so on. You define the record number field as a fullword binary item, like this:

```
01  INVMAST-RRN          PIC S9(8)   COMP.
```

Then, you specify this field in the RIDFLD option.

You can also read a record from an entry-sequenced data set by specifying the record's relative byte address, or RBA. Frankly, though, it's unlikely that you'll use the READ command for entry-sequenced

```
2100-READ-ACCOUNT-RECORD.
*
     EXEC CICS
         READ DATASET('ACCOUNT')
              INTO(ACCOUNT-RECORD)
              RIDFLD(AR-ACCOUNT-NUMBER)
              RESP(RESPONSE-CODE)
     END-EXEC.
     IF RESPONSE-CODE = DFHRESP(NORMAL)
         MOVE 'Y' TO ACCOUNT-RECORD-FOUND-SW
     ELSE IF RESPONSE-CODE = DFHRESP(NOTFND)
         MOVE 'N' TO ACCOUNT-RECORD-FOUND-SW
     ELSE
         EXEC CICS
              ABEND
         END-EXEC.
```

Figure 8-2   Typical coding for a read module

data sets. The READ command is used only for random retrieval, and entry-sequenced data sets are usually processed sequentially. I'll cover the CICS commands you use for sequential retrieval in *Part 2: An Advanced Course.*

The LENGTH option is required only when you read a record from a file that contains variable-length records. Before you issue the READ command, you should set the field you name on the LENGTH option to the longest record length your program can accommodate (in other words, the length of the INTO area). When CICS reads the record, it sets the LENGTH field to the actual length of the record that was read.

If you intend to update the record a READ command returns, you must specify the UPDATE option. The UPDATE option causes the requested record to be reserved by your task until you issue a REWRITE, DELETE, or UNLOCK command or until your task ends. (Actually, it's not just the record that's reserved, but the entire control interval that contains it.) Coding the READ command with the UPDATE option insures that no other task can modify the record while your task is updating it. You'll see in a moment how the REWRITE, DELETE, and UNLOCK commands are used.

The WRITE command

The WRITE command, shown in figure 8-3, adds a record to a file. As you can see, the WRITE command is similar in format to the READ command. The DATASET option indicates the name of the data set, the FROM option names the program area that contains the output record to be written, and RIDFLD provides the record's key value. Again, the RIDFLD data area can be a part of the record or a separate field defined in working storage.

For relative record files, you must specify the RRN option and define the record number field as a fullword binary item. Then, before you

The WRITE command

```
EXEC CICS
    WRITE   DATASET(filename)
            FROM(data-area)
            RIDFLD(data-area)
        [ RRN | RBA ]
        [ LENGTH(data-value) ]
END-EXEC
```

Explanation

DATASET — Specifies the name of the data set to which the record is to be written. This name must be defined in the File Control Table (FCT).

FROM — Specifies the data area from which data is to be written.

RIDFLD — For a keyed file, specifies the key of the record to be written. If RRN or RBA is specified, this field is interpreted as a relative record number or a relative byte address.

RRN — Specifies that the file is a relative record file, and the RIDFLD option should be interpreted as a relative record number.

RBA — Specifies that the file is an entry-sequenced data set. The record will be written to the end of the file without regard to the contents of the RIDFLD field. When the command completes, the RIDFLD field will be set to the RBA of the new record.

LENGTH — Specifies a binary halfword (PIC S9(4) COMP) that indicates the length of the record to be written. Not required for fixed-length records or under VS COBOL II.

Figure 8-3 The WRITE command

issue the WRITE statement, you move the appropriate record number to the RIDFLD field. For entry-sequenced files, you must specify RBA. Then, the initial value of the RIDFLD field has no effect. Instead, the record is added to the end of the data set and the relative byte address of the new record is returned to your program via the RIDFLD field.

The LENGTH option is used to indicate record lengths for files that allow variable-length records. For fixed-length records, you can omit LENGTH. And if you're using VS COBOL II, you can omit LENGTH unless the length of the record is different than the length of the working-storage field specified in the FROM field.

Figure 8-4 shows a typical write module. Here, the IF statements following the WRITE command evaluate the response code field. If the WRITE command tries to write a record using a key that's already in the file, the DUPREC condition will be indicated in the response code field.

```
3100-WRITE-ACCOUNT-RECORD.
*
    EXEC CICS
        WRITE DATASET('ACCOUNT')
              FROM(ACCOUNT-RECORD)
              RIDFLD(AR-ACCOUNT-NUMBER)
              RESP(RESPONSE-CODE)
    END-EXEC.
    IF RESPONSE-CODE = DFHRESP(NORMAL)
        MOVE 'Y' TO ACCOUNT-RECORD-WRITTEN-SW
    ELSE IF RESPONSE-CODE = DFHRESP(DUPREC)
        MOVE 'N' TO ACCOUNT-RECORD-WRITTEN-SW
    ELSE
        EXEC CICS
            ABEND
        END-EXEC.
```

Figure 8-4 Typical coding for a write module

The REWRITE command

The REWRITE command, shown in figure 8-5, updates a record in a file. Before you issue a REWRITE command, you must first issue a READ command with the UPDATE option.

To illustrate, figure 8-6 shows a typical update module that includes both a READ/UPDATE command and a REWRITE command. This module is performed after the user has entered the required modifications and the new record has been formatted in the field named NEW-ACCOUNT-RECORD. (The previous execution of the program issued a READ command that retrieved the original record and displayed it for modification.) Following the READ/UPDATE command, IF statements evaluate the response code to make sure no errors have occurred. If the account record is found, the REWRITE command is issued, and the response code is checked for errors once again.

Notice in this example that I didn't code the READ and REWRITE commands in separate modules. That's because you can consider the READ/UPDATE and REWRITE commands as a single function: update the customer record. The only reason I'd code them in separate modules is if the same READ/UPDATE command is needed at more than one point in the program.

As for the READ and WRITE commands, the LENGTH option specifies the length of the record to be updated. It's required only if the file allows variable-length records, and under VS COBOL II only if the record length is different from the actual length of the FROM field. In addition, you should be aware that when you rewrite a record in an ESDS, you cannot change its length. So the length value should be the same as the length value CICS returned with the READ/UPDATE command.

The REWRITE command

```
EXEC CICS
    REWRITE  DATASET(filename)
             FROM(data-area)
           [ LENGTH(data-value) ]
END-EXEC
```

Explanation

DATASET   Specifies the name of the data set that contains the record to be updated. This name must be defined in the File Control Table (FCT).

FROM   Specifies the data area from which data is to be written.

LENGTH   Specifies a binary halfword field (PIC S9(4) COMP) that indicates the length of the record to be rewritten. Not required for fixed-length records or under VS COBOL II.

Note: The record must be previously read with a READ command with the UPDATE option.

Figure 8-5   The REWRITE command

```
    4100-UPDATE-ACCOUNT-RECORD.
*
        EXEC CICS
            READ DATASET('ACCOUNT')
                 INTO(ACCOUNT-RECORD)
                 RIDFLD(AR-ACCOUNT-NUMBER)
                 UPDATE
                 RESP(RESPONSE-CODE)
        END-EXEC.

        IF RESPONSE-CODE = DFHRESP(NORMAL)
            MOVE 'Y' TO ACCOUNT-RECORD-FOUND-SW
        ELSE IF RESPONSE-CODE = DFHRESP(NOTFND)
            MOVE 'N' TO ACCOUNT-RECORD-FOUND-SW
        ELSE
            EXEC CICS
                ABEND
            END-EXEC.

        IF ACCOUNT-RECORD-FOUND
            EXEC CICS
                REWRITE DATASET('ACCOUNT')
                        FROM(NEW-ACCOUNT-RECORD)
                        RESP(RESPONSE-CODE)
            END-EXEC.

        IF RESPONSE-CODE = DFHRESP(NORMAL)
            MOVE 'Y' TO ACCOUNT-RECORD-UPDATED-SW
        ELSE
            EXEC CICS
                ABEND
            END-EXEC.
```

Figure 8-6   Typical coding for an update module

The DELETE command

```
EXEC CICS
    DELETE  DATASET(filename)
            RIDFLD(data-area)
          [ RRN | RBA ]
END-EXEC
```

Explanation

DATASET	Specifies the name of the data set that contains the record to be deleted. This name must be defined in the File Control Table (FCT).
RIDFLD	For a keyed file, specifies the key of the record to be deleted. If RRN or RBA is specified, this field is interpreted as a relative record number or a relative byte address.
RRN	Specifies that the file is a relative record file, and the RIDFLD option should be interpreted as a relative record number.
RBA	Specifies that the RIDFLD option should be interpreted as a relative byte address. Valid only for key-sequenced data sets.

Figure 8-7   The DELETE command

The DELETE command

The DELETE command, shown in figure 8-7, deletes a record from a VSAM file. You can delete records from a KSDS or an RRDS, but not from an ESDS.

You can use the DELETE command in two ways. The first is to issue a READ command with the UPDATE option, and then issue a DELETE command like this one:

```
EXEC CICS
    DELETE DATASET('ACCOUNT')
END-EXEC.
```

Since the READ command identified the record, the RIDFLD option isn't required for this DELETE command.

The second way to use the DELETE command is to code the RIDFLD on the DELETE command, as shown in the typical delete module in figure 8-8. After the DELETE command, this module evaluates the response code to see if the NOTFND condition or some other, more serious, error occurred.

```
 5100-DELETE-ACCOUNT-RECORD.
*
     EXEC CICS
         DELETE DATASET('ACCOUNT')
                RIDFLD(AR-ACCOUNT-NUMBER)
                RESP(RESPONSE-CODE)
     END-EXEC.
     IF RESPONSE-CODE = DFHRESP(NORMAL)
         MOVE 'Y' TO ACCOUNT-RECORD-DELETED-SW
     ELSE IF RESPONSE-CODE = DFHRESP(NOTFND)
         MOVE 'N' TO ACCOUNT-RECORD-DELETED-SW
     ELSE
         EXEC CICS
             ABEND
         END-EXEC.
```

Figure 8-8   Typical coding for a delete module

The UNLOCK command

If you issue a READ/UPDATE command and then discover that the record doesn't need to be updated or deleted, you can release the record to other tasks by issuing an UNLOCK command, like this:

```
     EXEC CICS
         UNLOCK DATASET('ACCOUNT')
     END-EXEC.
```

Figure 8-9 gives the format of the UNLOCK command.

You'll probably never use the UNLOCK command, for two reasons. First, a record held by a READ/UPDATE command is released when your task is terminated. Since a pseudo-conversational update program terminates shortly after reading the record anyway, there's little point in issuing an UNLOCK command. Second, the UNLOCK command has no effect for files that are defined in the File Control Table as recoverable. And any file you intend to update is likely to be defined as recoverable. I included the UNLOCK command here only for completeness.

File-control exceptional conditions

Throughout this topic, I've referred to two exceptional conditions that often occur for file control commands: NOTFND and DUPREC. NOTFND occurs for READ, REWRITE, or DELETE commands when a specified record cannot be found. DUPREC occurs for a WRITE command if the specified record already exists or for a REWRITE command under special circumstances. Whenever you issue one of these commands, you should test the response code field to see if a NOTFND or DUPREC condition occurred.

Besides these two conditions, CICS file control commands can lead to a number of other exceptional conditions. Figure 8-10 summarizes the ones you should know about. In most cases, there's no need to check specifically for these conditions in your programs. Instead, you'll handle them as I have in the models in this topic: by terminating the program if

The UNLOCK command

```
EXEC CICS
    UNLOCK   DATASET(filename)
END-EXEC
```

Explanation

DATASET   Specifies the name of the data set that contains the record to be released. This name
                                 must be defined in the File Control Table (FCT).

Figure 8-9   The UNLOCK command

any response other than NORMAL, NOTFND, or DUPREC is encountered.

Design considerations

If you're designing a program that updates VSAM files, there are two considerations I want you to be aware of. First, you must realize that the UPDATE option reserves a record only for the duration of a task. To hold a record across executions of a pseudo-conversational program, additional programming techniques are required. Otherwise, while a record is displayed on the screen at one terminal, a user at another terminal may modify or delete the record before the first user's task is restarted.

There are two basic approaches to solving this problem: You can *prevent* it, or you can simply try to *detect* it. To prevent someone from accessing a record while a pseudo-conversational program is trying to update it, you must provide some way of indicating that the record is in the process of being updated. For example, you could designate the first byte of a record as an "update in progress" switch. Then, when a pseudo-conversational program first accesses the record, it turns this switch on. It turns the switch off again when the update is completed. Every program that updates the file must then test the switch to see if the record is available.

There are three disadvantages with this scheme. First, it will only work if all other programs that access the file obey the rules. Second, it adds unnecessary file I/O: Any program that needs to update the file must actually update it twice, once to set the switch, and again to update the record. And third, it's possible that the program that initially sets the switch will be unable to reset it. (The program might abend, the system might abend, or the network might go down.) If that happens, the record will be locked out indefinitely unless a special program is written to clear the "update in progress" switch.

Condition	READ	WRITE	REWRITE	DELETE	UNLOCK	Explanation
DISABLED	✓	✓	✓	✓	✓	The data set has been disabled by a master terminal operator.
DUPREC		✓	✓			A record with the specified key already exists in the file.
FILENOTFND	✓	✓	✓	✓	✓	The data set isn't defined in the FCT.
ILLOGIC	✓	✓	✓	✓	✓	A VSAM error has occurred.
INVREQ	✓	✓	✓	✓		The request is invalid.
IOERR	✓	✓	✓	✓	✓	An I/O error has occurred.
LENGERR	✓	✓	✓			The length of the record exceeds the maximum length allowed for the file (WRITE or REWRITE) or the length of the INTO area (READ).
NOSPACE		✓	✓			There is not enough space allocated to the data set to hold the record.
NOTAUTH	✓	✓	✓	✓	✓	The user is not authorized to access the data set.
NOTFND	✓		✓	✓		The record does not exist.

Figure 8-10 Exceptional conditions for file control commands

A more common technique doesn't prevent the problem, but simply detects it. Instead of indicating that a record is being updated, each pseudo-conversational program that updates a record saves an image of the record between task executions, either in the communication area or in temporary storage. Then, when the program issues a READ/UPDATE command, it compares the newly read record with the one saved in the communication area. If the records differ, it means another program has changed the record, so the update attempt is cancelled. You'll see this technique in the customer maintenance program later in this book.

The second consideration arises when your program must update records from more than one file. If you're not careful, it's possible to encounter a situation known as *deadlock*. Deadlock occurs when two tasks are each waiting for a resource that the other is holding. For example, suppose one program attempts to update records 100 and 200, and at the same time another program tries to update the same records, but in reverse order. The first program reads and holds record 100, and the second program reads and holds record 200. Then, the first program tries to read record 200, but can't because the second program is holding it for update. At the same time, the second program tries to read record 100, but can't because the first program is holding it. Each program is waiting for the other, and neither program can progress until CICS intervenes by cancelling one of them.

The simple way to avoid deadlock is to establish a standard order for file updates. Most shops simply say that all files should be updated in alphabetical order and, within the same file, records should be accessed in ascending key sequence. This simple technique avoids most deadlock situations.

Discussion   In this topic, I've briefly presented the formats of the basic CICS file control commands. If you understand how standard COBOL file handling statements work, you should have no trouble understanding the CICS file control elements I've presented here. Of course, there are many other CICS file handling features I haven't covered here, including alternate indexes and sequential file browsing. These topics will be covered in *Part 2: An Advanced Course.*

Objective

Given the specifications for a CICS program involving the file control commands presented in this topic, code a workable solution.

Term

deadlock

Program control commands

When CICS initiates a task, either when the user directly enters a trans-id or when the user presses an attention key to trigger pseudo-conversational processing, CICS loads a program and transfers control to it. In most cases, that program will perform whatever processing is required to respond to the event that caused its execution. Then, it will return to CICS using a RETURN command with the TRANSID option.

The RETURN command, which I introduced in chapter 6, is one of several program control commands that control the execution of programs within a task. XCTL, which I also introduced in chapter 6, is another. In this topic, I'll quickly review the RETURN command, then I'll discuss XCTL and a third program control command, LINK, in detail. XCTL and LINK let one program within a task invoke another program, which executes as a part of the same task.

The RETURN command

Figure 8-11 shows the format of the RETURN command. Here, I want to point out a few aspects of the TRANSID and COMMAREA options that might not have been apparent when you first encountered them in chapter 6. To begin, neither of these options is required. They are coded only when you use the RETURN command to end one interaction with a pseudo-conversational program and to set up the subsequent execution of the program to process the next user input event.

If you omit the TRANSID and COMMAREA options, what happens depends on how your program was invoked. If your program was invoked directly from CICS as a result of the user entering a trans-id, the task ends and control returns directly to CICS. Then, if the user wants to run another program, he or she must enter another trans-id. On the other hand, if the program was invoked by a LINK or XCTL command, the RETURN command behaves differently. I'll explain why when I present those commands in just a moment.

Strictly speaking, the TRANSID and COMMAREA options are independent of one another. Thus, you can code the COMMAREA option without the TRANSID option. Then, control will be returned to CICS, and the communication area will be passed to whatever program the user invokes next. There's little reason to do this, however, so you'll probably never code COMMAREA without TRANSID.

Incidentally, if you're using OS/VS COBOL, you must code the LENGTH option when you use the COMMAREA option. Under VS

The RETURN command

```
EXEC CICS
    RETURN    [ TRANSID(name) ]
              [ COMMAREA(data-area) ]
              [ LENGTH(data-value) ]
END-EXEC
```

Options

TRANSID   Specifies the one- to four-character name of the transaction to be invoked when the user presses an attention key. The trans-id must be defined in the Program Control Table (PCT).

COMMAREA   Specifies a data area that's passed to the next execution of a pseudo-conversational program. The next program execution accesses the communication area via its DFHCOMMAREA field.

LENGTH   Specifies a binary halfword (PIC S9(4) COMP) or numeric literal that indicates the length of the data area specified in the COMMAREA option. Under OS/VS COBOL, LENGTH is required if you code COMMAREA.

Figure 8-11 The RETURN command

COBOL II, CICS will use the defined length of the COMMAREA field if you omit the LENGTH option.

The LINK command and logical levels

Figure 8-12 shows that when a program is invoked by a trans-id, there are two *logical levels* of program execution involved. CICS is at the highest logical level, which I identified as level 0 in the figure. When CICS invokes Program A, Program A runs at level 1. When Program A issues a RETURN command, control returns to CICS at level 0.

Just as CICS loads and executes Program A subordinate to it in level 1, your application programs can use the LINK command to invoke programs at levels subordinate to them. For example, figure 8-13 shows what happens if Program A uses a LINK command to invoke Program B. Here, you can see that Program B executes at level 2, subordinate to Program A at level 1. When Program B issues a RETURN command, control is passed not back to CICS, but back to the program that was executing at the next higher level: Program A.

At this point, I want to be sure you understand the difference between a task and a program within a task. The programs in figure 8-13 (Program A and Program B) are a part of a single task. For the entire task to be pseudo-conversational, only the program at level 1 (in this example, Program A) can issue a RETURN command with the TRANSID and COMMAREA options. In fact, if a program at level 2 (or

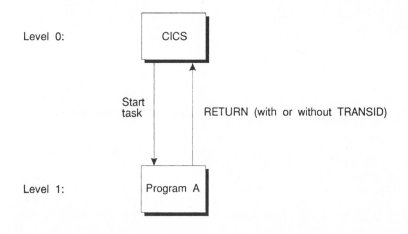

Figure 8-12 Operation of the RETURN command

below) issues a RETURN command with one of these options, the task terminates abnormally. So in programs that execute at logical level 2 or below, always code the RETURN command with no options.

Figure 8-14 shows the format of the LINK command. As you can see, it has three options. The PROGRAM option supplies the name of the program being invoked. This name must appear in the Processing Program Table (PPT). This is similar to the TRANSID option on the RETURN command. The difference is that the TRANSID option on the RETURN command requires a four-character transaction-identifier, but the PROGRAM option on the LINK command requires an eight-character program name. Also, you can omit the TRANSID option on the RETURN command, but PROGRAM is required on the LINK command.

The COMMAREA option works the same way for the LINK command as it does for the RETURN command. The data in the Working-Storage Section communication area is passed to the linked program's Linkage Section DFHCOMMAREA.

If the program specified in the PROGRAM option doesn't exist, the PGMIDERR condition is raised. Depending on the application, it might be appropriate to code the RESP option on the LINK command, and follow the LINK command with IF statements to check the response code for NORMAL or PGMIDERR. Note that these IF statements won't execute until *after* the linked program finishes. If the response code is NORMAL, it means the linked program has executed successfully and returned control to the invoking program. If the response code is PGMIDERR, it means the linked program could not be found, so it was not executed. Any other response code means a serious error occurred and should probably be dealt with by immediately terminating the task. (If you omit the RESP option, any condition other than NORMAL will automatically cause the task to be terminated.)

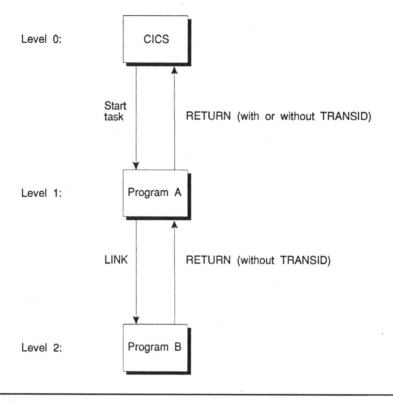

Figure 8-13 Operation of the LINK command

You may be wondering why Program A doesn't invoke Program B as a subprogram, using a standard COBOL CALL statement. Under older releases of CICS, subprograms called with CALL statements could not issue any CICS commands, so CALL statements were rarely used. With VS COBOL II, this restriction was lifted. Now, you can invoke a subprogram with a CICS LINK statement or with a COBOL CALL statement. In addition, the COBOL CALL statement can invoke a static subprogram (one that has been link-edited into the same load module with the calling program) or a dynamic subprogram (one that stands alone as a separate load module). In either case, a subprogram invoked by a CALL statement does not return control to its caller by issuing a CICS RETURN command. Instead, it should use a standard COBOL GOBACK or EXIT PROGRAM statement.

In general, all three of these methods are inefficient ways to invoke another program. That's because while the invoked program is executing, the program that invoked it still occupies main storage. It has to remain in storage so that control can be passed back to it when the invoked program ends.

In many applications, however, a program doesn't need to return to the program that invoked it. For example, in a menu program, you want

The LINK command

```
EXEC CICS
    LINK    PROGRAM(name)
        [ COMMAREA(data-area) ]
        [ LENGTH(data-value) ]
END-EXEC
```

Options

PROGRAM

Specifies the one- to eight-character name of the program to be invoked. This name must be defined in the Processing Program Table (PPT).

COMMAREA

Specifies a data area that's passed to the invoked program as a communication area. The invoked program accesses the communication area via its DFHCOMMAREA field.

LENGTH

Specifies a binary halfword (PIC S9(4) COMP) or numeric literal that indicates the length of the data area specified in the COMMAREA option. Under OS/VS COBOL, LENGTH is required if you code COMMAREA.

Figure 8-14   The LINK command

to transfer control to the program the user selects. In this case, a LINK command would be inappropriate. Instead, you use an XCTL command.

The XCTL command   Unlike LINK, the XCTL command (sometimes pronounced *X-control* or *X-kettle*) transfers control to another program *without* setting up a return mechanism. As a result, control doesn't return to a program that issues an XCTL command. The critical distinction between LINK and XCTL is that while the LINK command transfers control to a program at the *next lower* logical level, the XCTL command transfers control to a program at the *same* logical level.

To illustrate, consider figure 8-15. Here, CICS invokes Program A at level 1. Next, Program A issues a LINK command to invoke Program B at level 2. Then, Program B issues an XCTL command to invoke Program C at the same level. When Program C issues a RETURN command (without the TRANSID option), control is returned to the next higher level. So, execution continues with the statement in Program A after the LINK command that invoked Program B.

The XCTL command, shown in figure 8-16, is similar in format to the LINK command. The PROGRAM option specifies the name of the program you want to invoke, and the COMMAREA option lets you pass data to the program's communication area.

Although the XCTL command's COMMAREA option is useful, you may want to omit it when invoking a program from a menu program. That way, the program will be invoked as if it were invoked directly by

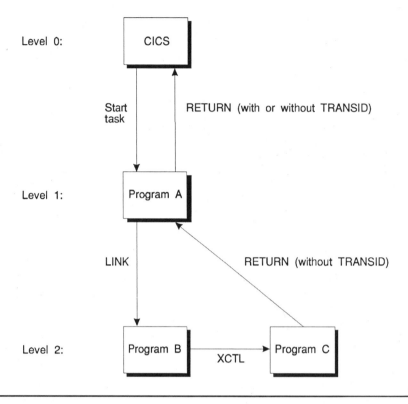

Figure 8-15 Operation of the XCTL command

the user (that is, by typing a trans-id). The program can then detect the first time condition when it evaluates the length of the communication area and respond by displaying its initial map and returning. Similarly, an application program can return control to a menu by issuing an XCTL command that specifies the menu program without a communication area. Then, the menu program will detect its first time condition, display its map, and return. That's how the sample programs in this book work.

If the program specified in the PROGRAM option doesn't exist, the PGMIDERR condition is raised just as it is for the LINK command. So, again depending on the application, you may want to use the RESP option and follow the XCTL command with IF statements to evaluate the response code. When you do, however, keep in mind that the XCTL command will never return a NORMAL response code to your program. After all, if the XCTL command is successful, control will never return to your program.

The XCTL command

```
EXEC CICS
    XCTL    PROGRAM(name)
         [ COMMAREA(data-area) ]
         [ LENGTH(data-value) ]
END-EXEC
```

Options

PROGRAM Specifies the one- to eight-character name of the program to be invoked. This name must be defined in the Processing Program Table (PPT).

COMMAREA Specifies a data area that's passed to the invoked program as a communication area. The invoked program accesses the communication area via its DFHCOMMAREA field.

LENGTH Specifies a binary halfword (PIC S9(4) COMP) or numeric literal that indicates the length of the data area specified in the COMMAREA option. Under OS/VS COBOL, LENGTH is required if you code COMMAREA.

Figure 8-16 The XCTL command

Term

logical level

Objectives

1. Explain the notion of logical levels, and describe the effects RETURN, LINK, and XCTL commands have on the current level.

2. Given a programming problem that requires the use of RETURN, LINK, or XCTL commands, code an appropriate solution.

Terminal handling techniques

Among the most challenging aspects of learning CICS is mastering the techniques for interacting with the terminal user in an efficient manner. How do you control the position of the cursor on the terminal screen? How do you change the attributes of individual screen fields to highlight errors? What is the most efficient way to send data to the terminal? How do you edit numeric input data? In this chapter, I'll present the techniques you use to solve these basic problems.

I'll conclude this chapter by presenting an outdated technique for detecting the use of attention keys: the HANDLE AID command. Unlike the other techniques presented in this topic, I do *not* recommend that you use the HANDLE AID command. But you need to know about it nevertheless, because many existing programs use it.

How to position the cursor

Whenever you issue a SEND MAP command, you should make sure that the cursor is positioned properly. By default, CICS will place the cursor in the top left corner of the screen. In almost all cases, this forces the user to press the Tab key to move the cursor to the first data entry field. For starters, your program should save the user this keystroke by placing the cursor in the first data entry field automatically. Beyond that, if your program detects a data entry error, it should place the cursor in the field that's in error. That way, the user won't have to tab over to the field to make the correction.

CICS provides three techniques to set the cursor position. The first is to specify the IC option in the BMS DFHMDF macro for the field where you want the cursor to be positioned. (IC stands for *Initial Cursor*.) Then, when you issue a SEND MAP command, CICS will position the cursor in the IC field. If you specify IC for more than one map field, CICS positions the cursor in the last one.

The IC technique is appropriate for maps that have only one input field, such as the map for the customer inquiry program presented in chapters 5 and 6. For maps with more than one input field, however, the IC technique isn't flexible enough. So you'll need to use one of the two remaining techniques: direct cursor positioning and symbolic cursor positioning. Both require that you specify the CURSOR option on the SEND MAP command. (You can look back to figure 6-16 to refresh your memory about SEND MAP's format.)

To use *direct cursor positioning*, specify a cursor position in the CURSOR option of the SEND MAP command. This cursor position is a displacement from the start of the screen, not a row/column address. As a result, it must be a number from 0 to 1919 (for a 24 X 80 screen), where 0 is row 1/column 1 and 1919 is row 24/column 80.

To calculate the displacement for a row/column address, subtract 1 from the row address and multiply the result by 80. Then, subtract 1 from the column address. Add the results of the first two steps. The sum is the displacement you code in the CURSOR option of the SEND MAP command.

To illustrate, suppose you want to place the cursor in column 17 of row 12. The correct displacement is 896:

$$(12 - 1) \times 80 + (17 - 1) = 896$$

Then, you code the cursor option like this:

```
CURSOR(896)
```

Or, you can move the value 896 to a binary halfword field (PIC S9(4) COMP) that's specified in the CURSOR option. Either way, the cursor will be placed in column 17 of row 12.

Direct cursor positioning has two major drawbacks. First, cursor displacements are awkward to use. Second, and perhaps more important, direct cursor positioning ties your program to specific screen locations. So, if you change your mapset by moving a field from one screen location to another, you have to change your program as well. It's because of these drawbacks that you'll use symbolic cursor positioning more often than direct cursor positioning.

To use *symbolic cursor positioning*, you specify the position of the cursor by field rather than by displacement. To tell CICS in which field to place the cursor, you move -1 to the corresponding length field in the symbolic map. Then, you issue a SEND MAP command with the CURSOR option specified, but without a displacement value.

If you move -1 to more than one length field in the symbolic map, the cursor is positioned at the *first* field containing -1. So, when you edit data entry fields, it's common to move -1 to the length fields of all input fields that contain invalid data. That way, when the program issues a SEND MAP command, the cursor is automatically positioned at the start of the first field that's in error. You'll see examples of this later in this topic, when I present the techniques you use to edit input fields.

It is also sometimes useful to know the position of the cursor when the user pressed the Enter key (or any other attention key, for that matter.) The cursor position is made available to your program in the Execute Interface Block field EIBCPOSN, a halfword binary item that contains the cursor displacement from the start of the screen. So, you'll have to do some simple calculations to interpret its value properly. Like EIBAID, EIBCPOSN is updated at the start of the task, so you don't have to issue a RECEIVE MAP command before using it.

How to modify attribute bytes

As you already know, the symbolic map definition for each screen field includes an attribute byte field. Before you do a SEND MAP command, you can move an attribute byte value to this field. The result is that the new attribute byte value will be applied to the data displayed on the screen.

A good example of the use of this technique is the customer maintenance program I described in chapter 7. That program uses the same map to let the user enter data for a new customer, enter changes to data for an existing customer, or confirm the deletion of an existing customer. The BMS definition for this map creates a number of unprotected fields so the user can enter data for an addition or a change. For a deletion, however, those fields should be protected. After all, it doesn't make sense to let the user type changes in the fields of a record that's to be deleted. So the program sets the attribute bytes for those fields to protected whenever it displays the map for a customer to be deleted.

There are three possible sources for the attribute that will be used for a field: the symbolic map, the physical map, and the terminal itself. If you issue a SEND MAP command with the MAPONLY option, the attribute byte for every screen field is set to the attribute specified in the physical map. Any attribute byte values in the symbolic map are ignored, because the MAPONLY option tells CICS not to use the symbolic map. If you move a value to an attribute field in the symbolic map and issue a SEND MAP command without the MAPONLY option, that value is used as the attribute byte for the field. If you move LOW-VALUE to an attribute field, the resulting field attribute depends on the options you code for the SEND MAP command. If you code DATAONLY, the attribute byte currently on the screen will remain unchanged, since low values aren't sent to the terminal. If you don't code DATAONLY, the attribute specified in the physical map will be used.

One way to set an attribute field in the symbolic map is to move a literal value to it, like this:

```
MOVE 'Q' TO CUSTNOA.
```

Here, I set the attribute for the customer number field to unprotected, numeric, and highlighted. (The letter Q is the EBCDIC character for the bit combination that specifies those attributes.) The only problem with this method is that you have to know the EBCDIC character for each attribute combination you need to use. And since not all attribute combinations have an EBCDIC equivalent, you can't code all attribute bytes this way.

To make it easier for you to modify attribute bytes, IBM supplies a standard copy member named DFHBMSCA. This member, shown in figure 8-17, defines many attribute bytes. It has some severe limitations, however. First, the names assigned to the various attributes are cryptic.

```
01          DFHBMSCA.
  02        DFHBMPEM   PICTURE X    VALUE IS   '.'.
  02        DFHBMPNL   PICTURE X    VALUE IS   '.'.
  02        DFHBMASK   PICTURE X    VALUE IS   '0'.
  02        DFHBMUNP   PICTURE X    VALUE IS   ' '.
  02        DFHBMUNN   PICTURE X    VALUE IS   '&'.
  02        DFHBMPRO   PICTURE X    VALUE IS   '-'.
  02        DFHBMBRY   PICTURE X    VALUE IS   'H'.
  02        DFHBMDAR   PICTURE X    VALUE IS   '<'.
  02        DFHBMFSE   PICTURE X    VALUE IS   'A'.
  02        DFHBMPRF   PICTURE X    VALUE IS   '/'.
  02        DFHBMASF   PICTURE X    VALUE IS   '1'.
  02        DFHBMASB   PICTURE X    VALUE IS   '8'.
  02        DFHBMEOF   PICTURE X    VALUE IS   '.'.
  02        DFHBMDET   PICTURE X    VALUE IS   '.'.
  02        DFHBMPSO   PICTURE X    VALUE IS   '.'.
  02        DFHBMPSI   PICTURE X    VALUE IS   '.'.
  02        DFHSA      PICTURE X    VALUE IS   '.'.
  02        DFHCOLOR   PICTURE X    VALUE IS   '.'.
  02        DFHPS      PICTURE X    VALUE IS   '.'.
  02        DFHHLT     PICTURE X    VALUE IS   '.'.
  02        DFH3270    PICTURE X    VALUE IS   '{'.
  02        DFHVAL     PICTURE X    VALUE IS   'A'.
  02        DFHOUTLN   PICTURE X    VALUE IS   'B'.
  02        DFHBKTRN   PICTURE X    VALUE IS   '.'.
  02        DFHALL     PICTURE X    VALUE IS   '.'.
  02        DFHERROR   PICTURE X    VALUE IS   '.'.
  02        DFHDFT     PICTURE X    VALUE IS   '.'.
  02        DFHDFCOL   PICTURE X    VALUE IS   '.'.
  02        DFHBLUE    PICTURE X    VALUE IS   '1'.
  02        DFHRED     PICTURE X    VALUE IS   '2'.
  02        DFHPINK    PICTURE X    VALUE IS   '3'.
  02        DFHGREEN   PICTURE X    VALUE IS   '4'.
  02        DFHTURQ    PICTURE X    VALUE IS   '5'.
  02        DFHYELLO   PICTURE X    VALUE IS   '6'.
  02        DFHNEUTR   PICTURE X    VALUE IS   '7'.
  02        DFHBASE    PICTURE X    VALUE IS   '.'.
  02        DFHDFHI    PICTURE X    VALUE IS   '.'.
  02        DFHBLINK   PICTURE X    VALUE IS   '1'.
  02        DFHREVRS   PICTURE X    VALUE IS   '2'.
  02        DFHUNDLN   PICTURE X    VALUE IS   '4'.
  02        DFHMFIL    PICTURE X    VALUE IS   '.'.
  02        DFHMENT    PICTURE X    VALUE IS   '.'.
  02        DFHMFE     PICTURE X    VALUE IS   '.'.
  02        DFHUNNOD   PICTURE X    VALUE IS   '('.
  02        DFHUNIMD   PICTURE X    VALUE IS   'I'.
  02        DFHUNNUM   PICTURE X    VALUE IS   'J'.
  02        DFHUNINT   PICTURE X    VALUE IS   'R'.
  02        DFHUNNON   PICTURE X    VALUE IS   ')'.
  02        DFHPROTI   PICTURE X    VALUE IS   'Y'.
  02        DFHPROTN   PICTURE X    VALUE IS   '%'.
  02        DFHMT      PICTURE X    VALUE IS   '.'.
  02        DFHMFT     PICTURE X    VALUE IS   '.'.
  02        DFHMET     PICTURE X    VALUE IS   '.'.
  02        DFHMFET    PICTURE X    VALUE IS   '.'.
  02        DFHDFFR    PICTURE X    VALUE IS   '.'.
  02        DFHLEFT    PICTURE X    VALUE IS   '.'.
  02        DFHOVER    PICTURE X    VALUE IS   '.'.
  02        DFHRIGHT   PICTURE X    VALUE IS   '.'.
  02        DFHUNDER   PICTURE X    VALUE IS   '.'.
  02        DFHBOX     PICTURE X    VALUE IS   '.'.
  02        DFHSOSI    PICTURE X    VALUE IS   '.'.
  02        DFHTRANS   PICTURE X    VALUE IS   '0'.
  02        DFHOPAQ    PICTURE X    VALUE IS   '.'.
```

Figure 8-17 The IBM-supplied copy member DFHBMSCA

For example, DFHBMASB is the name for auto-skip and highlighted. Second, IBM's copy member doesn't include some of the most commonly used attribute bytes, and most of the definitions it does include are rarely used. For example, the attribute byte for unprotected, numeric, and highlighted isn't supplied, yet attributes for special features like the light pen are.

Rather than use IBM's copy member, I recommend you create your own, if your shop hasn't already done so. Figure 8-18 shows the one I use. In it, each attribute combination has a meaningful name. For example, the name for unprotected, numeric, and highlighted is ATTR-UNPROT-NUM-BRT.

So then, to change an attribute, you simply move the correct value to the attribute field. For example:

```
MOVE ATTR-PROT TO CUSTNOA
```

changes the attribute byte for the customer number field to protected.

Once you've changed an attribute value, you must be able to restore it to its original value. You can do this in several ways. One method is to send the map with the MAPONLY option, so the field attributes are restored from the physical map. However, since the labels and constant data in the physical map are sent as well, this is usually unacceptably inefficient. Another method is to move LOW-VALUE to the symbolic map, and issue a SEND MAP command without the DATAONLY or MAPONLY option. This has the same inefficiencies as the first method, however, so I don't recommend it.

The third technique is to move the original values of the attribute bytes to the attribute fields in the symbolic map and issue a SEND MAP command with the DATAONLY option. That way, the attribute bytes in the symbolic map will be sent to the terminal. For efficiency reasons, this is usually the best technique.

Incidentally, there is a peculiar problem that often arises because of the way the BMS symbolic map is structured. As you know, the BMS symbolic map includes a flag field (suffix F) that indicates whether or not the user has cleared the field. If the user has not modified the field, the flag field contains hexadecimal 00 (LOW-VALUE). However, if the user modified the field by erasing it, the flag field is set to hexadecimal 80. Unfortunately, the flag field occupies the same storage position as the attribute byte field. So if the user clears a field, hex 80 will be placed in the attribute byte field when you issue a RECEIVE MAP command. If you then issue a SEND MAP command without replacing this hex 80 with LOW-VALUE or a valid attribute byte, the results will be unpredictable. So be sure to move an attribute byte or LOW-VALUE to each attribute field (or to the entire symbolic map) before you issue a SEND MAP command.

```
  01   ATTRIBUTE-DEFINITIONS.
  *
       05   ATTR-UNPROT                         PIC X    VALUE X'40'.
       05   ATTR-UNPROT-MDT                     PIC X    VALUE X'C1'.
       05   ATTR-UNPROT-BRT                     PIC X    VALUE X'C8'.
       05   ATTR-UNPROT-BRT-MDT                 PIC X    VALUE X'C9'.
       05   ATTR-UNPROT-DARK                    PIC X    VALUE X'4C'.
       05   ATTR-UNPROT-DARK-MDT                PIC X    VALUE X'4D'.
       05   ATTR-UNPROT-NUM                     PIC X    VALUE X'50'.
       05   ATTR-UNPROT-NUM-MDT                 PIC X    VALUE X'D1'.
       05   ATTR-UNPROT-NUM-BRT                 PIC X    VALUE X'D8'.
       05   ATTR-UNPROT-NUM-BRT-MDT             PIC X    VALUE X'D9'.
       05   ATTR-UNPROT-NUM-DARK                PIC X    VALUE X'5C'.
       05   ATTR-UNPROT-NUM-DARK-MDT            PIC X    VALUE X'5D'.
       05   ATTR-PROT                           PIC X    VALUE X'60'.
       05   ATTR-PROT-MDT                       PIC X    VALUE X'61'.
       05   ATTR-PROT-BRT                       PIC X    VALUE X'E8'.
       05   ATTR-PROT-BRT-MDT                   PIC X    VALUE X'E9'.
       05   ATTR-PROT-DARK                      PIC X    VALUE X'6C'.
       05   ATTR-PROT-DARK-MDT                  PIC X    VALUE X'6D'.
       05   ATTR-PROT-SKIP                      PIC X    VALUE X'F0'.
       05   ATTR-PROT-SKIP-MDT                  PIC X    VALUE X'F1'.
       05   ATTR-PROT-SKIP-BRT                  PIC X    VALUE X'F8'.
       05   ATTR-PROT-SKIP-BRT-MDT              PIC X    VALUE X'F9'.
       05   ATTR-PROT-SKIP-DARK                 PIC X    VALUE X'7C'.
       05   ATTR-PROT-SKIP-DARK-MDT             PIC X    VALUE X'7D'.
  *
       05   ATTR-NO-HIGHLIGHT                   PIC X    VALUE X'FF'.
       05   ATTR-BLINK                          PIC X    VALUE '1'.
       05   ATTR-REVERSE                        PIC X    VALUE '2'.
       05   ATTR-UNDERSCORE                     PIC X    VALUE '4'.
  *
       05   ATTR-DEFAULT-COLOR                  PIC X    VALUE X'FF'.
       05   ATTR-BLUE                           PIC X    VALUE '1'.
       05   ATTR-RED                            PIC X    VALUE '2'.
       05   ATTR-PINK                           PIC X    VALUE '3'.
       05   ATTR-GREEN                          PIC X    VALUE '4'.
       05   ATTR-TURQUOISE                      PIC X    VALUE '5'.
       05   ATTR-YELLOW                         PIC X    VALUE '6'.
       05   ATTR-NEUTRAL                        PIC X    VALUE '7'.
```

Figure 8-18 An improved copy member for attribute definitions

How to modify extended attributes

You may remember from chapter 5 that some 3270 terminals support extended attributes. If you're developing applications according to the CUA Entry Model standard, you'll need to use two types of extended attributes: extended highlighting and color. CUA says that whenever you detect an entry error, you should redisplay the incorrect data in reverse video. To do that, you need to use the extended highlighting attribute. And when you display a message to the user, CUA says the message should be white, yellow, or red, depending on whether it is simple information, a warning, or requires user action. To do that, you need to use the extended color attribute.

Changing an extended attribute under program control is similar to changing a standard attribute. You simply move the correct extended attribute value to the appropriate extended attribute field in the symbolic map. Keep in mind that extended attribute fields are not included automatically in the symbolic map BMS generates. To tell BMS to include symbolic map fields for the extended highlighting and color attributes, you should include two lines in the DFHMSD macro for the mapset:

```
MAPATTS=(HILIGHT,COLOR),
DSATTS=(HILIGHT,COLOR)
```

Then, for each screen field, BMS will include a field for extended highlighting attributes (suffix H) and a field for color attributes (suffix C). For example, BMS would generate attribute fields named LNAMEH and LNAMEC for a screen field named LNAME.

The copy members in figures 8-17 and 8-18 both include definitions for extended highlighting and color attribute values. To change an extended attribute, you simply move one of these extended attribute values to the appropriate symbolic map field. Thus, to change the highlighting of the LNAME field to reverse video, you would use a MOVE statement like this one:

```
MOVE ATTR-REVERSE TO LNAMEH.
```

The equivalent attribute name in the IBM-supplied copy member (DFHBMSCA) is DFHREVRS. Similarly, to change the color of the MSG1 field to red, you would use this statement:

```
MOVE ATTR-RED TO MSG1C.
```

The equivalent attribute name in DFHBMSCA is DFHRED.

Like standard attributes, you must be careful to reset any extended attributes that you change. To reset the extended highlighting attribute, move ATTR-NO-HILIGHT to the extended highlight attribute field. To reset the color attribute, move the original color value to the color attribute field. For example, if the field was originally turquoise, move ATTR-TURQUOISE to the color field.

How to optimize data transmission

For the sake of efficiency, you should try to optimize the transmission of data to and from the terminal. Next to using pseudo-conversational programming, optimizing data transmission will probably improve overall performance more than any other efficiency technique. So although it will take some extra programming effort, the effort will usually be justified by the resulting performance improvement.

In general, there are two levels where you can optimize data transmission. The first is to optimize data that is sent from your program to the terminal. For example, suppose a user running a data entry program enters data for 15 fields. When the user presses the Enter key, the data for all 15 fields is sent to the program and edited. If the program detects an error in one of the fields, is it necessary to send all 15 fields back to the terminal? Of course not. Instead, the program should send just the error message and the attribute bytes necessary to highlight the field that's in error. Sending the contents of the 15 fields back to the terminal is unnecessary, since that data is already displayed on the screen.

The techniques for minimizing data sent to the terminal are relatively straightforward. To begin, you should use the DATAONLY option of the SEND MAP command whenever you send data using a map that's already on the screen. If your program uses only one map, that means you'll specify DATAONLY for all but the first SEND MAP command. If your program uses more than one map, you'll have to send both the physical and the symbolic map whenever the display changes from one map to another. But whenever you redisplay the same map (for example, to display an error message), you should specify DATAONLY.

In addition, you should move LOW-VALUE to map fields that are already present on the screen. (Remember, low values are never transmitted to the terminal.) I usually do this immediately before invoking the send module. For example, consider these lines of code from the customer maintenance program I described in chapter 7:

```
MOVE LOW-VALUE TO CUSTNO1O
                   ACTIONO
SET SEND-DATAONLY-ALARM TO TRUE
PERFORM 1400-SEND-KEY-MAP.
```

These statements are executed when the program has detected an error in one of the two fields of the maintenance program's key map (CUSTNO1 or ACTION). The error message field has already been formatted by the edit module. Also, the cursor position has been set to the field that contains invalid data, and that field's attributes have been set to indicate it's in error. Just before performing module 1400 to send the error message back to the terminal, I move LOW-VALUE to the symbolic map's two output fields (CUSTNO1O and ACTIONO) and set the send control flag to SEND-DATAONLY-ALARM. That way, the customer number and action code won't be sent back to the terminal.

The second level of optimization is to reduce the amount of data sent to your program when the user presses an attention key. For example, suppose a user enters 15 fields, and the program detects an error in one of them and sends an error message back to the terminal. If the user then corrects the field in error and presses the Enter key again, how many of the fields are sent back to the program? Using the techniques presented in this book, all 15 fields are sent, even though the user entered data for only one field. That's because the modified data tags of all the fields remain unchanged from the last interaction.

Although it is possible to eliminate this inefficiency, the programming techniques are a bit complicated for an introductory CICS book. In short, what you must do is maintain a copy of all fields on the screen in the communication area. Then, when you issue a SEND MAP command, you specify the FRSET option so that the modified data tags of all the unprotected fields on the screen will be reset. That way, the next time the user presses the Enter key, only those fields that he or she has modified will be transmitted to the program. As a result, when the program issues a RECEIVE MAP command, it must merge the fields entered by the user with the fields saved in the communication area before it edits the data.

How to identify data entry fields with underscores

IBM's Common User Access guidelines state that data entry fields should be clearly identified on the screen by underlining them. For terminals that support extended highlighting, this is easy. All you do is specify HILIGHT=UNDERLINE in the DFHMDF macro for a field, and the terminal will underline the field for you. If the terminal does not support extended highlighting, the HILIGHT=UNDERLINE specification will be ignored.

CUA says that for terminals that don't support underlining, you can simulate underlining by filling a field with underscores if you wish. Although the result is similar to the use of underline attributes, it is different in that the underscores are a part of the field's contents. When the user types data into the field, the characters he or she types replace the underscores. Then, when the user presses the Enter key, any underscore characters remaining in the field are transmitted to the program as a part of the data.

To provide underscore fill characters, you must do the three things shown in figure 8-19. First, you must initially fill all data entry fields with underscores. To do that, you specify the INITIAL parameter on the DFHMDF macro for each unprotected map field. Second, you must remove any underscores from the symbolic map after you issue a RECEIVE MAP command, replacing them with spaces. The easiest way to do that is with an INSPECT statement like the one shown. And third, before you send the data back to the terminal, you should replace any spaces with underscore characters using another INSPECT statement.

(If you're using OS/VS COBOL, you cannot use INSPECT statements because of CICS restrictions. So you'll have to code your own routine that processes the symbolic map, accessing each character position individually by using a subscript or index.)

Ideally, you should code your programs so that they use the underline attribute for terminals that support extended highlighting, but fill entry fields with underscores for terminals that don't. To do that, you must first determine whether or not the terminal supports extended highlighting. You can find this out by issuing an ASSIGN command, which lets you access information about a wide variety of CICS facilities. Figure 8-20 shows an abbreviated format for the ASSIGN command. Although the IBM manual documents more than 60 options for the

To fill an entry field with underscores

```
CUSTNO     DFHMDF POS=(5,26),
                  LENGTH=6,
                  ATTRB=(NORM,UNPROT,IC),
                  COLOR=TURQUOISE,
                  INITIAL='_____'
```

To replace underscores with spaces after RECEIVE MAP

```
INSPECT MNTMAP1I
    REPLACING ALL '_' BY SPACE.
```

To replace spaces with underscores before SEND MAP

```
INSPECT MNTMAP1I
    REPLACING ALL SPACE BY '_'.
```

Figure 8-19 Programming techniques for filling input fields with underscores

ASSIGN command, I included just the ones that provide information about the terminal's characteristics in figure 8-20.

To find out if the terminal supports extended highlighting, you use the ASSIGN command's HILIGHT option. This option returns a single byte that's set to HIGH-VALUE (hex FF) if the terminal supports extended highlighting or LOW-VALUE (hex 00) if the terminal does not. If you define this switch field in the communication area, you can issue the ASSIGN command in response to the first-time event and pass the switch forward to each subsequent program execution. Then, the program can evaluate this switch to determine whether it should execute the statements used to insert and remove underscore characters for input fields.

How to edit input data

One of the most important aspects of CICS programming is thoroughly editing data entered by the user. Unfortunately, this can also be one of the most detailed and tedious aspects of CICS programming. For each data entry field, you'll need one or more IF statements that check for various error situations. For example, in the maintenance program, all of the data entry fields are required; if the user omits a field, the program must respond by displaying an error message and highlighting the field in error. The programs in this book follow CUA standards, highlighting error fields with reverse video.

Figure 8-21 summarizes the more common error conditions that should be tested and gives a sample IF statement for each test, except the test to determine if a field contains data in proper numeric format. Unfortunately, CICS provides no built-in support for editing numeric

The ASSIGN command

```
EXEC CICS
    ASSIGN [ COLOR(data-area) ]
           [ HILIGHT(data-area) ]
           [ SCRNHT(data-area) ]
           [ SCRNWD(data-area) ]
END-EXEC
```

Explanation

COLOR	Returns a one-byte field that's set to HIGH-VALUE (hex FF) if the terminal supports extended color or LOW-VALUE (hex 00) if it does not.
HILIGHT	Returns a one-byte field that's set to HIGH-VALUE (hex FF) if the terminal supports extended highlighting or LOW-VALUE (hex 00) if it does not.
SCRNHT	Returns a binary halfword (PIC S9(4) COMP) that indicates the screen height in lines.
SCRNWD	Returns a binary halfword (PIC S9(4) COMP) that indicates the screen width in columns.

Figure 8-20 The ASSIGN command

data. As a result, most shops have developed specialized numeric editing routines that evaluate a field byte by byte. I'll show you two examples of routines that do that, one for decimal values, the other for integers, in a few moments. But first, we'll focus on editing alphanumeric data.

Besides the conditions in figure 8-21, certain fields have specific editing requirements. For example, you should test a state code field to be sure it contains a valid state code. (For example, CA is a valid state code, but CB isn't.) Similarly, you should test a social security number to make sure the user entered nine digits.

In addition, you'll need to code IF statements that test whether related data entry fields agree with one another. For example, if a data entry screen includes both a state code and a zip code field, you may want to make sure the zip code entered by the user is a valid zip code for the state the user entered. For example, 93722 is a valid zip code for CA, but 23110 is not.

The basic structure of an edit module For all but the simplest programs, you should isolate the editing function in its own module. That module can thoroughly edit the entry fields, then set a switch (such as VALID-DATA-SW) to Y or N, depending on whether it detects any errors. The program should invoke this module after receiving map data, and it should continue processing the data only if the edit module detects no errors.

Error condition	COBOL statements to test it
Field was not entered	IF CUSTNOL = ZERO
Field contains spaces	IF CUSTNOI = SPACE
Field is not numeric	(Call appropriate numeric editing routine)
Field is not positive	IF AMOUNTI NOT > ZERO
Field is zero	IF AMOUNTI = ZERO

Figure 8-21 Common field edits

Figure 8-22 illustrates the basic structure of an edit module. It starts by resetting the extended highlighting attribute for all screen fields. Then, it edits each field with a series of nested IF statements, like this:

```
IF error-condition-1
    error processing
ELSE IF error-condition-2
    error-processing
ELSE ...
```

Finally, it performs any required cross-validation checks. To avoid long strings of nested IF statements, each field should have its own series of them.

Figure 8-23 shows a typical editing module that follows this form. This code is from the customer maintenance program, which you'll see in the next chapter. This module edits data entered on the customer data map, which contains six fields: last name (LNAME), first name (FNAME), address (ADDR), city (CITY), state (STATE), and zip code (ZIPCODE). For this simple program, the only editing requirement is that all of the fields must be entered. The program does not check the state code to make sure it is valid, nor does it check the zip code to make sure it's consistent with the state code.

Notice in figure 8-23 that the program edits the data entry fields from the bottom of the screen to the top. As a result, all of the invalid fields are highlighted, but the error message the program displays relates to the first invalid field on the screen. If the program edited the fields from top to bottom, the error message would relate to the *last* invalid field on the screen. Although you can code an edit module so it edits fields in the same order they appear on the screen, editing from the bottom to the top results in the simplest code.

When you detect an error, you need to do four things: (1) highlight the field by modifying its attributes; (2) move -1 to the length field so the cursor will be placed under the field in error; (3) move an appropriate

```
MOVE ATTR-NO-HIGHLIGHT TO extended highlight field for all map fields.

IF error-condition-1 for field-1
    MOVE ATTR-REVERSE  TO extended highlight field for field-1
    MOVE -1            TO length field for field-1
    MOVE error-message TO message field
    MOVE 'N'           TO VALID-DATA-SW
ELSE IF error-condition-2 for field-1
    .
    .
    .


IF error-condition-1 for field-2
    .
    .
    .


IF tests for cross-validation conditions
    .
    .
    .
```

Figure 8-22 General structure of an edit module

error message to the message field; and (4) set a switch to indicate that the data is invalid.

If you code the editing module as shown in figure 8-22, you must do these four steps for each IF statement for each data entry field on the screen. Counting the IF statement, then, you must code five statements for each edit condition. For a screen with 20 input fields, each requiring an average of three field edits, the edit module will contain 300 lines of code. You might be tempted to break this module into several smaller modules, but it's unnecessary. Even though the module is long, it's repetitive and its structure is clear. Breaking it into smaller modules won't improve the program's readability, so I recommend that you code simple field edits in one straightforward module.

You should, however, consider creating a separate module for complicated edits. For example, you should code edits that require table or file lookups in separate modules. The point is to keep the program clear. As long as the edits are simple, keep them in one module. When they become complex, isolate them in separate modules.

Incidentally, you can shave a few lines off of an editing module by omitting the MOVE statement that sets VALID-DATA-SW from each of the IF statements. Then, you add a statement like this to the end of the editing module:

```
IF MSGO NOT = LOW-VALUE
    MOVE 'N' TO VALID-DATA-SW.
```

This will set VALID-DATA-SW to N if any error is detected. It works because when you issue a RECEIVE MAP command, CICS moves

```
2200-EDIT-CUSTOMER-DATA.
*
     MOVE ATTR-NO-HIGHLIGHT TO ZIPCODEH
                              STATEH
                              CITYH
                              ADDRH
                              FNAMEH
                              LNAMEH.

     IF      ZIPCODEI = SPACE
        OR ZIPCODEL = ZERO
        MOVE ATTR-REVERSE TO ZIPCODEH
        MOVE -1 TO ZIPCODEL
        MOVE 'You must enter a zip code.' TO MSG20
        MOVE 'N' TO VALID-DATA-SW.

     IF      STATEI = SPACE
        OR STATEL = ZERO
        MOVE ATTR-REVERSE TO STATEH
        MOVE -1 TO STATEL
        MOVE 'You must enter a state.' TO MSG20
        MOVE 'N' TO VALID-DATA-SW.

     IF      CITYI = SPACE
        OR CITYL = ZERO
        MOVE ATTR-REVERSE TO CITYH
        MOVE -1 TO CITYL
        MOVE 'You must enter a city.' TO MSG20
        MOVE 'N' TO VALID-DATA-SW.

     IF      ADDRI = SPACE
        OR ADDRL = ZERO
        MOVE ATTR-REVERSE TO ADDRH
        MOVE -1 TO ADDRL
        MOVE 'You must enter an address.' TO MSG20
        MOVE 'N' TO VALID-DATA-SW.

     IF      FNAMEI = SPACE
        OR FNAMEL = ZERO
        MOVE ATTR-REVERSE TO FNAMEH
        MOVE -1 TO FNAMEL
        MOVE 'You must enter a first name.' TO MSG20
        MOVE 'N' TO VALID-DATA-SW.

     IF      LNAMEI = SPACE
        OR LNAMEL = ZERO
        MOVE ATTR-REVERSE TO LNAMEH
        MOVE -1 TO LNAMEL
        MOVE 'You must enter a last name.' TO MSG20
        MOVE 'N' TO VALID-DATA-SW.
*
```

Figure 8-23 An edit module from the customer maintenance program

LOW-VALUE to any field in the symbolic map that isn't entered by the user, including protected fields such as the message field. If the edit module detects an error, the program moves data into the message field. So a value other than LOW-VALUE in the message field means the edit module detected an error.

How to edit numeric input data   Editing numeric input data is a bit more challenging than editing alphanumeric input data. You might expect that specifying NUM in the ATTRB parameter of the DFHMDF macro insures that the user can enter only a valid number into a field. Unfortunately, that's not the case. The NUM option does two things. First, it forces the terminal into numeric shift, if the terminal supports that feature. When in numeric shift, the user can type only numbers, the decimal point, and hyphens. However, nothing prevents the user from inadvertently typing two decimal points, or some other invalid combination of numeric characters. Furthermore, the user can easily take the keyboard out of numeric shift and enter alpha-numeric data.

Second, the NUM option causes BMS to right-justify data in the field and pad the field on the left with zeros as necessary. This is helpful, unless your program fills the field with underscore characters to mark its location on the screen. Suppose the user types the number 123 into a five-byte field that's filled with underscores. In that case, the remaining two underscore characters are treated as part of the data, so right-justification has no effect. Although the user typed the three characters '123,' CICS places the five-character value '123__' in the symbolic map input field.

CICS provides no support at all for decimal-aligned input. For example, if you assign a PICIN picture of 9(5)V99 to a field, the user must enter 10000 to obtain a value of 100.00. If the user enters simply 100, the value 1.00 will be placed in the field. And the user cannot use a decimal point to indicate the decimal position.

Because of these problems, most shops have developed specialized routines for editing numeric input data. Typically, these routines are invoked with CALL statements or are included in the program with COPY statements. They accept an unedited field as input and evaluate it to determine if it contains a valid number. If so, they return an edited field in valid numeric format with an indication that the number is valid.

Figure 8-24 presents the calling conventions for two typical numeric editing routines. The first, called INTEDIT, edits integer data. It accepts a five-byte alphanumeric field as input, and it returns a five-byte numeric field and a switch that indicates whether or not the input field contained a valid integer. The second, called NUMEDIT, edits numbers that may include a decimal point. It accepts a 10-byte alphanumeric field as input and returns a decimal-aligned edited number (PIC 9(7)V99) and a switch to indicate whether the input contained a valid number. Notice that DFHEIBLK and DFHCOMMAREA are coded as the first two parameters on both CALL statements. This is a requirement for calling VS COBOL II subprograms.

Figure 8-25 shows how NUMEDIT might be used in an editing module. Here, AMOUNT is a 10-byte map field. The first IF statement checks to see if the user entered any data by evaluating the length field, AMOUNTL. If so, NUMEDIT is called using AMOUNTI,

Calling INTEDIT

```
CALL 'INTEDIT' USING DFHEIBLK
                     DFHCOMMAREA
                     UNEDITED-NUMBER
                     EDITED-NUMBER
                     VALID-NUMBER-SW.
```

Calling NUMEDIT

```
CALL 'NUMEDIT' USING DFHEIBLK
                     DFHCOMMAREA
                     UNEDITED-NUMBER
                     EDITED-NUMBER
                     VALID-NUMBER-SW.
```

Explanation

DFHEIBLK	The address of the Execute Interface Block.
DFHCOMMAREA	The address of the communication area.
UNEDITED-NUMBER	The value entered by the user. For INTEDIT, PIC X(5). For NUMEDIT, PIC X(10).
EDITED-NUMBER	The resulting number in valid numeric format. For INTEDIT, PIC 9(5). For NUMEDIT, PIC 9(7)V99.
VALID-NUMBER-SW	PIC X. Set to Y if the value in UNEDITED-NUMBER is a valid number; otherwise, set to N.

Figure 8-24 Calling the INTEDIT and NUMEDIT subprograms

```
IF AMOUNTL = ZERO
    MOVE ATTR-REVERSE TO AMOUNTH
    MOVE -1 TO AMOUNTL
    MOVE 'You must enter an amount.' TO MSGO
    MOVE 'N' TO VALID-DATA-SW
ELSE
    CALL 'NUMEDIT' USING DFHEIBLK
                         DFHCOMMAREA
                         AMOUNTI
                         EDITED-AMOUNT
                         VALID-AMOUNT-SW
    IF NOT VALID-AMOUNT
        MOVE ATTR-REVERSE TO AMOUNTH
        MOVE -1 TO AMOUNTL
        MOVE 'Amount must be numeric' TO MSGO
        MOVE 'N' TO VALID-DATA-SW
    ELSE IF EDITED-AMOUNT NOT > ZERO
        MOVE ATTR-REVERSE TO AMOUNTH
        MOVE -1 TO AMOUNTL
        MOVE 'Amount must be greater than zero' TO MSGO
        MOVE 'N' TO VALID-DATA-SW.
```

Figure 8-25 Editing numeric data

EDITED-AMOUNT (a working-storage field whose picture is 9(7)V99), and VALID-AMOUNT-SW. The next two IF statements format error messages if the amount field is not numeric or not greater than zero.

```
 IDENTIFICATION DIVISION.
*
 PROGRAM-ID.  NUMEDIT.
*
 ENVIRONMENT DIVISION.
*
 DATA DIVISION.
*
 WORKING-STORAGE SECTION.
*
 01  WORK-FIELDS.
*
     05  INTEGER-PART        PIC 9(10).
     05  INTEGER-PART-X      REDEFINES    INTEGER-PART.
         10  INTEGER-CHAR    PIC X        OCCURS 10.
     05  DECIMAL-PART        PIC V9(10).
     05  DECIMAL-PART-X      REDEFINES    DECIMAL-PART.
         10  DECIMAL-CHAR    PIC X        OCCURS 10.
     05  DECIMAL-POS         PIC S999     COMP-3.
     05  INTEGER-LENGTH      PIC S999     COMP-3.
     05  INTEGER-SUB         PIC S999     COMP-3.
     05  DECIMAL-SUB         PIC S999     COMP-3.
     05  UNEDIT-SUB          PIC S999     COMP-3.
*
 LINKAGE SECTION.
*
 01  UNEDITED-NUMBER.
     05  UNEDITED-CHAR       OCCURS 10    PIC X.
*
 01  EDITED-NUMBER           PIC 9(7)V99.
*
 01  VALID-NUMBER-SW         PIC X.
     88  VALID-NUMBER        VALUE 'Y'.
*
 PROCEDURE DIVISION USING UNEDITED-NUMBER
                          EDITED-NUMBER
                          VALID-NUMBER-SW.
*
 0000-EDIT-NUMBER.
*
     MOVE 'Y' TO VALID-NUMBER-SW.
     MOVE ZERO TO INTEGER-PART
                  DECIMAL-PART
                  DECIMAL-POS.
     INSPECT UNEDITED-NUMBER
         TALLYING DECIMAL-POS FOR CHARACTERS
             BEFORE INITIAL '.'.
     IF DECIMAL-POS < 10
         PERFORM 1000-EDIT-DECIMAL-NUMBER
     ELSE
         PERFORM 2000-EDIT-INTEGER.
     IF VALID-NUMBER
         COMPUTE EDITED-NUMBER = INTEGER-PART + DECIMAL-PART.
*
 0000-EXIT.
*
     EXIT PROGRAM.
```

Figure 8-26   The NUMEDIT subprogram (part 1 of 2)

```
*
 1000-EDIT-DECIMAL-NUMBER.
*
     MOVE 10 TO INTEGER-SUB.
     PERFORM 1100-EDIT-INTEGER-PART
         VARYING UNEDIT-SUB FROM DECIMAL-POS BY -1
           UNTIL UNEDIT-SUB < 1.
     MOVE 1 TO DECIMAL-SUB.
     ADD 2 TO DECIMAL-POS.
     PERFORM 1200-EDIT-DECIMAL-PART
         VARYING UNEDIT-SUB FROM DECIMAL-POS BY 1
           UNTIL UNEDIT-SUB > 10.
*
 1100-EDIT-INTEGER-PART.
*
     IF UNEDITED-CHAR(UNEDIT-SUB) NUMERIC
         MOVE UNEDITED-CHAR(UNEDIT-SUB)
             TO INTEGER-CHAR(INTEGER-SUB)
         SUBTRACT 1 FROM INTEGER-SUB
     ELSE IF UNEDITED-CHAR(UNEDIT-SUB) NOT = SPACE
         MOVE 'N' TO VALID-NUMBER-SW.
*
 1200-EDIT-DECIMAL-PART.
*
     IF UNEDITED-CHAR(UNEDIT-SUB) NUMERIC
         MOVE UNEDITED-CHAR(UNEDIT-SUB)
             TO DECIMAL-CHAR(DECIMAL-SUB)
         ADD 1 TO DECIMAL-SUB
     ELSE IF UNEDITED-CHAR(UNEDIT-SUB) NOT = SPACE
         MOVE 'N' TO VALID-NUMBER-SW.
*
 2000-EDIT-INTEGER.
*
     INSPECT UNEDITED-NUMBER
         REPLACING LEADING SPACE BY ZERO.
     MOVE ZERO TO INTEGER-LENGTH.
     INSPECT UNEDITED-NUMBER
         TALLYING INTEGER-LENGTH FOR CHARACTERS
             BEFORE INITIAL SPACE.
     MOVE 10 TO INTEGER-SUB.
     PERFORM 1100-EDIT-INTEGER-PART
         VARYING UNEDIT-SUB FROM INTEGER-LENGTH BY -1
           UNTIL UNEDIT-SUB < 1.
     MOVE ZERO TO DECIMAL-PART.
```

Figure 8-26   The NUMEDIT subprogram (part 2 of 2)

Figure 8-26 presents the source code for the NUMEDIT subprogram. Since your shop probably has its own standard routine for editing numeric data, you don't need to study this code unless you're interested in seeing how this type of routine works. Simply put, NUMEDIT works by locating a decimal point and treating the characters on the left of the decimal point as the "integer part" and the numbers to the right of the decimal point as the "decimal part." Then, it moves characters one at a time to working-storage fields named INTEGER-PART and DECIMAL-PART, and it ends by adding these fields together. To facilitate this, UNEDITED-NUMBER, INTEGER-PART, and DECIMAL-PART are all redefined as one-character tables.

```
 IDENTIFICATION DIVISION.
*
 PROGRAM-ID.  INTEDIT.
*
 ENVIRONMENT DIVISION.
*
 DATA DIVISION.
*
 WORKING-STORAGE SECTION.
*
 01  WORK-FIELDS.
*
     05  INTEGER-PART        PIC 9(5).
     05  INTEGER-LENGTH      PIC S999  COMP-3.
*
 LINKAGE SECTION.
*
 01  UNEDITED-NUMBER         PIC X(5).
*
 01  EDITED-NUMBER           PIC 9(5).
*
 01  VALID-NUMBER-SW         PIC X.
     88  VALID-NUMBER        VALUE 'Y'.
*
 PROCEDURE DIVISION USING UNEDITED-NUMBER
                          EDITED-NUMBER
                          VALID-NUMBER-SW.
*
 0000-EDIT-NUMBER.
*
     MOVE ZERO TO INTEGER-LENGTH.
     INSPECT UNEDITED-NUMBER
         REPLACING LEADING SPACE BY ZERO.
     INSPECT UNEDITED-NUMBER
         TALLYING INTEGER-LENGTH FOR CHARACTERS
             BEFORE INITIAL SPACE.
     IF UNEDITED-NUMBER(1:INTEGER-LENGTH) NUMERIC
         MOVE UNEDITED-NUMBER(1:INTEGER-LENGTH)
             TO EDITED-NUMBER
         MOVE 'Y' TO VALID-NUMBER-SW
     ELSE
         MOVE 'N' TO VALID-NUMBER-SW.
*
 0000-EXIT.
*
     EXIT PROGRAM.
```

Figure 8-27   The INTEDIT subprogram

Figure 8-27 shows the source code for the INTEDIT subprogram. It's considerably simpler than the NUMEDIT program for two reasons. First, it doesn't have to contend with decimal points. And second, it uses the VS COBOL II facility called *reference modification* to directly refer to substrings within the unedited number. So it doesn't require a PERFORM VARYING statement to process the unedited number byte by byte.

You should notice that neither subprogram provides for the DFHEIBLK and DFHCOMMAREA fields that are passed by the calling program. That's because the CICS translator automatically adds these

The SEND TEXT command

```
EXEC CICS
    SEND TEXT FROM(data-area)
              [LENGTH(data-value)]
              [ERASE]
              [FREEKB]
END-EXEC
```

Explanation

FROM   Specifies the name of the field containing the data to be displayed on the terminal.

LENGTH   Specifies the number of characters to be sent. Usually coded as a numeric literal, but may be a data-name. May be omitted under VS COBOL II; the length of the FROM area will be used.

ERASE   Specifies that the screen should be erased before the data is displayed.

FREEKB   Specifies that the terminal keyboard should be unlocked after the data is sent. If FREEKB is omitted, the user will have to press the Reset key to unlock the keyboard.

Figure 8-28   The SEND TEXT command

fields to the Linkage Section of the subprogram and to the USING phrase of the Procedure Division statement. So no special code is required.

How to use the SEND TEXT command

In many cases, you'll want to send a simple message to the terminal without having to create a BMS mapset. For example, when a program ends without transferring control to a menu program, you may want to display a brief message telling the user that the program has ended. To do that, you use the SEND TEXT command, shown in figure 8-28. The FROM option specifies the field in the Working-Storage Section that contains the message. If you're using the OS/VS COBOL compiler, you must also specify the LENGTH option to tell CICS the length of the FROM area; under VS COBOL II, the LENGTH option is not required.

The message will be displayed starting at the top left corner of the screen. If you specify the ERASE option, the screen is erased before the message is displayed; otherwise, the message overlays whatever was on the screen before. If you specify the FREEKB option, the keyboard will be released after the message is sent. Otherwise, the user has to press the Reset key to continue.

Figure 8-29 shows how you use the SEND TEXT command. Here, the message to be displayed is defined as a 14-byte working-storage item named TERMINATION-MESSAGE. When the SEND TEXT command is executed, the screen will be erased and the message "Session ended." will be displayed at the top left of the screen.

```
     WORKING-STORAGE SECTION.
     *
     01  TERMINATION-MESSAGE       PIC X(14)   VALUE 'Session ended.'.
     *
          .
          .
          .
     *
     PROCEDURE DIVISION.
     *
          .
          .
          .

          EXEC CICS
              SEND TEXT FROM(TERMINATION-MESSAGE)
                        ERASE
                        FREEKB
          END-EXEC.
          .
          .
          .
```

Figure 8-29 Using the SEND TEXT command to display a termination message.

How to use the HANDLE AID command

The last CICS terminal handling technique I want to teach you in this topic is how to use the HANDLE AID command. The HANDLE AID command is an alternative technique for detecting the use of attention keys. I want you to realize from the start that I recommend that you do not use this command in your programs. Instead, I suggest you detect the use of attention keys by evaluating the EIBAID field in the Execute Interface Block. That's the technique used by all of the programs in this book, and it has many advantages over the HANDLE AID technique. However, because many existing programs use HANDLE AID, you may come across it if you're involved in maintaining those programs. So you need to understand how it works.

Figure 8-30 shows the format of the HANDLE AID command. The HANDLE AID command tells your program what to do when the user presses an attention key. The HANDLE AID command itself does not detect the use of the AID key; it's the RECEIVE MAP command that does that. As a result, the HANDLE AID key is always used alongside a RECEIVE MAP command. In effect, the HANDLE AID command sets up the processing to be done if the RECEIVE MAP command detects the use of an AID key.

To code a HANDLE AID command, you list one or more attention keys, along with the name of the paragraph that will process each key. Then, when a subsequent RECEIVE MAP command detects that an attention key has been used, CICS simply transfers control to the corresponding label specified in a previous HANDLE AID command. CICS transfers control to the appropriate label with a GO TO.

The HANDLE AID command

```
EXEC CICS
    HANDLE AID
        option(procedure-name)...
END-EXEC
```

Explanation

option   The name of the attention key to be handled. Up to 12 options may be specified in a single command. More than 12 options may be specified by multiple HANDLE AID commands. Common options are:

PA1-PA3	Program attention keys
PF1-PF24	Program function keys
ENTER	The Enter key
CLEAR	The Clear key
ANYKEY	Any attention key not previously specified in a HANDLE AID command, except the Enter key

Control is passed to procedure-name when the use of the specified attention key is detected; this occurs when the program issues a RECEIVE MAP command. If procedure-name is omitted, no action is taken when the specified key is detected, even if ANYKEY is also specified.

Figure 8-30 The HANDLE AID command

For example, consider this HANDLE AID command:

```
EXEC CICS
    HANDLE AID PF3(1100-PF3)
               CLEAR(1100-CLEAR)
END-EXEC.
```

Here, control is passed to the paragraph named 1100-PF3 if the user presses PF3. If the user presses the Clear key, control is passed to 1100-CLEAR. If the user presses any other key, no special action is taken, so control falls through to the statement following the RECEIVE MAP command.

The ANYKEY option is provided to process attention keys not specifically mentioned in the HANDLE AID command. For example, consider this HANDLE AID command:

```
EXEC CICS
    HANDLE AID PF3(1100-PF3)
               ANYKEY(1100-ANYKEY)
END-EXEC.
```

Here, control is passed to 1100-PF3 if the user presses PF3. If any other key is pressed, control is passed to 1100-ANYKEY. Note, however, that the Enter key is not handled by the ANYKEY option. To handle the Enter key, you must specify ENTER as an option. Usually, though, you don't want to do any special processing for the Enter key, so you don't code ENTER as an option on a HANDLE AID command.

If you specify an attention key without a label, that key isn't included as a part of the ANYKEY option, and any previous HANDLE AID for that key is ignored. For example, consider these two HANDLE AID commands:

```
EXEC CICS
    HANDLE AID PF3(1100-PF3)
               CLEAR(1100-CLEAR)
END-EXEC.
EXEC CICS
    HANDLE AID PF12(1100-PF12)
               ANYKEY(1100-ANYKEY)
               CLEAR
END-EXEC.
```

After the execution of the second of these HANDLE AID commands, the PF3 key is processed by 1100-PF3, the PF12 key is handled by 1100-PF12, and any other attention key besides the Enter key and the Clear key is handled by 1100-ANYKEY. Since I coded CLEAR without a label, no action is taken for it, even though I specified it explicitly in the first command and implicitly in the ANYKEY option in the second.

To help you see how the HANDLE AID command is paired with the RECEIVE MAP command, figure 8-31 shows typical coding for a receive module that uses HANDLE AID. Here, you can see that the HANDLE AID command sets up attention key processing for PF3, PF12, the Clear key, and any other key besides Enter. Then, a RECEIVE MAP command receives the map and detects the use of AID keys.

Notice that I coded the entire receive module as a section. Using HANDLE AID commands forces you to code all of the functional modules in your program as sections rather than paragraphs. In addition, GO TO statements are required to branch from the end of each attention key paragraph to the end of the section, marked by the 1100-EXIT paragraph name. If you study this coding for a moment, you'll see that all of the processing for attention keys is contained within the same section. As a result, you can invoke this section with a PERFORM statement, and rest assured that control will always fall through to the EXIT statement at the end of the section and then return to the statement following the invoking PERFORM statement.

I hope you can see why I recommend you don't use the HANDLE AID command. There are at least three compelling reasons to avoid it. First, it forces you to develop your programs using a mix of sections, paragraphs, and GO TO statements. By using EIBAID instead, you can avoid this confusion.

Second, it forces you to issue a RECEIVE MAP command just to detect the use of an attention key. In many cases, you don't need the input data retrieved by the RECEIVE MAP command to process the

```
1100-RECEIVE-INQUIRY-MAP SECTION.
*
    EXEC CICS
        HANDLE AID PF3     1100-PF3
                   PF12    1100-PF3
                   CLEAR   1100-CLEAR
                   ANYKEY  1100-ANYKEY
    END-EXEC.
    EXEC CICS
        RECEIVE MAP('INQMAP1')
                MAPSET('INQSET1')
                INTO(INQMAP1I)
    END-EXEC.
    GO TO 1100-EXIT.
*
 1100-PF3.
*
    MOVE 'Y' TO END-SESSION-SW.
    GO TO 1100-EXIT.
*
 1100-CLEAR.
*
    MOVE 'Y' TO CLEAR-KEY-SW.
    GO TO 1100-EXIT.
*
 1100-ANYKEY.
*
    MOVE 'Invalid key pressed.' TO MSGO.
    MOVE 'N' TO VALID-DATA-SW.
*
 1100-EXIT.
*
    EXIT.
*
```

Figure 8-31 A receive module that uses the HANDLE AID command

attention key. For example, if the user presses PF3 to end the program, all your program has to do is issue an XCTL command to transfer to a menu program. In this case, issuing a RECEIVE MAP command is simply a waste of processing time.

The third reason not to use HANDLE AID is the most significant: It forces you to bury the key event-processing logic of your program deep within the program's structure. For example, if a receive module detects the use of the PF3 key to end the program, it will have to set a switch that will probably have to be evaluated several times in other modules higher up in the program's structure. Your program will be considerably easier to develop and maintain if it responds to attention keys in the top modules.

Terms

direct cursor positioning
symbolic cursor positioning
reference modification

Objectives

1. Use the direct and symbolic cursor positioning techniques to control the position of the cursor when you issue a SEND MAP command.

2. Code appropriate MOVE statements to change standard and extended field attributes.

3. Explain the techniques used to optimize the transmission of data from SEND MAP commands.

4. Code appropriate INSPECT statements to add and remove underscore characters from a symbolic map.

5. Given editing requirements for the fields in a symbolic map, code an appropriate edit module to detect and indicate each possible error.

6. Use the SEND TEXT command to display a short message on the terminal.

7. Describe how the HANDLE AID command works, and explain why testing EIBAID is the preferred technique for detecting the use of attention keys.

Error processing techniques

As you already know, when CICS encounters an error situation from which it cannot recover, it raises an exceptional condition. Each exceptional condition has a name. For example, NOTFND is the name of the condition that's raised if you attempt to read a file record that doesn't exist. Some exceptional conditions, such as NOTFND, represent conditions from which your program should be able to recover. Most exceptional conditions, however, do not. For example, if the IOERR condition is raised, it means an I/O error has occurred. Your program can do nothing to correct this type of error.

For most conditions, CICS's default action is to terminate your task abnormally. This is true even for the conditions that represent recoverable errors, such as NOTFND. As a result, your programs must explicitly deal with these exceptional conditions to prevent CICS from abending your task when they occur. CICS provides two ways to do this: the HANDLE CONDITION command and response code checking. Although the programs in this book use response code checking, I'll present both techniques in this topic. But first, I want to show you the exceptional conditions you're most likely to encounter.

Exceptional conditions In all, the IBM manual lists more than 70 exceptional conditions that can be raised by CICS commands. Most of these conditions represent obscure errors from which your program cannot recover. So you only need to deal with a few of them in your programs. Figure 8-32 lists the exceptional conditions that are most likely to occur for the commands I've presented so far in this book.

Most of these conditions should be self-explanatory. The condition that causes the most confusion is the MAPFAIL condition. This condition is raised whenever you issue a RECEIVE MAP command and there is no data to be mapped. This can happen for two reasons: (1) the user presses the Enter key or a PF key without entering any data and there are no fields on the screen with the Modified Data Tag (MDT) set; or (2) the user presses the Clear key or one of the PA keys. The best way to deal with the MAPFAIL condition is to prevent it from occurring. You can do that by: (1) not issuing a RECEIVE MAP command if EIBAID indicates that the Clear key or a PA key was pressed; and (2) always including in the mapset a one-byte DUMMY field with FSET specified, so at least one byte of data is sent to the program when the user presses the Enter key or a PF key.

Condition	Related CICS command	Caused by
DUPREC	WRITE	The record already exists.
MAPFAIL	RECEIVE MAP	No data was sent by the user.
NOSPACE	WRITE REWRITE	The data set does not have enough allocated space to hold the record.
NOTOPEN	READ WRITE REWRITE DELETE UNLOCK	The data set is not open.
NOTFND	READ REWRITE DELETE	The requested record is not in the file.
PGMIDERR	LINK XCTL	The requested program is not in the Processing Program Table.

Figure 8-32   Commonly occurring exceptional conditions

The HANDLE CONDITION command

One way to deal with exceptional conditions is by using the HANDLE CONDITION command, whose format is shown in figure 8-33. If you're familiar with the HANDLE AID command, you'll have no trouble understanding how the HANDLE CONDITION command works. Like the HANDLE AID command, the HANDLE CONDITION command sets up processing to be done if a subsequent command encounters an exceptional condition.

The HANDLE CONDITION command specifies a procedure name (a paragraph or section name) that's given control if a specified condition occurs. For example, the HANDLE CONDITION command

```
EXEC CICS
    HANDLE CONDITION NOTFND(2100-NOTFND)
END-EXEC.
```

causes control to pass immediately to 2100-NOTFND if the NOTFND condition is raised. Note that 2100-NOTFND is *not* given control when the HANDLE CONDITION command is executed, but only when the NOTFND condition is raised by a subsequent command. If effect, a GO TO is done to 2100-NOTFND from whatever part of the program is executing when the NOTFND condition is raised.

The HANDLE CONDITION command

```
EXEC CICS
    HANDLE CONDITION condition-name(procedure-name) ...
END-EXEC
```

Explanation

condition-name   The name of a CICS exceptional condition. Up to 16 condition names may be specified
                      in a single command. More than 16 may be handled by multiple HANDLE CONDITION
                      commands. The special condition name ERROR traps all exceptional conditions not
                      otherwise listed.

procedure-name   A paragraph or section name. Control is passed to procedure-name when the specified
                      condition occurs. If procedure-name is omitted, the effect of any previous HANDLE
                      CONDITION command for the condition is nullified.

Figure 8-33   The HANDLE CONDITION command

A single HANDLE CONDITION command can specify actions for up to 16 exceptional conditions. For example, the command

```
EXEC CICS
    HANDLE CONDITION DUPREC(3100-DUPKEY)
                     NOSPACE(3100-NOSPACE)
                     NOTOPEN(3100-NOTOPEN)
END-EXEC.
```

handles three conditions: DUPREC, NOSPACE, and NOTOPEN.

You can nullify the effect of a HANDLE CONDITION action by listing a condition name without a paragraph or section name. For example,

```
EXEC CICS
    HANDLE CONDITION NOSPACE
END-EXEC.
```

reverses the effect of any previous HANDLE CONDITION command for the NOSPACE condition. As a result, if NOSPACE is raised after the execution of this command, the task is terminated.

You can use a special condition name, ERROR, to trap any errors not specifically named in a HANDLE CONDITION command. The routine you specify for the ERROR condition will be invoked for *any* exceptional condition that isn't specifically handled. For example, suppose this command is issued:

```
EXEC CICS
    HANDLE CONDITION DUPKEY(3100-DUPKEY)
                     NOTOPEN(3100-NOTOPEN)
                     ERROR(3100-ERROR)
END-EXEC.
```

```
 2100-READ-ACCOUNT-RECORD SECTION.
*
     EXEC CICS
         HANDLE CONDITION NOTFND(2100-NOTFND)
     END-EXEC.
     EXEC CICS
         READ DATASET('ACCOUNT')
              INTO(ACCOUNT-RECORD)
              RIDFLD(AR-ACCOUNT-NUMBER)
     END-EXEC.
     MOVE 'Y' TO RECORD-FOUND-SW.
     GO TO 2100-RESET.
*
 2100-NOTFND.
*
     MOVE 'N' TO RECORD-FOUND-SW.
*
 2100-RESET.
*
     EXEC CICS
         HANDLE CONDITION NOTFND
     END-EXEC.
*
 2100-EXIT.
*
     EXIT.
```

Figure 8-34 A READ module that uses the HANDLE CONDITION command

Then, if the NOSPACE condition is raised, control is transferred to 3100-ERROR since I coded ERROR, but not NOSPACE. However, the DUPKEY and NOTOPEN conditions are still processed by their respective paragraphs.

In general, I do *not* recommend that you code ERROR on the HANDLE CONDITION command. Any error you can correct requires its own paragraph. For all other errors, it's best to let the system terminate the task. So don't bother with the ERROR condition.

Figure 8-34 shows how a HANDLE CONDITION command is typically used in a program. Here, I've paired a HANDLE CONDITION command with a READ command in a module that reads a record from a file named ACCOUNT. Because several paragraph labels and GO TO statements are required to code this module, I implemented it as a section. That way, you can issue a PERFORM statement to perform the section and rest assured that control will return to the statement following the PERFORM statement.

Look carefully at the structure of this section. First, a HANDLE CONDITION command specifies that if the NOTFND condition is raised by any subsequent command, control should be passed to 2100-NOTFND. Then, a READ command attempts to read the record. If the read is successful, control falls through to the next statement, which sets RECORD-FOUND-SW to Y. Then, a GO TO statement transfers control to 2100-RESET. There, another HANDLE CONDITION command deactivates the condition handling for the NOTFND command, and control falls through to 2100-EXIT, which marks the end of the section.

If the NOTFND condition is raised during execution of the READ command, control is transferred immediately to 2100-NOTFND. There, a MOVE statement sets RECORD-FOUND-SW to N. Then, control falls through to 2100-RESET and 2100-EXIT. The MOVE and GO TO statements following the READ command are bypassed because of the NOTFND condition.

The HANDLE CONDITION command in the paragraph labelled 2100-RESET is important because it deactivates the condition handling established by the first HANDLE CONDITION command. If you don't deactivate this condition handling, a CICS command later in the program might inadvertently cause control to be transferred into this section. To prevent that from happening, I recommend you always deactivate any condition handling before you exit from a module. (I would have placed this final HANDLE CONDITION command in the 2100-EXIT paragraph, but COBOL requires that the EXIT statement be in a paragraph by itself.)

You may be wondering what happens if both a HANDLE CONDITION command and a HANDLE AID command are in effect. In other words, which has precedence? The HANDLE AID command does. If both a HANDLE CONDITION and a HANDLE AID command are in effect when you issue a RECEIVE MAP command and an AID key is detected, control will be transferred to the procedure specified for the AID key. Any HANDLE CONDITION command in effect will be ignored.

Response code checking

With release 1.7 of CICS, IBM introduced an alternative to the HANDLE CONDITION command: response code checking with the RESP option. The RESP option eliminates the need for the HANDLE CONDITION command, GO TO statements, paragraph labels to process specific exceptional conditions, and sections. Instead, you simply follow each CICS command with IF statements that test the response code to determine if errors have occurred. All of the programming examples in this book use response code checking rather than the HANDLE CONDITION command. Even though you've already seen how it works in the inquiry program I presented in chapter 6, I want to review it now.

To use response code checking, you must first define a binary fullword item (PIC S9(8) COMP) in working storage. Then, you name this field in the RESP option on your CICS commands. When you specify RESP on a CICS command, you instruct CICS to ignore any exceptional conditions that are raised by the command. Instead, CICS places a numeric value that represents the condition status of the command in the response code field.

It's up to you to evaluate this field to make sure the command executed properly. To do that, you use the DFHRESP keyword in an IF statement, like this:

```
IF RESPONSE-CODE = DFHRESP(NOTFND)
```

Here, the IF statement checks the response code field to see if the NOTFND condition was raised. To check for normal completion, code an IF statement like this:

```
IF RESPONSE-CODE = DFHRESP(NORMAL)
```

The CICS translator translates the DFHRESP specification into a numeric constant that corresponds to the condition you specify.

I want to be sure you understand the fundamental difference between response code checking and the HANDLE CONDITION command. When you use the HANDLE CONDITION command, you specify the exceptional conditions you want to process *before* you issue the command that might raise those conditions. If a condition that isn't specifically listed in a HANDLE CONDITION command is raised, CICS takes its default action, which in most cases abends your program. In contrast, when you use response code checking, you test for specific conditions *after* you issue the command that might raise those conditions. With response code checking, CICS *never* takes its default action for exceptional conditions, because it doesn't know in advance which conditions you want to handle in your program.

This means that your program is responsible for handling all CICS exceptional conditions, not just certain conditions like NOTFND and DUPREC. So whenever you use the RESP option, you have to add extra code to deal with exceptional conditions your program can't handle. Most shops have a standard way of dealing with these errors, often in the form of code you can copy into your Procedure Division or a standardized error processing program you can invoke with a LINK or XCTL command. I'll show you an example of a simple error processing program in a moment.

CICS also provides a second response code option, RESP2, which in some cases provides additional error information. To use it, you should define another fullword field (PIC S9(8) COMP) in working storage. Then, you name that field in the RESP2 option. Although you can specify RESP2 for any CICS command, only a few commands actually place a value in this field. Unless your error handling needs are very specialized, you won't need to use RESP2. The response code the RESP option returns provides enough diagnostic information for most purposes.

You should also realize that both response code fields are available in the Execute Interface Block as EIBRESP and EIBRESP2. These fields are updated at the completion of each CICS command, so they always contain the response codes for the most recently executed command.

Incidentally, CICS 1.6 introduced a NOHANDLE option that can also be coded on every CICS command. It tells CICS to ignore any HANDLE CONDITION commands in effect and to skip the default action if an exceptional condition is raised. However, it doesn't return a response code. Instead, you have to test the response code in the Execute Interface Block. Unfortunately, there is no EIBRESP field in the Execute Interface Block under CICS 1.6. Instead, you have to test the EIBRCODE field. Like EIBRESP, EIBRCODE indicates the exceptional condition that was raised. But unlike EIBRESP, the exceptional condition information in EIBRCODE is stored as a binary value that's not easily accessible to COBOL programs. So if you're using CICS 1.6, I recommend you use the HANDLE CONDITION command rather than the NOHANDLE option.

A generalized error handling program

Earlier, I mentioned that most shops have standards for handling unrecoverable errors. Although these standards vary from shop to shop, it's not uncommon to provide a generic error handling program that can be branched to if an unrecoverable error is detected. The error handling program then displays an error message to the user and perhaps writes detailed error information to an error log, reverses any changes that were made to recoverable files, produces a dump, abends the program, or just ends with a RETURN command.

Figures 8-35 through 8-38 present a simple error processing program that will be used by two of the model programs I'll present in the next chapter. This error processing program, called SYSERR, is not intended to provide the type of error recovery that's necessary in a production environment. In fact, all it does is display an error message like the one in figure 8-35 and end by issuing a RETURN command without the TRANSID option. But it does illustrate the concept of branching to a standard error processing routine when an unrecoverable error occurs.

Figure 8-36 shows a copy member that the model programs include in their Working-Storage Sections. This copy member defines an 01-level item named ERROR-PARAMETERS that will be passed to SYSERR when an unrecoverable error occurs. It contains four fields: the two response codes (RESP and RESP2), the current transaction identifier, and the resource that was being used by the command that produced the error (such as a file or mapset). All four of these values can be obtained from Execute Interface Block fields (EIBRESP, EIBRESP2, EIBTRNID, and EIBRSRCE).

Figure 8-37 shows how a program can invoke SYSERR. Here, you can see that an IF statement following a CICS command evaluates the response code. If the response is not normal, the program branches to a paragraph labelled 9999-TERMINATE-PROGRAM. This paragraph simply moves fields from the Execute Interface Block to the

```
A serious error has occurred.   Please contact technical support.

EIBRESP  =         19
EIBRESP2 =          0
EIBTRNID = MNT1
EIBRSRCE = CUSTMAS
```

Figure 8-35 Error message displayed by the SYSERR program

```
01    ERROR-PARAMETERS.
*
      05    ERR-RESP          PIC S9(8)    COMP.
      05    ERR-RESP2         PIC S9(8)    COMP.
      05    ERR-TRNID         PIC X(4).
      05    ERR-RSRCE         PIC X(8).
```

Figure 8-36 The ERRPARM copy member

```
        IF RESPONSE-CODE NOT = DFHRESP(NORMAL)
            GO TO 9999-TERMINATE-PROGRAM.
        .
        .
        .
*
  9999-TERMINATE-PROGRAM.
*
      MOVE EIBRESP   TO ERR-RESP.
      MOVE EIBRESP2  TO ERR-RESP2.
      MOVE EIBTRNID  TO ERR-TRNID.
      MOVE EIBRSRCE  TO ERR-RSRCE.
      EXEC CICS
          XCTL PROGRAM('SYSERR')
              COMMAREA(ERROR-PARAMETERS)
      END-EXEC.
```

Figure 8-37 Invoking the SYSERR error handling program

ERROR-PARAMETERS fields, then issues an XCTL command to transfer control to the SYSERR program. The ERROR-PARAMETERS field is passed to SYSERR via the COMMAREA option.

Although you could include the 9999-TERMINATE-PROGRAM paragraph on the program structure chart, I don't think it's necessary. It's not really a function of the program, but merely a common point for terminating the program from any program module that does response code checking. If you included it in the structure chart, you would have to draw it as a subordinate to any module that issues a CICS command. This would clutter the chart without clarifying the program's design in any substantial way.

Figure 8-38 shows the source code for the SYSERR program. Most of it is devoted to defining the seven-line error message in the Working-Storage Section. In the Procedure Division, the program starts by moving DFHCOMMAREA to its working-storage copy of ERROR-PARAMETERS. Then, it moves fields individually to the appropriate error message fields. Next, it issues a SEND TEXT command to erase the screen, display the error message, and sound the alarm. Finally, it terminates the task by issuing a RETURN command without options. Thus, to continue work, the user will have to clear the screen by pressing the Clear key, then type in a new trans-id.

Objectives

1. Code a program module that issues a CICS command and uses the HANDLE CONDITION command to trap and process exceptional conditions.

2. Code a program module that issues a CICS command and uses response code checking to handle exceptional conditions.

```
       IDENTIFICATION DIVISION.
      *
       PROGRAM-ID.  SYSERR.
      *
       ENVIRONMENT DIVISION.
      *
       DATA DIVISION.
      *
       WORKING-STORAGE SECTION.
      *
       01  ERROR-MESSAGE.
      *
           05  ERROR-LINE-1.
               10  FILLER       PIC X(20)   VALUE 'A serious error has '.
               10  FILLER       PIC X(20)   VALUE 'occurred.  Please co'.
               10  FILLER       PIC X(20)   VALUE 'ntact technical supp'.
               10  FILLER       PIC X(19)   VALUE 'ort.               '.
           05  ERROR-LINE-2     PIC X(79)   VALUE SPACE.
           05  ERROR-LINE-3.
               10  FILLER       PIC X(11)   VALUE 'EIBRESP  = '.
               10  EM-RESP      PIC Z(8)9.
               10  FILLER       PIC X(59)   VALUE SPACE.
           05  ERROR-LINE-4.
               10  FILLER       PIC X(11)   VALUE 'EIBRESP2 = '.
               10  EM-RESP2     PIC Z(8)9.
               10  FILLER       PIC X(59)   VALUE SPACE.
           05  ERROR-LINE-5.
               10  FILLER       PIC X(11)   VALUE 'EIBTRNID = '.
               10  EM-TRNID     PIC X(4).
               10  FILLER       PIC X(64)   VALUE SPACE.
           05  ERROR-LINE-6.
               10  FILLER       PIC X(11)   VALUE 'EIBRSRCE = '.
               10  EM-RSRCE     PIC X(8).
               10  FILLER       PIC X(60)   VALUE SPACE.
           05  ERROR-LINE-7     PIC X(79)   VALUE SPACE.
      *
       COPY ERRPARM.
      *
       LINKAGE SECTION.
      *
       01  DFHCOMMAREA          PIC X(20).
      *
       PROCEDURE DIVISION.
      *
       0000-DISPLAY-ERROR-MESSAGE.
      *
           MOVE DFHCOMMAREA TO ERROR-PARAMETERS.
           MOVE ERR-RESP  TO EM-RESP.
           MOVE ERR-RESP2 TO EM-RESP2.
           MOVE ERR-TRNID TO EM-TRNID.
           MOVE ERR-RSRCE TO EM-RSRCE.
           EXEC CICS
               SEND TEXT FROM(ERROR-MESSAGE)
                         ERASE
                         ALARM
                         FREEKB
           END-EXEC.
           EXEC CICS
               RETURN
           END-EXEC.
```

Figure 8-38 Source listing for the SYSERR program

How to access data using the Linkage Section

In this topic, you'll learn how to access storage that's outside your program's Working-Storage Section by using the Linkage Section. Although you've already seen examples of accessing data in the communication area and the Execute Interface Block, this topic begins by explaining in greater depth how you use those Linkage Section areas. Then, it shows you how to access data in other CICS areas using the Linkage Section. As you'll see, the coding requirements to do that vary depending on whether you're using the OS/VS COBOL compiler or VS COBOL II.

How to use the communication area

In chapter 6, I showed you how to evaluate the length of the communication area to identify the first execution of a program in a pseudo-conversational session. In that example, I didn't use the communication area to pass data between executions of the program. I just passed a one-byte dummy field so that the length of the communication area would not be zero.

In many cases, however, you need to keep data between program executions. For example, you saw in chapter 7 that the communication area should be used to keep track of the state of a pseudo-conversational program, so that you can determine the context in which user input events should be interpreted. And in topic 1 of this chapter, you saw that when a pseudo-conversational program updates a file record, it can save a copy of that record in the communication area to make sure it isn't updated between pseudo-conversational interactions. Depending on the application program's requirements, there may be other data that should be saved across executions, as well. For example, a program that accumulates control totals (such as a count of the number of transactions entered) must pass the totals forward from one execution to the next.

As a general rule, you should define the communication area with its fields in the Working-Storage Section, something like this:

```
 01   COMMUNICATION-AREA.
 *
      05   CA-CONTEXT-FLAG          PIC X.
           88   CA-KEY-MAP                    VALUE '1'.
           88   CA-ADD-CUSTOMER               VALUE '2'.
           88   CA-CHANGE-CUSTOMER            VALUE '3'.
           88   CA-DELETE-CUSTOMER            VALUE '4'.
      05   CA-CUSTOMER-RECORD       PIC X(118).
```

Here, I defined two fields in the communication area: a one-byte flag used to manage the program's event context and a 118-byte area used to hold an image of a record from a customer file. The total length of this communication area is 119 bytes.

Next, you define DFHCOMMAREA in the Linkage Section so it has the same length as the working-storage COMMUNICATION-AREA field. In this case, I'd code:

```
01  DFHCOMMAREA            PIC X(119).
```

Notice that I didn't define the individual fields in DFHCOMMAREA. As you'll see in a moment, you move DFHCOMMAREA to COMMUNICATION-AREA to access the individual fields of the communication area.

It's important to realize that these two fields define two distinct areas of storage. For any given execution of your program except the first, the working-storage area represents storage freshly allocated for your program, while the Linkage Section area represents storage saved from the *previous* execution of the program. Each time your program ends, the storage held by DFHCOMMAREA in the Linkage Section is released, and the contents of the working-storage definition of the communication area are saved and accessed via the Linkage Section in the next execution of the program. (The first time your program is executed, the Linkage Section DFHCOMMAREA doesn't exist.)

To access the data saved by the previous execution of your program, you should move it to the newly allocated storage defined in the Working-Storage Section. You can do that easily by placing this statement at the beginning of the Procedure Division:

```
IF EIBCALEN > ZERO
    MOVE DFHCOMMAREA TO COMMUNICATION-AREA.
```

Here, the MOVE is performed only if EIBCALEN is greater than zero. If there is no communication area, you shouldn't attempt to access it. Once this MOVE statement has completed, the program can access the individual fields in COMMUNICATION-AREA in subsequent statements.

When you use the communication area with the OS/VS COBOL compiler, you have to specify its correct length in the RETURN command. For example, to pass a 119-byte communication area forward to the next execution using OS/VS COBOL, you would use a RETURN command like

```
EXEC CICS
    RETURN TRANSID('MNT1')
           COMMAREA(COMMUNICATION-AREA)
           LENGTH(119)
END-EXEC.
```

If you specify an incorrect length, your program won't operate properly. If you're using VS COBOL II, the LENGTH parameter isn't required. If you omit it, CICS uses the actual length of the field specified in the COMMAREA option.

How to use fields in the Execute Interface Block

As I explained in chapter 6, the Execute Interface Block (EIB) is a CICS area that contains information related to the current task. Figure 8-39 lists all of the fields contained in the Execute Interface Block, their COBOL pictures, and a brief description of each field. The shaded fields are the ones you're likely to use in coding and debugging your programs. Some of these fields are initialized when the task is started; others are updated each time certain CICS commands are executed.

The CICS command-level translator automatically inserts the EIB into your program's Linkage Section immediately after the DFHCOMMAREA entry, so you don't have to do anything special to access these fields. You learned how to use EIBCALEN and EIBAID in chapter 6, and I presented EIBCPOSN in topic 3 of this chapter. Now, I want to explain how to use some of the other fields.

EIBDATE and EIBTIME   EIBDATE contains the date the task was started. The format of EIBDATE is 00YYDDD, where DDD represents the three digits that indicate what number day in the year it is. Thus, July 1, 1993 is stored as 0093182 (the 182nd day of 1993).

EIBTIME contains the time of day your task was started. The time is stored as a seven-digit packed-decimal number in the form 0HHMMSS (one leading zero followed by two-digit hours, minutes, and seconds). This assumes a 24-hour clock, so 2:00 p.m. is hour 14. As a result, 38 seconds after 2:41 p.m. is stored as 0144138. Midnight is stored as 0000000; one second before midnight is 0235959.

Although the YYDDD date format is useful for date comparisons, it's inappropriate for display purposes. And two time values can only be compared if you're confident that both represent the same day. As a result, with CICS version 1.7, IBM introduced a new command, FORMATTIME, designed specifically to convert times and dates to and from various formats. I'll present the FORMATTIME command in *Part 2: An Advanced Course.*

EIBTRNID   EIBTRNID contains the transaction identifier that started the current task. One of the common uses of EIBTRNID is to determine how your program was started. For example, suppose you want to insure that a program is invoked only from a menu. In other words, you don't want the program to be started by entering the transaction identifier at a terminal. (Remember that a task is started by a single transaction identifier, even though it may consist of several different programs.) Figure 8-40 shows a simple test you could place in the EVALUATE statement of a program's top module to check this. Here, if

Field name	COBOL PIC	Description
EIBAID	X(1)	Most recent AID character
EIBATT	X(1)	RU attach header flag
EIBCALEN	S9(4) COMP	Length of DFHCOMMAREA
EIBCOMPL	X(1)	RECEIVE command completion flag
EIBCONF	X(1)	LU 6.2 comfirmation flag
EIBCPOSN	S9(4) COMP	Most recent cursor address
EIBDATE	S9(7) COMP-3	Task start date
EIBDS	X(8)	Most recent data set name
EIBEOC	X(1)	RU end-of-chain flag
EIBERR	X(1)	LU 6.2 error flag
EIBERRCD	X(4)	LU 6.2 error code
EIBFMH	X(1)	FMH flag
EIBFN	X(2)	Most recent CICS command code
EIBFREE	X(1)	Free facility flag
EIBNODAT	X(1)	LU 6.2 no data flag
EIBRCODE	X(6)	CICS response code
EIBRECV	X(1)	RECEIVE command more-data flag
EIBREQID	X(8)	Interval control request-id
EIBRESP	S9(8) COMP	Exceptional condition code
EIBRESP2	S9(8) COMP	Exceptional condition extended code
EIBRLDBK	X(1)	Rollback flag (CICS 2.1 and later)
EIBRSRCE	X(8)	Last resource (file, queue, etc.)
EIBSIG	X(1)	SIGNAL flag
EIBSYNC	X(1)	Syncpoint flag
EIBSYNRB	X(1)	Syncpoint rollback flag
EIBTASKN	S9(7) COMP-3	Task number
EIBTIME	S9(7) COMP-3	Task starting time
EIBTRMID	X(4)	Terminal-id
EIBTRNID	X(4)	Transaction-id

Figure 8-39 Fields in the Execute Interface Block

```
0000-MAINTAIN-CUSTOMER-FILE.
*
    IF EIBCALEN > ZERO
        MOVE DFHCOMMAREA TO COMMUNICATION-AREA.

    EVALUATE TRUE

        WHEN EIBCALEN = ZERO AND EIBTRNID NOT = 'MENU'
                EXEC CICS
                    RETURN
                END-EXEC

        WHEN EIBCALEN = ZERO
                .
                .
                .
```

Figure 8-40 Using EIBTRNID to insure that a program is started from a menu

the first time condition is detected and EIBTRNID is anything other than MENU (the transaction-id that starts the menu program), a RETURN command is issued to terminate the task.

EIBTRMID   This field supplies the name of the terminal running the task. The terminal name that appears in EIBTRMID isn't a physical device type like 3270-2, but rather a symbolic name assigned to a terminal in the Terminal Control Table (TCT). (An example of a terminal name is L131.) You might use this field for security purposes. For example, if you want to restrict a program to certain terminals, you can test EIBTRMID to make sure the terminal is eligible to run the task. If not, your program would issue a RETURN command to terminate the task.

EIB fields used for debugging   Several of the Execute Interface Block fields are particularly useful when debugging a command-level CICS program. EIBFN indicates which CICS command was executed last, and EIBRESP, EIBRESP2, and EIBRCODE represent that command's completion status. The CICS *Application Programming Reference* manual lists possible values for these fields.

EIBRSRCE contains the name of the most recently used resource. For BMS commands (SEND MAP and RECEIVE MAP), the resource is the map name. For program control commands (LINK and XCTL), the resource is the program name specified in the PROGRAM option. And for file control commands, the resource is the file name. (The file name can also be found in the field EIBDS.)

The rest of the fields in the Execute Interface Block are seldom used, so I won't describe them here. You can find a complete explanation of them in the CICS *Application Programming Reference* manual.

The ADDRESS command

```
EXEC CICS
    ADDRESS [ CWA(pointer) ]
            [ CSA(pointer) ]
            [ TWA(pointer) ]
            [ TCTUA(pointer) ]
END-EXEC
```

Explanation

CWA   Establishes addressability to the Common Work Area, a user-defined storage area
                    common to all tasks in a CICS system.

CSA   Establishes addressability to the Common System Area, an internal CICS control block.

TWA   Establishes addressability to the Transaction Work Area, an area of storage assigned to
                    the current task.

TCTUA   Establishes addressability to the Terminal Control Table User Area, an area of storage
                    associated with the terminal.

Figure 8-41 The ADDRESS command

How to access CICS areas

Command-level COBOL lets you access areas of storage that are owned by CICS rather than by your application program. The two CICS area I've already described in this topic (the communication area and the Execute Interface Block) are provided automatically. But others must be set up explicitly. CICS lets you access some of these areas by using the ADDRESS command, shown in figure 8-41.

As you can see, the ADDRESS command lets you access four CICS areas: the *CWA* (*Common Work Area*), the *CSA* (*Common System Area*), the *TWA* (*Transaction Work Area*), and the *TCTUA* (*Terminal Control Table User Area*). You'll hear and read about the last three of these areas, but they're largely holdovers from macro-level CICS and are seldom used in command-level programming. However, you may need to use the CWA in your programs.

The CWA is an area of storage that's available to all tasks in a CICS system. Typically, the CWA is used to store limited amounts of information that might be useful to many or all programs in an installation. For example, a typical CWA might contain fields for the current date in various formats (such as "10/12/93" or "November 12, 1993") and the company name for use in report headings. The CWA might also contain fields such as the day of the week, the system start-up time, the time zone, the job name, and so on. The actual contents of the CWA vary from installation to installation.

```
LINKAGE SECTION

01 DFHCOMMAREA ...

01 BLL-CELLS.
    05 FILLER          PIC S9(8)  COMP.
    05 BLL-FIELD-1     PIC S9(8)  COMP.
    05 BLL-FIELD-2     PIC S9(8)  COMP.
    05 BLL-FIELD-3     PIC S9(8)  COMP.
01 FIELD-1 ...

01 FIELD-2 ...

01 FIELD-3 ...
```

Figure 8-42   BLL cells in the Linkage Section

Since these storage areas exist outside of your program's working storage, you must access them via the Linkage Section. When CICS loads and executes your program, it automatically provides *addressability* to the first two Linkage Section fields: DFHCOMMAREA and the Execute Interface Block. However, if you define any other field in the Linkage Section (such as the CWA), you must establish addressability to it yourself. If you don't, your program will abend with an addressing exception when you try to access the field.

The technique you use to establish addressability to Linkage Section fields depends on whether you're using the OS/VS COBOL compiler or the newer VS COBOL II compiler. Because the techniques are completely different from one another, I'll present them separately here.

How to access Linkage Section data using OS/VS COBOL   To establish addressability to a field in the Linkage Section using the OS/VS COBOL compiler, you must use a convention called *Base Locator for Linkage* (or *BLL*). Figure 8-42 illustrates this convention. Quite simply, you must define an 01-level item in the Linkage Section following DFHCOMMAREA. In figure 8-42, I called this item BLL-CELLS, but the name doesn't matter. Each field in BLL-CELLS is a pointer that stores the address of a Linkage Section field. These pointers must be defined as PIC S9(8) COMP. The first pointer points to the BLL-CELLS item itself. Then, each subsequent pointer points to an 01-level item that follows in the Linkage Section. In figure 8-42, the pointer named BLL-FIELD-1 is used to establish addressability to FIELD-1. Similarly, BLL-FIELD-2 is used for FIELD-2, and BLL-FIELD-3 is used for FIELD-3. But it's not the names of the BLL cells that matter; it's the order in which you code them.

```
 LINKAGE SECTION.
*
 01   DFHCOMMAREA              PIC X.
*
 01   BLL-CELLS.
*
      05   FILLER              PIC S9(8)  COMP.
      05   BLL-CWA             PIC S9(8)  COMP.
*
 01   COMMON-WORK-AREA.
*
      05   CWA-CURRENT-DATE    PIC X(8).
      05   CWA-COMPANY-NAME    PIC X(30).
*
 PROCEDURE DIVISION.
*
 0000-PROCESS-CUSTOMER-INQUIRY.
*
         .
         .
         .
      EXEC CICS
          ADDRESS CWA(BLL-CWA)
      END-EXEC.
      SERVICE RELOAD COMMON-WORK-AREA.
      MOVE CWA-COMPANY-NAME TO COMPO.
         .
         .
         .
```

Figure 8-43   Accessing the CWA under OS/VS COBOL

Coding the BLL cells in the Linkage Section defines the pointers that will be used to address fields in the Linkage Section. However, before you can use these fields, you must load the pointers with the correct addresses. That's where the ADDRESS command comes in. It simply loads the address of the named field in the specified BLL cell. For example, if you code this ADDRESS command:

```
EXEC CICS
    ADDRESS CWA(BLL-CWA)
END-EXEC.
```

the address of the CWA is placed in BLL-CWA.

Before you can access the CWA in your program, you must add one additional statement:

```
SERVICE RELOAD COMMON-WORK-AREA.
```

SERVICE RELOAD is neither a COBOL statement or a CICS command. Instead, it's a compiler directive that's necessary because of the optimizing features of the OS/VS COBOL compiler. In short, any time your program changes the contents of a BLL cell, it should follow with a SERVICE RELOAD statement that names the field that the BLL cell refers to.

```
 LINKAGE SECTION.
 *
 01   DFHCOMMAREA               PIC X.
 *
 01   COMMON-WORK-AREA.
 *
      05   CWA-CURRENT-DATE     PIC X(8).
      05   CWA-COMPANY-NAME     PIC X(30).
 *
 PROCEDURE DIVISION.
 *
 0000-PROCESS-CUSTOMER-INQUIRY.
 *

          .
          .
          .
      EXEC CICS
          ADDRESS CWA(ADDRESS OF COMMON-WORK-AREA)
      END-EXEC.
      MOVE CWA-COMPANY-NAME TO COMPO.
          .
          .
          .
```

Figure 8-44   Accessing the CWA under VS COBOL II

Figure 8-43 shows how you put these techniques together to access the CWA under OS/VS COBOL. Here, BLL-CWA is the name of the pointer that will be used for COMMON-WORK-AREA. The ADDRESS command places the address of the CWA in BLL-CWA, and the SERVICE RELOAD statement ensures that addressability is established. Then, the fields in COMMON-WORK-AREA are accessible, so the MOVE statement that references CWA-COMPANY-NAME will work properly.

How to access Linkage Section data using VS COBOL II   Under VS COBOL II, it's much easier to access data via the Linkage Section. Instead of using the BLL cell convention, you use the special register ADDRESS OF to set the address of any field in the Linkage Section. So you don't have to code a BLL-CELLS entry in the Linkage Section. In addition, the SERVICE RELOAD statement isn't required.

Figure 8-44 shows how to access the CWA under VS COBOL II. As you can see, I omitted the BLL-CELLS entry in the Linkage Section. Then, I coded the ADDRESS command like this:

```
EXEC CICS
    ADDRESS CWA(ADDRESS OF COMMON-WORK-AREA)
END-EXEC.
```

Here, I used the ADDRESS OF register to set the address of the Linkage Section field COMMON-WORK-AREA to the address of the CWA supplied by the CICS ADDRESS command.

Discussion   Besides addressing the communication area, the Execute Interface Block, and CICS areas like the CWA, the Linkage Section can be used for two other types of storage areas: (1) pre-defined constant tables and (2) buffers used for locate-mode I/O. A CICS *constant table* is an area of storage that contains values for a table many programs use. Rather than code the table in the Working-Storage Section of each program, the table is loaded into storage once and accessed by each program via the Linkage Section. You'll learn how to create and access constant tables in *Part 2: An Advanced Course.*

Locate-mode I/O is an I/O technique that uses I/O areas in the Linkage Section rather than in working storage. When you use locate-mode I/O, your program processes data while it's still in a CICS buffer. To access the CICS buffer, you use the SET option on I/O commands such as SEND MAP, RECEIVE MAP, READ, WRITE, and so on. The alternative to locate-mode I/O is *move-mode I/O,* in which CICS moves data to and from working-storage fields you specify in the FROM and INTO options. Although locate-mode I/O is the more efficient technique, move-mode I/O is more widely used because it is both safer and easier to use.

Terms

CWA
Common Work Area
CSA
Common System Area
TWA
Transaction Work Area
TCTUA
Terminal Control Table User Area
addressability
Base Locator for Linkage
BLL
constant table
locate-mode I/O
move-mode I/O

Objectives

1. Code the COBOL statements necessary to define individual fields within a communication area, to pass that communication area forward to the next execution of the program, and to access the data passed from a previous execution.

2. Identify the contents of the following Execute Interface Block fields:

    EIBAID
    EIBCALEN
    EIBCPOSN
    EIBDATE
    EIBDS
    EIBFN
    EIBRESP
    EIBRESP2
    EIBRSRCE
    EIBTIME
    EIBTRMID
    EIBTRNID

3. Code the CICS commands necessary to access the Common Work Area using both the OS/VS COBOL compiler and the VS COBOL II compiler.

Section 3

A sample CICS application

Now that you've learned a basic subset of CICS commands and programming techniques, you're ready to analyze several model programs. The two chapters in this section present a simple invoicing system that's implemented in command-level CICS. Chapter 9 describes the system design background you need to understand this sample system. Then, chapter 10 presents three model programs: a menu program, a program that maintains a file of customer records, and a program that accepts orders from the user and writes them to an invoice file.

Chapter 9

An overview of the sample application

This chapter presents a brief overview of an invoicing application that lets a user enter orders and maintain a file of customer records. I've simplified the design of this application to make it easier to understand. Nevertheless, it illustrates how the CICS elements this book presents work together.

System design for the sample application

Figure 9-1 is a *data flow diagram* (or *DFD*) for the sample application. Quite simply, the data flow diagram shows the relationships between *processes* (or programs), indicated by circles, and *data stores* (or files), indicated by parallel lines. The link between a process and a data store, called a *data flow*, is indicated by an arrow.

If you're not familiar with data flow diagrams, I recommend you read *How to Design and Develop Business Systems* by Steve Eckols, available from Mike Murach & Associates. But even if you don't know how to create data flow diagrams, I think you'll find that figure 9-1 is a good overview of the sample application.

The key program in this application is the order entry program. It accepts orders from the user and writes them to an invoice file, using three other files for reference information: products, customers, and

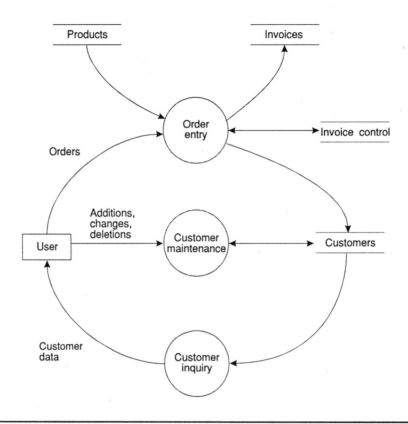

Figure 9-1   Data flow diagram for the sample application

invoice control. The customer maintenance program lets the user add new customers and change or delete existing customers. And the inquiry program lets the user display information about specific customers. (I presented the inquiry program in chapter 6.)

As I've already mentioned, I simplified this application to make it easier to understand. As a result, many critical functions have been omitted. For example, the application doesn't print the invoices, post sales to accounts receivable, or update the inventory status in the product file. These and other functions would certainly be provided in a real CICS application.

Figure 9-2 is the *system structure chart* for the sample application. You can use a system structure chart such as this one to organize system functions, design a menu structure, plan program development, and document your progress towards completing a system. *How to Design and Develop Business Systems* describes how to use the system structure chart throughout design and implementation.

I use the system structure chart here to document the sample application's menu structure. As you can see, the sample application

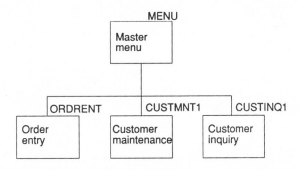

Figure 9-2 System structure chart for the sample application

includes a menu program that invokes the programs that provide the three functions in the data flow diagram in figure 9-1. The menu program itself isn't part of the data flow diagram because its only purpose is to let the user control the execution the other programs; it doesn't make any changes to the application's data files.

Program control in the sample application

Figure 9-3 illustrates the relationships between the sample application's menu structure and the program control commands each program issues. Here, the boxes represent programs and the arrows connecting the boxes represent the flow of control. At the highest level, CICS is the program in control. Four application programs are at the next level: the order entry program (ORDRENT), the menu program (INVMENU), the maintenance program (CUSTMNT1) and the inquiry program (CUSTINQ1). (To simplify the chart, I represented the maintenance program and the inquiry program as a single box, because their program control processing is the same. Also, the maintenance and inquiry program names end with 1 because I'll present alternative versions of those programs in *Part 2: An Advanced Course*.)

The sample application starts when the user enters the trans-id MENU at the terminal. That causes CICS to invoke the menu program INVMENU. When the user makes a selection, the menu program issues an XCTL command to transfer control to the order entry program (ORDRENT), the maintenance program (CUSTMNT1), or the inquiry program (CUSTINQ1). These programs are executed at the same logical level as the menu program.

Control returns to the menu program in one of two ways. The maintenance and inquiry programs return to the menu program by issuing an XCTL command that specifies PROGRAM('INVMENU'). In contrast, the order entry program issues a RETURN command with TRANSID('MENU') specified. That's because the order entry program

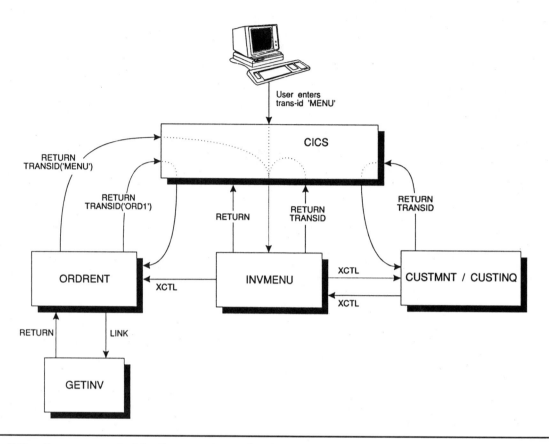

Figure 9-3 Program control for the sample application

displays a termination message before returning to the menu, but the maintenance and inquiry programs do not.

Notice that the ORDRENT program uses a subprogram called GETINV. The order entry program invokes this subprogram to obtain the next sequential invoice number for the invoice file. ORDRENT invokes GETINV by issuing a LINK command, and GETINV returns to ORDRENT by issuing a RETURN command.

The program control for the sample application is complicated because all of its programs (except the subprogram GETINV) are pseudo-conversational. Consider, for example, what this forces the order entry program to do. As you've seen, when the user ends a pseudo-conversational order entry session, control passes back to the menu because ORDRENT issues the command RETURN TRANSID('MENU'). But during a pseudo-conversational order entry session, ORDRENT must end and be restarted over and over again. To do this, ORDRENT ends by issuing the command RETURN TRANSID('ORD1'). This command passes control back to CICS, and the task ends. The next time the user presses an attention key, CICS uses the trans-id ORD1 to restart the ORDRENT program directly, without going through the master menu program. As you can see in figure 9-3, the maintenance and inquiry programs work the same way.

Data sets for the sample application

As you can see in the data flow diagram in figure 9-1, the sample application uses four data sets: products (PRODUCT), invoices (INVOICE), invoice control (INVCTL), and customers (CUSTMAS). Figure 9-4 shows the record layouts for each of these files. Each of these record layouts is contained in a copy member.

Naturally, the record layouts presented here are simplified; in a production system, they'd probably be more complicated. For example, the customer file might contain sales history data, and the invoice file ' might contain shipping information as well as freight and sales tax charges. In addition, alternate index relationships might exist among the files. For example, the customer number field might be an alternate index in the invoice file. Still, the simplified record formats shown in figure 9-4 are adequate for the model programs presented in the next chapter.

Resource definitions for the sample application

For an application like this to work, the CICS system tables must contain definitions for the application's resources: files, programs, and transactions. In most installations, systems programmers add these definitions to the CICS tables when new programs are developed, or they change them when existing programs are modified. So, as an application programmer, it's not your responsibility. Still, seeing the table entries for the sample application will help you understand how its resources relate to one another.

How the systems programmer makes these changes depends on which release of CICS is being used and whether the installation uses resource definition macros or on-line resource definition. If the installation uses macros, the systems programmer must code and assemble a set of macro instructions similar in format to those used to create BMS mapsets. If the installation uses *Resource Definition Online*, or *RDO*, the systems programmer runs a special CICS transaction (CEDA) to make changes to the CICS resource tables using full-screen panels. RDO was introduced with CICS version 1.7, but macros were still required for file definitions until version 3.1.

Figures 9-5 through 9-7 present the macros that create the table definitions for the sample application. If your shop uses RDO, the information contained in these macros would be supplied on-line using the CEDA transaction.

```
01   CUSTOMER-MASTER-RECORD.
*
     05   CM-CUSTOMER-NUMBER            PIC  X(6).
     05   CM-FIRST-NAME                PIC  X(20).
     05   CM-LAST-NAME                 PIC  X(30).
     05   CM-ADDRESS                   PIC  X(30).
     05   CM-CITY                      PIC  X(20).
     05   CM-STATE                     PIC  X(2).
     05   CM-ZIP-CODE                  PIC  X(10).
*


01   PRODUCT-MASTER-RECORD.
*
     05   PRM-PRODUCT-CODE             PIC  X(10).
     05   PRM-PRODUCT-DESCRIPTION      PIC  X(20).
     05   PRM-UNIT-PRICE               PIC  S9(7)V99     COMP-3.
     05   PRM-QUANTITY-ON-HAND         PIC  S9(7)        COMP-3.
*


01   INVOICE-RECORD.
*
     05   INV-INVOICE-NUMBER           PIC  9(6).
     05   INV-INVOICE-DATE             PIC  9(6).
     05   INV-CUSTOMER-NUMBER          PIC  X(6).
     05   INV-PO-NUMBER                PIC  X(10).
     05   INV-LINE-ITEM                OCCURS  10.
          10   INV-PRODUCT-CODE        PIC  X(10).
          10   INV-QUANTITY            PIC  S9(7)        COMP-3.
          10   INV-UNIT-PRICE          PIC  S9(7)V99     COMP-3.
          10   INV-AMOUNT              PIC  S9(7)V99     COMP-3.
     05   INV-INVOICE-TOTAL            PIC  S9(7)V99     COMP-3.
*


01   INVCTL-RECORD.
*
     05   INVCTL-RECORD-KEY            PIC  X.
     05   INVCTL-NEXT-INVOICE-NUMBER   PIC  9(6).
*
```

Figure 9-4   Record layouts for the data files in the sample application

File Control Table entries

Figure 9-5 shows the File Control Table (FCT) entries required for the sample application. As you can see, one DFHFCT macro defines each data set. Each entry includes TYPE=DATASET. Then, the DATASET parameter provides the data set name you code in CICS file-control commands. The ACCMETH option in these examples specifies that the files are VSAM key-sequenced data sets (KSDS). The SERVREQ option specifies the operations that are allowed for these files. ADD, DELETE, and UPDATE indicate that you can issue the CICS commands WRITE, DELETE, and REWRITE for the data set. BROWSE enables sequential access to the data set. I'll explain the CICS commands for sequential access in *Part 2: An Advanced Course*. Finally, the RECFORM option specifies that the files have fixed-length records.

```
DFHFCT TYPE=DATASET,                                          X
       DATASET=CUSTMAS,                                       X
       ACCMETH=(VSAM,KSDS),                                   X
       SERVREQ=(ADD,DELETE,UPDATE,BROWSE),                    X
       RECFORM=(FIXED,BLOCKED)
*
DFHFCT TYPE=DATASET,                                          X
       DATASET=PRODUCT,                                       X
       ACCMETH=(VSAM,KSDS),                                   X
       SERVREQ=(ADD,DELETE,UPDATE,BROWSE),                    X
       RECFORM=(FIXED,BLOCKED)
*
DFHFCT TYPE=DATASET,                                          X
       DATASET=INVOICE,                                       X
       ACCMETH=(VSAM,KSDS),                                   X
       SERVREQ=(ADD,DELETE,UPDATE,BROWSE),                    X
       RECFORM=(FIXED,BLOCKED)
*
DFHFCT TYPE=DATASET,                                          X
       DATASET=INVCTL,                                        X
       ACCMETH=(VSAM,KSDS),                                   X
       SERVREQ=(ADD,DELETE,UPDATE,BROWSE),                    X
       RECFORM=(FIXED,BLOCKED)
*
```

Figure 9-5   File Control Table entries for the sample application

Besides creating the FCT entries, the systems programmer must allocate each data set in the job stream that starts CICS. Under MVS, that means that a DD statement must be added for each data set. Under VSE, a DLBL statement is required. The DATASET name specified for the file must match the ddname (MVS) or DLBL file name (VSE) specified in the JCL. (As an application programmer, you don't create these JCL statements yourself. I mention them here only so you'll have a better understanding of how the FCT entries relate CICS files to actual data sets.)

Processing Program Table entries

Figure 9-6 shows the Processing Program Table (PPT) entries for the sample application. An entry is required for each program in the system, regardless of the level where it's invoked. That includes mapsets as well as application programs. TYPE=ENTRY is coded for each macro. The PROGRAM option identifies the CICS program or mapset name, and the PGMLANG option specifies its language. If you omit PGMLANG, assembler is assumed. That's why I didn't code PGMLANG on the macros that define mapsets.

```
        DFHPPT TYPE=ENTRY,                                        X
               PROGRAM=INVMENU,                                  X
               PGMLANG=COBOL
 *
        DFHPPT TYPE=ENTRY,                                        X
               PROGRAM=CUSTMNT1,                                 X
               PGMLANG=COBOL
 *
        DFHPPT TYPE=ENTRY,                                        X
               PROGRAM=CUSTINQ1,                                 X
               PGMLANG=COBOL
 *
        DFHPPT TYPE=ENTRY,                                        X
               PROGRAM=ORDRENT,                                  X
               PGMLANG=COBOL
 *
        DFHPPT TYPE=ENTRY,                                        X
               PROGRAM=GETINV,                                   X
               PGMLANG=COBOL
 *
        DFHPPT TYPE=ENTRY,                                        X
               PROGRAM=MENUSET1
 *
        DFHPPT TYPE=ENTRY,                                        X
               PROGRAM=MNTSET1
 *
        DFHPPT TYPE=ENTRY,                                        X
               PROGRAM=INQSET1
 *
        DFHPPT TYPE=ENTRY,                                        X
               PROGRAM=ORDSET1
 *
```

Figure 9-6 Processing Program Table entries for the sample application

Program Control Table entries

Figure 9-7 shows the Program Control Table (PCT) entries that define the trans-ids used by the sample application. Again, TYPE=ENTRY is always coded. Then, the TRANSID option specifies the transaction identifier used to invoke a task. Finally, the PROGRAM option specifies the program associated with the trans-id. Figure 9-7 defines four trans-ids: MENU, INQ1, MNT1, and ORD1 for, respectively, the menu, inquiry, maintenance, and order entry programs.

Other table entries

You should be aware that there are dozens of table entry options I haven't mentioned here. Obviously, the table entries I've presented here are simplified. The exact options coded for each entry depend on factors unique to your installation. In any event, those options are generally the responsibility of the systems programmer.

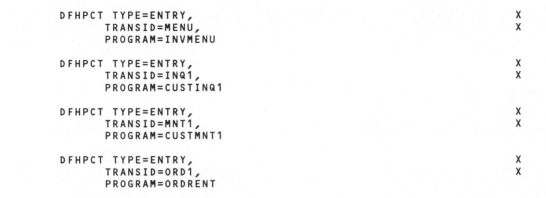

```
          DFHPCT TYPE=ENTRY,                              X
                 TRANSID=MENU,                            X
                 PROGRAM=INVMENU
*
          DFHPCT TYPE=ENTRY,                              X
                 TRANSID=INQ1,                            X
                 PROGRAM=CUSTINQ1
*
          DFHPCT TYPE=ENTRY,                              X
                 TRANSID=MNT1,                            X
                 PROGRAM=CUSTMNT1
*
          DFHPCT TYPE=ENTRY,                              X
                 TRANSID=ORD1,                            X
                 PROGRAM=ORDRENT
*
```

Figure 9-7   Program Control Table entries for the sample application

Discussion   Now that you've been introduced to the sample application, you're ready to study three model programs from it in the next chapter. You've already seen the customer inquiry program; it was presented in chapter 6. In the next chapter, then, you'll see the designs and the complete program listings for the menu program, the maintenance program, and the order entry program.

Terms

data flow diagram
DFD
process
data store
data flow
system structure chart
Resource Definition Online
RDO

Objectives

1. Describe the sample application presented in this chapter.

2. Explain the CICS table entries required to support this application.

Chapter 10

Three model programs

In the last chapter, you saw an overview of a simple invoicing application. You've already seen the inquiry program from that application. In this chapter, I'll present the other three programs: the master menu program, the customer maintenance program, and the order entry program. These programs illustrate most of the CICS commands and programming techniques I've described in this book, and they're good models for many application programs you'll be called upon to write.

I'll present each program in a separate topic. In each topic, you'll find a complete program specification, design documents such as event/response charts and program structure charts, a mapset listing, and the program source code itself. (The order entry program in topic 3 uses a subprogram named GETINV; you'll find the source listing for that subprogram in topic 3 as well.) The source code I'll present in this chapter was developed under VS COBOL II. I've included OS/VS COBOL versions of the programs in Appendix D.

When you study these programs, don't get discouraged if you don't understand every line of code immediately. These programs combine many CICS and COBOL elements that are new to you, so it's natural that you'll need to read through them more than once to understand them. Each time you read through one of these model programs, the CICS and COBOL elements it illustrates will become clearer.

I'd like to offer three suggestions for studying these programs. First, study each program using the accompanying event/response chart as a guide. In other words, read through the program once for each input event, studying how the program responds to the event. Second, if possible, run the program using a debugger such as EDF, Intertest, or (if you're using a PC) Animator. That way, you can trace the execution of the program and observe the results of each statement or CICS command. And third, design and develop your own CICS programs using one or more of these model programs for guidance. By experimenting with the CICS commands and the related COBOL statements, you'll rapidly come to understand how they work.

The master menu program

Figure 10-1 (on page 238) gives the specifications for the master menu program. As you can see, the menu program asks the user to select one of three functions: customer inquiry, customer maintenance, or order entry. When the user has made a selection (by entering 1, 2, or 3 in the Action field), the menu program issues an XCTL command to load and execute the correct program. If the user presses the PF3 or PF12 key, the program displays a message and terminates without branching to another program.

Figure 10-2 (on page 239) shows an event/response chart for the menu program. If you'll study this chart for a moment, you'll see that every possible input event is accounted for. The only one that requires extensive processing is when the user presses the Enter key. Then, the program must evaluate the action code entered by the user to determine which program to transfer control to. If the user doesn't enter a valid action code, the program simply displays an error message.

Figure 10-3 (on page 239) shows the program structure chart I developed for the menu program. Here, I created two modules subordinate to the 0000 module. I created module 1000 because the processing required to respond to the Enter key is complex. It has subordinates to receive the menu map, edit the action code, branch to the selected program, and send the menu map if the action code is invalid. I created module 2000 only to remove the CICS command necessary to send the termination message from module 0000. And module 1400 is called from module 0000 to handle responses to other input events (such as "Start the program").

Figure 10-4 (on pages 240-241) presents the mapset listing for the menu program, and figure 10-5 (on page 242) presents the symbolic map BMS generated from the mapset program. There's nothing unusual about this mapset, so you shouldn't have any trouble understanding it.

Figure 10-6 (on pages 243-245) presents the source code for the master menu program. The Working-Storage and Linkage Sections are straightforward enough. I included a switch (VALID-DATA-SW) that's set by module 1200 when it edits the action code field and a flag (SEND-FLAG) that's used to control which SEND MAP options should be used by the general-purpose send module (module 1400). I defined the termination message as a working-storage field, and because this program doesn't pass data forward to the next execution of the program, the communication area is just one byte long.

The one working-storage field that might confuse you is the PROGRAM-TABLE entry:

```
01   PROGRAM-TABLE.
*
     05   PROGRAM-LIST.
          10   PROGRAM-1            PIC X(8)   VALUE 'CUSTINQ1'.
          10   PROGRAM-2            PIC X(8)   VALUE 'CUSTMNT1'.
          10   PROGRAM-3            PIC X(8)   VALUE 'ORDRENT '.
     05   PROGRAM-NAME              REDEFINES PROGRAM-LIST
                                    OCCURS 3
                                    PIC X(8).
```

This is a simple table that defines the names of the three programs the menu program can branch to, then redefines the names with PROGRAM-NAME, which occurs 3 times. This PROGRAM-NAME field is then used along with a subscript in the PROGRAM option of the XCTL statement to transfer control to the appropriate program.

The subscript value will be the number the user enters in the Action field. The program uses the next two working-storage items, ACTION-ALPHA and ACTION-NUM, for the subscript.

The last three items in the Working-Storage Section are COPY statements. The first copies MENSET1, the symbolic map for the menu screen in figure 10-5. The second includes the DFHAID copy member, which I introduced in figure 6-8. And the third copies the code in ATTR, my customized copy member that contains attribute byte definitions; I presented ATTR in figure 8-18.

In the Procedure Division, module 0000 manages the program's event processing. Here, an EVALUATE statement determines which event has occurred and responds to each accordingly. The "Start the program" event is detected if EIBCALEN=ZERO (that is, no communication area was passed to the program). The program responds by displaying the menu map. The program responds to the Clear key the same way. The PA keys are ignored. If EIBAID indicates that the user pressed PF3 or PF12, module 2000 is invoked to send the termination message, and a RETURN statement with no options is issued to terminate the program. If the Enter key was pressed, module 1000 is invoked to process the menu map. Finally, if any other event caused the program to start, the program responds by displaying an error message.

In module 1000, a PERFORM statement invokes module 1100 to receive the menu map. Then, module 1200 is invoked to edit the action code field. If the action code is valid, module 1300 is invoked to branch to the selected program; otherwise, module 1400 is invoked to send an error message back to the terminal.

Module 1300 is worth a closer look. It begins with this command:

```
EXEC CICS
    XCTL PROGRAM(PROGRAM-NAME(ACTION-NUM))
         RESP(RESPONSE-CODE)
END-EXEC.
```

This command transfers control to the program specified by PROGRAM-NAME, subscripted by the action code. Thus, if ACTION-NUM is 1, the XCTL command invokes CUSTINQ1; if it's 2, CUSTMNT1 is invoked; and if it's 3, ORDRENT is invoked. If ACTION-NUM has any value other than 1, 2, or 3, the error would have been detected in module 1200, and module 1300 would not have been invoked.

If the XCTL command executes successfully, control will not return to the menu program. So what's the point of the MOVE statement that follows the XCTL command? It's there because the XCTL command might fail. Because I coded the RESP option on the XCTL command, control will return to the menu program if an exceptional condition is raised. If that happens, the MOVE statement moves an appropriate error message to MESSAGEO. Then, if you'll look back to module 1000, you'll see that execution will continue with the statements that set SEND-FLAG and invoke module 1400 to display the error message.

From the point of view of structured programming, you might object to placing the XCTL command in module 1300. After all, one of the basic premises of structured programming is that every module should have one entry point and one exit point. So shouldn't the XCTL command be placed in module 0000, thus maintaining the structural integrity of the program?

I think not. If you place the XCTL command in module 0000, you'll have to create a switch that module 1000 sets to tell module 0000 whether or not it should issue the XCTL command. Then, you'll have to provide for exceptional conditions in module 0000. That means you'll have to follow the XCTL command with code that formats and displays an error message. In short, if you code the XCTL command in module 0000, module 0000 becomes overly complicated and its primary purpose of responding to events is obscured. So in this case, it's best to compromise strict adherence to the rules of structured programming for the sake of program clarity and simplicity.

Objective

Given specifications for a menu program, design and code it using the program in this topic as a model.

Program INVMENU

Overview Displays a menu and lets the user select which program to run: customer inquiry, customer maintenance, or order entry.

Input/output specifications MENMAP1 Menu map

Processing specifications

1. The menu program is invoked when the user enters the trans-id MENU or when another program branches to it via an XCTL command with no communication area. Either way, it should respond by displaying the menu map.

2. On the menu map, the user enters an Action code. If the Action code is valid (1, 2, or 3), the program should XCTL to the inquiry program, the maintenance program, or the order entry program. If the action code is not valid, the program should display an error message.

3. If the user presses PF3 or PF12, the program should display the message "Session ended" and terminate by issuing a RETURN command without a trans-id.

Figure 10-1 Specifications for the menu program (part 1 of 2)

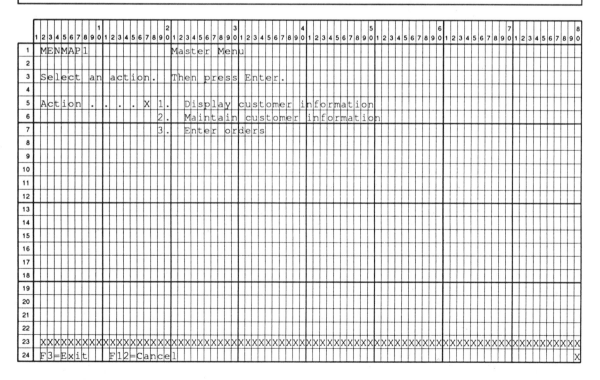

Figure 10-1 Specifications for the menu program (part 2 of 2)

Event	Response
Start the program	Display the menu map.
PF3	Display a termination message and end.
PF12	Display a termination message and end.
Enter	If the action code is 1, XCTL to the inquiry program. If the action code is 2, XCTL to the maintenance program. If the action code is 3, XCTL to the order entry program. Otherwise, display an error message.
Clear	Redisplay the menu map.
PA1, PA2, or PA3	Ignore the key.
Any other key	Display an appropriate error message.

Figure 10-2 An event/response chart for the menu program

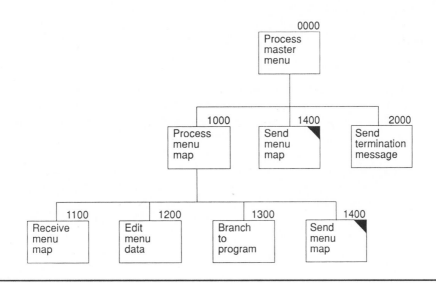

Figure 10-3 Structure chart for the menu program

```
          PRINT NOGEN
MENSET1   DFHMSD TYPE=&SYSPARM,                                          X
                 LANG=COBOL,                                            X
                 MODE=INOUT,                                            X
                 TERM=3270-2,                                           X
                 CTRL=FREEKB,                                           X
                 STORAGE=AUTO,                                          X
                 DSATTS=(COLOR,HILIGHT),                                X
                 MAPATTS=(COLOR,HILIGHT),                               X
                 TIOAPFX=YES
*****************************************************************
MENMAP1   DFHMDI SIZE=(24,80),                                          X
                 LINE=1,                                                X
                 COLUMN=1
*****************************************************************
          DFHMDF POS=(1,1),                                            X
                 LENGTH=7,                                             X
                 ATTRB=(NORM,PROT),                                    X
                 COLOR=BLUE,                                           X
                 INITIAL='MENMAP1'
          DFHMDF POS=(1,20),                                           X
                 LENGTH=11,                                            X
                 ATTRB=(NORM,PROT),                                    X
                 COLOR=BLUE,                                           X
                 INITIAL='Master Menu'
*****************************************************************
          DFHMDF POS=(3,1),                                            X
                 LENGTH=36,                                            X
                 ATTRB=(NORM,PROT),                                    X
                 COLOR=GREEN,                                          X
                 INITIAL='Select an action.  Then press Enter.'
          DFHMDF POS=(5,1),                                            X
                 LENGTH=14,                                            X
                 ATTRB=(NORM,PROT),                                    X
                 COLOR=GREEN,                                          X
                 INITIAL='Action . . . .'
ACTION    DFHMDF POS=(5,16),                                           X
                 LENGTH=1,                                             X
                 ATTRB=(NORM,NUM),                                     X
                 COLOR=TURQUOISE,                                      X
                 INITIAL='_'
          DFHMDF POS=(5,18),                                           X
                 LENGTH=32,                                            X
                 ATTRB=(NORM,ASKIP),                                   X
                 COLOR=NEUTRAL,                                        X
                 INITIAL='1.  Display customer information'
          DFHMDF POS=(6,18),                                           X
                 LENGTH=33,                                            X
                 ATTRB=(NORM,PROT),                                    X
                 COLOR=NEUTRAL,                                        X
                 INITIAL='2.  Maintain customer information'
          DFHMDF POS=(7,18),                                           X
                 LENGTH=16,                                            X
                 ATTRB=(NORM,PROT),                                    X
                 COLOR=NEUTRAL,                                        X
                 INITIAL='3.  Enter orders'
```

Figure 10-4 Mapset listing for the menu program (part 1 of 2)

```
******************************************************************
MESSAGE   DFHMDF POS=(23,1),                                        X
                 LENGTH=79,                                         X
                 COLOR=YELLOW,                                      X
                 ATTRB=(BRT,PROT)
          DFHMDF POS=(24,1),                                        X
                 LENGTH=20,                                         X
                 ATTRB=(NORM,PROT),                                 X
                 COLOR=BLUE,                                        X
                 INITIAL='F3=Exit    F12=Cancel'
DUMMY     DFHMDF POS=(24,79),                                       X
                 LENGTH=1,                                          X
                 ATTRB=(DRK,PROT,FSET),                             X
                 INITIAL=' '
******************************************************************
          DFHMSD TYPE=FINAL
          END
```

Figure 10-4 Mapset listing for the menu program (part 2 of 2)

```
01   MENMAP1I.
     02    FILLER     PIC X(12).
     02    ACTIONL    PIC S9(4) COMP.
     02    ACTIONF    PIC X.
     02    FILLER REDEFINES ACTIONF.
      03   ACTIONA    PIC X.
     02    FILLER     PIC X(0002).
     02    ACTIONI    PIC X(0001).
     02    MESSAGEL   PIC S9(4) COMP.
     02    MESSAGEF   PIC X.
     02    FILLER REDEFINES MESSAGEF.
      03   MESSAGEA   PIC X.
     02    FILLER     PIC X(0002).
     02    MESSAGEI   PIC X(0079).
     02    DUMMYL     PIC S9(4) COMP.
     02    DUMMYF     PIC X.
     02    FILLER REDEFINES DUMMYF.
      03   DUMMYA     PIC X.
     02    FILLER     PIC X(0002).
     02    DUMMYI     PIC X(0001).
01   MENMAP1O REDEFINES MENMAP1I.
     02    FILLER     PIC X(12).
     02    FILLER     PIC X(3).
     02    ACTIONC    PIC X.
     02    ACTIONH    PIC X.
     02    ACTIONO    PIC X(0001).
     02    FILLER     PIC X(3).
     02    MESSAGEC   PIC X.
     02    MESSAGEH   PIC X.
     02    MESSAGEO   PIC X(0079).
     02    FILLER     PIC X(3).
     02    DUMMYC     PIC X.
     02    DUMMYH     PIC X.
     02    DUMMYO     PIC X(0001).
```

Figure 10-5 BMS-generated symbolic map for the menu program

```
 IDENTIFICATION   DIVISION.
*
 PROGRAM-ID.  INVMENU.
*
 ENVIRONMENT DIVISION.
*
 DATA DIVISION.
*
 WORKING-STORAGE SECTION.
*
 01   SWITCHES.
*
     05   VALID-DATA-SW          PIC X      VALUE 'Y'.
          88   VALID-DATA                   VALUE 'Y'.
*
 01   FLAGS.
*
     05   SEND-FLAG              PIC X.
          88   SEND-ERASE                   VALUE '1'.
          88   SEND-DATAONLY                VALUE '2'.
          88   SEND-DATAONLY-ALARM          VALUE '3'.
*
 01   PROGRAM-TABLE.
*
     05   PROGRAM-LIST.
          10   PROGRAM-1         PIC X(8)   VALUE 'CUSTINQ1'.
          10   PROGRAM-2         PIC X(8)   VALUE 'CUSTMNT1'.
          10   PROGRAM-3         PIC X(8)   VALUE 'ORDRENT '.
     05   PROGRAM-NAME           REDEFINES PROGRAM-LIST
                                 OCCURS 3
                                 PIC X(8).
*
 01   ACTION-ALPHA.
*
     05   ACTION-NUM             PIC 9.
*
 01   END-OF-SESSION-MESSAGE     PIC X(13) VALUE 'Session ended'.
*
 01   RESPONSE-CODE             PIC S9(8) COMP.
*
 01   COMMUNICATION-AREA        PIC X.
*
 COPY MENSET1.
*
 COPY DFHAID.
*
 COPY ATTR.
*
 LINKAGE SECTION.
*
 01   DFHCOMMAREA               PIC X.
```

Figure 10-6 Source listing for the menu program (part 1 of 3)

```
/
 PROCEDURE DIVISION.
*
 0000-PROCESS-MASTER-MENU.
*
     EVALUATE TRUE

         WHEN EIBCALEN = ZERO
             MOVE LOW-VALUE TO MENMAP1O
             MOVE -1 TO ACTIONL
             SET SEND-ERASE TO TRUE
             PERFORM 1400-SEND-MENU-MAP

         WHEN EIBAID = DFHCLEAR
             MOVE LOW-VALUE TO MENMAP1O
             MOVE -1 TO ACTIONL
             SET SEND-ERASE TO TRUE
             PERFORM 1400-SEND-MENU-MAP

         WHEN EIBAID = DFHPA1 OR DFHPA2 OR DFHPA3
             CONTINUE

         WHEN EIBAID = DFHPF3 OR DFHPF12
             PERFORM 2000-SEND-TERMINATION-MESSAGE
             EXEC CICS
                 RETURN
             END-EXEC

         WHEN EIBAID = DFHENTER
             PERFORM 1000-PROCESS-MENU-MAP

         WHEN OTHER
             MOVE 'Invalid key pressed.' TO MESSAGEO
             MOVE -1 TO ACTIONL
             SET SEND-DATAONLY-ALARM TO TRUE
             PERFORM 1400-SEND-MENU-MAP

     END-EVALUATE.

     EXEC CICS
         RETURN TRANSID('MENU')
                COMMAREA(COMMUNICATION-AREA)
                LENGTH(1)
     END-EXEC.
*
 1000-PROCESS-MENU-MAP.
*
     PERFORM 1100-RECEIVE-MENU-MAP.
     PERFORM 1200-EDIT-MENU-DATA.
     IF VALID-DATA
         PERFORM 1300-BRANCH-TO-PROGRAM.
     SET SEND-DATAONLY-ALARM TO TRUE.
     PERFORM 1400-SEND-MENU-MAP.
```

Figure 10-6   Source listing for the menu program (part 2 of 3)

```
/
 1100-RECEIVE-MENU-MAP.
*
     EXEC CICS
         RECEIVE MAP('MENMAP1')
                 MAPSET('MENSET1')
                 INTO(MENMAP1I)
     END-EXEC.
*
 1200-EDIT-MENU-DATA.
*
     IF ACTIONI NOT = '1' AND '2' AND '3'
         MOVE ATTR-REVERSE TO ACTIONH
         MOVE 'You must enter 1, 2, or 3.' TO MESSAGEO
         MOVE 'N' TO VALID-DATA-SW
     ELSE
         MOVE ACTIONI TO ACTION-ALPHA.
*
 1300-BRANCH-TO-PROGRAM.
*
     EXEC CICS
         XCTL PROGRAM(PROGRAM-NAME(ACTION-NUM))
              RESP(RESPONSE-CODE)
     END-EXEC.
     MOVE 'That program is not available.' TO MESSAGEO.
*
 1400-SEND-MENU-MAP.
*
     IF SEND-ERASE
         EXEC CICS
             SEND MAP('MENMAP1')
                  MAPSET('MENSET1')
                  FROM(MENMAP1O)
                  ERASE
                  CURSOR
         END-EXEC
     ELSE IF SEND-DATAONLY
         EXEC CICS
             SEND MAP('MENMAP1')
                  MAPSET('MENSET1')
                  FROM(MENMAP1O)
                  DATAONLY
                  CURSOR
         END-EXEC
     ELSE IF SEND-DATAONLY-ALARM
         EXEC CICS
             SEND MAP('MENMAP1')
                  MAPSET('MENSET1')
                  FROM(MENMAP1O)
                  DATAONLY
                  CURSOR
                  ALARM
         END-EXEC.
*
 2000-SEND-TERMINATION-MESSAGE.
*
     EXEC CICS
         SEND TEXT FROM(END-OF-SESSION-MESSAGE)
                   ERASE
                   FREEKB
     END-EXEC.
```

Figure 10-6 Source listing for the menu program (part 3 of 3)

The customer maintenance program

Figure 10-7 (on pages 252-253) presents the specifications for the customer maintenance program, which lets the user maintain the customer master file by adding, changing, or deleting records. As you can see, the program uses two screens. On the first, the user enters a customer number and an action code (1 to add a customer, 2 to change a customer, or 3 to delete a customer). Then, the program displays the second screen. For an addition, the user types new data into the fields on this screen. For a change, the program displays data from the existing record and the user types any changes. And for a deletion, the program displays data from the existing record so the user can verify that he or she is deleting the correct record.

Figures 10-8 and 10-9 present the design for this program. Figure 10-8 (on page 254) shows the structure chart I derived from the event/response chart in figure 10-9 (on page 256). Because I presented the design for this program in chapter 7, I won't review it in detail here. However, I do want to remind you of the four contexts the program uses to interpret input events. Whenever the key map is displayed on the screen, the "Get key" context is current. Whenever the data map is displayed, the context is "Add customer," "Change customer," or "Delete customer," depending on the action code the user entered on the previous key map.

The mapset

Figure 10-10 (on pages 257-260) is the mapset for this program. Although this mapset is straightforward, I want you to notice three things about it. First, it contains two map definitions: one (MNTMAP1) for the key map, the other (MNTMAP2) for the data map. Whenever you include more than one map in a mapset, you must be sure to use unique names for all fields within the mapset. Since both maps have a customer number field, I used the names CUSTNO1 and CUSTNO2 to avoid confusion. And since both maps have a message field, I used the names MSG1 and MSG2.

Second, notice that the input fields in MNTMAP2 all specify the FSET attribute. That way, they will always be transmitted to the program, whether or not the user enters data into them. This is probably not the most efficient way to handle screen transmission for this program, but it is the most straightforward. At this point, I'd rather you concentrate on learning more basic aspects of CICS programming than the nuances of efficient data transmission.

Third, notice that the instructions for MNTMAP2 are not defined as a constant. Instead, I created a 79-byte field that the program can change by moving a value to INSTR2O. This is necessary because the instructions that appear on the data map depend on whether the user is entering data for a new customer, changing data for an existing customer, or confirming a deletion.

Figure 10-11 (on pages 261-263) shows the BMS-generated copy member for this mapset. Notice that this copy member contains four 01-level group items. The first two, MNTMAP1I and MNTMAP1O, are for the first map in the mapset (MNTMAP1). The second two, MNTMAP2I and MNTMAP2O, are for the second map (MNTMAP2).

The source listing

Figure 10-12 (on pages 264-272) shows the source listing for the maintenance program. If you understand the program design presented in figures 10-8 and 10-9, you should have little trouble understanding how this program works.

How the maintenance program manages its event context

The key to understanding how the maintenance program works is understanding how it manages its response to various input events in their contexts. When you first look at module 0000, you may be intimidated by the EVALUATE statement. After all, this single statement is more than 50 lines long. However, this EVALUATE statement is easy to understand when you consider how closely it corresponds to the event/response chart in figure 10-8. In short, each WHEN clause represents the program's response to one input event. Taken by itself, each of these WHEN clauses is easy enough to understand.

The maintenance program uses the communication area field CA-CONTEXT-FLAG to keep track of the current context. Thus, for those events that can occur in one of several contexts, the WHEN clause includes a series of IF statements that evaluate CA-CONTEXT-FLAG. CA-CONTEXT-FLAG is set at appropriate points in the program, whenever the context changes.

The key WHEN clause in module 0000 is the one that responds to the Enter key:

```
WHEN EIBAID = DFHENTER
    IF PROCESS-KEY-MAP
        PERFORM 1000-PROCESS-KEY-MAP
    ELSE IF PROCESS-ADD-CUSTOMER
        PERFORM 2000-PROCESS-ADD-CUSTOMER
    ELSE IF PROCESS-CHANGE-CUSTOMER
        PERFORM 3000-PROCESS-CHANGE-CUSTOMER
    ELSE IF PROCESS-DELETE-CUSTOMER
        PERFORM 4000-PROCESS-DELETE-CUSTOMER
```

This WHEN clause invokes one of the program's second-level modules, depending on which context was current when the user pressed the Enter key. All of the other WHEN clauses in this EVALUATE statement deal with less common events, such as starting or ending the program or handling an unassigned function key.

How the maintenance program processes the key map

Module 1000 processes data from the key map using the typical receive-edit-send processing cycle. First, if performs module 1100 to receive the key map. Then, module 1200 edits the map data. If the data is valid, module 1400 is invoked to send the data map to the terminal. Otherwise, module 1500 sends the key map back to the terminal with an error message.

Notice the processing in module 1200, which edits the data entered in the key map. It begins by performing simple field edits to make sure both fields are entered. Then, it uses an EVALUATE statement to perform the edits specific to each action code. If the action code is 1, the specified customer must not already exist in the customer file. So module 1200 performs module 1300 to read the customer file, expecting the result to be a NOTFND condition. If NOTFND does not occur, an error message is issued. Similarly, if the action code is 2 or 3, the specified customer must already exist in the customer file. So module 1200 performs module 1300, this time expecting the result to be NORMAL.

Notice how this EVALUATE statement sets CA-CONTEXT-FLAG to reflect the program's new context. If the user selects action 1 and the record does not already exist, the PROCESS-ADD-CUSTOMER condition is set to true. If the user selects action 2 and the record exists, PROCESS-CHANGE-CUSTOMER is set to true. And if the user selects action 3 and the record exists, PROCESS-DELETE-CUSTOMER is set to true. In any other case, CA-CONTEXT-FLAG is left at its original setting of PROCESS-KEY-MAP.

There are four other things I want you to notice here. First, notice that when ACTIONI is 3 and the record to be deleted does exist, the program moves ATTR-PROT to the attribute bytes for each unprotected field on the data map. That way, when the program displays the customer data, the user won't be able to change it. Instead, he or she can examine the data to make sure that the correct record is going to be deleted.

Second, notice the INSPECT statements in modules 1100 and 1000. The INSPECT statement in module 1100 immediately follows the RECEIVE MAP command. It removes any underscores that were in any of the map's input fields. In module 1000, a similar INSPECT statement is used to replace any spaces with underscores before the data is sent back to the terminal.

Third, notice that when module 1300 reads a record from the customer file, it moves it to the field CA-CUSTOMER-RECORD in the communication area. Subsequent executions of the program can then read the customer record and compare it with the record stored in the communication area. If the two records aren't identical, it means another user has updated the record between this program's pseudo-conversational interactions. In that event, the change or deletion request should be denied and an appropriate error message should be displayed.

Finally, notice how modules 1400 and 1500 serve as general-purpose send modules for the key map and the data map. Both evaluate the field SEND-FLAG to determine which combination of options to use on the SEND MAP commands. For the customer map, only two combinations are required: SEND-ERASE and SEND-DATAONLY-ALARM. SEND-ERASE is used when the program changes from the key map to the data map, and SEND-DATAONLY-ALARM is used when an error has been detected in one of the data map's input fields.

For the key map, three SEND-FLAG settings are required: SEND-ERASE, SEND-ERASE-ALARM, and SEND-DATAONLY-ALARM. SEND-ERASE is used to display a new key map, and SEND-DATAONLY-ALARM is used when the user enters an invalid customer number or action code. SEND-ERASE-ALARM is used when module 3000 or 4000 reads a customer record and discovers that it's not the same as the customer record saved in the communication area. In that case, the module redisplays the key map with an appropriate error message.

How the maintenance program adds a new customer

Module 2000 is invoked to add a customer to the customer file. It performs module 2100 to receive the data map, then performs module 2200 to edit the customer data. Although module 2200 is long, it's not complicated. The only editing requirement for this program is that every field must be entered. If the data is valid, the program calls module 2300 to write a record to the customer file. Then, it sets the context to PROCESS-KEY-MAP and calls module 1500 to redisplay the key map. If the data is invalid, it moves low values to the output fields (since they're already displayed at the terminal, there's no point in sending them again), sets SEND-DATAONLY-ALARM to true, and calls module 1500 to send the data map.

The only complication to this processing occurs if the WRITE command detects the DUPREC condition. This can only happen if another user has added a record with the same key between pseudo-conversational interactions. If DUPREC is detected, module 2000 formats an appropriate error message and displays the key map, this time sounding the terminal alarm to draw the user's attention to this unusual error.

How the maintenance program changes an existing customer

Module 3000 is much like module 2000. It too performs module 2100 to receive the data map, then performs module 2200 to edit the data. However, instead of invoking module 2300 to write the record, it invokes module 3100 to read the record for update and module 3200 to rewrite the record.

The complication here, as before, is determining if something has happened to the record between pseudo-conversations. Module 3000 checks for this in two ways. First, if the NOTFND condition is detected by the READ/UPDATE command, it means that someone has deleted the record between executions. Second, if the record read by the READ/UPDATE command is not equal to the record previously read and saved in the communication area, it means that someone has changed the record between executions. Either way, the record is not updated. Instead, an error message is formatted and the key map is sent.

How the maintenance program deletes an existing customer

Module 4000 processes the delete function. Unlike the add and change functions, the delete function does not require that data be received from the terminal. So module 4000 does not call module 2100 or 2200. Instead, it calls module 3100 to read the record for update. If the record exists, and if it's identical to the record stored in the communication area, module 4100 is then called to delete the record. Otherwise, an error message is displayed.

Discussion
As you might guess, there are other ways to implement a maintenance program. For example, instead of requiring the user to enter an action code on the first screen, you could ask for just a customer number. Then, if the user enters a customer number that doesn't exist, you could assume that he or she wants to add a new customer. If the user enters a number that does exist, you could display the data and let the user update the record by typing changes and pressing the Enter key or delete the record by pressing a PF key. Alternatively, you could develop separate programs to add, change, and delete customers. In any event, the customer maintenance program presented here illustrates the basic requirements of any file maintenance program.

Objective

Given specifications for a file maintenance program, design and code it using the program in this topic as a model.

Program CUSTMNT1

Overview Maintains customer information in the customer master file by allowing the user to enter new customers, change existing customers, or delete existing customers.

Input/output specifications

CUSTMAS   Customer master file
MNTMAP1   Customer maintenance key map
MNTMAP2   Customer maintenance data map

Processing specifications

1. Control is transferred to this program via XCTL from the menu program INVMENU with no communication area. The user can also start the program by entering the trans-id MNT1. In either case, the program should respond by displaying the customer maintenance key map.

2. On the key map, the user selects a processing action (Add, Change, or Delete) and enters a customer number. Both the action field and the customer number field must be entered. If the user selects Add, the customer number entered must not exist in the file. For Change or Delete, the customer number must exist in the file.

3. If the user enters a valid combination of action and customer number, the program displays the customer maintenance data map. For an addition or a change request, all data fields must be entered. For a delete request, all fields should be set to protected so the user cannot enter changes.

4. If the user presses PF3 from either the key map or the data map, return to the menu program INVMENU by issuing an XCTL command. If the user presses PF12 from the key map, return to the menu program. However, if the user presses PF12 from the data map, redisplay the key map without processing any data that was entered.

5. For a change or deletion, maintain an image of the customer record in the communication area between program executions. If the record is changed in any way between program executions, notify the user and do not complete the change or delete operation.

Figure 10-7   Specifications for a maintenance program (part 1 of 2)

Map name ___MNTMAP1_____   Date ___5/1/92_____
Program name ___CUSTMNT1_____   Designer ___Doug Lowe_____

```
         1         2         3         4         5         6         7         8
 12345678901234567890123456789012345678901234567890123456789012345678901234567890
1  MNTMAP1              Customer Maintenance
2
3  Type a customer number.  Then select an action and press Enter.
4
5  Customer number. . . . . XXXXXX
6
7  Action . . . . . . . . . X  1. Add a new customer
8                              2. Change an existing customer
9                              3. Delete an existing customer
10
11
12
13
14
15
16
17
18
19
20
21
22
23 XXXXXXXXXXXXXXXXXXXXXXXXXXXXXXXXXXXXXXXXXXXXXXXXXXXXXXXXXXXXXXXXXXXXXXXXXXXXXXXX
24 F3=Exit    F12=Cancel                                                         X
```

Map name ___MNTMAP2_____   Date ___5/1/92_____
Program name ___CUSTMNT1_____   Designer ___Doug Lowe_____

```
         1         2         3         4         5         6         7         8
 12345678901234567890123456789012345678901234567890123456789012345678901234567890
1  MNTMAP2              Customer Maintenance
2
3  XXXXXXXXXXXXXXXXXXXXXXXXXXXXXXXXXXXXXXXXXXXXXXXXXXXXXXXXXXXXXXXXXXXXXXXXXXXXXXXX
4
5  Customer number. . . . : XXXXXX
6
7  Last name. . . . . . . XXXXXXXXXXXXXXXXXXXXXXXXXXXXX
8  First name . . . . . . XXXXXXXXXXXXXXXXXXXX
9  Address. . . . . . . . XXXXXXXXXXXXXXXXXXXXXXXXXXXXXX
10 City . . . . . . . . . XXXXXXXXXXXXXXXXXXXXX
11 State. . . . . . . . . XX
12 Zip Code . . . . . . . XXXXXXXXXX
13
14
15
16
17
18
19
20
21
22
23 XXXXXXXXXXXXXXXXXXXXXXXXXXXXXXXXXXXXXXXXXXXXXXXXXXXXXXXXXXXXXXXXXXXXXXXXXXXXXXXX
24 F3=Exit    F12=Cancel                                                         X
```

Figure 10-7 Specifications for a maintenance program (part 2 of 2)

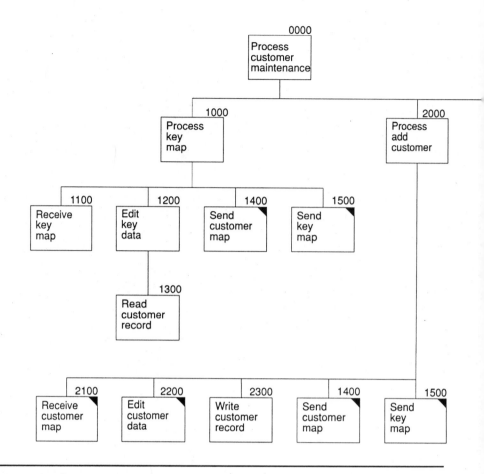

Figure 10-8 Structure chart for the maintenance program

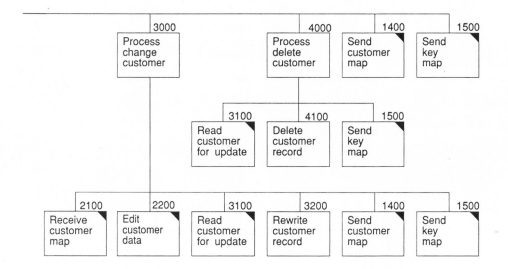

Event	Context	Response	New context
Start the program	n/a	Display the key map.	Get key
PF3	All	Transfer control to the menu program.	n/a
PF12	Get key	Transfer control to the menu program.	n/a
	Add customer Change customer Delete customer	Cancel the operation and display the key map.	Get key

Enter	Get key	Edit input data.
		If valid
		   read customer record
		   display data map
		
		else
		   display an error message.
			Add customer,
			Change customer, or
			Delete customer
			
			Get key

	Add customer	Edit input data.
		If valid
		   add the customer record
		   display the key map
		else
		   display an error message.
			Get key
			
			Add customer

	Change customer	Edit input data.
		If valid
		   change the customer record
		   display the key map
		else
		   display an error message.
			Get key
			
			Change customer

	Delete customer	Delete the customer record. Display the key map.	Get key
Clear	All	Redisplay the current map.	Unchanged
PA1, PA2, or PA3	All	Ignore the key.	Unchanged
Any other key	All	Display an appropriate error message.	Unchanged

Figure 10-9 An event/response chart for the maintenance program

```
           PRINT NOGEN
MNTSET1   DFHMSD TYPE=&SYSPARM,                                         X
                 LANG=COBOL,                                           X
                 MODE=INOUT,                                           X
                 TERM=3270-2,                                          X
                 CTRL=FREEKB,                                          X
                 STORAGE=AUTO,                                         X
                 DSATTS=(COLOR,HILIGHT),                               X
                 MAPATTS=(COLOR,HILIGHT),                              X
                 TIOAPFX=YES
***********************************************************************
MNTMAP1   DFHMDI SIZE=(24,80),                                         X
                 LINE=1,                                               X
                 COLUMN=1
***********************************************************************
          DFHMDF POS=(1,1),                                           X
                 LENGTH=7,                                            X
                 ATTRB=(NORM,PROT),                                   X
                 COLOR=BLUE,                                          X
                 INITIAL='MNTMAP1'
          DFHMDF POS=(1,20),                                          X
                 LENGTH=20,                                           X
                 ATTRB=(NORM,PROT),                                   X
                 COLOR=BLUE,                                          X
                 INITIAL='Customer Maintenance'
***********************************************************************
          DFHMDF POS=(3,1),                                           X
                 LENGTH=63,                                           X
                 ATTRB=(NORM,PROT),                                   X
                 COLOR=GREEN,                                         X
                 INITIAL='Type a customer number.  Then select an action X
                 and press Enter.'
          DFHMDF POS=(5,1),                                           X
                 LENGTH=24,                                           X
                 ATTRB=(NORM,PROT),                                   X
                 COLOR=GREEN,                                         X
                 INITIAL='Customer number. . . . .'
CUSTNO1   DFHMDF POS=(5,26),                                          X
                 LENGTH=6,                                            X
                 ATTRB=(NORM,UNPROT,FSET,IC),                         X
                 COLOR=TURQUOISE,                                     X
                 INITIAL='_____'
          DFHMDF POS=(5,33),                                          X
                 LENGTH=1,                                            X
                 ATTRB=ASKIP
          DFHMDF POS=(7,1),                                           X
                 LENGTH=24,                                           X
                 ATTRB=(NORM,PROT),                                   X
                 COLOR=GREEN,                                         X
                 INITIAL='Action . . . . . . . . .'
ACTION    DFHMDF POS=(7,26),                                          X
                 LENGTH=1,                                            X
                 ATTRB=(NORM,UNPROT,FSET),                            X
                 COLOR=TURQUOISE,                                     X
                 INITIAL='_'
          DFHMDF POS=(7,28),                                          X
                 LENGTH=21,                                           X
                 ATTRB=(NORM,ASKIP),                                  X
                 COLOR=NEUTRAL,                                       X
                 INITIAL='1. Add a new customer'
```

Figure 10-10   Mapset listing for the maintenance program (part 1 of 4)

```
          DFHMDF POS=(8,28),                                               X
                 LENGTH=30,                                                X
                 ATTRB=(NORM,ASKIP),                                       X
                 COLOR=NEUTRAL,                                            X
                 INITIAL='2. Change an existing customer'
          DFHMDF POS=(9,28),                                               X
                 LENGTH=21,                                                X
                 ATTRB=(NORM,ASKIP),                                       X
                 COLOR=NEUTRAL,                                            X
                 INITIAL='3. Delete an existing customer'
MSG1      DFHMDF POS=(23,1),                                               X
                 LENGTH=79,                                                X
                 ATTRB=(BRT,PROT),                                         X
                 COLOR=YELLOW
          DFHMDF POS=(24,1),                                               X
                 LENGTH=20,                                                X
                 ATTRB=(NORM,PROT),                                        X
                 COLOR=BLUE,                                               X
                 INITIAL='F3=Exit    F12=Cancel'
DUMMY1    DFHMDF POS=(24,79),                                              X
                 LENGTH=1,                                                 X
                 ATTRB=(DRK,PROT,FSET),                                    X
                 INITIAL=' '
*********************************************************************
MNTMAP2   DFHMDI SIZE=(24,80),                                            X
                 LINE=1,                                                  X
                 COLUMN=1
*********************************************************************
          DFHMDF POS=(1,1),                                               X
                 LENGTH=7,                                                X
                 ATTRB=(NORM,PROT),                                       X
                 COLOR=BLUE,                                              X
                 INITIAL='MNTMAP2'
          DFHMDF POS=(1,20),                                              X
                 LENGTH=20,                                               X
                 ATTRB=(NORM,PROT),                                       X
                 COLOR=BLUE,                                              X
                 INITIAL='Customer Maintenance'
*********************************************************************
INSTR2    DFHMDF POS=(3,1),                                               X
                 LENGTH=79,                                               X
                 ATTRB=(NORM,PROT),                                       X
                 COLOR=GREEN
          DFHMDF POS=(5,1),                                               X
                 LENGTH=24,                                               X
                 ATTRB=(NORM,PROT),                                       X
                 COLOR=GREEN,                                             X
                 INITIAL='Customer number. . . . :'
CUSTNO2   DFHMDF POS=(5,26),                                              X
                 LENGTH=6,                                                X
                 ATTRB=(NORM,PROT,FSET,IC),                               X
                 COLOR=TURQUOISE
*********************************************************************
          DFHMDF POS=(7,1),                                               X
                 LENGTH=24,                                               X
                 ATTRB=(NORM,PROT),                                       X
                 COLOR=GREEN,                                             X
                 INITIAL='Last name. . . . . . . .'
LNAME     DFHMDF POS=(7,26),                                              X
                 LENGTH=30,                                               X
                 ATTRB=(NORM,UNPROT,FSET),                                X
                 COLOR=TURQUOISE
```

Figure 10-10   Mapset listing for the maintenance program (part 2 of 4)

```
          DFHMDF POS=(7,57),                                        X
                 LENGTH=1,                                          X
                 ATTRB=ASKIP
*********************************************************************
          DFHMDF POS=(8,1),                                         X
                 LENGTH=24,                                         X
                 ATTRB=(NORM,PROT),                                 X
                 COLOR=GREEN,                                       X
                 INITIAL='First name . . . . . . .'
FNAME     DFHMDF POS=(8,26),                                        X
                 LENGTH=20,                                         X
                 ATTRB=(NORM,UNPROT,FSET),                          X
                 COLOR=TURQUOISE
          DFHMDF POS=(8,47),                                        X
                 LENGTH=1,                                          X
                 ATTRB=ASKIP
*********************************************************************
          DFHMDF POS=(9,1),                                         X
                 LENGTH=24,                                         X
                 ATTRB=(NORM,PROT),                                 X
                 COLOR=GREEN,                                       X
                 INITIAL='Address. . . . . . . . .'
ADDR      DFHMDF POS=(9,26),                                        X
                 LENGTH=30,                                         X
                 ATTRB=(NORM,UNPROT,FSET),                          X
                 COLOR=TURQUOISE
          DFHMDF POS=(9,57),                                        X
                 LENGTH=1,                                          X
                 ATTRB=ASKIP
*********************************************************************
          DFHMDF POS=(10,1),                                        X
                 LENGTH=24,                                         X
                 ATTRB=(NORM,PROT),                                 X
                 COLOR=GREEN,                                       X
                 INITIAL='City . . . . . . . . . .'
CITY      DFHMDF POS=(10,26),                                       X
                 LENGTH=20,                                         X
                 ATTRB=(NORM,UNPROT,FSET),                          X
                 COLOR=TURQUOISE
          DFHMDF POS=(10,47),                                       X
                 LENGTH=1,                                          X
                 ATTRB=ASKIP
*********************************************************************
          DFHMDF POS=(11,1),                                        X
                 LENGTH=24,                                         X
                 ATTRB=(NORM,PROT),                                 X
                 COLOR=GREEN,                                       X
                 INITIAL='State. . . . . . . . . .'
STATE     DFHMDF POS=(11,26),                                       X
                 LENGTH=2,                                          X
                 ATTRB=(NORM,UNPROT,FSET),                          X
                 COLOR=TURQUOISE
          DFHMDF POS=(11,29),                                       X
                 LENGTH=1,                                          X
                 ATTRB=ASKIP
*********************************************************************
          DFHMDF POS=(12,1),                                        X
                 LENGTH=24,                                         X
                 ATTRB=(NORM,PROT),                                 X
                 COLOR=GREEN,                                       X
                 INITIAL='Zip Code . . . . . . . .'
```

Figure 10-10 Mapset listing for the maintenance program (part 3 of 4)

```
ZIPCODE   DFHMDF POS=(12,26),                                          X
                 LENGTH=10,                                            X
                 ATTRB=(NORM,UNPROT,FSET),                             X
                 COLOR=TURQUOISE
          DFHMDF POS=(12,37),                                          X
                 LENGTH=1,                                             X
                 ATTRB=ASKIP
*************************************************************************
MSG2      DFHMDF POS=(23,1),                                           X
                 LENGTH=79,                                            X
                 ATTRB=(BRT,PROT),                                     X
                 COLOR=YELLOW
          DFHMDF POS=(24,1),                                           X
                 LENGTH=20,                                            X
                 ATTRB=(NORM,PROT),                                    X
                 COLOR=BLUE,                                           X
                 INITIAL='F3=Exit    F12=Cancel'
DUMMY2    DFHMDF POS=(24,79),                                          X
                 LENGTH=1,                                             X
                 ATTRB=(DRK,PROT,FSET),                                X
                 INITIAL=' '
*************************************************************************
          DFHMSD TYPE=FINAL
          END
```

Figure 10-10   Mapset listing for the maintenance program (part 4 of 4)

```
01   MNTMAP1I.
     02   FILLER     PIC X(12).
     02   CUSTNO1L   PIC S9(4) COMP.
     02   CUSTNO1F   PIC X.
     02   FILLER REDEFINES CUSTNO1F.
      03   CUSTNO1A   PIC X.
     02   FILLER     PIC X(0002).
     02   CUSTNO1I   PIC X(0006).
     02   ACTIONL    PIC S9(4) COMP.
     02   ACTIONF    PIC X.
     02   FILLER REDEFINES ACTIONF.
      03   ACTIONA    PIC X.
     02   FILLER     PIC X(0002).
     02   ACTIONI    PIC X(0001).
     02   MSG1L      PIC S9(4) COMP.
     02   MSG1F      PIC X.
     02   FILLER REDEFINES MSG1F.
      03   MSG1A      PIC X.
     02   FILLER     PIC X(0002).
     02   MSG1I      PIC X(0079).
     02   DUMMY1L    PIC S9(4) COMP.
     02   DUMMY1F    PIC X.
     02   FILLER REDEFINES DUMMY1F.
      03   DUMMY1A    PIC X.
     02   FILLER     PIC X(0002).
     02   DUMMY1I    PIC X(0001).
01   MNTMAP1O REDEFINES MNTMAP1I.
     02   FILLER     PIC X(12).
     02   FILLER     PIC X(3).
     02   CUSTNO1C   PIC X.
     02   CUSTNO1H   PIC X.
     02   CUSTNO1O   PIC X(0006).
     02   FILLER     PIC X(3).
     02   ACTIONC    PIC X.
     02   ACTIONH    PIC X.
     02   ACTIONO    PIC X(0001).
     02   FILLER     PIC X(3).
     02   MSG1C      PIC X.
     02   MSG1H      PIC X.
     02   MSG1O      PIC X(0079).
     02   FILLER     PIC X(3).
     02   DUMMY1C    PIC X.
     02   DUMMY1H    PIC X.
     02   DUMMY1O    PIC X(0001).
01   MNTMAP2I.
     02   FILLER     PIC X(12).
     02   INSTR2L    PIC S9(4) COMP.
     02   INSTR2F    PIC X.
     02   FILLER REDEFINES INSTR2F.
      03   INSTR2A    PIC X.
     02   FILLER     PIC X(0002).
     02   INSTR2I    PIC X(0079).
     02   CUSTNO2L   PIC S9(4) COMP.
     02   CUSTNO2F   PIC X.
     02   FILLER REDEFINES CUSTNO2F.
      03   CUSTNO2A   PIC X.
     02   FILLER     PIC X(0002).
     02   CUSTNO2I   PIC X(0006).
     02   LNAMEL     PIC S9(4) COMP.
     02   LNAMEF     PIC X.
     02   FILLER REDEFINES LNAMEF.
      03   LNAMEA     PIC X.
     02   FILLER     PIC X(0002).
     02   LNAMEI     PIC X(0030).
```

Figure 10-11   BMS-generated symbolic map for the maintenance program (part 1 of 3)

```
02    FNAMEL    PIC S9(4) COMP.
02    FNAMEF    PIC X.
02    FILLER REDEFINES FNAMEF.
 03   FNAMEA    PIC X.
02    FILLER    PIC X(0002).
02    FNAMEI    PIC X(0020).
02    ADDRL     PIC S9(4) COMP.
02    ADDRF     PIC X.
02    FILLER REDEFINES ADDRF.
 03   ADDRA     PIC X.
02    FILLER    PIC X(0002).
02    ADDRI     PIC X(0030).
02    CITYL     PIC S9(4) COMP.
02    CITYF     PIC X.
02    FILLER REDEFINES CITYF.
 03   CITYA     PIC X.
02    FILLER    PIC X(0002).
02    CITYI     PIC X(0020).
02    STATEL    PIC S9(4) COMP.
02    STATEF    PIC X.
02    FILLER REDEFINES STATEF.
 03   STATEA    PIC X.
02    FILLER    PIC X(0002).
02    STATEI    PIC X(0002).
02    ZIPCODEL  PIC S9(4) COMP.
02    ZIPCODEF  PIC X.
02    FILLER REDEFINES ZIPCODEF.
 03   ZIPCODEA  PIC X.
02    FILLER    PIC X(0002).
02    ZIPCODEI  PIC X(0010).
02    MSG2L     PIC S9(4) COMP.
02    MSG2F     PIC X.
02    FILLER REDEFINES MSG2F.
 03   MSG2A     PIC X.
02    FILLER    PIC X(0002).
02    MSG2I     PIC X(0079).
02    DUMMY2L   PIC S9(4) COMP.
02    DUMMY2F   PIC X.
02    FILLER REDEFINES DUMMY2F.
 03   DUMMY2A   PIC X.
02    FILLER    PIC X(0002).
02    DUMMY2I   PIC X(0001).
01 MNTMAP2O REDEFINES MNTMAP2I.
02    FILLER    PIC X(12).
02    FILLER    PIC X(3).
02    INSTR2C   PIC X.
02    INSTR2H   PIC X.
02    INSTR2O   PIC X(0079).
02    FILLER    PIC X(3).
02    CUSTNO2C  PIC X.
02    CUSTNO2H  PIC X.
02    CUSTNO2O  PIC X(0006).
02    FILLER    PIC X(3).
02    LNAMEC    PIC X.
02    LNAMEH    PIC X.
02    LNAMEO    PIC X(0030).
02    FILLER    PIC X(3).
02    FNAMEC    PIC X.
02    FNAMEH    PIC X.
02    FNAMEO    PIC X(0020).
02    FILLER    PIC X(3).
02    ADDRC     PIC X.
02    ADDRH     PIC X.
02    ADDRO     PIC X(0030).
```

Figure 10-11   BMS-generated symbolic map for the maintenance program (part 2 of 3)

```
02    FILLER      PIC X(3).
02    CITYC       PIC X.
02    CITYH       PIC X.
02    CITYO       PIC X(0020).
02    FILLER      PIC X(3).
02    STATEC      PIC X.
02    STATEH      PIC X.
02    STATEO      PIC X(0002).
02    FILLER      PIC X(3).
02    ZIPCODEC    PIC X.
02    ZIPCODEH    PIC X.
02    ZIPCODEO    PIC X(0010).
02    FILLER      PIC X(3).
02    MSG2C       PIC X.
02    MSG2H       PIC X.
02    MSG2O       PIC X(0079).
02    FILLER      PIC X(3).
02    DUMMY2C     PIC X.
02    DUMMY2H     PIC X.
02    DUMMY2O     PIC X(0001).
```

Figure 10-11   BMS-generated symbolic map for the maintenance program (part 3 of 3)

```
IDENTIFICATION DIVISION.
*
PROGRAM-ID.  CUSTMNT1.
*
ENVIRONMENT DIVISION.
*
DATA DIVISION.
*
WORKING-STORAGE SECTION.
*
01   SWITCHES.
*
     05   VALID-DATA-SW               PIC X   VALUE 'Y'.
          88   VALID-DATA                     VALUE 'Y'.
*
01   FLAGS.
*
     05   SEND-FLAG                   PIC X.
          88   SEND-ERASE                     VALUE '1'.
          88   SEND-ERASE-ALARM               VALUE '2'.
          88   SEND-DATAONLY                  VALUE '3'.
          88   SEND-DATAONLY-ALARM            VALUE '4'.
*
01   WORK-FIELDS.
*
     05   RESPONSE-CODE               PIC S9(8) COMP.
*
01   COMMUNICATION-AREA.
*
     05   CA-CONTEXT-FLAG             PIC X.
          88   PROCESS-KEY-MAP                VALUE '1'.
          88   PROCESS-ADD-CUSTOMER           VALUE '2'.
          88   PROCESS-CHANGE-CUSTOMER        VALUE '3'.
          88   PROCESS-DELETE-CUSTOMER        VALUE '4'.
     05   CA-CUSTOMER-RECORD.
          10   CA-CUSTOMER-NUMBER     PIC X(6).
          10   FILLER                 PIC X(112).
*
COPY CUSTMAS.
*
COPY MNTSET1.
*
COPY DFHAID.
*
COPY ATTR.
*
COPY ERRPARM.
*
LINKAGE SECTION.
*
01   DFHCOMMAREA                     PIC X(119).
```

Figure 10-12 Source listing for the maintenance program (part 1 of 9)

```
/
 PROCEDURE DIVISION.
*
 0000-PROCESS-CUSTOMER-MAINT.
*
     MOVE DFHCOMMAREA TO COMMUNICATION-AREA.

     EVALUATE TRUE

         WHEN EIBCALEN = ZERO
             MOVE LOW-VALUE TO MNTMAP1O
             MOVE -1 TO CUSTNO1L
             SET SEND-ERASE TO TRUE
             PERFORM 1500-SEND-KEY-MAP
             SET PROCESS-KEY-MAP TO TRUE

         WHEN EIBAID = DFHPF3
             EXEC CICS
                 XCTL PROGRAM('INVMENU')
             END-EXEC

         WHEN EIBAID = DFHPF12
             IF PROCESS-KEY-MAP
                 EXEC CICS
                     XCTL PROGRAM('INVMENU')
                 END-EXEC
             ELSE
                 MOVE LOW-VALUE TO MNTMAP1O
                 MOVE -1 TO CUSTNO1L
                 SET SEND-ERASE TO TRUE
                 PERFORM 1500-SEND-KEY-MAP
                 SET PROCESS-KEY-MAP TO TRUE

         WHEN EIBAID = DFHCLEAR
             IF PROCESS-KEY-MAP
                 MOVE LOW-VALUE TO MNTMAP1O
                 MOVE -1 TO CUSTNO1L
                 SET SEND-ERASE TO TRUE
                 PERFORM 1500-SEND-KEY-MAP
             ELSE
                 MOVE LOW-VALUE TO MNTMAP2O
                 MOVE -1 TO CUSTNO2L
                 SET SEND-ERASE TO TRUE
                 PERFORM 1400-SEND-CUSTOMER-MAP

         WHEN EIBAID = DFHPA1 OR DFHPA2 OR DFHPA3
             CONTINUE

         WHEN EIBAID = DFHENTER
             IF PROCESS-KEY-MAP
                 PERFORM 1000-PROCESS-KEY-MAP
             ELSE IF PROCESS-ADD-CUSTOMER
                 PERFORM 2000-PROCESS-ADD-CUSTOMER
             ELSE IF PROCESS-CHANGE-CUSTOMER
                 PERFORM 3000-PROCESS-CHANGE-CUSTOMER
             ELSE IF PROCESS-DELETE-CUSTOMER
                 PERFORM 4000-PROCESS-DELETE-CUSTOMER
```

Figure 10-12   Source listing for the maintenance program (part 2 of 9)

```
/
                WHEN OTHER
                    IF PROCESS-KEY-MAP
                        MOVE LOW-VALUE TO MNTMAP10
                        MOVE -1 TO CUSTNO1L
                        MOVE 'That key is unassigned.' TO MSG10
                        SET SEND-DATAONLY-ALARM TO TRUE
                        PERFORM 1500-SEND-KEY-MAP
                    ELSE
                        MOVE LOW-VALUE TO MNTMAP20
                        MOVE -1 TO CUSTNO2L
                        MOVE 'That key is unassigned.' TO MSG20
                        SET SEND-DATAONLY-ALARM TO TRUE
                        PERFORM 1400-SEND-CUSTOMER-MAP

        END-EVALUATE.

        EXEC CICS
            RETURN TRANSID('MNT1')
                    COMMAREA(COMMUNICATION-AREA)
        END-EXEC.
*
 1000-PROCESS-KEY-MAP.
*
        PERFORM 1100-RECEIVE-KEY-MAP.
        PERFORM 1200-EDIT-KEY-DATA.
        IF VALID-DATA
            INSPECT CUSTOMER-MASTER-RECORD
                REPLACING ALL SPACE BY '_'
            MOVE CUSTNO1I       TO CUSTNO2O
            MOVE CM-LAST-NAME   TO LNAMEO
            MOVE CM-FIRST-NAME  TO FNAMEO
            MOVE CM-ADDRESS     TO ADDRO
            MOVE CM-CITY        TO CITYO
            MOVE CM-STATE       TO STATEO
            MOVE CM-ZIP-CODE    TO ZIPCODEO
            MOVE -1             TO LNAMEL
            SET SEND-ERASE TO TRUE
            PERFORM 1400-SEND-CUSTOMER-MAP
        ELSE
            MOVE LOW-VALUE TO CUSTNO1O
                             ACTIONO
            SET SEND-DATAONLY-ALARM TO TRUE
            PERFORM 1500-SEND-KEY-MAP.
*
 1100-RECEIVE-KEY-MAP.
*
        EXEC CICS
            RECEIVE MAP('MNTMAP1')
                    MAPSET('MNTSET1')
                    INTO(MNTMAP1I)
        END-EXEC.
        INSPECT MNTMAP1I
            REPLACING ALL '_' BY SPACE.
```

Figure 10-12 Source listing for the maintenance program (part 3 of 9)

```
/
 1200-EDIT-KEY-DATA.
*
     MOVE ATTR-NO-HIGHLIGHT TO ACTIONH
                           CUSTNO1H.

     IF ACTIONI NOT = '1' AND '2' AND '3'
         MOVE ATTR-REVERSE TO ACTIONH
         MOVE -1 TO ACTIONL
         MOVE 'Action must be 1, 2, or 3.' TO MSG10
         MOVE 'N' TO VALID-DATA-SW.

     IF       CUSTNO1L = ZERO
         OR CUSTNO1I = SPACE
         MOVE ATTR-REVERSE TO CUSTNO1H
         MOVE -1 TO CUSTNO1L
         MOVE 'You must enter a customer number.' TO MSG10
         MOVE 'N' TO VALID-DATA-SW.

     IF VALID-DATA
         EVALUATE ACTIONI
             WHEN '1'
                 PERFORM 1300-READ-CUSTOMER-RECORD
                 IF RESPONSE-CODE = DFHRESP(NOTFND)
                     MOVE 'Type information for new customer.  The
-                        'n Press Enter.' TO INSTR20
                     SET PROCESS-ADD-CUSTOMER TO TRUE
                     MOVE SPACE TO CUSTOMER-MASTER-RECORD
                 ELSE
                     MOVE 'That customer already exists.'
                         TO MSG10
                     MOVE 'N' TO VALID-DATA-SW
             WHEN '2'
                 PERFORM 1300-READ-CUSTOMER-RECORD
                 IF RESPONSE-CODE = DFHRESP(NORMAL)
                     MOVE 'Type changes.  Then press Enter.'
                         TO INSTR20
                     SET PROCESS-CHANGE-CUSTOMER TO TRUE
                 ELSE
                     MOVE 'That customer does not exist.' TO MSG10
                     MOVE 'N' TO VALID-DATA-SW
             WHEN '3'
                 PERFORM 1300-READ-CUSTOMER-RECORD
                 IF RESPONSE-CODE = DFHRESP(NORMAL)
                     MOVE 'Press Enter to delete this customer or
-                        'press F12 to cancel.' TO INSTR20
                     SET PROCESS-DELETE-CUSTOMER TO TRUE
                     MOVE ATTR-PROT TO LNAMEA
                                      FNAMEA
                                      ADDRA
                                      CITYA
                                      STATEA
                                      ZIPCODEA
                 ELSE
                     MOVE 'That customer does not exist.' TO MSG10
                     MOVE 'N' TO VALID-DATA-SW
         END-EVALUATE.
*
```

Figure 10-12   Source listing for the maintenance program (part 4 of 9)

```
/
 1300-READ-CUSTOMER-RECORD.
*
     EXEC CICS
         READ DATASET('CUSTMAS')
              INTO(CUSTOMER-MASTER-RECORD)
              RIDFLD(CUSTNO1I)
              RESP(RESPONSE-CODE)
     END-EXEC.
     IF        RESPONSE-CODE NOT = DFHRESP(NORMAL)
          AND  RESPONSE-CODE NOT = DFHRESP(NOTFND)
         GO TO 9999-TERMINATE-PROGRAM.
     MOVE CUSTOMER-MASTER-RECORD TO CA-CUSTOMER-RECORD.
*
 1400-SEND-CUSTOMER-MAP.
*
     EVALUATE TRUE
         WHEN SEND-ERASE
             EXEC CICS
                 SEND MAP('MNTMAP2')
                      MAPSET('MNTSET1')
                      FROM(MNTMAP2O)
                      ERASE
                      CURSOR
             END-EXEC
         WHEN SEND-DATAONLY-ALARM
             EXEC CICS
                 SEND MAP('MNTMAP2')
                      MAPSET('MNTSET1')
                      FROM(MNTMAP2O)
                      DATAONLY
                      ALARM
                      CURSOR
             END-EXEC
     END-EVALUATE.
*
 1500-SEND-KEY-MAP.
*
     EVALUATE TRUE
         WHEN SEND-ERASE
             EXEC CICS
                 SEND MAP('MNTMAP1')
                      MAPSET('MNTSET1')
                      FROM(MNTMAP1O)
                      ERASE
                      CURSOR
             END-EXEC
         WHEN SEND-ERASE-ALARM
             EXEC CICS
                 SEND MAP('MNTMAP1')
                      MAPSET('MNTSET1')
                      FROM(MNTMAP1O)
                      ERASE
                      ALARM
                      CURSOR
             END-EXEC
         WHEN SEND-DATAONLY-ALARM
             EXEC CICS
                 SEND MAP('MNTMAP1')
                      MAPSET('MNTSET1')
                      FROM(MNTMAP1O)
                      DATAONLY
                      ALARM
                      CURSOR
             END-EXEC
     END-EVALUATE.
```

Figure 10-12   Source listing for the maintenance program (part 5 of 9)

```
/
 2000-PROCESS-ADD-CUSTOMER.
*
     PERFORM 2100-RECEIVE-CUSTOMER-MAP.
     PERFORM 2200-EDIT-CUSTOMER-DATA.
     IF VALID-DATA
         PERFORM 2300-WRITE-CUSTOMER-RECORD
         IF RESPONSE-CODE = DFHRESP(NORMAL)
             MOVE 'Customer record added.' TO MSG10
             SET SEND-ERASE TO TRUE
         ELSE
             MOVE 'Another user has added a record with that custo
-                    'mer number.' TO MSG10
             SET SEND-ERASE-ALARM TO TRUE
         END-IF
         PERFORM 1500-SEND-KEY-MAP
         SET PROCESS-KEY-MAP TO TRUE
     ELSE
         MOVE LOW-VALUE TO LNAMEO
                          FNAMEO
                          ADDRO
                          CITYO
                          STATEO
                          ZIPCODEO
         SET SEND-DATAONLY-ALARM TO TRUE
         PERFORM 1400-SEND-CUSTOMER-MAP.
*
 2100-RECEIVE-CUSTOMER-MAP.
*
     EXEC CICS
         RECEIVE MAP('MNTMAP2')
                 MAPSET('MNTSET1')
                 INTO(MNTMAP2I)
     END-EXEC.
     INSPECT MNTMAP2I
         REPLACING ALL '_' BY SPACE.
*
 2200-EDIT-CUSTOMER-DATA.
*
     MOVE ATTR-NO-HIGHLIGHT TO ZIPCODEH
                             STATEH
                             CITYH
                             ADDRH
                             FNAMEH
                             LNAMEH.

     IF       ZIPCODEI = SPACE
         OR ZIPCODEL = ZERO
         MOVE ATTR-REVERSE TO ZIPCODEH
         MOVE -1 TO ZIPCODEL
         MOVE 'You must enter a zip code.' TO MSG20
         MOVE 'N' TO VALID-DATA-SW.

     IF       STATEI = SPACE
         OR STATEL = ZERO
         MOVE ATTR-REVERSE TO STATEH
         MOVE -1 TO STATEL
         MOVE 'You must enter a state.' TO MSG20
         MOVE 'N' TO VALID-DATA-SW.
```

Figure 10-12 Source listing for the maintenance program (part 6 of 9)

```
/
        IF        CITYI = SPACE
              OR CITYL = ZERO
           MOVE ATTR-REVERSE TO CITYH
           MOVE -1 TO CITYL
           MOVE 'You must enter a city.' TO MSG20
           MOVE 'N' TO VALID-DATA-SW.
        IF        ADDRI = SPACE
              OR ADDRL = ZERO
           MOVE ATTR-REVERSE TO ADDRH
           MOVE -1 TO ADDRL
           MOVE 'You must enter an address.' TO MSG20
           MOVE 'N' TO VALID-DATA-SW.

        IF        FNAMEI = SPACE
              OR FNAMEL = ZERO
           MOVE ATTR-REVERSE TO FNAMEH
           MOVE -1 TO FNAMEL
           MOVE 'You must enter a first name.' TO MSG20
           MOVE 'N' TO VALID-DATA-SW.

        IF        LNAMEI = SPACE
              OR LNAMEL = ZERO
           MOVE ATTR-REVERSE TO LNAMEH
           MOVE -1 TO LNAMEL
           MOVE 'You must enter a last name.' TO MSG20
           MOVE 'N' TO VALID-DATA-SW.
*
    2300-WRITE-CUSTOMER-RECORD.
*
        MOVE CUSTNO2I TO CM-CUSTOMER-NUMBER.
        MOVE LNAMEI   TO CM-LAST-NAME.
        MOVE FNAMEI   TO CM-FIRST-NAME.
        MOVE ADDRI    TO CM-ADDRESS.
        MOVE CITYI    TO CM-CITY.
        MOVE STATEI   TO CM-STATE.
        MOVE ZIPCODEI TO CM-ZIP-CODE.
        EXEC CICS
            WRITE DATASET('CUSTMAS')
                  FROM(CUSTOMER-MASTER-RECORD)
                  RIDFLD(CM-CUSTOMER-NUMBER)
                  RESP(RESPONSE-CODE)
        END-EXEC.
        IF        RESPONSE-CODE NOT = DFHRESP(NORMAL)
              AND RESPONSE-CODE NOT = DFHRESP(DUPREC)
           GO TO 9999-TERMINATE-PROGRAM.
*
    3000-PROCESS-CHANGE-CUSTOMER.
*
        PERFORM 2100-RECEIVE-CUSTOMER-MAP.
        PERFORM 2200-EDIT-CUSTOMER-DATA.
        IF VALID-DATA
           MOVE CUSTNO2I TO CM-CUSTOMER-NUMBER
           PERFORM 3100-READ-CUSTOMER-FOR-UPDATE
           IF RESPONSE-CODE = DFHRESP(NORMAL)
              IF CUSTOMER-MASTER-RECORD = CA-CUSTOMER-RECORD
                 PERFORM 3200-REWRITE-CUSTOMER-RECORD
                 MOVE 'Customer record updated.' TO MSG10
                 SET SEND-ERASE TO TRUE
              ELSE
                 MOVE 'Another user has updated the record.  Try a
                      'gain.' TO MSG10
                 SET SEND-ERASE-ALARM TO TRUE
```

Figure 10-12 Source listing for the maintenance program (part 7 of 9)

```
/
            ELSE
                MOVE 'Another user has deleted the record.' TO MSG10
                SET SEND-ERASE-ALARM TO TRUE
            END-IF
            PERFORM 1500-SEND-KEY-MAP
            SET PROCESS-KEY-MAP TO TRUE
        ELSE
            SET SEND-DATAONLY-ALARM TO TRUE
            PERFORM 1400-SEND-CUSTOMER-MAP.
*
 3100-READ-CUSTOMER-FOR-UPDATE.
*
        EXEC CICS
            READ DATASET('CUSTMAS')
                INTO(CUSTOMER-MASTER-RECORD)
                RIDFLD(CM-CUSTOMER-NUMBER)
                UPDATE
                RESP(RESPONSE-CODE)
        END-EXEC.
        IF        RESPONSE-CODE NOT = DFHRESP(NORMAL)
            AND RESPONSE-CODE NOT = DFHRESP(NOTFND)
            GO TO 9999-TERMINATE-PROGRAM.
*
 3200-REWRITE-CUSTOMER-RECORD.
*
        MOVE LNAMEI    TO CM-LAST-NAME.
        MOVE FNAMEI    TO CM-FIRST-NAME.
        MOVE ADDRI     TO CM-ADDRESS.
        MOVE CITYI     TO CM-CITY.
        MOVE STATEI    TO CM-STATE.
        MOVE ZIPCODEI TO CM-ZIP-CODE.
        EXEC CICS
            REWRITE DATASET('CUSTMAS')
                    FROM(CUSTOMER-MASTER-RECORD)
                    RESP(RESPONSE-CODE)
        END-EXEC.
        IF RESPONSE-CODE NOT = DFHRESP(NORMAL)
            GO TO 9999-TERMINATE-PROGRAM.
*
 4000-PROCESS-DELETE-CUSTOMER.
*
        MOVE CA-CUSTOMER-NUMBER TO CM-CUSTOMER-NUMBER.
        PERFORM 3100-READ-CUSTOMER-FOR-UPDATE.
        IF RESPONSE-CODE = DFHRESP(NORMAL)
            IF CUSTOMER-MASTER-RECORD = CA-CUSTOMER-RECORD
                PERFORM 4100-DELETE-CUSTOMER-RECORD
                MOVE 'Customer deleted.' TO MSG10
                SET SEND-ERASE TO TRUE
            ELSE
                MOVE 'Another user has updated the record.  Try again
-                   '.' TO MSG10
                SET SEND-ERASE-ALARM TO TRUE
        ELSE
            MOVE 'Another user has deleted the record.' TO MSG10
            SET SEND-ERASE-ALARM TO TRUE.
        PERFORM 1500-SEND-KEY-MAP.
        SET PROCESS-KEY-MAP TO TRUE.
*
 4100-DELETE-CUSTOMER-RECORD.
*
        EXEC CICS
            DELETE DATASET('CUSTMAS')
                    RESP(RESPONSE-CODE)
        END-EXEC.
```

Figure 10-12 Source listing for the maintenance program (part 8 of 9)

```
/
        IF          RESPONSE-CODE NOT = DFHRESP(NORMAL)
            GO TO 9999-TERMINATE-PROGRAM.
*
 9999-TERMINATE-PROGRAM.
*
        MOVE EIBRESP  TO ERR-RESP.
        MOVE EIBRESP2 TO ERR-RESP2.
        MOVE EIBTRNID TO ERR-TRNID.
        MOVE EIBRSRCE TO ERR-RSRCE.
        EXEC CICS
            XCTL PROGRAM('SYSERR')
                COMMAREA(ERROR-PARAMETERS)
        END-EXEC.
```

Figure 10-12 Source listing for the maintenance program (part 9 of 9)

The order entry program

Figure 10-13 (on pages 281-282) presents the specifications for an order entry program. Simply put, this program accepts orders from the user and writes them to the order file, a VSAM indexed file keyed by invoice number. The data for each order consists of a customer number, an optional purchase order number, and up to 10 line items. Each line item must include a product code and a quantity. In addition, the user can enter a net price for a line item to override the unit price stored in the product record.

After the user enters the data for an order, the program edits it. If the program detects no entry errors, it redisplays the order data so the user can sight-verify the order. On this verification screen, the entry fields are protected so the user cannot make changes. To post the order, the user presses the Enter key. Alternatively, the user can press PF4 to make corrections to the order before posting it. Or, the user can press PF12 to cancel the order altogether. When the user exits the order entry program, the program displays a message showing how many orders were entered before it returns to the menu.

The editing requirements for this program are more demanding than for the programs you've seen so far. To begin, the customer number must be in the customer file, and any product codes entered must be in the product file. In addition, any quantity and net price fields entered must be valid numbers. Beyond these simple requirements, the program has a number of cross-validation editing requirements. For example, if the user enters a product code, he or she must also enter a quantity. Similarly, if the user enters a quantity, he or she must also enter a product code. The net price field is optional, but if the user enters it, he or she must also enter a product code. Finally, the user must enter at least one line item.

Although this program could be implemented with two maps, I decided to use the same map for the entry screen and the verify screen. To display the verify screen, the program simply sets the attribute bytes of each entry field to protected. Then, to redisplay the entry screen, the program restores the attribute bytes to unprotected.

The design   Figure 10-14 (on page 283) shows the event/response chart I created as I designed this program. As you can see, I identified two event contexts, which correspond to the entry and verify operations of the program. The program's responses to three of the input events (PF12, Enter, and PF4) depend on which of these contexts is current. If the user presses PF12 when the context is "Process entry," the program returns to the menu; on the other hand, if the context is "Process verify," the program cancels the current order and redisplays the entry screen.

If the user presses Enter when the context is "Process entry," the program edits the input data. If the data is valid, the program displays the verify screen. To do that, it simply protects all the data entry fields and displays a message asking the user to confirm the order. Then, it changes the context to "Process verify." If the data is invalid, the program simply displays an error message without changing the context. If the user presses Enter when the context is "Process verify," the program posts the order, redisplays the entry screen, and changes the context to "Process entry."

If the user presses PF4 when the context is "Process entry," the program displays an "invalid key pressed" message, since PF4 has no meaning when the entry screen is displayed. But if the user presses PF4 when the context is "Process verify," the program redisplays the entry screen with the data entry fields unprotected and changes the context to "Process entry." That way, the user can make changes to the order data.

Figure 10-15 (on page 284) shows the structure chart I created for this program. I created modules 1000 and 2000 to handle the program's response to the Enter key for both contexts. The other program responses will be handled directly by module 0000.

Module 1000 is called when the user presses the Enter key after entering order data. It first calls module 1100 to receive the order data, then it calls module 1200 to edit the order data. If module 1200 indicates that the data is valid, module 1000 then calls module 1300 to format an invoice record, which will be passed forward to the next program execution via the communication area. Then, module 1400 is called to display the order map.

Because the editing requirements of this program are complex, module 1200 has several subordinates. First, I added a subordinate module (1210) to read a record from the customer file using the customer number entered by the user. Then, I added a module (1220) to edit each line item. This module will be invoked repeatedly with a PERFORM VARYING statement. It, in turn, calls module 1230 to read a record from the product file using the product code entered by the user.

Module 1400 also has subordinates. As before, this program uses a single send module to handle several variations of the SEND command for a single map. In this program, the send module has the added responsibility of setting and resetting the attribute bytes. To display the verify screen, module 1400 calls module 1410 to move protected attributes to the attribute byte fields of each entry field. To redisplay the entry screen, module 1400 calls module 1420 to restore those attribute fields to their original values. The operation of these modules will become apparent when you see the source listing, so don't worry if it isn't clear now.

Module 2000 is called when the user confirms an order by pressing the Enter key while the verify screen is displayed. Its operation is straightforward. Because the invoice record to be written was formatted by module 1300 and passed to this execution in the communication area, module 2000 doesn't need to receive data from the map. So it doesn't perform a receive module. Instead, it performs the GETINV subprogram to obtain the invoice number for the invoice record, then performs module 2100 to write the invoice record. Finally, it performs module 1400 to send a fresh entry map so the user can enter another order.

The mapset   Figure 10-16 (on pages 285-287) shows a portion of the BMS mapset I created for this program. Since the coding for the line items is repetitious, I include the coding for only the first one. The coding for the second through tenth line items is similar, but the field names are different (for example, PCODE2 instead of PCODE1) and the POS parameters are different.

For this program, I chose to discard the symbolic map BMS generated and create my own instead. That way, I can use an OCCURS clause to process the line item data efficiently. Figure 10-17 (on pages 288-289) shows the symbolic map I created. Notice how I used the OCCURS clause to create 10 groups of line item fields. Whenever you create your own symbolic map like this, it must have the same structure as the BMS-generated symbolic map. Thus, following the 12-byte filler item, I created five COBOL fields for each map field: a length field, an attribute field, an extended color attribute field, an extended highlighting attribute field, and the data field itself. (The color and highlight attribute fields are required because I specified DSATTS=(COLOR,HIGHLIGHT) in the DFHMSD macro for the mapset.)

Notice the coding I used for the QTY data field:

```
10   ORD-D-QTY                 PIC ZZZZ9
                               BLANK WHEN ZERO.
10   ORD-D-QTY-ALPHA           REDEFINES ORD-D-QTY
                               PIC X(5).
```

This coding simulates the effect of coding PICIN and PICOUT in the DFHMDF macro. It lets me access the field as alphanumeric (using ORD-D-QTY-ALPHA) so I can edit the input data. For output, I can move the edited quantity field to ORD-D-QTY so the quantity will be displayed right-justified with leading zeros suppressed. I used similar coding for the NET data field.

I hope you can appreciate the need to create your own symbolic map in this type of situation. BMS provides no convenient way to group these repeating line items, so it generates separate fields for each. As a result, the symbolic map BMS generated for this map is 12 pages long.

The source listing

Figure 10-18 (on pages 290-299) shows the source listing for the order entry program. As you can see, it includes a number of copy members. If you want to review the contents of the first four of these copy members (INVOICE, CUSTMAS, PRODUCT, and INVCTL), you can look back to figure 9-4. You just saw the copy member for the symbolic map ORDSET1 in figure 10-17. The other three copy members appear in different figures: DFHAID is in figure 6-8, ATTR is in figure 8-18, and ERRPARM is in figure 8-36.

Before I describe the Procedure Division code, I want you to notice two things in the Data Division. First, notice that I defined two flags. As in the other model programs, SEND-FLAG is used to tell the general-purpose send module which form of the SEND MAP command to use. In this program, I also created ATTRIBUTE-SET-FLAG, which tells the send module whether to set or reset the attributes for the order screen. When the program needs to display the verify screen, it sets SET-ATTRIBUTES to true before calling module 1400. To redisplay the entry screen, it sets RESET-ATTRIBUTES to true before calling module 1400.

Second, notice the fields in the communication area. As usual, the communication area contains CA-CONTEXT-FLAG, which keeps track of the program's current context. In addition, the communication area contains a field named CA-TOTAL-ORDERS. The order entry program uses this field to keep a count of the number of orders entered by the user. The communication area also contains a complete copy of the invoice record. When module 1300 formats an invoice record, it stores it here. Then, when module 2000 prepares to write the invoice record, it retrieves it from here.

The last group in the communication area, CA-FIELDS-ENTERED, contains a switch for each data entry field on the screen. When the program detects that the user has entered data into a field, the corresponding switch is set. As you'll see, these switches are used in several places throughout the program, particularly in modules 1410 and 1420.

Module 0000: Process Order Entry

As in the other sample programs I've presented, module 0000 contains the program's event-processing logic in an EVALUATE statement. Although this EVALUATE statement is long, each of its WHEN clauses is manageable. The way to understand this program is to study the EVALUATE statement one WHEN clause at a time, making sure you understand how the program responds to each input event.

Probably the most important WHEN clauses in this EVALUATE statement are the ones that handle the Enter key and the PF4 key. The program handles the Enter key with this WHEN clause:

```
WHEN EIBAID = DFHENTER
    IF PROCESS-ENTRY
        PERFORM 1000-PROCESS-ORDER-MAP
    ELSE IF PROCESS-VERIFY
        PERFORM 2000-PROCESS-POST-ORDER
        SET PROCESS-ENTRY TO TRUE
```

This WHEN clause simply invokes module 1000 or 2000, depending on the context. If the context is "Process verify," the WHEN clause sets the context to "Process entry" after invoking module 2000. If the context is "Process entry," however, the WHEN clause doesn't set the context after invoking module 1000. Instead, module 1000 itself sets the new context, depending on whether the user entered valid data.

The WHEN clause that handles PF4 also checks the context. If the context is "Process verify," it formats the symbolic map with appropriate instructions, sets RESET-ATTRIBUTES and SEND-DATA-ONLY to true, calls module 1400 to redisplay the entry map, and sets the new context to "Process entry." If the context is not "Process verify," the program treats PF4 as an error and displays an appropriate message.

Module 1000: Process Order Map

Module 1000 itself is straightforward. It performs module 1100 to receive the order map data, then performs module 1200 to edit the data. If the data is valid, it performs module 1300 to format the invoice record, then performs module 1400 to display the verify map. If the data is invalid, it performs module 1400 to display an error message. Notice how module 1000 formats the instructions and function key area and sets the flags that control module 1400's operation. Also, notice that if the data is valid, module 1000 sets the context to "Process-verify;" if the data isn't valid, it leaves the context unchanged.

Module 1200: Edit Order Data

Most of the real work done to process the order map is done by module 1200 and its subordinates. Module 1200 edits the order map data. It starts by performing module 1220 repeatedly to edit each line item. Notice that the PERFORM statement varies the subscript backwards, from 10 to 1 by -1. That way, the line items will be edited from the bottom up. As a result, the error message in ORD-D-MESSAGE (if any) will reflect the error closest to the top of the screen.

Among other things, module 1220 counts the line items entered by the user so module 1200 can check to make sure at least one line item has been entered. It then checks to see if the purchase order field has been entered. Since this field is optional, no error message is formatted. This edit is done only to set CA-PO-ENTERED-SW, which will be used elsewhere in the program.

Next, module 1200 edits the customer number field. First, it checks to make sure the field was entered. If it was, it performs module 1210 to read the customer file. If the record is found, it moves the customer's name and address to the appropriate map fields. If not, it formats an error message and moves spaces to the map fields.

Module 1220 is the most complex module in the program. It's invoked once for each line item. It starts by checking to see if the user entered a product code, quantity, and net price for this line item, setting the communication area switches accordingly. Then, it performs various edits against the net price and quantity fields, calling NUMEDIT and INTEDIT to make sure they are valid numbers. (NUMEDIT and INTEDIT were presented in chapter 8; you may want to refer back to that chapter if you've forgotten how they work.)

Next, module 1220 edits the product code by calling module 1230 to read the product file. If the product code exists in the file, the product description and unit price from the product record are moved to the appropriate map fields. Finally, if the product code exists in the file and both the quantity and net price fields contain valid numbers, the arithmetic necessary to extend the line item and maintain the invoice total is performed. Note that even the MULTIPLY and ADD statements involve editing: If a size error occurs for either, an error message is displayed and the data is considered invalid.

Module 1300: Format Invoice Record

Module 1300 is relatively straightforward. However, I want you to notice three things. First, I coded an ADDRESS command to access the date stored in the Common Work Area. Second, I used an in-line PERFORM statement here to format each line item. Although I could have created a separate module and used a standard PERFORM VARYING statement, I don't think it's necessary here. Third, I used the CA-PCODE-ENTERED switch to determine whether or not the user entered data for a line item. If so, I moved data from the symbolic map to the corresponding invoice record line item. (It isn't necessary to move data to the INV-AMOUNT field here, because that field was set by the MULTIPLY statement in module 1220.) If the user didn't enter data for the line item, I moved space to the product code field and zero to the quantity, unit price, and amount fields.

Module 1400: Send Order Map

Module 1400 itself is also straightforward, but I want to point out a few details in its subordinate modules, 1410 and 1420. Module 1410 is called to set up the verify screen. It does this by moving a protected attribute byte to the attribute field of each unprotected field on the map. If you'll study this code for a moment, you'll see that the attribute byte value it moves to each attribute field depends on whether the user has entered data for the field. If the user has entered data, the program moves ATTR-PROT to the attribute field. That way, the field will be protected so the user can't change it. On the other hand, if the user has *not* entered data for the field, the program moves ATTR-PROT-DARK to the attribute field. As a result, not only will the field be protected, but its contents will be hidden. I used this coding to remove the underscores that identify the unprotected fields so the user won't be confused by their appearance on the verify screen.

Module 1420's job is similar. You might expect that it could simply move ATTR-UNPROT to each attribute byte field. Unfortunately, that's not the case. The order entry program expects each field entered by the operator to be transmitted to the program whenever the user presses the Enter key. Unfortunately, when we moved ATTR-PROT to the attribute bytes of these fields in module 1410, we overwrote the modified data tags for these fields. So, module 1420 must move ATTR-UNPROT to each field that wasn't entered by the user, and ATTR-UNPROT-MDT to each field that was. That way, the modified data tags will be restored, and all of the entered fields will be sent to the program. Like module 1410, module 1420 uses the switches in CA-FIELDS-ENTERED to determine which fields were entered and which were not.

Module 2000: Post Order

Because module 1200 and its subordinates thoroughly edited the order data and module 1300 formatted the invoice record and saved it in the communication area, module 2000 is deceptively simple. First, it invokes the GETINV subprogram with a LINK command to retrieve an invoice number from the invoice control file. GETINV returns the invoice number via its communication area, so the LINK command simply specifies INV-INVOICE-NUMBER in its COMMAREA option. Then, module 2000 calls module 2100 to write the invoice record to the invoice file. Finally, it calls module 1400 to display the order map. Because it specifies SEND-ERASE, it doesn't have to worry about resetting the protected attribute bytes that were set by module 1410.

The GETINV subprogram
Figure 10-19 (on page 300) shows the source listing for the GETINV subprogram. As you can see, this program simply reads a record from the invoice control file, moves the invoice number to the communication area, adds 1 to the invoice number in the invoice control record, and rewrites the record. By using this subprogram, the order entry program produces invoices with unique ascending invoice numbers, even if many users are entering orders at once.

Frankly, calling the GETINV subprogram with a LINK command is probably the least efficient way to invoke it. In a production environment, you would probably invoke it with a CALL statement or code its function directly in the ORDRENT program. But I wanted to illustrate the use of program control commands here, so I decided to invoke it with a LINK command even though it's probably not the most efficient choice.

Discussion   The order entry program I've presented here is the most complex CICS program this book presents. If you thoroughly understand it, you're well underway to developing CICS applications of professional quality. If you don't understand every aspect of it, don't worry too much. CICS is complicated, and understanding this program requires you to keep track of a lot of details. Your understanding will improve as you apply what you've learned to developing your own programs.

Objective

Given specifications for a data entry program, design and code it using the order entry program presented in this topic as a model.

Program	ORDRENT

Overview	Writes orders to an invoice file based on data entered by the user.	

Input/output specifications	INVOICE	Invoice file
	CUSTMAS	Customer master file
	PRODUCT	Product (inventory) file
	ORDMAP1	Order entry map

Processing specifications

1. Control is transferred to this program via XCTL from the menu program INVMENU with no communication area. The user can also start the program by entering the trans-id ORD1. In either case, the program should respond by displaying the order entry map.

2. On the order entry map, the user enters a customer number, a p/o number, and data for up to 10 line items. The order entry program edits the data according to the rules listed in step 3. If the data is valid, the program redisplays the map with all fields protected. Then, the user can post the order by pressing the Enter key or make additional changes by pressing PF4. If the user presses PF4, the program should unprotect the entry fields and let the user enter changes. If the user presses PF12, the program should cancel the order and redisplay the entry screen with blank fields. The user ends the program by pressing PF3.

3. Order data should be edited according to the following rules:

customer number	must be in the customer file
product code	must be in the product file
quantity	must be a valid integer
net price	must be a valid decimal number

   In addition, the following cross-validation requirements must be checked:

   a. If the user enters a product code, he or she must also enter a quantity for that line item;

   b. The user cannot enter a quantity or net price on a line where he or she did not enter a product code;

   c. The user must enter at least one line item.

4. If the user does not enter a net price, use the list price from the appropriate product record.

5. To obtain the invoice number, invoke the GETINV program with a LINK command.

6. Use the date stored in the CWA for the invoice date field.

7. When the user exits the program, display a total of the number of orders entered before returning to the menu.

Figure 10-13   Specifications for the order entry program (part 1 of 2)

Map name ____ORDMAP1_____   Date ____5-1-92_____
Program name _ORDRENT_____   Designer _Doug Lowe_____

```
     1         1         2         3         4         5         6         7         8
   1234567890123456789012345678901234567890123456789012345678901234567890123456789 0
 1 ORDMAP1              Order Entry
 2
 3 XXXXXXXXXXXXXXXXXXXXXXXXXXXXXXXXXXXXXXXXXXXXXXXXXXXXXXXXXXXXXXXXXXXXXXXXXXXXXXXXXX
 4
 5 Customer number . . . XXXXXX        Customer: XXXXXXXXXXXXXXXXXXXXXXXXXXXXXX
 6 P.O. number . . . . . XXXXXXXXXX              XXXXXXXXXXXXXXXXXXXXXX
 7                                               XXXXXXXXXXXXXXXXXXXXXXXXXXXXXX
 8                                               XXXXXXXXXXXXXXXXXXXX XX XXXXXXXXXXX
 9
10 Prod code     Qty   Description              List         Net        Amount
11 XXXXXXXXXX   XXXXX   XXXXXXXXXXXXXXXXXXXXX  Z,ZZZ,ZZ9.99  XXXXXXXXXX  Z,ZZZ,ZZ9.99
12 XXXXXXXXXX   XXXXX   XXXXXXXXXXXXXXXXXXXXX  Z,ZZZ,ZZ9.99  XXXXXXXXXX  Z,ZZZ,ZZ9.99
13 XXXXXXXXXX   XXXXX   XXXXXXXXXXXXXXXXXXXXX  Z,ZZZ,ZZ9.99  XXXXXXXXXX  Z,ZZZ,ZZ9.99
14 XXXXXXXXXX   XXXXX   XXXXXXXXXXXXXXXXXXXXX  Z,ZZZ,ZZ9.99  XXXXXXXXXX  Z,ZZZ,ZZ9.99
15 XXXXXXXXXX   XXXXX   XXXXXXXXXXXXXXXXXXXXX  Z,ZZZ,ZZ9.99  XXXXXXXXXX  Z,ZZZ,ZZ9.99
16 XXXXXXXXXX   XXXXX   XXXXXXXXXXXXXXXXXXXXX  Z,ZZZ,ZZ9.99  XXXXXXXXXX  Z,ZZZ,ZZ9.99
17 XXXXXXXXXX   XXXXX   XXXXXXXXXXXXXXXXXXXXX  Z,ZZZ,ZZ9.99  XXXXXXXXXX  Z,ZZZ,ZZ9.99
18 XXXXXXXXXX   XXXXX   XXXXXXXXXXXXXXXXXXXXX  Z,ZZZ,ZZ9.99  XXXXXXXXXX  Z,ZZZ,ZZ9.99
19 XXXXXXXXXX   XXXXX   XXXXXXXXXXXXXXXXXXXXX  Z,ZZZ,ZZ9.99  XXXXXXXXXX  Z,ZZZ,ZZ9.99
20 XXXXXXXXXX   XXXXX   XXXXXXXXXXXXXXXXXXXXX  Z,ZZZ,ZZ9.99  XXXXXXXXXX  Z,ZZZ,ZZ9.99
21
22                                      Invoice total:      Z,ZZZ,ZZ9.99
23 XXXXXXXXXXXXXXXXXXXXXXXXXXXXXXXXXXXXXXXXXXXXXXXXXXXXXXXXXXXXXXXXXXXXXXXXXXXXXXXXXX
24 XXXXXXXXXXXXXXXXXXXXXXXXXXXXXXXXXXXXXXXXX                                        X
```

Figure 10-13   Specifications for the order entry program (part 2 of 2)

Event	Context	Response	New context
Start the program	n/a	Display the order map.	Process entry
PF3	All	Transfer control to the menu program.	n/a
PF12	Process entry	Transfer control to the menu program.	n/a
	Process verify	Cancel the order and redisplay the order map with entry fields unprotected.	Process entry

Enter	Process entry	Edit input data.
		If valid
		  protect all fields
		  display confirmation message.
		If not valid
		  display error message.
			Process verify
			
			Process entry

	Process verify	Get the invoice number. Write the order record. Redisplay the order map with entry fields unprotected.	Process entry
PF4	Process entry	Display an "invalid key pressed" message.	Unchanged
	Process verify	Redisplay the order map with entry fields unprotected.	Process entry
Clear	All	Redisplay the map.	Process entry
PA1, PA2, or PA3	All	Ignore the key.	Unchanged
Any other key	All	Display an appropriate error message.	Unchanged

Figure 10-14 An event/response chart for the order entry program

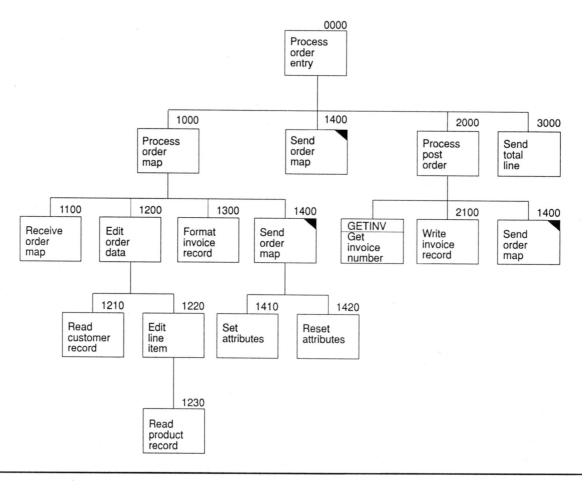

Figure 10-15 Structure chart for the order entry program

```
          PRINT NOGEN
ORDSET1   DFHMSD TYPE=&SYSPARM,                                            X
                 LANG=COBOL,                                               X
                 MODE=INOUT,                                               X
                 TERM=3270-2,                                              X
                 CTRL=FREEKB,                                              X
                 STORAGE=AUTO,                                             X
                 DSATTS=(COLOR,HILIGHT),                                   X
                 MAPATTS=(COLOR,HILIGHT),                                  X
                 TIOAPFX=YES
****************************************************************************
ORDMAP1   DFHMDI SIZE=(24,80),                                            X
                 LINE=1,                                                   X
                 COLUMN=1
****************************************************************************
          DFHMDF POS=(1,1),                                               X
                 LENGTH=7,                                                 X
                 ATTRB=(NORM,PROT),                                        X
                 COLOR=BLUE,                                               X
                 INITIAL='ORDMAP1'
          DFHMDF POS=(1,20),                                              X
                 LENGTH=11,                                                X
                 ATTRB=(NORM,PROT),                                        X
                 COLOR=BLUE,                                               X
                 INITIAL='Order Entry'
****************************************************************************
INSTR     DFHMDF POS=(3,1),                                               X
                 LENGTH=79,                                                X
                 ATTRB=(NORM,PROT),                                        X
                 COLOR=GREEN
          DFHMDF POS=(5,1),                                               X
                 LENGTH=21,                                                X
                 ATTRB=(NORM,PROT),                                        X
                 COLOR=GREEN,                                              X
                 INITIAL='Customer number . . .'
CUSTNO    DFHMDF POS=(5,23),                                              X
                 LENGTH=6,                                                 X
                 ATTRB=(NORM,UNPROT),                                      X
                 COLOR=TURQUOISE,                                          X
                 INITIAL='_____'
          DFHMDF POS=(5,30),                                              X
                 LENGTH=1,                                                 X
                 ATTRB=ASKIP
          DFHMDF POS=(5,36),                                              X
                 LENGTH=9,                                                 X
                 ATTRB=(NORM,PROT),                                        X
                 COLOR=GREEN,                                              X
                 INITIAL='Customer:'
LNAME     DFHMDF POS=(5,46),                                              X
                 LENGTH=30,                                                X
                 ATTRB=(NORM,PROT),                                        X
                 COLOR=TURQUOISE
          DFHMDF POS=(6,1),                                               X
                 LENGTH=21,                                                X
                 ATTRB=(NORM,PROT),                                        X
                 COLOR=GREEN,                                              X
                 INITIAL='P.O. number . . . . .'
```

Figure 10-16 BMS mapset for the order entry program (part 1 of 3)

```
PO         DFHMDF POS=(6,23),                                                      X
                  LENGTH=10,                                                       X
                  ATTRB=(NORM,UNPROT),                                             X
                  COLOR=TURQUOISE,                                                 X
                  INITIAL='_____'
           DFHMDF POS=(6,34),                                                      X
                  LENGTH=1,                                                        X
                  ATTRB=ASKIP
FNAME      DFHMDF POS=(6,46),                                                      X
                  LENGTH=20,                                                       X
                  ATTRB=(NORM,PROT),                                               X
                  COLOR=TURQUOISE
ADDR       DFHMDF POS=(7,46),                                                      X
                  LENGTH=30,                                                       X
                  ATTRB=(NORM,PROT),                                               X
                  COLOR=TURQUOISE
CITY       DFHMDF POS=(8,46),                                                      X
                  LENGTH=20,                                                       X
                  ATTRB=(NORM,PROT),                                               X
                  COLOR=TURQUOISE
STATE      DFHMDF POS=(8,67),                                                      X
                  LENGTH=2,                                                        X
                  ATTRB=(NORM,PROT),                                               X
                  COLOR=TURQUOISE
ZIPCODE    DFHMDF POS=(8,70),                                                      X
                  LENGTH=10,                                                       X
                  ATTRB=(NORM,PROT),                                               X
                  COLOR=TURQUOISE
           DFHMDF POS=(10,1),                                                      X
                  LENGTH=30,                                                       X
                  ATTRB=(NORM,PROT),                                               X
                  COLOR=BLUE,                                                      X
                  INITIAL='Prod code     Qty   Description'
           DFHMDF POS=(10,49),                                                     X
                  LENGTH=29,                                                       X
                  ATTRB=(NORM,PROT),                                               X
                  COLOR=BLUE,                                                      X
                  INITIAL='List          Net       Amount'
********************************************************************************
*          LINE ITEM  1                                                        *
********************************************************************************
PCODE1     DFHMDF POS=(11,1),                                                      X
                  LENGTH=10,                                                       X
                  ATTRB=(NORM,UNPROT),                                             X
                  COLOR=TURQUOISE,                                                 X
                  INITIAL='_____'
           DFHMDF POS=(11,12),                                                     X
                  LENGTH=1,                                                        X
                  ATTRB=ASKIP
QTY1       DFHMDF POS=(11,13),                                                     X
                  LENGTH=5,                                                        X
                  ATTRB=(NORM,UNPROT,NUM),                                         X
                  COLOR=TURQUOISE,                                                 X
                  INITIAL='_____'
           DFHMDF POS=(11,19),                                                     X
                  LENGTH=1,                                                        X
                  ATTRB=ASKIP
DESC1      DFHMDF POS=(11,20),                                                     X
                  LENGTH=20,                                                       X
                  ATTRB=(NORM,PROT),                                               X
                  COLOR=TURQUOISE
```

Figure 10-16   BMS mapset for the order entry program (part 2 of 3)

```
LIST1     DFHMDF POS=(11,41),                                          X
               LENGTH=12,                                              X
               ATTRB=(NORM,PROT),                                      X
               COLOR=TURQUOISE,                                        X
               PICOUT='Z,ZZZ,ZZ9.99'
NET1      DFHMDF POS=(11,55),                                          X
               LENGTH=10,                                              X
               ATTRB=(NORM,NUM),                                       X
               COLOR=TURQUOISE,                                        X
               PICOUT='ZZZZZZ9.99',                                    X
               INITIAL='_____'
AMT1      DFHMDF POS=(11,66),                                          X
               LENGTH=12,                                              X
               ATTRB=(NORM,PROT),                                      X
               COLOR=TURQUOISE,                                        X
               PICOUT='Z,ZZZ,ZZ9.99'
```

> The BMS macro instructions that define line items 2 through 10
> are similar to those that define line item 1.

```
************************************************************************
          DFHMDF POS=(22,44),                                          X
               LENGTH=14,                                              X
               ATTRB=(NORM,PROT),                                      X
               COLOR=GREEN,                                            X
               INITIAL='Invoice total:'
TOTAL     DFHMDF POS=(22,66),                                          X
               LENGTH=12,                                              X
               ATTRB=(NORM,PROT),                                      X
               COLOR=TURQUOISE,                                        X
               PICOUT='Z,ZZZ,ZZ9.99'
************************************************************************
MSG       DFHMDF POS=(23,1),                                           X
               LENGTH=79,                                              X
               ATTRB=(BRT,PROT),                                       X
               COLOR=YELLOW
FKEY      DFHMDF POS=(24,1),                                           X
               LENGTH=40,                                              X
               ATTRB=(NORM,PROT),                                      X
               COLOR=BLUE
DUMMY     DFHMDF POS=(24,79),                                          X
               LENGTH=1,                                               X
               ATTRB=(DRK,PROT,FSET),                                  X
               INITIAL=' '
************************************************************************
          DFHMSD TYPE=FINAL
          END
```

Figure 10-16   BMS mapset for the order entry program (part 3 of 3)

```
01   ORDMAP1.
*
     05   FILLER                      PIC X(12).
*
     05   ORD-L-INSTR                 PIC S9(4)  COMP.
     05   ORD-A-INSTR                 PIC X.
     05   ORD-C-INSTR                 PIC X.
     05   ORD-H-INSTR                 PIC X.
     05   ORD-D-INSTR                 PIC X(79).
*
     05   ORD-L-CUSTNO                PIC S9(4)  COMP.
     05   ORD-A-CUSTNO                PIC X.
     05   ORD-C-CUSTNO                PIC X.
     05   ORD-H-CUSTNO                PIC X.
     05   ORD-D-CUSTNO                PIC X(6).
*
     05   ORD-L-LNAME                 PIC S9(4)  COMP.
     05   ORD-A-LNAME                 PIC X.
     05   ORD-C-LNAME                 PIC X.
     05   ORD-H-LNAME                 PIC X.
     05   ORD-D-LNAME                 PIC X(30).
*
     05   ORD-L-PO                    PIC S9(4)  COMP.
     05   ORD-A-PO                    PIC X.
     05   ORD-C-PO                    PIC X.
     05   ORD-H-PO                    PIC X.
     05   ORD-D-PO                    PIC X(10).
*
     05   ORD-L-FNAME                 PIC S9(4)  COMP.
     05   ORD-A-FNAME                 PIC X.
     05   ORD-C-FNAME                 PIC X.
     05   ORD-H-FNAME                 PIC X.
     05   ORD-D-FNAME                 PIC X(20).
*
     05   ORD-L-ADDR                  PIC S9(4)  COMP.
     05   ORD-A-ADDR                  PIC X.
     05   ORD-C-ADDR                  PIC X.
     05   ORD-H-ADDR                  PIC X.
     05   ORD-D-ADDR                  PIC X(30).
*
     05   ORD-L-CITY                  PIC S9(4)  COMP.
     05   ORD-A-CITY                  PIC X.
     05   ORD-C-CITY                  PIC X.
     05   ORD-H-CITY                  PIC X.
     05   ORD-D-CITY                  PIC X(20).
*
     05   ORD-L-STATE                 PIC S9(4)  COMP.
     05   ORD-A-STATE                 PIC X.
     05   ORD-C-STATE                 PIC X.
     05   ORD-H-STATE                 PIC X.
     05   ORD-D-STATE                 PIC X(2).
*
     05   ORD-L-ZIPCODE               PIC S9(4)  COMP.
     05   ORD-A-ZIPCODE               PIC X.
     05   ORD-C-ZIPCODE               PIC X.
     05   ORD-H-ZIPCODE               PIC X.
     05   ORD-D-ZIPCODE               PIC X(10).
*

     05   ORD-LINE-ITEM               OCCURS 10.
*
          10   ORD-L-PCODE            PIC S9(4)  COMP.
          10   ORD-A-PCODE            PIC X.
          10   ORD-C-PCODE            PIC X.
          10   ORD-H-PCODE            PIC X.
          10   ORD-D-PCODE            PIC X(10).
```

Figure 10-17 Programmer-generated symbolic map for the order entry program (part 1 of 2)

```
*
          10   ORD-L-QTY                PIC S9(4)  COMP.
          10   ORD-A-QTY                PIC X.
          10   ORD-C-QTY                PIC X.
          10   ORD-H-QTY                PIC X.
          10   ORD-D-QTY                PIC ZZZZ9
                                        BLANK WHEN ZERO.
          10   ORD-D-QTY-ALPHA          REDEFINES ORD-D-QTY
                                        PIC X(5).
*
          10   ORD-L-DESC               PIC S9(4)  COMP.
          10   ORD-A-DESC               PIC X.
          10   ORD-C-DESC               PIC X.
          10   ORD-H-DESC               PIC X.
          10   ORD-D-DESC               PIC X(20).
*
          10   ORD-L-LIST               PIC S9(4)  COMP.
          10   ORD-A-LIST               PIC X.
          10   ORD-C-LIST               PIC X.
          10   ORD-H-LIST               PIC X.
          10   ORD-D-LIST               PIC Z,ZZZ,ZZ9.99
                                        BLANK WHEN ZERO.
*
          10   ORD-L-NET                PIC S9(4)  COMP.
          10   ORD-A-NET                PIC X.
          10   ORD-C-NET                PIC X.
          10   ORD-H-NET                PIC X.
          10   ORD-D-NET                PIC ZZZ,ZZ9.99
                                        BLANK WHEN ZERO.
          10   ORD-D-NET-ALPHA          REDEFINES ORD-D-NET
                                        PIC X(10).
*
          10   ORD-L-AMOUNT             PIC S9(4)  COMP.
          10   ORD-A-AMOUNT             PIC X.
          10   ORD-C-AMOUNT             PIC X.
          10   ORD-H-AMOUNT             PIC X.
          10   ORD-D-AMOUNT             PIC Z,ZZZ,ZZ9.99
                                        BLANK WHEN ZERO.
*
       05   ORD-L-TOTAL                 PIC S9(4)  COMP.
       05   ORD-A-TOTAL                 PIC X.
       05   ORD-C-TOTAL                 PIC X.
       05   ORD-H-TOTAL                 PIC X.
       05   ORD-D-TOTAL                 PIC Z,ZZZ,ZZ9.99
                                        BLANK WHEN ZERO.
*
       05   ORD-L-MESSAGE               PIC S9(4)  COMP.
       05   ORD-A-MESSAGE               PIC X.
       05   ORD-C-MESSAGE               PIC X.
       05   ORD-H-MESSAGE               PIC X.
       05   ORD-D-MESSAGE               PIC X(79).
*
       05   ORD-L-FKEY                  PIC S9(4)  COMP.
       05   ORD-A-FKEY                  PIC X.
       05   ORD-C-FKEY                  PIC X.
       05   ORD-H-FKEY                  PIC X.
       05   ORD-D-FKEY                  PIC X(40).
*
       05   ORD-L-DUMMY                 PIC S9(4)  COMP.
       05   ORD-A-DUMMY                 PIC X.
       05   ORD-C-DUMMY                 PIC X.
       05   ORD-H-DUMMY                 PIC X.
       05   ORD-D-DUMMY                 PIC X.
*
```

Figure 10-17 Programmer-generated symbolic map for the order entry program (part 2 of 2)

```
      IDENTIFICATION DIVISION.
      *
      PROGRAM-ID.  ORDRENT.
      *
      ENVIRONMENT DIVISION.
      *
      DATA DIVISION.
      *
      WORKING-STORAGE SECTION.
      *
      01   SWITCHES.
      *
           05   VALID-DATA-SW                 PIC X    VALUE 'Y'.
                88   VALID-DATA                         VALUE 'Y'.
           05   CUSTOMER-FOUND-SW             PIC X    VALUE 'Y'.
                88   CUSTOMER-FOUND                     VALUE 'Y'.
           05   PRODUCT-FOUND-SW             PIC X    VALUE 'Y'.
                88   PRODUCT-FOUND                      VALUE 'Y'.
           05   VALID-QUANTITY-SW            PIC X    VALUE 'Y'.
                88   VALID-QUANTITY                     VALUE 'Y'.
           05   VALID-NET-SW                 PIC X    VALUE 'Y'.
                88   VALID-NET                          VALUE 'Y'.
      *
      01   FLAGS.
      *
           05   SEND-FLAG                     PIC X.
                88   SEND-ERASE                         VALUE '1'.
                88   SEND-DATAONLY                      VALUE '2'.
                88   SEND-DATAONLY-ALARM                VALUE '3'.
           05   ATTRIBUTE-SET-FLAG            PIC X.
                88   SET-ATTRIBUTES                     VALUE '1'.
                88   RESET-ATTRIBUTES                   VALUE '2'.
      *
      01   WORK-FIELDS.
      *
           05   ITEM-SUB         PIC S9(3)   COMP-3   VALUE ZERO.
           05   LINE-ITEM-COUNT  PIC S9(3)   COMP-3   VALUE ZERO.
           05   NET-NUMERIC      PIC 9(7)V99.
           05   QTY-NUMERIC      PIC 9(5).
      *
      01   RESPONSE-CODE         PIC S9(8)   COMP.
      *
      01   COMMUNICATION-AREA.
      *
           05   CA-CONTEXT-FLAG               PIC X.
                88   PROCESS-ENTRY                      VALUE '1'.
                88   PROCESS-VERIFY                     VALUE '2'.
           05   CA-TOTAL-ORDERS              PIC S9(3) COMP-3.
           05   CA-INVOICE-RECORD            PIC X(318).
           05   CA-FIELDS-ENTERED.
                10   CA-PO-ENTERED-SW         PIC X.
                     88   CA-PO-ENTERED                 VALUE 'Y'.
                10   CA-LINE-ITEM            OCCURS 10.
                     15   CA-PCODE-ENTERED-SW PIC X.
                          88   CA-PCODE-ENTERED         VALUE 'Y'.
                     15   CA-QTY-ENTERED-SW   PIC X.
                          88   CA-QTY-ENTERED           VALUE 'Y'.
                     15   CA-NET-ENTERED-SW   PIC X.
                          88   CA-NET-ENTERED           VALUE 'Y'.
      *
      01   TOTAL-LINE.
      *
           05   TL-TOTAL-ORDERS  PIC ZZ9.
           05   FILLER           PIC X(20) VALUE ' Orders entered.  Pr'.
           05   FILLER           PIC X(20) VALUE 'ess Enter to continu'.
           05   FILLER           PIC X(2)  VALUE 'e.'.
```

Figure 10-18 Source listing for the order entry program (part 1 of 10)

```
/
 COPY INVOICE.
*
 COPY CUSTMAS.
*
 COPY PRODUCT.
*
 COPY INVCTL.
*
 COPY ORDSET1.
*
 COPY DFHAID.
*
 COPY ATTR.
*
 COPY ERRPARM.
*
 LINKAGE SECTION.
*
 01   DFHCOMMAREA              PIC X(352).
*
 01   COMMON-WORK-AREA.
*
     05   CWA-DATE             PIC X(6).
     05   CWA-COMPANY-NAME     PIC X(40).
*
 PROCEDURE DIVISION.
*
 0000-PROCESS-ORDER-ENTRY.
*
     MOVE DFHCOMMAREA TO COMMUNICATION-AREA.

     EVALUATE TRUE

         WHEN EIBCALEN = ZERO
             MOVE LOW-VALUE TO ORDMAP1
             MOVE LOW-VALUE TO COMMUNICATION-AREA
             MOVE ZERO       TO CA-TOTAL-ORDERS
             MOVE 'Type order details.  Then press Enter.'
                 TO ORD-D-INSTR
             MOVE 'F3=Exit   F12=Cancel' TO ORD-D-FKEY
             MOVE -1 TO ORD-L-CUSTNO
             SET SEND-ERASE TO TRUE
             PERFORM 1400-SEND-ORDER-MAP
             SET PROCESS-ENTRY TO TRUE


         WHEN EIBAID = DFHCLEAR
             MOVE LOW-VALUE TO ORDMAP1
             MOVE LOW-VALUE TO CA-INVOICE-RECORD
                               CA-FIELDS-ENTERED
             MOVE 'Type order details.  Then press Enter.'
                 TO ORD-D-INSTR
             MOVE 'F3=Exit   F12=Cancel' TO ORD-D-FKEY
             MOVE -1 TO ORD-L-CUSTNO
             SET SEND-ERASE TO TRUE
             PERFORM 1400-SEND-ORDER-MAP
             SET PROCESS-ENTRY TO TRUE

         WHEN EIBAID = DFHPA1 OR DFHPA2 OR DFHPA3
             CONTINUE

         WHEN EIBAID = DFHPF3
             PERFORM 3000-SEND-TOTAL-LINE
             EXEC CICS
                 RETURN TRANSID('MENU')
             END-EXEC
```

Figure 10-18   Source listing for the order entry program (part 2 of 10)

```
/                   WHEN EIBAID = DFHPF12
                        IF PROCESS-VERIFY
                            MOVE LOW-VALUE TO ORDMAP1
                            MOVE LOW-VALUE TO CA-INVOICE-RECORD
                                             CA-FIELDS-ENTERED
                            MOVE 'Type order details.  Then press Enter.'
                                TO ORD-D-INSTR
                            MOVE 'F3=Exit    F12=Cancel' TO ORD-D-FKEY
                            MOVE -1 TO ORD-L-CUSTNO
                            SET SEND-ERASE TO TRUE
                            PERFORM 1400-SEND-ORDER-MAP
                            SET PROCESS-ENTRY TO TRUE
                        ELSE
                            PERFORM 3000-SEND-TOTAL-LINE
                            EXEC CICS
                                RETURN TRANSID('MENU')
                            END-EXEC

                    WHEN EIBAID = DFHENTER
                        IF PROCESS-ENTRY
                            PERFORM 1000-PROCESS-ORDER-MAP
                        ELSE IF PROCESS-VERIFY
                            PERFORM 2000-PROCESS-POST-ORDER
                            SET PROCESS-ENTRY TO TRUE

                    WHEN EIBAID = DFHPF4
                        IF PROCESS-VERIFY
                            MOVE LOW-VALUE TO ORDMAP1
                            MOVE 'Type corrections.  Then press Enter.'
                                TO ORD-D-INSTR
                            MOVE 'F3=Exit    F12=Cancel' TO ORD-D-FKEY
                            MOVE -1 TO ORD-L-CUSTNO
                            SET RESET-ATTRIBUTES TO TRUE
                            SET SEND-DATAONLY      TO TRUE
                            PERFORM 1400-SEND-ORDER-MAP
                            SET PROCESS-ENTRY TO TRUE
                        ELSE
                            MOVE LOW-VALUE TO ORDMAP1
                            MOVE 'Invalid key pressed.' TO ORD-D-MESSAGE
                            MOVE -1 TO ORD-L-CUSTNO
                            SET SEND-DATAONLY-ALARM TO TRUE
                            PERFORM 1400-SEND-ORDER-MAP

                    WHEN OTHER
                        MOVE LOW-VALUE TO ORDMAP1
                        MOVE 'Invalid key pressed.' TO ORD-D-MESSAGE
                        MOVE -1 TO ORD-L-CUSTNO
                        SET SEND-DATAONLY-ALARM TO TRUE
                        PERFORM 1400-SEND-ORDER-MAP

                END-EVALUATE.

                EXEC CICS
                    RETURN TRANSID('ORD1')
                           COMMAREA(COMMUNICATION-AREA)
                END-EXEC.
```

Figure 10-18   Source listing for the order entry program (part 3 of 10)

```
/
 1000-PROCESS-ORDER-MAP.
*
     PERFORM 1100-RECEIVE-ORDER-MAP.
     PERFORM 1200-EDIT-ORDER-DATA.
     IF VALID-DATA
         PERFORM 1300-FORMAT-INVOICE-RECORD
         MOVE 'Press Enter to post this order.  Or press F4 to ent
-            'er corrections.' TO ORD-D-INSTR
         MOVE 'F3=Exit    F4=Change    F12=Cancel' TO ORD-D-FKEY
         MOVE SPACE TO ORD-D-MESSAGE
         SET SEND-DATAONLY TO TRUE
         SET SET-ATTRIBUTES TO TRUE
         PERFORM 1400-SEND-ORDER-MAP
         SET PROCESS-VERIFY TO TRUE
     ELSE
         MOVE 'Type corrections.  Then press Enter.'
             TO ORD-D-INSTR
         MOVE 'F3=Exit    F12=Cancel' TO ORD-D-FKEY
         SET SEND-DATAONLY-ALARM TO TRUE
         PERFORM 1400-SEND-ORDER-MAP.
*
 1100-RECEIVE-ORDER-MAP.
*
     EXEC CICS
         RECEIVE MAP('ORDMAP1')
                 MAPSET('ORDSET1')
                 INTO(ORDMAP1)
     END-EXEC.
     INSPECT ORDMAP1 REPLACING ALL '_' BY SPACE.
*
 1200-EDIT-ORDER-DATA.
*
     MOVE ATTR-NO-HIGHLIGHT TO ORD-H-CUSTNO
                               ORD-H-PO.
     MOVE ZERO TO LINE-ITEM-COUNT
                  INV-INVOICE-TOTAL.
     PERFORM 1220-EDIT-LINE-ITEM
         VARYING ITEM-SUB FROM 10 BY -1
             UNTIL ITEM-SUB < 1.
     MOVE INV-INVOICE-TOTAL TO ORD-D-TOTAL.
     IF        LINE-ITEM-COUNT = ZERO
           AND VALID-DATA
         MOVE ATTR-REVERSE TO ORD-H-PCODE(1)
         MOVE -1 TO ORD-L-PCODE(1)
         MOVE 'You must enter at least one line item'
             TO ORD-D-MESSAGE
         MOVE 'N' TO VALID-DATA-SW.

     IF        ORD-L-PO = ZERO
           OR ORD-D-PO = SPACE
         MOVE 'N' TO CA-PO-ENTERED-SW
     ELSE
         MOVE 'Y' TO CA-PO-ENTERED-SW.

     IF        ORD-L-CUSTNO = ZERO
           OR ORD-D-CUSTNO = SPACE
         MOVE ATTR-REVERSE TO ORD-H-CUSTNO
         MOVE -1 TO ORD-L-CUSTNO
         MOVE 'You must enter a customer number'
             TO ORD-D-MESSAGE
         MOVE 'N' TO VALID-DATA-SW
     ELSE
```

Figure 10-18 Source listing for the order entry program (part 4 of 10)

```
/                PERFORM 1210-READ-CUSTOMER-RECORD
                 IF CUSTOMER-FOUND
                     MOVE CM-LAST-NAME   TO ORD-D-LNAME
                     MOVE CM-FIRST-NAME  TO ORD-D-FNAME
                     MOVE CM-ADDRESS     TO ORD-D-ADDR
                     MOVE CM-CITY        TO ORD-D-CITY
                     MOVE CM-STATE       TO ORD-D-STATE
                     MOVE CM-ZIP-CODE    TO ORD-D-ZIPCODE
                 ELSE
                     MOVE SPACE TO ORD-D-LNAME
                                   ORD-D-FNAME
                                   ORD-D-ADDR
                                   ORD-D-CITY
                                   ORD-D-STATE
                                   ORD-D-ZIPCODE
                     MOVE ATTR-REVERSE TO ORD-H-CUSTNO
                     MOVE -1 TO ORD-L-CUSTNO
                     MOVE 'That customer does not exist'
                         TO ORD-D-MESSAGE
                     MOVE 'N' TO VALID-DATA-SW.
             IF VALID-DATA
                 MOVE -1 TO ORD-L-CUSTNO.
*
 1210-READ-CUSTOMER-RECORD.
*
         EXEC CICS
             READ DATASET('CUSTMAS')
                  INTO(CUSTOMER-MASTER-RECORD)
                  RIDFLD(ORD-D-CUSTNO)
                  RESP(RESPONSE-CODE)
         END-EXEC.
         IF RESPONSE-CODE = DFHRESP(NORMAL)
             MOVE 'Y' TO CUSTOMER-FOUND-SW
         ELSE IF RESPONSE-CODE = DFHRESP(NOTFND)
             MOVE 'N' TO CUSTOMER-FOUND-SW
         ELSE
             PERFORM 9999-TERMINATE-PROGRAM.
*
 1220-EDIT-LINE-ITEM.
*
         MOVE ATTR-NO-HIGHLIGHT TO ORD-H-PCODE(ITEM-SUB)
                                   ORD-H-QTY(ITEM-SUB)
                                   ORD-H-NET(ITEM-SUB).

         MOVE 'N' TO PRODUCT-FOUND-SW.

         IF          ORD-L-PCODE(ITEM-SUB) > ZERO
             AND ORD-D-PCODE(ITEM-SUB) NOT = SPACE
             MOVE 'Y' TO CA-PCODE-ENTERED-SW(ITEM-SUB)
         ELSE
             MOVE 'N' TO CA-PCODE-ENTERED-SW(ITEM-SUB).
         IF          ORD-L-QTY(ITEM-SUB) > ZERO
             AND ORD-D-QTY-ALPHA(ITEM-SUB) NOT = SPACE
             MOVE 'Y' TO CA-QTY-ENTERED-SW(ITEM-SUB)
         ELSE
             MOVE 'N' TO CA-QTY-ENTERED-SW(ITEM-SUB).
         IF          ORD-L-NET(ITEM-SUB) > ZERO
             AND ORD-D-NET-ALPHA(ITEM-SUB) NOT = SPACE
             MOVE 'Y' TO CA-NET-ENTERED-SW(ITEM-SUB)
         ELSE
             MOVE 'N' TO CA-NET-ENTERED-SW(ITEM-SUB).

         IF              CA-NET-ENTERED(ITEM-SUB)
             AND NOT CA-PCODE-ENTERED(ITEM-SUB)
             MOVE ATTR-REVERSE TO ORD-H-PCODE(ITEM-SUB)
             MOVE -1 TO ORD-L-PCODE(ITEM-SUB)
             MOVE 'You cannot enter a net price without a product code
-            '.' TO ORD-D-MESSAGE
             MOVE 'N' TO VALID-DATA-SW.
```

Figure 10-18 Source listing for the order entry program (part 5 of 10)

```
/           IF CA-NET-ENTERED(ITEM-SUB)
                CALL 'NUMEDIT' USING ORD-D-NET-ALPHA(ITEM-SUB)
                                     NET-NUMERIC
                                     VALID-NET-SW
                IF VALID-NET
                    MOVE NET-NUMERIC TO ORD-D-NET(ITEM-SUB)
                ELSE
                    MOVE ATTR-REVERSE TO ORD-H-NET(ITEM-SUB)
                    MOVE -1 TO ORD-L-NET(ITEM-SUB)
                    MOVE 'Net price must be numeric' TO ORD-D-MESSAGE
                    MOVE 'N' TO VALID-DATA-SW
                    MOVE 'N' TO VALID-QUANTITY-SW.

            IF           CA-QTY-ENTERED(ITEM-SUB)
                AND NOT CA-PCODE-ENTERED(ITEM-SUB)
                MOVE ATTR-REVERSE TO ORD-H-PCODE(ITEM-SUB)
                MOVE -1 TO ORD-L-PCODE(ITEM-SUB)
                MOVE 'You cannot enter a quantity without a product code'
                    TO ORD-D-MESSAGE
                MOVE 'N' TO VALID-DATA-SW.

            IF CA-QTY-ENTERED(ITEM-SUB)
                CALL 'INTEDIT' USING ORD-D-QTY-ALPHA(ITEM-SUB)
                                     QTY-NUMERIC
                                     VALID-QUANTITY-SW
                IF VALID-QUANTITY
                    IF QTY-NUMERIC > ZERO
                        MOVE QTY-NUMERIC TO ORD-D-QTY(ITEM-SUB)
                    ELSE
                        MOVE ATTR-REVERSE TO ORD-H-QTY(ITEM-SUB)
                        MOVE -1 TO ORD-L-QTY(ITEM-SUB)
                        MOVE 'Quantity must be greater than zero'
                            TO ORD-D-MESSAGE
                        MOVE 'N' TO VALID-DATA-SW
                        MOVE 'N' TO VALID-QUANTITY-SW
                ELSE
                    MOVE ATTR-REVERSE TO ORD-H-QTY(ITEM-SUB)
                    MOVE -1 TO ORD-L-QTY(ITEM-SUB)
                    MOVE 'Quantity must be numeric' TO ORD-D-MESSAGE
                    MOVE 'N' TO VALID-DATA-SW
                    MOVE 'N' TO VALID-QUANTITY-SW.

            IF           CA-PCODE-ENTERED(ITEM-SUB)
                AND NOT CA-QTY-ENTERED(ITEM-SUB)
                MOVE ATTR-REVERSE TO ORD-H-QTY(ITEM-SUB)
                MOVE -1 TO ORD-L-QTY(ITEM-SUB)
                MOVE 'You must enter a quantity' TO ORD-D-MESSAGE
                MOVE 'N' TO VALID-DATA-SW.

            IF NOT CA-PCODE-ENTERED(ITEM-SUB)
                MOVE SPACE TO ORD-D-DESC(ITEM-SUB)
                MOVE ZERO  TO ORD-D-LIST(ITEM-SUB)
                             ORD-D-AMOUNT(ITEM-SUB)
            ELSE
                ADD 1 TO LINE-ITEM-COUNT
                PERFORM 1230-READ-PRODUCT-RECORD
                IF PRODUCT-FOUND
                    MOVE PRM-PRODUCT-DESCRIPTION
                                        TO ORD-D-DESC(ITEM-SUB)
                    MOVE PRM-UNIT-PRICE TO ORD-D-LIST(ITEM-SUB)
                    IF NOT CA-NET-ENTERED(ITEM-SUB)
                        MOVE PRM-UNIT-PRICE TO ORD-D-NET(ITEM-SUB)
                                               NET-NUMERIC

                    END-IF
```

Figure 10-18   Source listing for the order entry program (part 6 of 10)

/

```
            IF VALID-QUANTITY AND VALID-NET
                MULTIPLY NET-NUMERIC BY QTY-NUMERIC
                    GIVING ORD-D-AMOUNT(ITEM-SUB)
                           INV-AMOUNT(ITEM-SUB)
                    ON SIZE ERROR
                        MOVE ATTR-REVERSE TO ORD-H-QTY(ITEM-SUB)
                        MOVE -1 TO ORD-L-QTY(ITEM-SUB)
                        MOVE 'Line item amount is too large'
                            TO ORD-D-MESSAGE
                        MOVE 'N' TO VALID-DATA-SW
                        MOVE ZERO TO ORD-D-AMOUNT(ITEM-SUB)
                                     INV-AMOUNT(ITEM-SUB)
                END-MULTIPLY
                ADD INV-AMOUNT(ITEM-SUB) TO INV-INVOICE-TOTAL
                    ON SIZE ERROR
                        MOVE ATTR-REVERSE TO ORD-H-QTY(ITEM-SUB)
                        MOVE -1 TO ORD-L-QTY(ITEM-SUB)
                        MOVE 'Invoice total is too large'
                            TO ORD-D-MESSAGE
                        MOVE 'N' TO VALID-DATA-SW
                        MOVE ZERO TO INV-INVOICE-TOTAL
                END-ADD
            END-IF
        ELSE
            MOVE SPACE TO ORD-D-DESC(ITEM-SUB)
            MOVE ZERO  TO ORD-D-LIST(ITEM-SUB)
                          ORD-D-AMOUNT(ITEM-SUB)
            MOVE ATTR-REVERSE TO ORD-H-PCODE(ITEM-SUB)
            MOVE -1    TO ORD-L-PCODE(ITEM-SUB)
            MOVE 'That product does not exist'
                          TO ORD-D-MESSAGE
            MOVE 'N'   TO VALID-DATA-SW.
*
 1230-READ-PRODUCT-RECORD.
*
     EXEC CICS
         READ DATASET('PRODUCT')
              INTO(PRODUCT-MASTER-RECORD)
              RIDFLD(ORD-D-PCODE(ITEM-SUB))
              RESP(RESPONSE-CODE)
     END-EXEC.
     IF RESPONSE-CODE = DFHRESP(NORMAL)
         MOVE 'Y' TO PRODUCT-FOUND-SW
     ELSE IF RESPONSE-CODE = DFHRESP(NOTFND)
         MOVE 'N' TO PRODUCT-FOUND-SW
     ELSE
         PERFORM 9999-TERMINATE-PROGRAM.
```

Figure 10-18 Source listing for the order entry program (part 7 of 10)

```
/
 1300-FORMAT-INVOICE-RECORD.
*
     EXEC CICS
         ADDRESS CWA(ADDRESS OF COMMON-WORK-AREA)
     END-EXEC.
     MOVE CWA-DATE      TO INV-INVOICE-DATE.
     MOVE ORD-D-CUSTNO TO INV-CUSTOMER-NUMBER.
     MOVE ORD-D-PO      TO INV-PO-NUMBER.
     PERFORM VARYING ITEM-SUB FROM 1 BY 1
             UNTIL ITEM-SUB > 10
         IF CA-PCODE-ENTERED(ITEM-SUB)
             MOVE ORD-D-PCODE(ITEM-SUB)
                     TO INV-PRODUCT-CODE(ITEM-SUB)
             MOVE ORD-D-QTY(ITEM-SUB)
                     TO INV-QUANTITY(ITEM-SUB)
             MOVE ORD-D-NET(ITEM-SUB)
                     TO INV-UNIT-PRICE(ITEM-SUB)
         ELSE
             MOVE SPACE TO INV-PRODUCT-CODE(ITEM-SUB)
             MOVE ZERO  TO INV-QUANTITY(ITEM-SUB)
                           INV-UNIT-PRICE(ITEM-SUB)
                           INV-AMOUNT(ITEM-SUB)
     END-PERFORM.
     MOVE INVOICE-RECORD TO CA-INVOICE-RECORD.
*
 1400-SEND-ORDER-MAP.
*
     IF SET-ATTRIBUTES
         PERFORM 1410-SET-ATTRIBUTES
     ELSE IF RESET-ATTRIBUTES
         PERFORM 1420-RESET-ATTRIBUTES.

     IF SEND-ERASE
         EXEC CICS
             SEND MAP('ORDMAP1')
                  MAPSET('ORDSET1')
                  FROM(ORDMAP1)
                  CURSOR
                  ERASE
         END-EXEC
     ELSE IF SEND-DATAONLY
         EXEC CICS
             SEND MAP('ORDMAP1')
                  MAPSET('ORDSET1')
                  FROM(ORDMAP1)
                  CURSOR
                  DATAONLY
         END-EXEC
     ELSE IF SEND-DATAONLY-ALARM
         EXEC CICS
             SEND MAP('ORDMAP1')
                  MAPSET('ORDSET1')
                  FROM(ORDMAP1)
                  CURSOR
                  DATAONLY
                  ALARM
         END-EXEC.
```

Figure 10-18   Source listing for the order entry program (part 8 of 10)

```
/
  1410-SET-ATTRIBUTES.
*
    MOVE ATTR-PROT TO ORD-A-CUSTNO.
    IF CA-PO-ENTERED
        MOVE ATTR-PROT TO ORD-A-PO
    ELSE
        MOVE ATTR-PROT-DARK TO ORD-A-PO.
    PERFORM VARYING ITEM-SUB FROM 1 BY 1
            UNTIL ITEM-SUB > 10
        IF CA-PCODE-ENTERED(ITEM-SUB)
            MOVE ATTR-PROT TO ORD-A-PCODE(ITEM-SUB)
        ELSE
            MOVE ATTR-PROT-DARK TO ORD-A-PCODE(ITEM-SUB)
        END-IF
        IF CA-QTY-ENTERED(ITEM-SUB)
            MOVE ATTR-PROT TO ORD-A-QTY(ITEM-SUB)
        ELSE
            MOVE ATTR-PROT-DARK TO ORD-A-QTY(ITEM-SUB)
        END-IF
        IF        CA-NET-ENTERED(ITEM-SUB)
              OR CA-PCODE-ENTERED(ITEM-SUB)
            MOVE ATTR-PROT TO ORD-A-NET(ITEM-SUB)
        ELSE
            MOVE ATTR-PROT-DARK TO ORD-A-NET(ITEM-SUB)
        END-IF
    END-PERFORM.
*
  1420-RESET-ATTRIBUTES.
*
    MOVE ATTR-UNPROT-MDT TO ORD-A-CUSTNO.
    IF CA-PO-ENTERED
        MOVE ATTR-UNPROT-MDT TO ORD-A-PO
    ELSE
        MOVE ATTR-UNPROT      TO ORD-A-PO.
    PERFORM VARYING ITEM-SUB FROM 1 BY 1
            UNTIL ITEM-SUB > 10
        IF CA-PCODE-ENTERED(ITEM-SUB)
            MOVE ATTR-UNPROT-MDT TO ORD-A-PCODE(ITEM-SUB)
        ELSE
            MOVE ATTR-UNPROT      TO ORD-A-PCODE(ITEM-SUB)
        END-IF
        IF CA-QTY-ENTERED(ITEM-SUB)
            MOVE ATTR-UNPROT-MDT TO ORD-A-QTY(ITEM-SUB)
        ELSE
            MOVE ATTR-UNPROT      TO ORD-A-QTY(ITEM-SUB)
        END-IF
        IF CA-NET-ENTERED(ITEM-SUB)
            MOVE ATTR-UNPROT-MDT TO ORD-A-NET(ITEM-SUB)
        ELSE
            MOVE ATTR-UNPROT      TO ORD-A-NET(ITEM-SUB)
        END-IF
    END-PERFORM.
```

Figure 10-18   Source listing for the order entry program (part 9 of 10)

```
/
 2000-PROCESS-POST-ORDER.
*
     MOVE CA-INVOICE-RECORD TO INVOICE-RECORD.
     EXEC CICS
         LINK PROGRAM('GETINV')
             COMMAREA(INV-INVOICE-NUMBER)
     END-EXEC.
     PERFORM 2100-WRITE-INVOICE-RECORD.
     ADD 1 TO CA-TOTAL-ORDERS.
     MOVE 'Type order details.  Then press Enter.'
         TO ORD-D-INSTR.
     MOVE 'Order posted.' TO ORD-D-MESSAGE.
     MOVE 'F3=Exit    F12=Cancel' TO ORD-D-FKEY.
     MOVE -1 TO ORD-L-CUSTNO.
     SET SEND-ERASE TO TRUE.
     PERFORM 1400-SEND-ORDER-MAP.
*
 2100-WRITE-INVOICE-RECORD.
*
     EXEC CICS
         WRITE DATASET('INVOICE')
             FROM(INVOICE-RECORD)
             RIDFLD(INV-INVOICE-NUMBER)
     END-EXEC.
*
 3000-SEND-TOTAL-LINE.
*
     MOVE CA-TOTAL-ORDERS TO TL-TOTAL-ORDERS.
     EXEC CICS
         SEND TEXT FROM(TOTAL-LINE)
                   ERASE
                   FREEKB
     END-EXEC.

 9999-TERMINATE-PROGRAM.
*
     MOVE EIBRESP  TO ERR-RESP.
     MOVE EIBRESP2 TO ERR-RESP2.
     MOVE EIBTRNID TO ERR-TRNID.
     MOVE EIBRSRCE TO ERR-RSRCE.
     EXEC CICS
         XCTL PROGRAM('SYSERR')
             COMMAREA(ERROR-PARAMETERS)
     END-EXEC.
```

Figure 10-18   Source listing for the order entry program (part 10 of 10)

```
 IDENTIFICATION DIVISION.
*
 PROGRAM-ID.  GETINV.
*
 ENVIRONMENT DIVISION.
*
 DATA DIVISION.
*
 WORKING-STORAGE SECTION.
*
 COPY INVCTL.
*
 LINKAGE SECTION.
*
 01  DFHCOMMAREA    PIC 9(6).
*
 PROCEDURE DIVISION.
*
 0000-GET-INVOICE-NUMBER.
*
     MOVE ZERO TO INVCTL-RECORD-KEY.
     EXEC CICS
         READ DATASET('INVCTL')
             INTO(INVCTL-RECORD)
             RIDFLD(INVCTL-RECORD-KEY)
             UPDATE
     END-EXEC.
     MOVE INVCTL-NEXT-INVOICE-NUMBER TO DFHCOMMAREA.
     ADD 1 TO INVCTL-NEXT-INVOICE-NUMBER.
     EXEC CICS
         REWRITE DATASET('INVCTL')
                 FROM(INVCTL-RECORD)
     END-EXEC.
     EXEC CICS
         RETURN
     END-EXEC.
```

Figure 10-19 The GETINV subprogram

Section 4

Testing and debugging

In this section, I'll present some useful techniques for testing and debugging CICS programs. This section has two chapters. Chapter 11 explains the process of testing a CICS program. Chapter 12 covers debugging techniques.

Chapter 11

Testing a CICS program

One of the major pitfalls of program development is inadequate testing. All too often, programs aren't tried on enough combinations of input data to be sure all of their routines work, but they're put into production anyway. Then, when a program produces inaccurate results or simply fails, a crisis can occur. It's your responsibility as a programmer to develop programs that work properly. As a result, you've got to take testing seriously.

Figure 11-1 summarizes four types of tests that are commonly done before CICS programs are put into production. In a *unit test*, the program is tested on its own to make sure it performs according to its specifications. During the unit test, the programmer makes sure that the screens are displayed properly, all field edits work as planned, files are updated correctly, and so on. As an application programmer, you'll most likely do the unit test yourself. The other types of tests might be done by a separate quality assurance group.

In a *concurrency test*, the program is run simultaneously at several terminals to make sure that multiple executions don't interfere with one another. For example, the maintenance program I presented in chapter 10 holds a copy of a record being updated from one execution to the

Test	Description
Unit test	The program is tested individually to ensure that it works according to specification.
Concurrency test	The program is tested simultaneously at several terminals to make sure that multiple executions of the same program don't interfere with one another.
Integration test	The program is tested in context with other programs in the application.
Regression test	Testing that was originally done against the program is repeated when the program undergoes maintenance.

Figure 11-1   Four types of testing for CICS programs

next. A concurrency test would ensure that this mechanism works, so that two users are not allowed to update the record at the same time.

In an *integration test*, the program is tested in combination with other programs to make sure the program works as a part of a complete system. Many programming errors aren't detected until the program is allowed to interact with other programs. In addition, the integration test often reveals inconsistencies in the application design.

Whenever a program is modified, the entire program must be retested...not just the portion of the program that was modified. That's the purpose of a *regression test*. In a regression test, the testing that was originally done on the program before it was approved for production is repeated to make sure the results are the same. Because 70 percent or more of all program development work is not developing new systems but maintaining and enhancing existing systems, the need for solid regression testing is clear. Unfortunately, regression testing is often overlooked because it is time-consuming.

The CICS testing environment

Most installations create a CICS testing environment that's separate from the production environment. That way, you can thoroughly unit test your programs without fear of affecting the production system. The testing environment consists of a CICS system dedicated to testing and test versions of production data sets. You'll work within this testing environment as you test your programs.

Some installations maintain several CICS testing environments for various levels of testing. For example, an installation might use one CICS system to let application programmers do unit testing and concurrency testing. When the unit test is complete, the programmer promotes the tested program to another CICS system, where integration and regression tests are performed by a separate quality assurance group. Only then is the program promoted into the production system.

When you're working in a CICS system dedicated to testing, there are a few things you need to find out. To begin, it's not uncommon for a each programmer to be assigned one or more generic transaction-identifiers and program names. That way, the CICS systems programmer doesn't have to define resources for every program that's under development. If that's the case, you'll use these generic names as you test the program. You'll replace them with actual names before the program is moved into production.

Also, you need to know what data sets exist for testing purposes. Usually, test versions of production data sets will be available. These test versions may contain small amounts of data extracted from the production files, or they may contain representative data created by a test data generator. Either way, you need to know what test files are available, and you need to know how to create test files of your own when necessary.

In addition, the security requirements for the test system will probably be more relaxed than those for the production system. That's because application programmers need access to CICS testing and debugging aids such as the CEMT, CECI, and CEDF transactions. Because these transactions give the user access to a wide range of CICS functions, they are usually off-limits to users of the production system. I'll show you how to use CEMT and CECI later in this chapter, and you'll learn how to use CEDF in chapter 12.

Finally, most installations have policies for how program testing is managed. Some shops just have a simple set of manual procedures for moving programs from test to production. But most larger shops use some sort of change management software to automate the process. Change management software keeps track of the status and location of each program within an application, and it helps ensure that two programmers don't modify a program at the same time. It also manages multiple versions of programs, so that when the current version of a program is taken from production for maintenance, a previous version can be temporarily installed in production until the maintenance is complete. In either case, you need to learn the change management procedures in place at your installation.

How to unit test a CICS program

As an application programmer, unit testing your programs is your responsibility. Before you begin testing your program, I suggest you develop a *test plan*. The test plan is a strategy you'll follow when you test your program. Since the burden of proof is on the programmer, you should prepare the test plan carefully.

Figure 11-2 lists a generalized test plan that can serve as a starting point for your test plans. As you can see, it has three steps. The first is to test the BMS map definitions. I suggest you do this before you begin coding the program. That way, you can dispense with trivial problems

1. Before coding the program, test the mapsets under CICS.

2. After coding the program, test with a carefully chosen set of valid transactions.

3. After testing with valid data, test the program's edit routines against every possible combination of errors.

Figure 11-2 A three-step plan for unit testing CICS programs

like misspelled words and misaligned data right away. The second step is to test your program using a small set of well-chosen input data and verify the results. The third step is to give the program a thorough workout, trying every combination of invalid input you can think of to make sure the program's editing routines work properly.

Figure 11-3 provides a list of things you should check for during each of these testing phases. Obviously, this isn't an exhaustive list. But it should give you an idea of the errors you should look for.

How to test a BMS map

To test the BMS maps, you must first define them to CICS (or use a generic map and mapset name assigned to you), assemble them, and display them to verify their format. There are several ways to display a map under CICS. One is to use the CECI transaction to issue a SEND MAP MAPONLY command interactively. I'll show you how to use CECI in a moment.

Another is to develop a program that accepts a map and mapset name from the command line, then issues a SEND MAP MAPONLY command to display the specified map. For example, if this program were started with the trans-id MAPS, you could type this CICS command:

```
MAPS MNTMAP2 MNTSET1
```

to display the map named MNTMAP2 that belongs to the mapset named MNTSET1.

If you're using CICS OS/2, you can start the transaction CSCA. This displays a list of all available maps, as shown in the first part of figure 11-4. Here, I've typed the name of the map and mapset I want to display (MNTMAP2 in MNTSET1). When I press the Enter key, CSCA displays the map, as shown in part 2 of figure 11-4.

Unfortunately, because the CSCA transaction uses the MAPONLY option to display the map, you can't determine if the map's variable fields are formatted properly. To do that, you can code a short program that's customized to display a specific map. Figure 11-5 shows the source

What to check for as you examine the appearance of the screen	Are all headings and captions placed correctly?
	Are the user instructions displayed properly?
	Is there any garbage on the screen?
	Are there any misspellings?
	Do all the fields have the correct attributes?
	Is the cursor in the correct initial location?
	Does the cursor move correctly from field to field?
What to check for as you enter valid data	Are all program screens displayed in the correct sequence?
	Do all attention keys work correctly?
	Are the user messages always correct?
	Are the functions of all attention keys indicated?
	Does the program properly acknowledge receipt of valid data?
	Are work fields properly cleared after each valid transaction?
	Are control totals accumulated properly?
	Are files updated properly?
What to check for as you enter invalid data	Does each case of invalid data for each field yield an appropriate error message?
	Do look-up routines work properly?
	Is the field in error highlighted?
	Is the cursor positioned at the field in error?
	When you correct the error, do the error message and highlighting go away?
	Does the program post transactions even though errors are detected?
	Does the program detect all possible cross-validation errors?
	Does the program properly detect and highlight multiple entry errors?

Figure 11-3 A checklist for program testing

code for a program that displays the MNTMAP2 map in the MNTSET1 mapset. As you can see, the program moves ALL 'X' to each field in the symbolic map before issuing the SEND MAP command. Figure 11-6 shows the display that this program produces.

Because this program is so simple, it takes just a few minutes to customize it for any map. You just change the name of the symbolic map in the COPY statement and the name of the map and mapset in the SEND MAP command. Then, you change the MOVE statement so it moves data to each field in the symbolic map. In figure 11-5, all of the fields are alphanumeric, so I moved ALL 'X' to each. If the symbolic map includes numeric fields, you should add another MOVE statement that moves numeric literals instead.

How to test with valid input

When you're ready to test a program, you should start by testing the program with valid data. To do that, you need to plan a small set of input transactions. For example, I tested the order entry program using the three transactions listed in figure 11-7. For this initial test, it isn't

Part 1

After starting the CSCA transaction, the user types the name of the map and mapset in the appropriate fields and presses the Enter key.

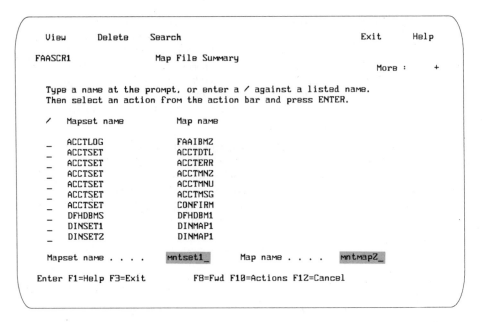

```
    View        Delete      Search                                Exit      Help

  FAASCR1                     Map File Summary
                                                               More :       +

     Type a name at the prompt, or enter a / against a listed name.
     Then select an action from the action bar and press ENTER.

     /     Mapset name          Map name

     _     ACCTLOG              FAAIBMZ
     _     ACCTSET              ACCTDTL
     _     ACCTSET              ACCTERR
     _     ACCTSET              ACCTMNZ
     _     ACCTSET              ACCTMNU
     _     ACCTSET              ACCTMSG
     _     ACCTSET              CONFIRM
     _     DFHDBMS              DFHDBM1
     _     DINSET1              DINMAP1
     _     DINSETZ              DINMAP1

     Mapset name . . . .   mntset1_      Map name . . . .   mntmapZ_

  Enter F1=Help F3=Exit           F8=Fwd F10=Actions F1Z=Cancel
```

Part 2

CSCA responds by displaying the requested map.

```
  MNTMAPZ              Customer Maintenance



  Customer number. . . . :

  Last name. . . . . . . .
  First name . . . . . . .
  Address. . . . . . . . .
  City . . . . . . . . . .
  State. . . . . . . . . .
  Zip Code . . . . . . . .







  F3=Exit    F1Z=Cancel
```

Figure 11-4 Using the CICS OS/2 CSCA transaction to display a map

```
 IDENTIFICATION DIVISION.
*
 PROGRAM-ID.  TESTMAP.
*
 ENVIRONMENT DIVISION.
*
 DATA DIVISION.
*
 WORKING-STORAGE SECTION.
*
 COPY MNTSET1.
*
 PROCEDURE DIVISION.
*
 0000-DISPLAY-TEST-MAP.
*
 MOVE ALL 'X' TO CUSTNO2O
                 LNAMEO
                 FNAMEO
                 ADDRO
                 CITYO
                 STATEO
                 ZIPCODEO
                 MSG2O.
 EXEC CICS
     SEND MAP('MNTMAP2')
          MAPSET('MNTSET1')
          FROM(MNTMAP2O)
          ERASE
 END-EXEC.
 EXEC CICS
     RETURN
 END-EXEC.
```

Figure 11-5 A program that displays the MNTMAP2 map

```
MNTMAP2              Customer Maintenance


   Customer number. . . . : XXXXX

   Last name. . . . . . . XXXXXXXXXXXXXXXXXXXXXXXXXXXX
   First name . . . . . . XXXXXXXXXXXXXXXXXX
   Address. . . . . . . . XXXXXXXXXXXXXXXXXXXXXXXXXXXX
   City . . . . . . . . . XXXXXXXXXXXXXXXXXX
   State. . . . . . . . . XX
   Zip Code . . . . . . . XXXXXXXXX







   XXXXXXXXXXXXXXXXXXXXXXXXXXXXXXXXXXXXXXXXXXXXXXXXXXXXXXXXXXXXXXXXXXXXXXXXXXXXX
   F3=Exit   F12=Cancel
```

Figure 11-6 Output from the TESTMAP program

Transaction 1

Customer number:		100000
P/O number:		ABC-1054

Product	Qty	Net
3000-001	5	

Transaction 2

Customer number:		100001
P/O number:		

Product	Qty	Net
3100-001	1	
3100-002	10	32.50
3100-003	5	

Transaction 3

Customer number:		100002
P/O number:		

Product	Qty	Net
3000-001	1	
3000-002	3	
3000-003	5	0.00
3000-004	7	
3000-005	9	
3000-006	11	50
3000-007	13	
3000-008	15	49.95
3000-009	17	
3000-010	19	

Figure 11-7   Three valid transactions for the order entry program

necessary to create a large amount of input data. Instead, the input data should represent the range of input that the program should accept. Thus, I included one order that has just one line item (the minimum), one that has three, and one that has ten (the maximum). I included some line items that omit the net price field so the list price will be used and some that override the list price by entering a net price value. And I omitted the P/O number on two orders, since this field is optional.

An important part of planning this test is planning how you will review the results. It's not sufficient to rely on the appearance of the screen alone. Since the order entry program writes records to a file named INVOICE, you need to examine the contents of the INVOICE file both before and after the test run. Otherwise, how will you know if the

```
//PRTFILE    JOB   (job-accounting information)
//           EXEC  PGM=IDCAMS
//SYSPRINT   DD    SYSOUT=A
//SYSIN      DD    *
 PRINT INDATASET(DLOWE2.TEST.INVOICE) DUMP
 PRINT INDATASET(DLOWE2.TEST.INVCTL)  DUMP
/*
//
```

Figure 11-8 An MVS IDCAMS job to print the contents of the INVOICE and INVCTL files

orders were posted properly? In addition, the order entry program invokes the GETINV program, which updates the INVCTL file. So you'll have to examine the contents of INVCTL before and after the test run, too.

How do you examine the contents of these test files? There are several ways. If the files are VSAM files, you can use the VSAM utility program IDCAMS to print the file contents. For example, figure 11-8 shows an MVS batch job that runs IDCAMS to print the contents of the INVOICE and INVCTL files. The output from this job will list the contents of each record in the two files, both in character and hexadecimal format. Before you can run this job, however, you must use the CEMT transaction to close the INVOICE and INVCTL files. You'll see how to do that later in this chapter.

Another way to examine the file contents is to develop a CICS program that displays or prints the contents of the file. Then, you can run this program before and after the test run. Or, you can use any of several non-IBM utility programs to display the contents of any VSAM file at a CICS terminal.

How to test with invalid input

When you've determined that the program works properly for valid input data, it's time to test the program's editing routines to make sure they don't allow any invalid data to go undetected. To do this, you should consider the editing requirements of every field. And you should consider editing requirements of fields in combination with one another.

When you test with invalid data, you should obviously look for errors in the way the program finds and indicates entry errors. Are the error messages appropriate? Are the incorrect fields highlighted? When you correct the errors, do the error message and the highlighting go away?

Beyond these cosmetic concerns, however, you want to make sure that your edit routines are comprehensive. In other words, they must not allow any form of incorrect data to pass through. The only way to do that is to enter every form of invalid data you can imagine into every field. For example, the quantity field for the order entry program must be a numeric integer that's greater than zero. What happens if you enter ABC? Spaces? A decimal point? Zero? A negative number? Nothing? You can be sure your editing routines work properly only if you test every input field with every type of invalid data.

You must be especially concerned with fields that require cross-validation. The order entry program has many cross-validation requirements. What happens if you enter a quantity without a product code? A product code without a quantity? A net price without a product code or quantity? And if you omit the net price but enter a product code and a quantity, does the program properly use the list price?

Top-down testing

One of the problems with testing a program is that it may contain dozens of bugs the first time it's run. As a result, it's often impossible to isolate each problem the first time around, so several test runs may be necessary. The idea of *top-down testing* is to simplify each test run by reducing the amount of code tested during each.

When you use top-down testing, you don't code the entire program and then test it. Instead, you code and test in increments. Event-driven program design lends itself especially well to top-down testing. You simply decide which events' responses you wish to implement first. For the order entry program, you might start by implementing the first-time and Enter key responses first. Then, after that code is thoroughly debugged, you might add the PF4 key response. You continue until all of the program responses have been coded and tested.

During top-down testing, you might decide to put off implementing a particularly complex module until you've tested the modules that surround it. For example, for the order entry program, I might decide to defer coding and testing the edit module (module 1200 and its subordinates) until I'm sure the basic operation of module 1000 (process-order-map) is sound. To do that, I'll create a *program stub* in module 1200's place.

The coding for a program stub is brief. It does the minimum amount of work necessary for the calling module to continue. For example, the program stub for module 1200 might contain a single MOVE statement, like this:

```
MOVE 'Y' TO VALID-DATA-SW.
```

In other words, the edit module always indicates that the data is valid, whether it is or not. You might take this program stub one step further and actually move valid data to critical program variables so that subsequent modules can operate on them.

To force a new program copy

```
CEMT SET PROGRAM(name) NEWCOPY
```

To open or close a data set

```
CEMT SET DATASET(name) {OPEN|CLOSED}
```

To disable a program

```
CEMT SET PROGRAM(name) {DISABLED|ENABLED}
```

To disable a transaction

```
CEMT SET TRANSACTION(name) {DISABLED|ENABLED}
```

Figure 11-9 CEMT commands commonly used for testing

CICS service transactions for testing

Now that you have a general idea of how to approach CICS testing, I want to show you how to use two CICS service transactions that are often useful during testing. The first, CEMT, lets you manage the status of CICS resources such as programs, transactions, data sets, and so on. The second, CECI, lets you interactively execute any CICS command.

CEMT: the master terminal transaction

The *master terminal transaction*, more commonly known as *CEMT*, lets you control a variety of CICS functions. To use the CEMT transaction, you type the trans-id CEMT followed by a CEMT command. CEMT then executes the command and displays a full-screen panel showing the results of the command. There, you can enter additional CEMT commands or leave CEMT by pressing PF3. Alternatively, you can enter the CEMT transaction without a CEMT command. Then, CEMT will help you construct a command by presenting command choices and prompting you for options.

Figure 11-9 shows the CEMT commands you'll use most often when testing application programs. Notice that I underlined certain letters in each command keyword. CEMT lets you abbreviate each keyword to as few characters as you wish, as long as you supply enough characters to distinguish one keyword from another. The underlining in figure 11-9 indicates the minimum abbreviations CEMT will accept for each keyword.

The first command in figure 11-9 tells CICS that you've updated an application program, so it should read a fresh copy of the program from disk. You should issue this command whenever you recompile a program while CICS is running. Otherwise, CICS may continue to use the older version of the program. To force CICS to access a new version of a program named CUSTMNT1, you would issue this command:

```
CEMT SET PROGRAM(CUSTMNT1) NEWCOPY
```

or its abbreviated form,

```
CEMT S PR(CUSTMNT1) N
```

Then, after you press the PF3 key to exit CEMT, you can test the new version of CUSTMNT1.

You use the next CEMT command, SET DATASET, when you need to print the contents of a CICS data set while CICS is running. To do that, you issue a command like this:

```
CEMT S DA(INVOICE) C
```

This closes and deallocates the file so it can be accessed by a batch job. After you've finished printing the file, you can open it again with this command:

```
CEMT S DA(INVOICE) OP
```

If you don't, however, CICS will automatically open the file the first time a program tries to access it.

The last two CEMT commands in figure 11-9 are useful when a programming error forces a pseudo-conversational program into a loop. Ordinarily, a simple programming loop (such as a PERFORM UNTIL statement whose UNTIL condition never becomes true) will be detected by CICS, and the task will be cancelled. However, sometimes a pseudo-conversational program will refuse to break its pseudo-conversational processing cycle. A loop like this can tie up a terminal indefinitely, restarting the same program over and over again every time you press an attention key.

To break this type of loop, you can use CEMT to disable either the program or the transaction that's causing the loop. The only catch is that you must enter the CEMT command from another terminal. For example, suppose the MNT1 transaction is in a loop. To disable this transaction, you would enter this command at another terminal:

```
CEMT S TRAN(MNT1) D
```

When you've corrected the problem, remember to use CEMT to enable the transaction or program.

CECI: the command-level interpreter

Another CICS service transaction that's useful for program development is *CECI*, the *command level interpreter*. You invoke it by typing the trans-id CECI, optionally followed by a CICS command (such as SEND MAP or READ). The command level interpreter checks the syntax of the command and displays a panel telling you it is about to execute the command. When you press the Enter key, CECI executes the command and displays a panel showing the result. Because you can execute just about any CICS command from within CECI, I think you'll come to find CECI to be one of most useful CICS testing aids.

I've already mentioned one possible use of CECI: issuing a SEND MAP command to test a map before you've written the program that will process it. The 13 parts of figure 11-10 show another common use: updating the contents of a file without developing a special-purpose program. Here, I use CECI to update the contents of the INVCTL file so the starting invoice number is 100000. To do this, I issue two commands from CECI: a READ UPDATE command to retrieve the current INVCTL record and a REWRITE command to update the record. Along the way, I use one of CECI's most powerful features, its ability to use variables, to store the retrieved record and the record key. (For this example, I used the OS/2 version of CECI. The mainframe version is nearly identical.)

Part 1 of figure 11-10 shows the CECI command I used to start the interpreter. Although you can follow the CECI trans-id with a command, in this case I didn't. As a result, CECI displayed its start-up panel, shown in part 2. This panel lists all of the CICS commands you can issue from CECI. Before typing a command, however, I pressed PF5 so I could define two variables that I'll use in the READ and REWRITE commands. CECI responded by displaying its Variables panel, shown in part 3 of figure 11-10.

All CECI variables begin with an ampersand (&). As you can see, CECI has five pre-defined variables: &DFHC, &DFHW, &DFHR, &LEN, and &DATA. To the right of each variable name is the variable's length (for &LEN, H indicates the variable is a binary halfword). The current contents of each variable is shown to the right of its length.

To define variables of your own, you simply add them to the list. In part 4 of figure 11-10, I added definitions for two variables: &REC, a 7-byte variable I'll use to hold the INVCTL record, and &KEY, a 1-byte variable I'll use for the record key. When I pressed the Enter key, CECI added these variables to its variable list. Then, as part 5 shows, I typed an initial value (0) for the &KEY variable.

Having defined the variables I'll need, I pressed the Enter key to return to the start-up screen. Here, as you can see in part 6 of figure 11-13, I typed a CICS READ command:

```
read dataset(invctl) into(&rec)
```

Notice that in CECI, apostrophes are not required to indicate literals. Whenever you use a variable value, however, the ampersand is required.

When I pressed the Enter key, CECI responded with the panel in part 7, which indicates that there is a problem with the command's syntax. When I pressed PF9 to see the syntax messages, CECI displayed the syntax messages panel shown in part 8. Here, you can see that I omitted

Part 1

The user starts the
command-level
interpreter by entering
the trans-id CECI.

```
ceci
```

Part 2

CECI displays its start-up
panel, which lists the
commands that can be
issued.

```
STATUS: Enter one of the following:
      CICS OS/Z Command Interpreter  CICS  OS/Z  Version  1.Z
ABEND         FREEMAIN     REWRITE
ADDRESS       GETMAIN      SEND
ALLOCATE      HANDLE       SET
ASKTIME       IGNORE       SIGNOFF
ASSIGN        INQUIRE      SIGNON
CANCEL        ISSUE        START
CONNECT       LINK         STARTBR
CONVERSE      LOAD         SUSPEND
DELAY         POP          SYNCPOINT
DELETE        POST         UNLOCK
DELETEQ       PUSH         WAIT
DEQ           READ         WRITE
DUMP          READNEXT     WRITEQ
ENDBR         READPREV     XCTL
ENQ           READQ
ENTER         RECEIVE
EXTRACT       RESETBR
FORMATTIME    RETRIEVE
FREE          RETURN


PF 1 Help Z HEX 3 End 4 EIB 5 VAR 6 User          9 MSG
```

Figure 11-10   Using the CECI transaction

Part 3

The user presses PF5, and CICS responds by displaying the Variables panel.

```
Variables:

&DFHC      +00030 EXEC CICS ASSIGN SYSID(&DATA)
&DFHW      +00040 WRITEQ TS QUEUE(CECIV123) FROM(&DFHC)
&DFHR      +00040 READQ TS QUEUE(CECIV123) INTO(&DFHC)
&LEN    H     +00030
&DATA      +00100




RESPONSE:
PF 1 Help 2 HEX 3 End 4 EIB 5 VAR 6 User          9 MSG
```

Part 4

The user adds two variables, &rec and &key, to the variable list and presses the Enter key.

```
Variables:

&DFHC      +00030 EXEC CICS ASSIGN SYSID(&DATA)
&DFHW      +00040 WRITEQ TS QUEUE(CECIV123) FROM(&DFHC)
&DFHR      +00040 READQ TS QUEUE(CECIV123) INTO(&DFHC)
&LEN    H     +00030
&DATA      +00100
&rec       7
&key       1




RESPONSE:
PF 1 Help 2 HEX 3 End 4 EIB 5 VAR 6 User          9 MSG
```

Figure 11-10 Using the CECI transaction (continued)

Part 5

CECI confirms that the variables have been defined. The user types an initial value of zero for the &KEY variable and presses the Enter key.

```
Variables:

&DFHC       +00030 EXEC CICS ASSIGN SYSID(&DATA)
&DFHW       +00040 WRITEQ TS QUEUE(CECIV123) FROM(&DFHC)
&DFHR       +00040 READQ TS QUEUE(CECIV123) INTO(&DFHC)
&LEN        H      +00030
&DATA       +00100
&REC        +00007
&KEY        +00001 0




RESPONSE:
PF 1 Help 2 HEX 3 End 4 EIB 5 VAR 6 User            9 MSG
```

Part 6

CECI redisplays its initial screen. The user types a READ command and presses the Enter key.

```
 read dataset(invctl) into(&rec)
STATUS: Enter one of the following:
     CICS OS/2 Command Interpreter  CICS  OS/2  Version  1.2
ABEND       FREEMAIN     REWRITE
ADDRESS     GETMAIN      SEND
ALLOCATE    HANDLE       SET
ASKTIME     IGNORE       SIGNOFF
ASSIGN      INQUIRE      SIGNON
CANCEL      ISSUE        START
CONNECT     LINK         STARTBR
CONVERSE    LOAD         SUSPEND
DELAY       POP          SYNCPOINT
DELETE      POST         UNLOCK
DELETEQ     PUSH         WAIT
DEQ         READ         WRITE
DUMP        READNEXT     WRITEQ
ENDBR       READPREV     XCTL
ENQ         READQ
ENTER       RECEIVE
EXTRACT     RESETBR
FORMATTIME  RETRIEVE
FREE        RETURN

PF 1 Help 2 HEX 3 End 4 EIB 5 VAR 6 User            9 MSG
```

Figure 11-10   Using the CECI transaction (continued)

Part 7

CECI indicates that
there is an error in the
READ command's
syntax. The user
presses PF9 to display
the syntax error
message.

```
 READ DATASET( INVCTL) INTO( &REC)
STATUS: Command syntax check                              NAME=
EXEC CICS READ
DATASET       INVCTL
EQUAL
FILE
GENERIC
GTEQ
INTO
KEYLENGTH
LENGTH
RBA
RIDFLD
RRN
SET
SYSID
UPDATE




RESPONSE: Error messages received.
PF 1 Help 2 HEX 3 End 4 EIB 5 VAR 6 User 7 SB 8 SF 9 MSG
```

Part 8

CECI displays the syntax
error messages. The user
presses the Enter key.

```
 READ DATASET( INVCTL) INTO( &REC)
        Syntax Messages:

FAA0267E READ command requires RIDFLD operand










PF 1 Help 2 HEX 3 End      5 VAR 6 User
```

Figure 11-10 Using the CECI transaction (continued)

Part 9

The user corrects the command and presses the Enter key. CECI indicates that it is about to execute the READ command.

```
 READ DATASET(INVCTL) INTO(&REC) RIDFLD(&KEY) UPDATE
STATUS: About to execute command                              NAME=
EXEC CICS READ
DATASET       INVCTL
EQUAL
FILE
GENERIC
GTEQ
INTO
KEYLENGTH
LENGTH
RBA
RIDFLD        0
RRN
SET
SYSID
UPDATE




RESPONSE:
PF 1 Help 2 HEX 3 End 4 EIB 5 VAR 6 User 7 SB 8 SF 9 MSG
```

Part 10

The user presses the Enter key. CECI executes the READ command and displays the results.

```
 READ DATASET(INVCTL) INTO(&REC) RIDFLD(&KEY) UPDATE
STATUS: Command execution complete                            NAME=
EXEC CICS READ
DATASET       INVCTL
EQUAL
FILE
GENERIC
GTEQ
INTO          0555555
KEYLENGTH
LENGTH
RBA
RIDFLD        0
RRN
SET
SYSID
UPDATE




RESPONSE: Normal                              EIBRESP=+0000000000
PF 1 Help 2 HEX 3 End 4 EIB 5 VAR 6 User 7 SB 8 SF 9 MSG
```

Figure 11-10 Using the CECI transaction (continued)

Part 11

The user changes the
READ command to a
REWRITE command
and presses the Enter
key. CECI indicates that
it is about to execute the
REWRITE command.

```
REWRITE DATASET(INVCTL) FROM(&REC)
STATUS: About to execute command                        NAME=
EXEC CICS REWRITE
DATASET     INVCTL
FILE
FROM        0555555
LENGTH
SYSID




RESPONSE:
PF 1 Help 2 HEX 3 End 4 EIB 5 VAR 6 User 7 SB 8 SF 9 MSG
```

Part 12

The user changes the
contents of the FROM field
and presses the Enter key.
CECI again indicates that it
is about to execute the
command.

```
REWRITE DATASET(INVCTL) FROM(&REC)
STATUS: About to execute command                        NAME=
EXEC CICS REWRITE
DATASET     INVCTL
FILE
FROM        0100000
LENGTH
SYSID




RESPONSE:
PF 1 Help 2 HEX 3 End 4 EIB 5 VAR 6 User 7 SB 8 SF 9 MSG
```

Figure 11-10 Using the CECI transaction (continued)

Part 13

The user presses the Enter key. CECI executes the REWRITE command and displays the results.

```
REWRITE DATASET( INVCTL) FROM(&REC)
STATUS: Command execution complete                          NAME=
EXEC CICS REWRITE
DATASET      INVCTL
FILE
FROM         0100000
LENGTH
SYSID




RESPONSE: Normal                              EIBRESP=+0000000000
PF 1 Help 2 HEX 3 End 4 EIB 5 VAR 6 User 7 SB 8 SF 9 MSG
```

Figure 11-10   Using the CECI transaction (continued)

the required parameter RIDFLD. Although it didn't generate a syntax error, I also omitted the UPDATE option, which will be required by the subsequent REWRITE command. So I returned to the status panel and typed in the complete READ command:

```
read dataset(invctl) into(&rec) ridfld(&key) update
```

Then, I pressed the Enter key and CECI displayed the "About to execute command" panel shown in part 9 of figure 11-10.

When I pressed the Enter key again, CECI executed the READ command and displayed the results in part 10. Here, you can see that the command was executed successfully, and you can see the value of the &REC variable next to the INTO keyword near the middle of the panel: 0555555. To update the record, I first typed over the READ command, replacing it with this rewrite command:

```
rewrite dataset(invctl) from(&rec)
```

Then, when I pressed the Enter key, CECI displayed the "About to execute command" panel shown in part 11. Rather than execute the command as is, however, I moved the cursor down to the FROM variable and typed the value 0100000 over the old value. When I pressed the Enter key, CECI display the "About to execute command" panel again, as shown in part 12. I pressed the Enter key once more to execute the command, and CECI displayed the results in part 13. Again, you can

the command, and CECI displayed the results in part 13. Again, you can see that the command executed normally, so the INVCTL record has been properly updated.

Terms

unit test
concurrency test
integration test
regression test
test plan
top-down testing
program stub
master terminal transaction
CEMT
CECI
command level interpreter

Objectives

1. Describe the four phases of testing mentioned in this chapter.

2. Explain the techniques used to test a BMS mapset definition before you've coded your program.

3. Given the specifications for a CICS program, develop an initial set of test data that consists of valid transactions.

4. Explain how using top-down testing can improve the testing process.

5. Use the CEMT transaction to perform the following functions:
   a. update the working copy of a CICS program
   b. open and close a data set
   c. disable and enable a transaction or program

6. Use the CECI transaction to execute CICS commands interactively.

Chapter 12

Debugging a CICS abend

When a CICS program encounters an error from which it cannot recover, it ends in an *abnormal termination*, or *abend*. This chapter presents two common techniques for finding the cause of an abend: (1) using an IBM-supplied debugging aid called the Execution Diagnostics Facility, or EDF, and (2) interpreting the storage dump that results from the abend. During testing, you use EDF to determine the cause of an abend. Storage dumps are normally used only to debug abends in production programs. Before I show you these two techniques, you need to know two things: the two most commonly encountered problems that lead to an abend and the compiler output that's useful for debugging.

Abend codes   When a CICS program terminates abnormally, an *abnormal termination message* (or just *abend message*) is sent to the terminal. Figure 12-1 shows a typical abend message. Here, the transaction DFXX was running the program DFXXP00A when the abend occurred. Each type of CICS abend has its own *abend code*; in this case, the abend code is ASRA. The "AT H400" indicates that the task was running at the terminal named H400. Almost always, it's the abend code that gives you the information you need to begin debugging your program.

IBM's *CICS Messages and Codes* manual documents the more than 300 possible abend codes. Fortunately, only a few of them occur regularly. And most of those fall into two categories: exceptional condition abends and program check abends.

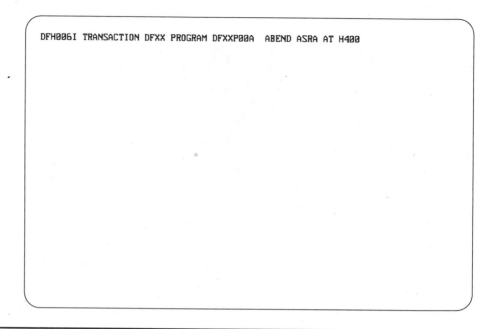

DFH0061 TRANSACTION DFXX PROGRAM DFXXP00A   ABEND ASRA AT H400

Figure 12-1   CICS transaction abend message

Exceptional condition abends

As you know, when a CICS command encounters an unusual situation, it generates an exceptional condition. For example, if a READ command tries to read a record that doesn't exist, the NOTFND condition is raised. If an exceptional condition occurs when no HANDLE CONDITION command for the condition is in effect or when you don't code the RESP option for the command, the task is abnormally terminated. Then, CICS displays an abend code that identifies the exceptional condition that caused the abend.

Figure 12-2 lists these codes. As you can see, all of the abend codes for exceptional conditions begin with the letters AEI or AEY. When you encounter one of these codes, you can refer to the list in figure 12-2 to see which condition was raised. In many cases, the abend code itself will be enough to solve the problem. For example, if the abend code AEIS is encountered, it means the program tried to access a file that isn't open. So all you have to do is check the status of each file accessed by the program to correct the problem.

Obviously, if you specify the RESP option on all of your CICS commands, you should never encounter AEI*x* or AEY*x* abends. In that case, your program's error processing routine should display a message that indicates which exceptional condition occurred.

Code	Condition	Code	Condition
AEIA	ERROR	AEI9	MAPFAIL
AEID	EOF	AEYA	INVERRTERM
AEIE	EODS	AEYB	INVMPSZ
AEIG	INBFMH	AEYC	IGREQID
AEIH	ENDINPT	AEYE	INVLDC
AEII	NONVAL	AEYG	JIDERR
AEIJ	NOSTART	AEYH	QIDERR
AEIK	TERMIDERR	AEYJ	DSSTAT
AEIL	DSIDERRR	AEYK	SELNERR
AEIM	NOTFND	AEYL	FUNCERR
AEIN	DUPREC	AEYM	UNEXPIN
AEIO	DUPKEY	AEYN	NOPASSBKRD
AEIP	INVREQ	AEYO	NOPASSBKWRR
AEIQ	IOERR	AEYP	SEQIDERR
AEIR	NOSPACE	SEYQ	SYSIDERR
AEIS	NOTOPEN	AEYR	ISINVREQ
AEIT	ENDFILE	AEYT	ENVDEFERR
AEIU	ILLOGIC	AEYU	IGREQCD
AEIV	LENGERRR	AEYV	SESSERR
AEIW	QZERO	AEYY	NOTALLOC
AEIZ	ITEMERR	AEYZ	CBIDERR
AEI0	PGMIDERR	AEY0	INVEXITREQ
AEI1	TRANSIDERR	AEY1	INVPARTNSET
AEI2	ENDDATA	AEY2	INVPARTN
AEI3	INVTSREQ	AEY3	PARTNFAIL
AEI8	TSIOERR	AEY7	NOTAUTH

Figure 12-2 AEI*x* and AEY*x* abend codes

Program check abends

When a program tries to perform an operation that isn't allowed by the hardware, a *program check* occurs. For example, trying to perform an arithmetic operation on non-numeric data results in a *data exception* program check. A program check always causes your program to abend with the code ASRA. As a result, ASRA is the abend code you'll probably see most often. Fifteen different types of program checks can occur on System/370-compatible machines. The technique you use to find out which program check occurred and to determine the exact cause of the program check depends on whether you're using EDF or a storage dump, as I'll explain later.

Other abend codes

Figure 12-3 lists a few other abend codes you might encounter. These abend codes represent errors other than program checks and exceptional conditions, so they're not covered by the ASRA, AEI*x* or AEY*x* codes. If

Code	Explanation
ABMB	You used the absolute cursor positioning technique and supplied a cursor position that's beyond the limit of the output device.
ABM0	The specified map isn't in the mapset. The map name is misspelled either in the program or in the mapset or the program specifies the wrong mapset.
AFCA	The data set has been disabled.
AICA	The task exceeded the execution time limit for runaway tasks; in other words, the task was looping.
AKCP	The task was canceled because it was suspended for a period longer than the transaction's defined deadlock timeout period. This is sometimes caused by programming practices that lead to deadlock situations, but it can also be caused by problems internal to CICS.
AKCT	The task was canceled because it was waiting for terminal input for a period longer than the transaction's defined terminal read timeout period. This happens when an operator starts a conversational program and then leaves the terminal unattended for a long period of time.
APCT	The program could not be found or is disabled.
ASRB	An operating system abend has occurred; CICS was able to abend the transaction and continue processing.
ATCH	A master terminal operator purged the task.
ATCI	A master terminal operator purged the task, specifying FORCEPURGE to force the task to be cancelled immediately.

Figure 12-3 Other CICS abend codes

you encounter one of these abends, the brief explanation in figure 12-3 should be enough to help you find the problem. If you encounter an abend code not listed here, you'll have to consult the IBM manual *CICS Messages and Codes*.

Compiler output used for debugging

Whether you use the Execution Diagnostics Facility or a CICS transaction dump to debug an abend, you need specific information from the program's compiler output. For example, to find out which COBOL statement was executing when the abend occured, you need to consult the *Condensed Procedure Listing*. To get this listing from the VS COBOL II compiler, you must specify the OFFSET compiler option. With OS/VS COBOL, you specify the CLIST option.

To locate specific fields in working storage, you need to examine the *Data Division Map*. The compiler option that causes VS COBOL II to generate this listing is MAP; for OS/VS COBOL, you use the DMAP option. In addition, if you're using VS COBOL II, you'll need the *TGT Memory Map* to find the start of working storage in a transaction dump. The TGT Memory Map is printed whenever you specify the OFFSET option. With OS/VS COBOL, you don't need the TGT Memory Map.

Figure 12-4 presents compiler output for a program named DFXXP00A that produces various CICS abends, depending on the PF key pressed by the user. The operation of this program is simple: On its first execution, it issues a SEND TEXT command that presents a menu that lets the user select a particular type of abend. On subsequent executions, it evaluates EIBAID to determine which PF key the user pressed and executes statements that will result in the selected abend. For example, if the user presses PF1 to force a data exception abend, the program moves invalid data to a numeric field, then uses the invalid data in a MULTIPLY statement.

Obviously, this program is not typical of the CICS programs you'll develop on the job. Nevertheless, it serves as a good example to use when learning how to debug CICS programs.

The listing in figure 12-4 was produced by Release 3.1 of the VS COBOL II compiler. Listings for other releases of the VS COBOL II compiler, and for the VS COBOL compiler, are similar enough that you shouldn't become confused if you're using one of those compilers instead. As you can see, the first 5 parts of the figure contain the source statement listing. (Keep in mind that the CICS translator processed the source file before the compiler was run, so the source listing in figure 12-4 includes many statements that were inserted by the translator.) Part 6 shows a portion of the Data Division Map, part 7 shows the Condensed Procedure Listing, and part 8 shows the beginning of the TGT Memory Map.

The Data Division Map lists the characteristics of each data field defined in your program. In part 6 of figure 12-4, I've shaded the entry for PACKED-FIELD-2. The main items you need to be concerned with in the Data Division Map are the *base locator*, found in the BASE LOCATOR column, and the *displacement* (or *offset*), found in the column labeled HEX-DISPLACEMENT BLK. You use these items to determine the address of a field in working storage. For PACKED-FIELD-2, the base locator is 0, and the displacement is 005.

You use the base locator and the displacement together to calculate the address of a particular field. To do that, you must find the base locator. VS COBOL II places its base locators in a control block called the *Task Global Table,* or *TGT*. The TGT Memory Map, shown in part 8 of figure 12-4, lists the offset of each field stored in the TGT. Here, I've shaded the entry for the working-storage base locators. As you can see, they are at offset 12C (hexadecimal) from the start of the TGT. Once

```
PP 5668-958 IBM VS COBOL II RELEASE 3.1 09/19/89          DFXXP00A  DATE 02/26/92   TIME 10:44:40  PAGE  2
LINEID PL SL ---+-*-A-1-B-+----2----+----3----+----4----+----5----+----6----+----7-|---+----8     MAP AND CROSS REFERENCE

000001 00010000     IDENTIFICATION DIVISION.
000002                   *
000003 00030000     PROGRAM-ID.              DFXXP00A.
000004                   *
000005 00050000     ENVIRONMENT DIVISION.
000006                   *
000007 00070000     DATA DIVISION.
000008                   *
000009 00090000     WORKING-STORAGE SECTION.
000010 00090134         *
000011 00090136     01  WORK-FIELDS.                                            OCL10
000012 00192000         *
000013 00192000     05  PACKED-FIELD-1          PIC S9(7)V99   COMP-3.  BLW=0000+000,0000000   5P
000014 00192000     05  PACKED-FIELD-2          PIC S9(7)V99   COMP-3.  BLW=0000+005,0000000   5P
000015 00192000     05  ALPHA-FIELD-2   REDEFINES PACKED-FIELD-2        BLW=0000+005,0000000   5C
000016                     PIC X(5).                                                           14
000017                   *
000018 00192000     01  I-O-AREA                PIC X(100).             BLW=0000+010         100C
000019 00192000         *
000020 00192000     01  START-UP-MESSAGE.                               BLW=0000+078      OCL948
000021 00192000         *
000022 00192000     05  FILLER PIC X(30)  VALUE 'ABEND TESTER         '.  BLW=0000+078,0000000  30C
000023 00000149     05  FILLER PIC X(49)  VALUE SPACE.                     BLW=0000+096,000001E  49C
000024 00192000     05  FILLER PIC X(79)  VALUE SPACE.                     IMP=0000+0C7,000004F  79C
000025 00000150     05  FILLER PIC X(30)  VALUE 'PRESS A PF KEY TO FORCE ONE OF'.  BLW=0000+116,000009E  30C
000026 00192000     05  FILLER PIC X(49)  VALUE 'THE FOLLOWING ABENDS:'.          BLW=0000+134,00000BC  49C
000027 00192000     05  FILLER PIC X(79)  VALUE SPACE.                            BLW=0000+165,00000ED  79C
000028 00192000     05  FILLER PIC X(30)  VALUE 'PF1 = ASRA (DATA EXCEPTION)'.    BLW=0000+1B4,000013C  30C
000029 00192000     05  FILLER PIC X(49)  VALUE SPACE.                            BLW=0000+1D2,000015A  49C
000030 00192000     05  FILLER PIC X(30)  VALUE 'PF2 = ASRA (DECIMAL DIVIDE EXC'. IMP
000031 00192000     05  FILLER PIC X(49)  VALUE 'EPTION)'.                        BLW=0000+203,000018B  30C
000032 00192000     05  FILLER PIC X(30)  VALUE 'PF3 = ASRA (PROTECTION EXCEPTI'. BLW=0000+221,00001A9  49C
000033 00192000     05  FILLER PIC X(49)  VALUE 'ON)'.                            BLW=0000+250,00001DA  30C
000034 00192000     05  FILLER PIC X(30)  VALUE 'PF4 = APCT (MISSING MAP)'.       BLW=0000+270,00001F8  49C
000035 00192000     05  FILLER PIC X(49)  VALUE SPACE.                            BLW=0000+2A1,0000229  30C
                                                                                  BLW=0000+2BF,0000247  49C
                                                                                  IMP
000036 00192000     05  FILLER PIC X(30)  VALUE 'PF5 = AEIO (PGMIDERR)'.          BLW=0000+2F0,0000278  30C
000037 00192000     05  FILLER PIC X(49)  VALUE SPACE.                            BLW=0000+30E,0000296  49C
000038 00192000     05  FILLER PIC X(30)  VALUE 'PF6 = AEIL (DSIDERR)'.           BLW=0000+33F,00002C7  30C
000039 00192000     05  FILLER PIC X(49)  VALUE SPACE.                            BLW=0000+35D,00002E5  49C
                                                                                  IMP
000040 00000173     05  FILLER PIC X(79)  VALUE SPACE.                            BLW=0000+38E,0000316  79C
000041 00192000     05  FILLER PIC X(30)  VALUE 'OR PRESS ENTER TO EXIT WITHOUT'. IMP
000042 00000178     05  FILLER PIC X(49)  VALUE 'ABENDING.'.                      BLW=0000+3DD,0000365  30C
                                                                                  BLW=0000+3FB,0000383  49C
000043 00000179         *
000044 00000180     01  TERMINATION-MESSAGE.                            BLW=0000+430         OCL9
000045 00000181         *
000046 00000182     05  FILLER PIC X(9)   VALUE 'GOOD BYE.'.            BLW=0000+430,0000000   9C
000047                   *
000048 00000183     01  COMMUNICATION-AREA      PIC X.                  BLW=0000+440           1C
```

Figure 12-4   Portions of the source listing for the abend tester program (part 1 of 8)

```
PP 5668-958 IBM VS COBOL II RELEASE 3.1 09/19/89              DFXXP00A  DATE 02/26/92  TIME 10:44:40  PAGE   3
LINEID PL SL  ----+--*A-1-B--+--1-+----2----+----3----+----4----+----5----+----6---+----7-|--+----8     MAP AND CROSS REFERENCE

000049              *
000050              COPY DFHAID.
000051C         01  DFHAID.                                   02000000   BLW=0000+448   0CL36
000052C         02  DFHNULL    PIC  X   VALUE IS ' '.         04000000   BLW=0000+449   0000000   1C
000053C         02  DFHENTER   PIC  X   VALUE IS QUOTE.       06000000   BLW=0000+44A   0000001   1C
000054C         02  DFHCLEAR   PIC  X   VALUE IS '_'.         08000000   BLW=0000+44B   0000002   1C
000055C         02  DFHCLRP    PIC  X   VALUE IS '='.         09000000   BLW=0000+44C   0000003   1C
000056C         02  DFHPEN     PIC  X   VALUE IS '='.         10000000   BLW=0000+44D   0000004   1C
000057C         02  DFHOPID    PIC  X   VALUE IS 'W'.         12000000   BLW=0000+44E   0000005   1C
000058C         02  DFHMSRE    PIC  X   VALUE IS 'X'.         14000000   BLW=0000+44F   0000006   1C
000059C         02  DFHSTRF    PIC  X   VALUE IS '='.         16000000   BLW=0000+450   0000007   1C
000060C         02  DFHTRIG    PIC  X   VALUE IS '"'.         18000000   BLW=0000+451   0000008   1C
000061C         02  DFHPA1     PIC  X   VALUE IS '%'.         20000000   BLW=0000+452   0000009   1C
000062C         02  DFHPA2     PIC  X   VALUE IS '>'.         22000000   BLW=0000+453   000000A   1C
000063C         02  DFHPA3     PIC  X   VALUE IS ','.         24000000   BLW=0000+454   000000B   1C
000064C         02  DFHPF1     PIC  X   VALUE IS '1'.         25000000   BLW=0000+455   000000C   1C
000065C         02  DFHPF2     PIC  X   VALUE IS '2'.         28000000   BLW=0000+456   000000D   1C
000066C         02  DFHPF3     PIC  X   VALUE IS '3'.         31000000   BLW=0000+457   000000E   1C
000067C         02  DFHPF4     PIC  X   VALUE IS '4'.         37000000   BLW=0000+458   000000F   1C
000068C         02  DFHPF5     PIC  X   VALUE IS '5'.         40000000   BLW=0000+459   0000010   1C
000069C         02  DFHPF6     PIC  X   VALUE IS '6'.         43000000   BLW=0000+45A   0000011   1C
000070C         02  DFHPF7     PIC  X   VALUE IS '7'.         46000000   BLW=0000+45B   0000012   1C
000071C         02  DFHPF8     PIC  X   VALUE IS '8'.         49000000   BLW=0000+45C   0000013   1C
000072C         02  DFHPF9     PIC  X   VALUE IS '9'.         52000000   BLW=0000+45D   0000014   1C
000073C         02  DFHPF10    PIC  X   VALUE IS ':'.         55000000   BLW=0000+45E   0000015   1C
000074C         02  DFHPF11    PIC  X   VALUE IS '#'.         58000000   BLW=0000+45F   0000016   1C
000075C         02  DFHPF12    PIC  X   VALUE IS '@'.         61000000   BLW=0000+460   0000017   1C
000076C         02  DFHPF13    PIC  X   VALUE IS 'A'.         67000000   BLW=0000+461   0000018   1C
000077C         02  DFHPF14    PIC  X   VALUE IS 'B'.         70000000   BLW=0000+462   0000019   1C
000078C         02  DFHPF15    PIC  X   VALUE IS 'C'.         73000000   BLW=0000+463   000001A   1C
000079C         02  DFHPF16    PIC  X   VALUE IS 'D'.         76000000   BLW=0000+464   000001B   1C
000080C         02  DFHPF17    PIC  X   VALUE IS 'E'.         79000000   BLW=0000+465   000001C   1C
000081C         02  DFHPF18    PIC  X   VALUE IS 'F'.         82000000   BLW=0000+466   000001D   1C
000082C         02  DFHPF19    PIC  X   VALUE IS 'G'.         85000000   BLW=0000+467   000001E   1C
000083C         02  DFHPF20    PIC  X   VALUE IS 'H'.         88000000   BLW=0000+468   000001F   1C
000084C         02  DFHPF21    PIC  X   VALUE IS 'I'.         91000000   BLW=0000+469   0000020   1C
000085C         02  DFHPF22    PIC  X   VALUE IS '¢'.         94000000   BLW=0000+46A   0000021   1C
000086C         02  DFHPF23    PIC  X   VALUE IS '.'.         97000000   BLW=0000+46B   0000022   1C
000087C         02  DFHPF24    PIC  X   VALUE IS '<'.         00000186   BLW=0000+46C   0000023   1C
000088              *
000089         01  DFHLDVER  PIC  X(22)  VALUE 'LD TABLE DFHEITAB 210.'.        BLW=0000+470   22C
000090         01  DFHEIDO   PICTURE S9(7)  COMPUTATIONAL-3 VALUE ZERO.         BLW=0000+488   4P
000091         01  DFHEIBO   PICTURE S9(4)  COMPUTATIONAL VALUE ZERO.           IMP           2C
000092         01  DFHEICB   PICTURE X(8)  VALUE IS ' '.            IMP    BLW=0000+498   8C
000093         01  DFHB0040  COMP  PIC  S9(8).                      BLW=0000+4A0   4C
000094         01  DFHB0041  COMP  PIC  S9(8).                      BLW=0000+4A8   4C
000095         01  DFHB0042  COMP  PIC  S9(8).                      BLW=0000+4B0   4C
000096         01  DFHB0043  COMP  PIC  S9(8).                      BLW=0000+4B8   4C
000097         01  DFHB0044  COMP  PIC  S9(8).                      BLW=0000+4C0   4C
000098         01  DFHB0045  COMP  PIC  S9(8).                      BLW=0000+4C8   4C
000099         01  DFHB0046  COMP  PIC  S9(8).                      BLW=0000+4D0   4C
000100         01  DFHB0047  COMP  PIC  S9(8).                      BLW=0000+4D8   4C
000101         01  DFHB0048  COMP  PIC  S9(8).                      BLW=0000+4E0   4C
000102
```

Figure 12-4 Portions of the source listing for the abend tester program (part 2 of 8)

```
PP 5668-958 IBM VS COBOL II RELEASE 3.1 09/19/89        DFXXP00A   DATE 02/26/92   TIME 10:44:40  PAGE   4
LINEID PL SL ---+--*-A-1-B--+--2---+---3---+----4---+----5---+----6---+----7-|---+----8    MAP AND CROSS REFERENCE

000103   01  DFHB0020  COMP PIC S9(4).                               BLW=0000+4E8      2C
000104   01  DFHB0021  COMP PIC S9(4).                               BLW=0000+4F0      2C
000105   01  DFHB0022  COMP PIC S9(4).                               BLW=0000+4F8      2C
000106   01  DFHB0023  COMP PIC S9(4).                               BLW=0000+500      2C
000107   01  DFHB0024  COMP PIC S9(4).                               BLW=0000+508      2C
000108   01  DFHB0025  COMP PIC S9(4).                               BLW=0000+510      2C
000109   01  DFHC0040  PIC X(4).                                     BLW=0000+518      4C
000110   01  DFHC0041  PIC X(4).                                     BLW=0000+520      4C
000111   01  DFHC0042  PIC X(4).                                     BLW=0000+528      4C
000112   01  DFHC0043  PIC X(4).                                     BLW=0000+530      4C
000113   01  DFHC0044  PIC X(4).                                     BLW=0000+538      4C
000114   01  DFHC0080  PIC X(8).                                     BLW=0000+540      8C
000115   01  DFHC0081  PIC X(8).                                     BLW=0000+548      8C
000116   01  DFHC0082  PIC X(8).                                     BLW=0000+550      8C
000117   01  DFHC0083  PIC X(8).                                     BLW=0000+558      8C
000118   01  DFHC0084  PIC X(8).                                     BLW=0000+560      8C
000119   01  DFHC0085  PIC X(8).                                     BLW=0000+568      8C
000120   01  DFHC0320  PIC X(32).                                    BLW=0000+570      32C
000121   01  DFHC0020  PIC X(2).                                     BLW=0000+590      2C
000122   01  DFHC0021  PIC X(2).                                     BLW=0000+598      2C
000123   01  DFHC0022  PIC X(2).                                     BLW=0000+5A0      2C
000124   01  DFHC0023  PIC X(2).                                     BLW=0000+5A8      2C
000125   01  DFHD0040  PIC S9(7)  COMP-3.                            BLW=0000+5B0      4P
000126   01  DFHC0010  PIC X(1).                                     BLW=0000+5B8      1C
000127   01  DFHC0011  PIC X(1).                                     BLW=0000+5C0      1C
000128   01  DFHC0060  PIC X(6).                                     BLW=0000+5C8      6C
000129   01  DFHC0070  PIC X(7).                                     BLW=0000+5D0      7C
000130   01  DFHC0071  PIC X(7).                                     BLW=0000+5D8      7C
000131   01  DFHC0440  PIC X(44).                                    BLW=0000+5E0      44C
000132   01  DFHDUMMY  COMP PIC S9(4).              00000187         BLW=0000+610      2C
000133   01  DFHEIVO   PICTURE X(29).               00000188         BLW=0000+618      29C
000134       LINKAGE SECTION.
000135   *
000136   01  DFHEIBLK.                                               BLL=0001+000      0CL85
000137   02  EIBTIME   PIC S9(7) COMP-3.                             BLL=0001+000      4P
000138   02  EIBDATE   PIC S9(7) COMP-3.                             BLL=0001+004      4P
000139   02  EIBTRNID  PIC X(4).                                     BLL=0001+008      4C
000140   02  EIBTASKN  PIC S9(7) COMP-3.                             BLL=0001+00C      4P
000141   02  DFHEIGDI  COMP PIC S9(4).                               BLL=0001+010      2C
000142   02  EIBCPOSN  COMP PIC S9(4).                               BLL=0001+012      2C
000143   02  EIBCALEN  COMP PIC S9(4).                               BLL=0001+014      2C
000144   02  EIBAID    PIC X(1).                                     BLL=0001+016      1C
000145   02  EIBFN     PIC X(2).                                     BLL=0001+017      2C
000146   02  EIBRCODE  PIC X(6).                                     BLL=0001+019      6C
000147   02  EIBDS     PIC X(8).                                     BLL=0001+01F      8C
000148   02  EIBREQID  PIC X(8).                                     BLL=0001+027      8C
000149   02  EIBRSRCE  PIC X(8).                                     BLL=0001+02F      8C
000150   02  EIBSYNC   PIC X(1).                                     BLL=0001+037      1C
000151   02  EIBFREE   PIC X(1).                                     BLL=0001+038      1C
000152   02  EIBRECV   PIC X(1).                                     BLL=0001+039      1C
000153   02  EIBFIL01  PIC X(1).                                     BLL=0001+03A      1C
000154   02  EIBATT    PIC X(1).                                     BLL=0001+03B      1C
000155   02  EIBEOC    PIC X(1).                                     BLL=0001+03C      1C
000156   02  EIBFMH    PIC X(1).                                     BLL=0001+03D      1C
000157   02  EIBCOMPL  PIC X(1).                                     BLL=0001+03E      1C
000158   02  EIBSIG    PIC X(1).                                     BLL=0001+03F      1C
000159   02                                                          BLL=0001+040
```

Figure 12-4 Portions of the source listing for the abend tester program (part 3 of 8)

```
PP 5668-958 IBM VS COBOL II RELEASE 3.1 09/19/89              DFXXP00A  DATE 02/26/92  TIME 10:44:40  PAGE    5
LINEID PL SL  ----+--*A-1-B---+----2----+----3----+----4----+----5----+----6----+----7-|----+----8   MAP AND CROSS REFERENCE

000160                  02  EIBCONF    PIC X(1).                                          BLL=0001+044,0000044  1C
000161                  02  EIBERR     PIC X(1).                                          BLL=0001+045,,0000045 1C
000162                  02  EIBERRCD   PIC X(4).                                          BLL=0001+046,0000046  4C
000163                  02  EIBSYNRB   PIC X(1).                                          BLL=0001+04A,0000004A 1C
000164                  02  EIBNODAT   PIC X(1).                                          BLL=0001+04B,0000004B 1C
000165                  02  EIBRESP    COMP PIC S9(8).                                    BLL=0001+04C,0000004C 4C
000166                  02  EIBRESP2   COMP PIC S9(8).                                    BLL=0001+050,0000050  4C
000167              01  EIBRLDBK   PIC X(1).    PIC X.                                    BLL=0001+054,0000054  1C
000168              01  DFHCOMMAREA         PIC X.                                        BLL=0002+000
000169          *
000170          01  COMMON-WORK-AREA.                                                     BLL=0003+000        0CL6
000171          *
000172              05  CWA-DATE            PIC 9(6).                                      BLL=0003+000,0000000  6C
000173          *
000174          PROCEDURE DIVISION USING DFHEIBLK DFHCOMMAREA.                            136 168
000175          *
000176          0000-FORCE-USER-ABEND.
000177          *
000178              EVALUATE TRUE
000179          *
000180          *EXEC CICS  WHEN EIBCALEN = ZERO                                          144 IMP
000181          **      SEND TEXT FROM(START-UP-MESSAGE)
000182          **      ERASE
000183          **      FREEKB
000184          *
000185          *END-EXEC
000186                  MOVE '  '    B  00067  ' TO DFHEIV0                               133
000187                  MOVE LENGTH OF START-UP-MESSAGE TO DFHB0020                       IMP  20  103
000188                  CALL 'DFHEI1' USING DFHEIV0 DFHDUMMY                              EXT 133 132
000189                  START-UP-MESSAGE DFHB0020                                         20  103
000190          *
000191              WHEN EIBAID = DFHPF1                                                  145  64
000192                  MOVE SPACE TO ALPHA-FIELD-2                                       IMP  15
000193                  MOVE 100 TO PACKED-FIELD-1                                        13   14
000194                  MULTIPLY PACKED-FIELD-1 BY PACKED-FIELD-2                         13   14
000195
000196              WHEN EIBAID = DFHPF2                                                  145  65
000197                  MOVE 100 TO PACKED-FIELD-1                                        13   15
000198                  MOVE ZERO TO PACKED-FIELD-2                                       IMP  14
000199                  DIVIDE PACKED-FIELD-2 INTO PACKED-FIELD-1                         14   13
000200
000201              WHEN EIBAID = DFHPF3                                                  145  66
000202                  SET ADDRESS OF COMMON-WORK-AREA TO NULL                           IMP 170 IMP
000203                  MOVE ZERO TO CWA-DATE                                             IMP 172
000204
000205              WHEN EIBAID = DFHPF4                                                  145  67
000206          *EXEC CICS  SEND MAP('NOMAP1')
000207          **      MAPSET('NOSET1')
000208          **      FROM(I-O-AREA)
000209          **      ERASE
000210          *
000211          *END-EXEC
000212                  MOVE ' 0 '   S  00088  ' TO DFHEIV0                               133
000213                  MOVE 'NOMAP1' TO DFHC0070                                         129
000214                  MOVE LENGTH OF I-O-AREA TO DFHB0020                               IMP  18  103
000215                  MOVE 'NOSET1' TO DFHC0071                                         130
000216
```

Figure 12-4 Portions of the source listing for the abend tester program (part 4 of 8)

```
PP 5668-958 IBM VS COBOL II RELEASE 3.1  09/19/89          DFXXP00A   DATE 02/26/92   TIME 10:44:40   PAGE   6
LINEID PL SL  ----+--*A-1-B--+----1----+----2----+----3----+----4----+----5----+----6----+----7-|--+----8  MAP AND CROSS REFERENCE

000217
000218   1            DFHB0020 CALL 'DFHEI1' USING DFHEIVO  DFHC0071  DFHC0070  I-O-AREA      EXT 133 129  18
000219   1                WHEN EIBAID = DFHPF5                                                103 130
000220              *EXEC CICS                                                                145  68
000221              *    XCTL PROGRAM('NOPGM1')
000222              *END-EXEC
000223
000224   1                MOVE '         00096 ' TO DFHEIVO                                   133
000225   1                MOVE 'NOPGM1' TO DFHC0080                                           114
000226   1                CALL 'DFHEI1' USING DFHEIVO  DFHC0080                           EXT 133 114
000227
000228              *EXEC CICS   WHEN EIBAID = DFHPF6                                         145  69
000229              *    READ DATASET('NOFILE')
000230              *       INTO(I-O-AREA)
000231                       RIDFLD(ALPHA-FIELD-2)
000232              *END-EXEC
000233
000234   1                MOVE '   0     00101 ' TO DFHEIVO                                   133
000235   1                MOVE 'NOFILE' TO DFHC0080                                           114
000236   1                MOVE LENGTH OF I-O-AREA TO DFHC0080                             IMP  18 103
000237   1                CALL 'DFHEI1' USING DFHEIVO  DFHC0080  I-O-AREA                 EXT 133 114  18
000238            DFHB0020 ALPHA-FIELD-2                                                      103  15
000239
000240              *EXEC CICS   WHEN EIBAID = DFHENTER OR DFHCLEAR                           145  53  54
000241              *    SEND TEXT FROM(TERMINATION-MESSAGE)
000242                       ERASE
000243                       FREEKB
000244              *END-EXEC
000245
000246   1                MOVE '     B   00108 ' TO DFHEIVO                                   133
000247   1                MOVE LENGTH OF TERMINATION-MESSAGE TO DFHB0020                  IMP  44 103
000248   1                CALL 'DFHEI1' USING DFHEIVO  DFHDUMMY                           EXT 133 132
000249                 TERMINATION-MESSAGE DFHB0020                                           44 103
000250
000251              *EXEC CICS                                                                133
000252              *    RETURN                                                           EXT 133
000253              *END-EXEC
000254   1                MOVE '         00114 ' TO DFHEIVO
000255   1                CALL 'DFHEI1' USING DFHEIVO
000256
000257                END-EVALUATE.
000258
000259              *EXEC CICS                                                                133
000260              *    RETURN TRANSID('DFXX')                                               109
000261              *       COMMAREA(COMMUNICATION-AREA)                                  IMP  48 103
000262              *END-EXEC.                                                            EXT 133 109  48
000263   1                MOVE '\        00120 ' TO DFHEIVO                                   103
000264   1                MOVE 'DFXX' TO DFHC0040
000265   1                MOVE LENGTH OF COMMUNICATION-AREA TO DFHB0020
000266   1                CALL 'DFHEI1' USING DFHEIVO  DFHC0040  COMMUNICATION-AREA
000267            DFHB0020.
```

Figure 12-4   Portions of the source listing for the abend tester program (part 5 of 8)

```
PP 5668-958 IBM VS COBOL II RELEASE 3.1 09/19/89              DFXXP00A  DATE 02/26/92  TIME 10:44:40   PAGE   12

DATA DIVISION MAP

DATA DEFINITION ATTRIBUTE CODES (RIGHTMOST COLUMN) HAVE THE FOLLOWING MEANINGS:
   D = OBJECT OF OCCURS DEPENDING     G = GLOBAL                         S = SPANNED FILE
   E = EXTERNAL                       O = HAS OCCURS CLAUSE              U = UNDEFINED FORMAT FILE
   F = FIXED LENGTH FILE              OG= GROUP HAS OWN LENGTH DEFINITION V = VARIABLE LENGTH FILE
   FB= FIXED LENGTH BLOCKED FILE      R = REDEFINES                     VB= VARIABLE LENGTH BLOCKED FILE


SOURCE  HIERARCHY AND                   BASE       HEX-DISPLACEMENT   ASMBLR DATA                    DATA DEF
LINEID  DATA NAME                       LOCATOR    BLK   STRUCTURE    DEFINITION    DATA TYPE        ATTRIBUTES
------------------------------------------------------------------------------------------------------------*

     3  PROGRAM-ID DFXXP00A
    11  01 WORK-FIELDS
    13    02 PACKED-FIELD-1 . . . . . .             000   0 000 000    DS 0CL10      GROUP
    14    02 PACKED-FIELD-2 . . . . . . BLW=0000    005   0 000 005    DS 5P         PACKED-DEC       R
    15    02 ALPHA-FIELD-2 . . . . . .  BLW=0000    005   0 000 005    DS 5C         PACKED-DEC       R
    18  01 I-O-AREA . . . . . . . . . . BLW=0000    010   0 000 010    DS 100C       DISPLAY
    20  01 START-UP-MESSAGE . . . . . . BLW=0000    078   0 000 000    DS 0CL948     GROUP
    22    02 FILLER . . . . . . . . . . BLW=0000    078   0 000 01E    DS 30C        DISPLAY
    23    02 FILLER . . . . . . . . . . BLW=0000    096   0 000 04F    DS 49C        DISPLAY
    24    02 FILLER . . . . . . . . . . BLW=0000    0C7   0 000 09C    DS 30C        DISPLAY
    25    02 FILLER . . . . . . . . . . BLW=0000    116   0 000 0BC    DS 49C        DISPLAY
    26    02 FILLER . . . . . . . . . . BLW=0000    134   0 000 0ED    DS 30C        DISPLAY
    27    02 FILLER . . . . . . . . . . BLW=0000    165   0 000 13C    DS 79C        DISPLAY
    28    02 FILLER . . . . . . . . . . BLW=0000    1B4   0 000 15A    DS 30C        DISPLAY
    29    02 FILLER . . . . . . . . . . BLW=0000    1D2   0 000 189    DS 49C        DISPLAY
    30    02 FILLER . . . . . . . . . . BLW=0000    203   0 000 1A9    DS 30C        DISPLAY
    31    02 FILLER . . . . . . . . . . BLW=0000    252   0 000 1D8    DS 49C        DISPLAY
    32    02 FILLER . . . . . . . . . . BLW=0000    270   0 000 1F8    DS 30C        DISPLAY
    33    02 FILLER . . . . . . . . . . BLW=0000    2A1   0 000 229    DS 49C        DISPLAY
    34    02 FILLER . . . . . . . . . . BLW=0000    2BF   0 000 247    DS 30C        DISPLAY
    35    02 FILLER . . . . . . . . . . BLW=0000    30E   0 000 296    DS 49C        DISPLAY
    36    02 FILLER . . . . . . . . . . BLW=0000    33F   0 000 2C7    DS 30C        DISPLAY
    37    02 FILLER . . . . . . . . . . BLW=0000    35D   0 000 2E5    DS 49C        DISPLAY
    38    02 FILLER . . . . . . . . . . BLW=0000    38E   0 000 316    DS 79C        DISPLAY
    39    02 FILLER . . . . . . . . . . BLW=0000    3DD   0 000 365    DS 30C        DISPLAY
    40    02 FILLER . . . . . . . . . . BLW=0000    3FB   0 000 383    DS 49C        DISPLAY
    41    02 FILLER . . . . . . . . . . BLW=0000                       DS 30C        DISPLAY
    42    02 FILLER . . . . . . . . . . BLW=0000                       DS 49C        DISPLAY
    46  01 TERMINATION-MESSAGE . . . .  BLW=0000    430   0 000 000    DS 0CL9       GROUP
    48    02 FILLER . . . . . . . . . . BLW=0000                       DS 9C         DISPLAY
    51  01 COMMUNICATION-AREA . . . . . BLW=0000    440                DS 1C         DISPLAY
    52  01 DFHAID . . . . . . . . . . . BLW=0000    448   0 000 000    DS 0CL36      GROUP
    53    02 DFHNULL . . . . . . . . .  BLW=0000    448   0 000 000    DS 1C         DISPLAY
    54    02 DFHENTER . . . . . . . . . BLW=0000    449   0 000 001    DS 1C         DISPLAY
    55    02 DFHCLEAR . . . . . . . . . BLW=0000    44A   0 000 002    DS 1C         DISPLAY
    56    02 DFHCLRP . . . . . . . . .  BLW=0000    44B   0 000 003    DS 1C         DISPLAY
    57    02 DFHPEN . . . . . . . . . . BLW=0000    44C   0 000 004    DS 1C         DISPLAY
    58    02 DFHOPID . . . . . . . . .  BLW=0000    44D   0 000 005    DS 1C         DISPLAY
    59    02 DFHMSRE . . . . . . . . .  BLW=0000    44E   0 000 006    DS 1C         DISPLAY
    60    02 DFHSTRF . . . . . . . . .  BLW=0000    44F   0 000 007    DS 1C         DISPLAY
    61    02 DFHTRIG . . . . . . . . .  BLW=0000    450   0 000 008    DS 1C         DISPLAY
    62    02 DFHPA1 . . . . . . . . . . BLW=0000    451   0 000 009    DS 1C         DISPLAY
    63    02 DFHPA2 . . . . . . . . . . BLW=0000    452   0 000 00A    DS 1C         DISPLAY
    64    02 DFHPA3 . . . . . . . . . . BLW=0000    453   0 000 00B    DS 1C         DISPLAY
    65    02 DFHPF1 . . . . . . . . . . BLW=0000    454   0 000 00C    DS 1C         DISPLAY
    66    02 DFHPF2 . . . . . . . . . . BLW=0000    455   0 000 00D    DS 1C         DISPLAY
    67    02 DFHPF3 . . . . . . . . . . BLW=0000    456   0 000 00E    DS 1C         DISPLAY
        02 DFHPF4 . . . . . . . . . . . BLW=0000    457   0 000 00F    DS 1C         DISPLAY
```

Figure 12-4   Portions of the source listing for the abend tester program (part 6 of 8)

```
PP 5668-958 IBM VS COBOL II RELEASE 3.1 09/19/89          DFXXP00A    DATE 02/26/92   TIME 10:4:40   PAGE   16

CONSTANT GLOBAL TABLE BEGINS AT LOCATION 0000A8 FOR 0002C6 BYTES
LITERAL POOL MAP FOR LITERALS IN THE CGT:

0000B0 (LIT+0)      00090064 00000001 00000000 00000000 C2C5D5C4 C9D5C74B C2CD5C4   .........ABENDING.
0000D0 (LIT+32)     40404040 4040E4E0 D6D940D7 D9C5E2E2 40C5D5E3 C5D940E3 D640C5E7  IT WITHOUTPF6 = AEIL (DSIDERR)
0000F0 (LIT+64)     C9E34040 C9E3C8D6 E4E3D7C6 F6F40406 C1C5C9D3 404DC4E2 D95D4040  PF5 = AEIO (PGMIDERR)
000110 (LIT+96)     40404040 40404040 D7C6F540 7C6F540 40D74C9 C4C5D9D9 C740D4D4   PF4 = APCT (MISSING MAP)
000130 (LIT+128)    40404040 40404040 F4407E40 C1D7C3E3 404040C1 404040C1 C740D4D4  ON)  PF3 = ASRA (PROTECTION EXCEPTI
000150 (LIT+160)    40404040 D6D55D40 F3407E40 C1E2D9C1 E2E2C9D5 40404040 4040D7C6  EPTION)  PF2 = ASRA (DECIMAL DIVIDE EXCPF1
000170 (LIT+192)    40404040 D6D55D40 C1E2D9C1 404DC4C5 E5C9C4C5 40C5E7C3 40D7C6C6  PF
000190 (LIT+224)    C5D7E3C9 F2407E40 C1E2D9C1 C3C9D9C1 D340C4C9 E5C9C4C5 C8C5540C6  2 = ASRA (DATA EXCEPTION)  PF
0001B0 (LIT+256)    7E40C1E2 D9C1404D C4C1E3C1 40C5E7C3 C5D7E3C9 D6D55D40 40404040  1 = ASRA (DATA EXCEPTION)  PF
0001D0 (LIT+288)    D6D3D3D6 E6C9D5C7 40C1C2C5 D5C4E27A 40404040 40404040 E24C540  OLLOWING ABENDS:  PRESS A
0001F0 (LIT+320)    7C640C3E3 40C3C540 40C1C2C5 D5C4E2E2 D7D9C5E2 4040404E E3C5E2E3  PF KEY TO FORCE ONE OF ABEND TEST
000210 (LIT+352)    40404040 40404040 40040407 18060000 0020C000 02000000 C1C2D3   ER ..00108 ..0...:.0088
000230 (LIT+384)    C5D94040 C5E84040 F0F1F0F8 40060000 F6F74000 40D3C440 E3C1C2D3  ....0....00067 ....LD TABL
000250 (LIT+416)    40401806 60000700 20F040F0 F0F0F0F0 F0406F40 40020F00 40F04040  E .DFHEITAB.210....00120
000270 (LIT+448)    C540C4C6 C8C5C9E3 C1C24B40 F0F0F0F0 F1F4F440 60D3C440 F1F0F140  ....00114 ...00101
000290 (LIT+480)    0E080004 07000000 00F6F6F6 F0F0F02F D5D6D7C9 E2E8D6E4 E3D6D6C9  LE .NOPGM1  DFXXP00ASYSOUT-NOFI
0002B0 (LIT+512)    D3C54040 80D5D6D7 D4C6F6F0 D7D6F0C1 E4E8C540 60D5D6C6 C9000200  T1 .NOMAP1 ... GOOD BYE-NOSE
0002D0 (LIT+544)    E3F14040 D5D6D4C1 D7F14000 10000040 00000060 00010020 00040020
000310 (LIT+608)    00000040 00000080 00000080 00000080 00250020 40000080
000350 (LIT+672)    02548000                                     0254
```

```
LINE #  HEXLOC  VERB                    LINE #  HEXLOC  VERB
000187  0005BD  MOVE                    000186  0005A4  MOVE
000188  0005B4  EVALUATE                000192  0005F6  WHEN
000193  000612  MOVE                    000195  00061E  MULTIPLY
000194  000618  CALL                    000199  00065C  MOVE
000197  00065C  MOVE                    000203  00069A  SET
000198  000656  MOVE                    000213  0006C2  MOVE
000202  00066E  WHEN                    000226  00074C  MOVE
000204  000662  DIVIDE                  000228  00077E  MOVE
000205  0006AE  WHEN                    000236  0007BC  MOVE
000214  0006D6  MOVE                    000246  000830  MOVE
000215  0006E2  MOVE                    000255  000874  MOVE
000217  000730  CALL                    000266  0008BA  MOVE
000226  00073E  MOVE
000234  0007B6  WHEN
000235  0007C2  CALL
000237  000842  CALL
000247  0008AE  MOVE
000256  0008AE  MOVE
000265  0008C6  CALL
000268  0008C0  MOVE
```

Figure 12-4 Portions of the source listing for the abend tester program (part 7 of 8)

```
PP 5668-958  IBM VS COBOL II RELEASE 3.1 09/19/89         DFXXP00A   DATE 02/26/92   TIME 10:44:40   PAGE   17

*** TGT MEMORY MAP ***
TGTLOC

000000   72 BYTE SAVE AREA
000048   TGT IDENTIFIER
000050   TGT LEVEL INDICATOR
000051   RESERVED - 3 SINGLE BYTE FIELDS
000054   32 BIT SWITCH
000058   POINTER TO RUNCOM
00005C   POINTER TO COBVEC
000060   POINTER TO PROGRAM DYNAMIC BLOCK TABLE
000064   NUMBER OF FCB'S
000068   WORKING STORAGE LENGTH
00006C   POINTER TO PREVIOUS TGT IN TGT CHAIN
000070   ADDRESS OF IGZESMG WORK AREA
000074   ADDRESS OF 1ST GETMAIN BLOCK (SPACE MGR)
000078   FULLWORD RETURN CODE
00007A   RETURN-CODE SPECIAL REGISTER
00007C   SORT-RETURN SPECIAL REGISTER
00007E   MERGE FILE NUMBER
000080   RESERVED - 4 HALF WORD FIELDS
000088   PROGRAM MASK OF CALLER OF THIS PROGRAM
000089   PROGRAM MASK USED BY THIS PROGRAM
00008A   RESERVED - 2 SINGLE BYTE FIELDS
00008C   NUMBER OF SECONDARY FCB CELLS
000090   LENGTH OF THE VN(VNI) VECTOR
000094   ADDRESS OF IGZEBST TERMINATION ROUTINE
000098   DDNAME FOR DISPLAY OUTPUT
0000A0   SORT-CONTROL SPECIAL REGISTER
0000A8   POINTER TO COM-REG SPECIAL REGISTER
0000AC   CALC ROUTINE REGISTER SAVE AREA
0000E0   ALTERNATE COLLATING SEQUENCE TABLE PTR.
0000E4   ADDRESS OF SORT G.N. ADDRESS BLOCK
0000EC   ADDRESS OF IGZCLNK DYNAMIC WORK AREA
0000F0   CURRENT INTERNAL PROGRAM NUMBER
0000F4   POINTER TO 1ST IPCB
0000F4   RESERVED
0000F8   POINTER TO ABEND INFORMATION TABLE
0000FC   POINTER TO FDMP/TEST FIELDS IN THE TGT
000100   ADDRESS OF START OF COBOL PROGRAM
000104   POINTER TO VN'S IN CGT
000108   POINTER TO VN'S IN TGT
00010C   POINTER TO FIRST PBL IN THE PGT
000110   POINTER TO FIRST FCB CELL
000114   WORKING STORAGE ADDRESS
000118   POINTER TO FIRST SECONDARY FCB CELL

*** VARIABLE PORTION OF TGT ***

00011C   BACKSTORE CELL FOR SYMBOLIC REGISTERS
000124   BASE LOCATORS FOR SPECIAL REGISTERS
00012C   BASE LOCATORS FOR WORKING-STORAGE
000130   BASE LOCATORS FOR LINKAGE-SECTION
00013C   CLLE ADR. CELLS FOR CALL LIT. SUB-PGMS.
00015C   VARIABLE NAME (VN) CELLS
000160   PERFORM SAVE CELLS
000164   INTERNAL PROGRAM CONTROL BLOCKS
000174   AREA FOR EVALUATE BOOLEAN VALUES
```

Figure 12-4 Portions of the source listing for the abend tester program (part 8 of 8)

you've found the base locator in storage, you add its contents to the displacement of the field you're looking for to determine the field's address. You'll see how this is done later in this chapter. (Because OS/VS COBOL assigns base locator cells to registers instead of storing them in the TGT, the procedure for finding a working-storage field under OS/VS COBOL is different. I'll explain it later in this chapter, too.)

The Condensed Procedure Listing for the DFXXP00A program is in the bottom portion of part 7 of figure 12-4. For each executable statement in the Procedure Division, the Condensed Procedure Listing shows three things: the statement number, the verb name, and the statement's offset from the beginning of the Procedure Division. The offset indicates the position of the first machine-language instruction generated for the statement. For example, the shaded portion of part 7 of figure 12-4 indicates that the first instruction generated for line 195, a MULTIPLY statement, begins at offset 61E. You use the Condensed Procedure Listing primarily to find out which statement was executing when an abend occurred. You'll also see how this works later in this chapter.

The Execution Diagnostics Facility

The *Execution Diagnostics Facility*, or *EDF*, is an on-line debugging tool that lets you trace the progress of a CICS program as it executes.   To illustrate how EDF is used, I'll present a series of screens from a terminal session where I run the DFXXP00A program to generate a data-exception abend. These screens are shown in figure 12-5.

You can use EDF in two ways. To use EDF in *same-terminal checkout* mode, you enter the transaction identifier CEDF at your terminal. When CICS responds with a message like this:

```
THIS TERMINAL: EDF MODE ON
```

you can type the trans-id to start the program you want to debug. Then, your terminal screen alternates between screens displayed by your program and screens displayed by EDF. The terminal session in figure 12-5 uses EDF in same-terminal checkout mode.

The second way to use EDF is called *two-terminal checkout* mode. When you use two-terminal checkout mode, you run EDF at one terminal and the program you're debugging at another. For example, suppose you want to debug a program that's running at the terminal named H400. To place your terminal into EDF mode, enter this transaction:

```
CEDF H400,ON
```

Then, EDF responds with this message:

```
TERMINAL H400: EDF MODE ON
```

Now you can debug the program running at terminal H400 from your own terminal.

Once you've started EDF and entered a trans-id to start your program, but before the first instruction of your program is executed, EDF displays a "Program initiation" screen like the one in part 1 of figure 12-5. This screen shows the contents of some of the fields in the Execute Interface Block. For example, you can see that the value of EIBCALEN is zero, indicating that no communication area was passed to the program.

The bottom lines of each EDF display show the meaning of each enabled attention key. For example, the Enter key lets you continue execution of the program, PF2 lets you switch the display from character mode to hex mode, PF3 ends the EDF session, and so on. For some EDF displays, there's more information than can be displayed on the screen at once. In that case, you can use the PF7 and PF8 keys to scroll the display backward or forward. For example, if you want to see additional EIB fields that aren't shown in the screen in part 1 of figure 12-5, you can press PF8.

As your program executes, EDF intercepts all CICS commands and displays two screens, one before and the other after the execution of the command. For example, suppose I press the Enter key after examining the screen in part 1 of figure 12-5. The DFXXP00A program begins execution and continues until it executes a CICS command. Then, EDF takes over and displays an "About to execute command" screen like the one in part 2 of figure 12-5. Here, DFXXP00A is about to execute a SEND TEXT command. As you can see, EDF shows you the command and all of its options along with their values. In addition, it shows you the command's line number from the translator listing (*not* the compiler listing).

To execute the CICS command, you press the Enter key. Part 3 of figure 12-5 shows the screen displayed by the SEND TEXT command. To continue with the debugging session, you press the Enter key. Then, EDF displays a "Command execution complete" screen like the one in part 4 of figure 12-5. Here, you can determine the results of the command. RESPONSE: NORMAL means that the command was successful. If an exceptional condition is raised by the command, the condition name (NOTFND, for example) is displayed as the RESPONSE.

(If you're using two-terminal checkout, the map sent by the SEND MAP won't appear on your terminal between the "About to execute command" screen and the "Command execution complete" screen. Instead, the map will be sent to the terminal where the program is executing.)

To continue execution of the DFXXP00A program, I pressed the Enter key. The program continued until it encountered the next CICS command: RETURN. Then, it displayed the "About to execute command" screen shown in part 5 of figure 12-5. To execute the RETURN command, I pressed the Enter key.

Next come two screens that EDF displays when a task ends. The first, shown in part 6 of figure 12-5, is the "Program termination" screen. It indicates that the current program is about to end. After the program termination screen, EDF displays the "Task termination" screen, shown in part 7. It indicates that the task is about to end. Notice the REPLY field. If you enter YES in this field, the EDF session will continue when the next task begins.

When you press the Enter key for the task termination screen, the current user screen is displayed again, as part 8 in figure 12-5 shows. Now, you can type data into map fields and use an appropriate attention key to restart the program. Since there's no data to be typed on this map, I simply restarted the program by pressing PF1. EDF responded by displaying the "Program initiation" screen, as shown in part 9.

When I pressed the Enter key again, the DFXXP00A program began its execution. This time, it detected the use of the PF1 key and executed statements that resulted in a data-exception abend. Part 10 of figure 12-5 shows the resulting screen displayed by EDF. Here, you can see that an ASRA abend has occurred. The offset of the instruction that caused the abend is 624 (hexadecimal), and the type of interrupt is DATA EXCEPTION. In other words, the instruction at offset 624 tried to perform an arithmetic operation with non-numeric data.

To find the COBOL statement that caused the abend, you look in the Condensed Procedure Listing for the statement with an offset closest to the offset in the EDF screen, but not exceeding it. In part 7 of figure 12-4, the shaded MULTIPLY statement has an offset of 61E, less than the offset on the EDF screen (624). Since the offset of the next statement (63A) is greater than 624, you can conclude that the abend occurred during execution of the MULTIPLY statement.

The MULTIPLY statement is highlighted in part 4 of figure 12-4. By examining this statement, you can conclude that PACKED-FIELD-1 or PACKED-FIELD-2 contains invalid data. To find out which, press PF5 to display the contents of working storage. Part 11 of figure 12-5 shows the resulting EDF display. Here, working-storage data is presented in columns: (1) the address of the data in hexadecimal, (2) the displacement (or offset) of each line of data in hexadecimal, (3) 16 bytes of working-storage data in hexadecimal (in four columns of four bytes each), and (4) the same 16 bytes of data in character format.

To find a particular field in the display, you first determine the field's displacement from the beginning of working storage as indicated by the Data Division Map in the compiler output. Then, you scan the offset column on the screen EDF displays, looking for a value that's closest to but not greater than the displacement of the field you're looking for. The field will be on that line, but you'll have to count over the correct number of bytes to find the exact position of the field. (If the correct line is beyond the last line displayed, use the PF8 key to scroll forward.)

For example, if you refer back to part 6 in figure 12-4, you'll see that the displacement of PACKED-FIELD-2 is 005. By scanning the offset column in part 11 of figure 12-5, you can see that offset 005 is contained

Part 1

EDF displays the
program initiation
screen, which shows
information from the
Execute Interface Block.

```
TRANSACTION: DFXX    PROGRAM: DFXXP00A    TASK NUMBER: 0004207    DISPLAY: 00
STATUS: PROGRAM INITIATION

   EIBTIME       = 155259
   EIBDATE       = 92056
   EIBTRNID      = 'DFXX'
   EIBTASKN      = 4207
   EIBTRMID      = 'G205'

   EIBCPOSN      = 4
   EIBCALEN      = 0
   EIBAID        = X'7D'                                   AT X'00107C42'
   EIBFN         = X'0000'                                 AT X'00107C43'
   EIBRCODE      = X'000000000000'                         AT X'00107C45'
   EIBDS         = '........'
 + EIBREQID      = '........'


ENTER:  CONTINUE
PF1 : UNDEFINED            PF2 : SWITCH HEX/CHAR      PF3 : END EDF SESSION
PF4 : SUPPRESS DISPLAYS    PF5 : WORKING STORAGE      PF6 : USER DISPLAY
PF7 : SCROLL BACK          PF8 : SCROLL FORWARD       PF9 : STOP CONDITIONS
PF10: PREVIOUS DISPLAY     PF11: UNDEFINED            PF12: UNDEFINED
```

Part 2

The user presses the Enter
key, and EDF indicates that
it is about to execute a
SEND TEXT command.

```
TRANSACTION: DFXX    PROGRAM: DFXXP00A    TASK NUMBER: 0004207    DISPLAY: 00
STATUS: ABOUT TO EXECUTE COMMAND

EXEC CICS SEND TEXT
 FROM ('ABEND TESTER                                                    '...)
 LENGTH (948)
 TERMINAL
 FREEKB
 ERASE




   OFFSET:X'0005E6'      LINE:00067         EIBFN=X'1806'


ENTER:  CONTINUE
PF1 : UNDEFINED            PF2 : SWITCH HEX/CHAR      PF3 : UNDEFINED
PF4 : SUPPRESS DISPLAYS    PF5 : WORKING STORAGE      PF6 : USER DISPLAY
PF7 : SCROLL BACK          PF8 : SCROLL FORWARD       PF9 : STOP CONDITIONS
PF10: PREVIOUS DISPLAY     PF11: UNDEFINED            PF12: ABEND USER TASK
```

Figure 12-5 The Execution Diagnostics Facility in use

Part 3

The user presses the
Enter key, and EDF
displays the output for
the SEND TEXT
command.

```
ABEND TESTER

PRESS A PF KEY TO FORCE ONE OF THE FOLLOWING ABENDS:

PF1 = ASRA (DATA EXCEPTION)
PF2 = ASRA (DECIMAL DIVIDE EXCEPTION)
PF3 = ASRA (PROTECTION EXCEPTION)
PF4 = ABM0 (MISSING MAP)
PF5 = AEIO (PGMIDERR)
PF6 = AEIL (DSIDERR)

OR PRESS ENTER TO EXIT WITHOUT ABENDING.
```

Part 4

The user presses the Enter
key, and EDF displays the
completion status of the
SEND TEXT command.

```
TRANSACTION: DFXX   PROGRAM: DFXXP00A   TASK NUMBER: 0004207   DISPLAY: 00
STATUS: COMMAND EXECUTION COMPLETE
EXEC CICS SEND TEXT
 FROM ('ABEND TESTER                                                  '...)
 LENGTH (948)
 TERMINAL
 FREEKB
 ERASE




   OFFSET:X'0005E6'    LINE:00067        EIBFN=X'1806'
   RESPONSE: NORMAL                      EIBRESP= 0

ENTER:  CONTINUE
PF1 : UNDEFINED          PF2 : SWITCH HEX/CHAR      PF3 : END EDF SESSION
PF4 : SUPPRESS DISPLAYS  PF5 : WORKING STORAGE      PF6 : USER DISPLAY
PF7 : SCROLL BACK        PF8 : SCROLL FORWARD       PF9 : STOP CONDITIONS
PF10: PREVIOUS DISPLAY   PF11: UNDEFINED            PF12: ABEND USER TASK
```

Figure 12-5 The Execution Diagnostics Facility in use (continued)

Part 5

The user presses the
Enter key, and EDF
indicates that it is about
to execute a RETURN
command.

```
  TRANSACTION: DFXX   PROGRAM: DFXXP00A   TASK NUMBER: 0004207   DISPLAY: 00
  STATUS: ABOUT TO EXECUTE COMMAND
  EXEC CICS RETURN
   TRANSID ('DFXX')
   COMMAREA ('.')
   LENGTH (1)




  OFFSET:X'0008F6'     LINE:000120          EIBFN=X'0E08'


  ENTER:   CONTINUE
  PF1 : UNDEFINED            PF2 : SWITCH HEX/CHAR      PF3 : UNDEFINED
  PF4 : SUPPRESS DISPLAYS    PF5 : WORKING STORAGE      PF6 : USER DISPLAY
  PF7 : SCROLL BACK          PF8 : SCROLL FORWARD       PF9 : STOP CONDITIONS
  PF10: PREVIOUS DISPLAY     PF11: UNDEFINED            PF12: ABEND USER TASK
```

Part 6

The user presses the Enter
key, and EDF displays its
program termination
screen.

```
  TRANSACTION: DFXX   PROGRAM: DFXXP00A   TASK NUMBER: 0004207   DISPLAY: 00
  STATUS:   PROGRAM TERMINATION










  ENTER:   CONTINUE
  PF1 : UNDEFINED            PF2 : SWITCH HEX/CHAR      PF3 : UNDEFINED
  PF4 : SUPPRESS DISPLAYS    PF5 : WORKING STORAGE      PF6 : USER DISPLAY
  PF7 : SCROLL BACK          PF8 : SCROLL FORWARD       PF9 : STOP CONDITIONS
  PF10: PREVIOUS DISPLAY     PF11: UNDEFINED            PF12: ABEND USER TASK
```

Figure 12-5 The Execution Diagnostics Facility in use (continued)

Part 7

The user presses the Enter key, and EDF displays its task termination screen. To continue the EDF session, the user types 'yes' in the REPLY field.

```
TRANSACTION: DFXX                          TASK NUMBER: 0004207   DISPLAY: 00
STATUS:    TASK TERMINATION




















TO CONTINUE EDF SESSION REPLY YES                              REPLY: yes
ENTER:    CURRENT DISPLAY
PF1 : UNDEFINED           PF2 : SWITCH HEX/CHAR     PF3 : END EDF SESSION
PF4 : SUPPRESS DISPLAYS   PF5 : WORKING STORAGE     PF6 : USER DISPLAY
PF7 : SCROLL BACK         PF8 : SCROLL FORWARD      PF9 : STOP CONDITIONS
PF10: PREVIOUS DISPLAY    PF11: UNDEFINED           PF12: UNDEFINED
```

Part 8

EDF responds by redisplaying the user screen.

```
ABEND TESTER

PRESS A PF KEY TO FORCE ONE OF THE FOLLOWING ABENDS:

PF1 = ASRA (DATA EXCEPTION)
PF2 = ASRA (DECIMAL DIVIDE EXCEPTION)
PF3 = ASRA (PROTECTION EXCEPTION)
PF4 = ABM0 (MISSING MAP)
PF5 = AEIO (PGMIDERR)
PF6 = AEIL (DSIDERR)

OR PRESS ENTER TO EXIT WITHOUT ABENDING.
```

Figure 12-5 The Execution Diagnostics Facility in use (continued)

Part 9

The user presses PF1, and EDF displays the program initiation screen.

```
TRANSACTION: DFXX   PROGRAM: DFXXP00A   TASK NUMBER: 0004239   DISPLAY: 00
STATUS: PROGRAM INITIATION
   COMMAREA      = '.'
   EIBTIME       = 155532
   EIBDATE       = 92056
   EIBTRNID      = 'DFXX'
   EIBTASKN      = 4239
   EIBTRMID      = 'G205'

   EIBCPOSN      = 1
   EIBCALEN      = 1
   EIBAID        = X'F1'                                    AT X'000F9C42'
   EIBFN         = X'0000'                                  AT X'000F9C43'
   EIBRCODE      = X'000000000000'                          AT X'000F9C45'
   EIBDS         = '........'
 + EIBREQID      = '........'



ENTER:  CONTINUE
PF1 : UNDEFINED              PF2 : SWITCH HEX/CHAR     PF3 : END EDF SESSION
PF4 : SUPPRESS DISPLAYS      PF5 : WORKING STORAGE     PF6 : USER DISPLAY
PF7 : SCROLL BACK            PF8 : SCROLL FORWARD      PF9 : STOP CONDITIONS
PF10: PREVIOUS DISPLAY       PF11: UNDEFINED           PF12: UNDEFINED
```

Part 10

The user presses the Enter key, and EDF indicates that an abend has occurred.

```
TRANSACTION: DFXX   PROGRAM: DFXXP00A   TASK NUMBER: 0004239   DISPLAY: 00
STATUS: AN ABEND HAS OCCURRED
   COMMAREA      = '.'
   EIBTIME       = 155532
   EIBDATE       = 92056
   EIBTRNID      = 'DFXX'
   EIBTASKN      = 4239
   EIBTRMID      = 'G205'

   EIBCPOSN      = 1
   EIBCALEN      = 1
   EIBAID        = X'F1'                                    AT X'000F9C42'
   EIBFN         = X'0000'                                  AT X'000F9C43'
   EIBRCODE      = X'000000000000'                          AT X'000F9C45'
   EIBDS         = '........'
 + EIBREQID      = '........'
 OFFSET:X'000624'                  INTERRUPT: DATA EXCEPTION
 ABEND:   ASRA                     PSW: X'078D2000 0031867A 00060007'

ENTER:  CONTINUE
PF1 : UNDEFINED              PF2 : SWITCH HEX/CHAR     PF3 : END EDF SESSION
PF4 : SUPPRESS DISPLAYS      PF5 : WORKING STORAGE     PF6 : USER DISPLAY
PF7 : SCROLL BACK            PF8 : SCROLL FORWARD      PF9 : STOP CONDITIONS
PF10: PREVIOUS DISPLAY       PF11: UNDEFINED           PF12: UNDEFINED
```

Figure 12-5 The Execution Diagnostics Facility in use (continued)

Part 11

The user presses PF5, and EDF responds by displaying the contents of Working Storage.

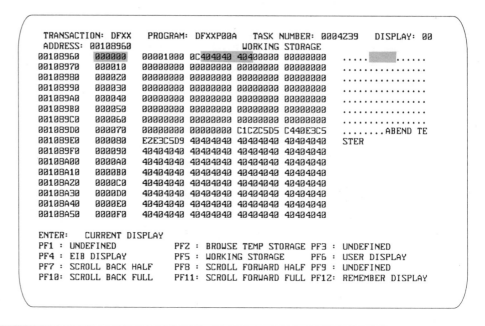

Figure 12-5   The Execution Diagnostics Facility in use (continued)

in the first row. Then, counting over five bytes, you can see that PACKED-FIELD-2 contains spaces (hex 4040404040). This is not valid numeric data, so it must be the cause of the abend. Looking at the source listing, of course, you can see that just before the MULTIPLY statement, a MOVE statement moved spaces to ALPHA-FIELD-2, which occupies the same storage locations as PACKED-FIELD-2.

Note that when you use EDF, you don't have to worry about the contents of the base locator to find a field in working storage. That's because EDF takes care of that automatically. As you'll soon see, finding a field in a transaction dump is more difficult.

As you can imagine, EDF is a powerful debugging tool. However, it has a built-in limitation: It traces only the execution of CICS commands. COBOL statements are not traced. Since there may be many COBOL statements between two CICS commands, it can sometimes be hard to isolate a bug. Because of this limitation, third-party source debuggers such as Intertest are often used in addition to (or instead of) EDF. If you're developing CICS programs under OS/2, you can use any of several source-level debuggers: Animator, Xilirator, or CodeView.

The transaction dump

When a CICS transaction abends, CICS formats the contents of storage associated with the transaction in a *transaction dump*. The detailed procedures for analyzing a dump could fill an entire book, so I won't cover them all here. But I will show you the basic techniques for (1) determining the type of program check that led to an ASRA abend, (2) determining the instruction that caused the program check, and (3) locating fields in working storage. But first, I want to show you how to obtain a transaction dump and give you a general overview of its contents.

The chances are that you'll need to deal with a transaction dump only when a program that's already in production fails. That shouldn't happen very often. As a result, don't worry if you don't master the rest of the material in this chapter the first time you read it. You can refer back to this chapter when you need to analyze a transaction dump.

How to obtain a transaction dump

When a CICS program abends, the transaction dump is written to the *dump data set*. Because all CICS transaction dumps are written to the same dump data set, it usually contains more than one transaction dump. Typically, the entire dump data set is printed when CICS is shut down at the end of the day. At some shops, the dump data set isn't actually printed, but held in the output queue so it can be viewed on-line. In either case, you'll usually need to search through the dump listing to find the particular dump you're interested in.

Although the dump data set is usually printed when CICS is shut down, it's possible to print it while CICS is still running. That's because CICS actually maintains two dump data sets, known as DFHDMPA and DFHDMPB. Normally, CICS writes transaction dumps to DFHDMPA, and switches to DFHDMPB only when DFHDMPA becomes full. However, you can force CICS to switch to DFHDMPB at any time by issuing this CEMT command:

```
CEMT SET DUMP SWITCH
```

Then, while CICS is writing to the alternate dump data set, you can run a batch job to print the contents of the main dump data set. After you print the dump data set, remember to issue the CEMT command again to switch back to DFHDMPA. And remember that any transaction dumps produced while the dump data set has been switched will be written to DFHDMPB.

The procedures for printing CICS transaction dumps vary from shop to shop, so be sure to find out what procedures are used at your shop and follow them. In most shops, a CICS systems programmer is responsible for printing the dump data sets. So you'll have to contact him or her if you want to print a transaction dump while CICS is running.

How to read a transaction dump

Although CICS transaction dumps can be intimidating at first, you'll quickly become familiar with them once you've worked with a few to solve actual problems. However, your first few attempts at reading a transaction dump will be easier if you understand the overall structure of the dump. Figure 12-6 presents a portion of a CICS transaction dump. This dump was actually 18 pages long, but the three pages I've included here include the dump information you'll use most.

The first page of a transaction dump always begins with basic diagnostic information, such as the CICS version (in this case, 2.1), the Program Status Word (PSW), and the register contents. Then, all of the areas of main storage that are associated with the abending task are listed, starting with a CICS control block called the Task Control Area.

As you page through a transaction dump, you'll notice that storage is grouped into sections. Each of these sections represents an area of storage that was allocated to your task for one purpose or another. The heading that precedes each section indicates the *storage class* associated with that storage. For example, the heading for the first section of storage in figure 12-6 indicates that the storage was allocated for the Task Control Area. Other storage classes you're likely to encounter in a transaction dump include Common System Area, Program Storage, Terminal Storage, and Transaction Storage. Your program's Working-Storage Section will be found in one of the sections identified as Transaction Storage.

Notice that the heading at the start of each section identifies the range of addresses it contains. Also notice that the rightmost column of each line shows the address of the first byte of data shown for the line. To locate specific data in a transaction dump, you must become adept at scanning this column to locate the line that contains a particular address, then counting over the appropriate number of bytes to find the correct data. For example, to find the data at address 108965, you would first find the line that contains address 108960 (item 9 in part 2 of figure 12-6). Then, you'd count over the remaining 5 bytes to find the field (item 10).

Two other portions of a transaction dump you may need are the *trace table* and the *module map*. The trace table appears midway through the dump, and lists the CICS activity that preceded the abend. It can be useful to determine the sequence of processing that lead to the abend. The module map appears near the end of the dump and lists all of the program modules known to CICS. You use it to determine the entry point of your program, which in turn enables you to determine which program statement caused the abend.

I want to make one final point about reading transaction dumps before I go on: To use a transaction dump effectively, you have to be comfortable working with hexadecimal numbers. Although the EBCDIC equivalent of storage is shown on the right-hand side of the page,

```
CICSTEST      --- CICS TRANSACTION DUMP ---      CODE=ASRA   TASK=DFXX            DATE=02/25/92   TIME=15:57:06    PAGE     1

SYMPTOMS= AB/UASRA PIDS/566540301 FLDS/F000KC RIDS/DFXXP00A

CICS/VS LEVEL = 0211

PSW                 078D2000   0031867A   00060007   00000000

REGS 14-4           00318554   C1E2D9C1   00006000   00000000          007D9340   003185C2   00785AA0

REGS 5-11           007D81BC   000F9800   000FA380   00201274          007DAD78   007DAC50   000F9AC0

TASK CONTROL AREA (USER AREA)               ADDRESS 000F9990 TO 000FA24F    LENGTH 000008C0

00000000   000F9800 0078268C 011D4EB4 00843A00   000F9D80 00000000 2000FE00 C42100A0   *..q.......+..d..............D...*   000F9990
00000020   5079A2F0 0078268C 00006000 00000000   0079A226 003185C2 00782670 007D81BC   *..sO......-........s...eB....'a.*   000F99B0
00000040   000F9800 000FA380 000F9800 007DAD78   0079B226 000F9AC0 5083FC4A 400FA430   *..q...t...q..'...........c.. .u.*   000F99D0
00000060   607D996A 00000000 00060007 0004E030   007D9340 A07D9650 00785AA0 007D81BC   *-'r...............'l .'o.....'a.*   000F99F0
00000080   FE000004 00004000 C4C6E700 C1E2D9C1   078D2000 0031867A 00060007 00000000   *...... .DFX.ASRA......f:........*   000F9A10
000000A0   00318554 C1E2D9C1 00006000 00000000   007D9340 003185C2 00785AA0 007D81BC   *..e.ASRA..-.......'l ..eB....'a.*   000F9A30
000000C0   000F9800 000FA380 00201274 007DAD78   007DAC50 000F9AC0 00000000 011D4EB4   *..q...t......'...'............+.*   000F9A50
000000E0   00000000 00000000 24000000 00000000   00000000 00000000 00000000 00000000   *................................*   000F9A70
00000100   00000028 000F9A90 00000000 00000000   00000000 00000000 00000000 00000000   *................................*   000F9A90
00000120   00000000 00000000 00000000 00000000   0000025C 000F9AC0 000F9C28 00000000   *.................*..............*   000F9AB0
00000140   00000000 00000000 00000000 40404040   00000000 00000000 00000000 00000000   *...........     ................*   000F9AD0
00000160   00000000 00000000 00000000 00000000   00000000 00000000 00000000 00000000   *................................*   000F9AF0
00000180   00000000 00000000 00000000 00000000   00000000 00000000 00000000 00000000   *................................*   000F9B10
000001A0   E2D7C3D6 E2D7C3D6 0084006C 00000000   000F9C80 00000000 00000000 00000100   *SPCOSPCO.d......................*   000F9B30
000001C0   00000000 00000000 00000000 00000000   00000000 00000006 00000000 00010000   *................................*   000F9B50
000001E0   00000000 000F9C28 000FA258 00000000   00000000 00000000 00785AB8 000FA278   *..........s....................s.*   000F9B70
00000200   00840632 8000EAA0 00785AB8 000F9C90   E2D7C3D6 000F9C80 E2D7C3D6 007DA238   *.d..............SPCO....SPCO.'s.*   000F9B90
00000220   00843A00 00318050 0084006C E2D7C3D6   00201274 000F9AC0 000F9990 00000000   *.d.......d..SPCO...........r....*   000F9BB0
00000240   00000000 00000000 00000000 00000000   000F9B74 800F9B78 00000000 00000000   *................................*   000F9BD0
00000260   00000000 00000000 00000000 00000000   00000000 00000000 000F9C28 00000000   *................................*   000F9BF0
00000280   00000000 00000000 00000000 FF000000   40C4C6C8 C5C9C240 0155532C 0092056F   *................ DFHEIB .....k..*   000F9C10
000002A0   C4C6E7E7 0004239C C7F2F0F5 00000001   0001F100 00000000 00000000 00000000   *DFXX....G205......1.............*   000F9C30
000002C0   00000000 00000000 00000040 40404040   40404000 00000000 00000000 00000000   *...........       ..............*   000F9C50
000002E0   00000000 00000000 00000000 00000000   00102E00 40404040 00000000 00000000   *....................    ........*   000F9C70
00000300   008407D8 00843C68 000F9C80 00318050   800F9B74 00000000 00000000 00000000   *.d.Q.d..........................*   000F9C90
00000320   001085D0 40404040 00000000 00000000   00000000 00843600 00000000 00000000   *..e.    ..........d.............*   000F9CB0
00000340   00000000 00000000 00000000 00000000   00000000 00000000 00000000 00000000   *................................*   000F9CD0
00000360   00000000 00000000 00000000 00000000   00000000 40000000 02D73A48 00000000   *....................    ....P...*   000F9CF0
00000380   0084375C 00000000 00000000 00000000   00000000 00000000 00000008 02920268   *.d.*.........................k..*   000F9D10
000003A0   00000001 029EB1F8 00000001 029BA638   00000002 029B9B14 00000002 00000000   *.......8.......W................*   000F9D30
000003C0   00000000 00000000 00000000 00000000   00000000 00000000 00000000 00000000   *................................*   000F9D50
000003E0   00000000 00000000 D3C9C6D6 E2E3D6D9   42000068 00000000 FF0F9DE8 0083C91E   *........LIFOSTOR...........Y.cI.*   000F9D70
00000400   00000000 0000B150 00000000 008451C8   0013F670 5083C8A2 0083D8A2 000F9800   *..............d.H..6..cHs.cQs..q.*   000F9D90
00000420   000FA380 000F9800 007DAD78 0079B226   000F9AC0 000F9990 00843600 FE0F9DE8   *..t...q..'...............r..d.....Y*   000F9DB0
00000440   F000D2C3 0083DB70 00000000 00000000   00000000 00000000 480001F0 000F9D80   *O.KC.c.........................O....*   000F9DD0
00000460   FF0F9FA0 00000000 00000000 0000B150   000F9DE8 008451C8 0013F670 4083C8A2   *...................Y.d.H..6. cHs*   000F9DF0
00000480   0083D8A2 80829C04 000F9DE8 00000000   001D4EB4 011D4EB4 007E91B8 000F9990   *.cQs.b.....Y......+...+..=j...r.*   000F9E10
000004A0   00843600 FE0F9FD8 EA00E3D4 007FA7F4   01000000 00000000 807FAAB2 00004000   *.d.....Q..TM..x4............... .*   000F9E30
000004C0   C4C6E700 C1E2D9C1 807FAAD6 0031867A   00000000 00000000 807FAB42 007FCF54   *DFX.ASRA...O..f:................*   000F9E50
000004E0   029B9B20 000F9F30 00000000 00000000   00000000 00000000 00000000 00000000   *................................*   000F9E70
00000500   00000000 00000000 00000000 00000000   00000000 00000000 00000000 00000000   *................................*   000F9E90
00000520   LINES TO 00000540 SAME AS ABOVE                                                                                         000F9EB0
```

Figure 12-6 Portions of a CICS transaction dump (part 1 of 3)

```
CICSTEST     --- CICS TRANSACTION DUMP ---     CODE=ASRA   TASK=DFXX          DATE=02/25/92   TIME=15:57:06   PAGE    5

TRANSACTION STORAGE -USER                 ADDRESS 00107800 TO 001097EF    LENGTH 00001FF0

00000E60   00000000 00000000 00000000 00000000  00000000 00000000 00000000 00000000   *................................*   00108660
00000E80   00000000 00000000 00000000 00000000  00000000 00000000 00000000 00000000   *................................*   00108680
00000EA0   00000000 00000000 00000000 00000000  00000000 00000000 00000000 43201000   *................................*   001086A0
00000EC0   1B33BF37 10014420 A1149110 10004710  A10E5830 30004A30 10044110 10024110   *..........j.....................*   001086C0
00000EE0   100407FE 1A300000 00000000 00000000  00000000 00000000 00000000 00000000   *................................*   001086E0
00000F00   00000000 00000000 00000000 00000000  00000000 00000000 00000000 00000000   *................................*   00108700
00000F20   00000000 00000000 00000050 20000000  00108778 001085B8 00108788 00000000   *...................g...e...gh...*   00108720
00000F40   C4C6E7E7 D7F0F0C1 00000000 00000000  94810000 00318050 00108790 00318050   *DFXXP00A........ma.........g....*   00108740
00000F60   00000000 00000000 00000000 00000000  00000000 00000000 000001A8 20000000   *...........................y    *   00108760
00000F80   00108920 00108728 00108930 00108738  00108001 000FA278 00000000 00000000   *..i...g...i...g........s.....   *   00108780
00000FA0   00000000 00000000 00000000 00000000  00000000 00000000 00000000 00000000   *................................*   001087A0
00000FC0   00000000 00000000 00000000 00000000  00000000 00000000 C3F2E3C7 E34EF4F8   *........................C2TGT+48*   001087C0
00000FE0   02000000 61010020 001085D0 000541A4  00108938 00000000 00000635 00000000   *..../.....e....u..i.............*   001087E0
00001000   00000000 00108FA8 00000000 00000000  00000000 00000000 30300000 00000000   *.......y........................*   00108800
00001020   00000001 0031A11A E2E8E2D6 E4E34040  C9C7E9E2 D9E3C3C4 00000000 00000000   *........SYSOUT  IGZSRTCD........*   00108820
00001040   00000000 00000000 00000000 00000000  00000000 00000000 00000000 00000000   *................................*   00108840
00001060   00000000 00000000 00000000 00000000  00000000 00000000 00000000 00000001   *................................*   00108860
00001080   001088F4 00000000 0031836F 00000000  00318050 003180FC 001088EC 003180F4   *..h4......c...............h....4*   00108880
000010A0   00000000 00108960 00000000 00000000  00000000 00000000 00108FB0 00108960   *......i-......................i-*   001088A0
000010C0   00000000 000F9C28 000FA258 00000000  00000000 00000000 00000000 00000000   *..........s.....................*   001088C0
000010E0   00000000 00000000 00000000 00318554  00318554 C0000000 00000000 00000000   *...............e...e............*   001088E0
00001100   00000000 01010000 0000     00000010  000C0000 00000000 00000000 00000000   *................................*   00108900
00001120   00000028 20000000 0010     00108778  00000000 00108788 00108790 00108960   *..........i...g.......gh..g...i-*   00108920
00001140   00108FB0 00000000 0000     20000000  00108F98 00108920 00108FA8 00000000   *....................q..i....y...*   00108940
00001160   00001000 0C404040 40400000 00000000  00000000 00000000 00000000 00000000   *.....        ...................*   00108960
00001180   00000000 00000000 00000000 00000000  00000000 00000000 00000000 00000000   *................................*   00108980
000011A0   00000000 00000000 00000000 00000000  00000000 00000000 00000000 00000000   *................................*   001089A0
000011C0   00000000 00000000 00000000 00000000  00000000 00000000 C1C2C5D5 C440E3C5   *........................ABEND TE*   001089C0
000011E0   E2E3C5D9 40404040 40404040 40404040  40404040 40404040 40404040 40404040   *STER                            *   001089E0
00001200   40404040 40404040 40404040 40404040  40404040 40404040 40404040 40404040   *                                *   00108A00
00001220   LINES TO 00001240 SAME AS ABOVE                                                                                    00108A20
00001260   40404040 40404040 40404040 40404040  40404040 4040D7D9 C5E2E240 C140D7C6   *                      PRESS A PF*   00108A60
00001280   40D2C5E8 40E3D640 C6D6D9C3 C540D6D5  C540D6C6 40E3C8C5 40C6D6D3 D3D6E6C9   * KEY TO FORCE ONE OF THE FOLLOWI*   00108A80
000012A0   D5C740C1 C2C5D5C4 E27A4040 40404040  40404040 40404040 40404040 40404040   *NG ABENDS:                      *   00108AA0
000012C0   40404040 40404040 40404040 40404040  40404040 40404040 40404040 40404040   *                                *   00108AC0
000012E0   40404040 40404040 40404040 40404040  40404040 40404040 40404040 40404040   *                                *   00108AE0
00001300   40404040 40404040 40404040 40404040  40404040 D7C6F140 7E40C1E2 D9C1404D   *                    PF1 = ASRA (*   00108B00
00001320   C4C1E3C1 40C5E7C3 C5D7E3C9 D6D55D40  40404040 40404040 40404040 40404040   *DATA EXCEPTION)                 *   00108B20
00001340   40404040 40404040 40404040 40404040  40404040 40404040 40404040 40404040   *                                *   00108B40
00001360   404040D7 C6F2407E 40C1E2D9 C1404DC4  C5C3C9D4 C1D340C4 C9E5C9C4 C540C5E7   *   PF2 = ASRA (DECIMAL DIVIDE EX*   00108B60
00001380   C3C5D7E3 C9D6D55D 40404040 40404040  40404040 40404040 40404040 40404040   *CEPTION)                        *   00108B80
000013A0   40404040 40404040 40404040 40404040  4040D7C6 F3407E40 C1E2D9C1 404DD7D9   *                  PF3 = ASRA (PR*   00108BA0
000013C0   D6E3C5C3 E3C9D6D5 40C5E7C3 C5D7E3C9  D6D55D40 40404040 40404040 40404040   *OTECTION EXCEPTION)             *   00108BC0
000013E0   40404040 40404040 40404040 40404040  40404040 40404040 40404040 40404040   *                                *   00108BE0
00001400   40D7C6F4 407E40C1 D7C3E340 4DD4C9E2  E2C9D5C7 40D4C1D7 5D404040 40404040   * PF4 = APCT (MISSING MAP)       *   00108C00
00001420   40404040 40404040 40404040 40404040  40404040 40404040 40404040 40404040   *                                *   00108C20
00001440   40404040 40404040 40404040 40404040  D7C6F540 7E40C1C5 C9D6404D D7C7D4C9   *                PF5 = AEIO (PGMI*   00108C40
00001460   C4C5D9D9 5D404040 40404040 40404040  40404040 40404040 40404040 40404040   *DERR)                           *   00108C60
00001480   40404040 40404040 40404040 40404040  40404040 40404040 40404040 404040D7   *                               P*   00108C80
000014A0   C6F6407E 40C1C5C9 D3404DC4 E2C9C4C5  D9D95D40 40404040 40404040 40404040   *F6 = AEIL (DSIDERR)             *   00108CA0
000014C0   40404040 40404040 40404040 40404040  40404040 40404040 40404040 40404040   *                                *   00108CC0
000014E0   LINES TO 00001500 SAME AS ABOVE                                                                                    00108CE0
00001520   40404040 40404040 40404040 40404040  40404040 40404040 40404040 40D6D940   *                             OR *   00108D20
00001540   D7D9C5E2 E240C5D5 E3C5D940 E3D640C5  E7C9E340 E6C9E3C8 D6E4E340 C1C2C5D5   *PRESS ENTER TO EXIT WITHOUT ABEN*   00108D40
00001560   C4C9D5C7 4B404040 40404040 40404040  40404040 40404040 40404040 40404040   *DING.                           *   00108D60
```

Figure 12-6 Portions of a CICS transaction dump (part 2 of 3)

```
CICSTEST   ---   CICS TRANSACTION DUMP   ---   CODE=ASRA   TASK=DFXX                    DATE=02/25/92   TIME=15:57:06   PAGE   15

ENTRY      LOAD
POINT      POINT      NAME       VERS'N  TIME    DATE    OPTIONS        ENTRY      LOAD
                                                                       POINT      POINT      NAME       VERS'N  TIME    DATE    OPTIONS

0001CD1C   0001CC40   DFHTRP                             F4            003D6808   003D6808   DVD933
0030F050   0030F008   EMSIDATE                                         003DB808   003DB808   DVD142
00312008   00312008   EMSM55B                                          003DC808   003DC808   DVD9210
00318050   00318008   DFXXP00A                                         003E0808   003E0808   DVD921
0031A850   0031A808   MLCSCCJP                                         003E3808   003E3808   DVD932
0031F808   0031F808   EMSM06C                                          003E4808   003E4808   DVD125
00327850   00327808   EMSO6A                                           003E6808   003E6808   DVD060
00327828   00327808   DFHEDFR    0211I   16:25   05/12                 003E8008   003E8008   DVD9200
00329008   00329008   DFHEITAB                                         003EA008   003EA008   DVD100
00333008   00333008   EMSM06                                           003ED008   003ED008   DVD912
00334008   00334008   EMSO6                                            003ED008   003ED008   DVD911
00336050   00336008   EMSM11                                           003F1008   003F1008   DVD310
0034C808   0034C808   EMSM11                                           003F3808   003F3808   DVD020
0034D050   0034D008   MLCSXFM                                          003F6008   003F6008   DVD344
0035D008   0035D008   MLCSSM                                           003F7008   003F7008   DVD342
0035D808   0035D808   MLCSMAP                                          003F7808   003F7808   DVD936
0035E008   0035E008   RACMAPB                                          003FA008   003FA008   DVD930
0035E850   0035E808   RACM11                                           003FC008   003FC008   DVD920
00362008   00362008   XAPLTBLS                                         003FE808   003FE808   DVD022
0036C008   0036C008   XAPLINTC                                         003FF808   003FF808   DVDDCT
0036D008   0036D008   RACMO9                                           00400808   00400808   DVDCMDT
00370008   00370008   RACMO9                                           00403008   00403008   DVD010
00378808   00378808   RACMAP8                                          00403808   00403808   DVDSGEN
00379808   00379808   RACMO8                                           00404808   00404808   DVD990C
0037E808   0037E808   RACMAP7                                          00405008   00405008   DVD9040
0037F808   0037F808   RACMO7                                           00406008   00406008   DVD901
00384808   00384808   RACMAPC                                          00407808   00407808   DVD9000
00385050   00385008   RACMAP12                                         0040C050   0040C008   DVD001C
00389008   00389008   RACMAP6                                          0040C850   0040C850   EMS21S
0038A050   0038A008   RACMO6                                           00411850   00411850   EMSITIME
0038D008   0038D008   MLCSHEL                                          00411808   00411808   EMS55
0038E008   0038E008   MLCSWNH                                          0041E808   0041E808   EMSM55
0038F008   0038F008   MLCSCMAP                                         00424808   00424808   FBCHP00A
00394850   00394808   FHHBP00A                                         00434808   00434808   MLCSW33
003A2030   003A2008   EMS42                                            00435808   00435808   MLCSWNE
003A7008   003A7008   DFHEDAD    0211I   17:07   12/14                 00436008   00436008   MLCSWQA
003BA008   003BA008   DFHEITSP                                         00436808   00436808   MLCSSMS
003BB008   003BB008   DFHEDAP    0211I   09:28   05/14                 00437050   00437050   EMS17
003BB008   003BB008   MLCSI60                                          00437008   00437008   EMS317E
003BE008   003BE008   MLCSWNX                                          00439808   00439808   DFHEIQSA   0211I   10:32   10/30
003BE808   003BE808   EMS53                                            0043A028   0043A008   EMSO1
003C7828   003C7828   DFHCRQ     0211I   03:15   05/12                 0043A850   0043A808   EMSDATE
003C8008   003C8008   SDMPMAO                                          00440808   00440808   EMSOOT
003C8508   003C8508   SDBXMNT                                          0042C850   0042C808   EMSDOT
003D0808   003D0808   DVD012                                           00445028   00445028   DFHEMIQDS  0211I   02:56   05/12
003D1008   003D1008   SDMPIQ3                                          00446008   00446008   DFHEIQDS   0211I   18:04   11/20
003D1808   003D1808   DVD140                                           00448008   00448008   SDMPMA1
```

⑪

Figure 12-6   Portions of a CICS transaction dump (part 3 of 3)

To determine the cause of an abend

1. Locate the correct dump in the dump listing.

   • TASK=xxxx in the dump heading (item 1 in figure 12-6) indicates the trans-id for the abending task.

   • DATE= and TIME= in the dump heading (item 2 in figure 12-6) indicate the date and time of the abend.

2. Note the abend code in the dump heading (item 3 in figure 12-6).

3. For ASRA abends, determine the type of program check.

   • Locate the program check code at the last hex character of the third fullword in the PSW (item 4 in figure 12-6).

   • Program check codes and their meanings:

     1 Operation exception
     2 Privileged operation
     3 Execute exception
     4 Protection exception
     5 Addressing exception
     6 Specification exception
     7 Data exception
     8 Fixed-point overflow
     9 Fixed-point divide exception
     A Decimal overflow
     B Decimal-divide exception
     C Exponent overflow
     D Exponent underflow
     E Significance exception
     F Floating-point divide exception

4. Note the program name that appears at the end of the SYMPTOMS line (item 5 in figure 12-6).

Figure 12-7 The procedure for determining the cause of an abend

working with a dump frequently requires you to add or subtract hexadecimal numbers to determine the address of a particular storage area or to interpret the contents of a packed-decimal or binary field.

How to determine the cause of an abend

Figure 12-7 summarizes the procedure for determining the cause of an abend. The first step is to make sure you're looking at the correct dump in the dump listing. You do that by verifying the trans-id, date, and time indicated in the heading that appears at the top of each page of the dump. In figure 12-6, I've marked the trans-id as item 1 and the date and time stamps as item 2.

**To locate the COBOL
statement that caused
the abend (ASRA abends)**

1. Determine the program entry point.

   • Find the module map near the end of the dump.

   • Locate the entry for the program that was executing.

   • Note the program's entry point (item 11 in figure 12-6).

2. Determine the interrupt address.

   • Note the second fullword in the PSW (item 6 in figure 12-6).

3. Determine the instruction offset by subtracting the program entry point from the interrupt address.

4. Use the Condensed Procedure Listing in the compiler output to determine which COBOL statement cause the abend.

   • Find the statement whose offset is closest to the result of step 3 without exceeding it.

   • The OFFSET option must be specified at compile time for the Condensed Procedure Listing to be printed.

Figure 12-8 The procedure for locating the statement that was executing when the interrupt occurred

Once you've found the correct dump, you can easily determine the abend code because it appears in the heading of each page of the transaction dump. In figure 12-6, item 3 shows that the abend code is ASRA, which indicates that the program abended because of a program check.

For ASRA abends, you need to determine which program check caused the abend. You can find this out by looking at the program check code in the program status word (PSW), item 4 in figure 12-6. Figure 12-7 lists the meaning of each program check code. In this example, 7 means that a data exception occurred. (These codes are the same codes as found in the S0Cx messages for batch program abends; S0C7 is the code for a data exception in a batch program.)

To find out which program was executing when the abend occurred, look at the end of the line labelled SYMPTOMS (item 5 in figure 12-6). Here, you can see that the program named DFXXP00A was executing. This information is particularly important if the transaction invokes more than one program by issuing XCTL or LINK commands.

How to determine the instruction that caused the abend

Figure 12-8 summarizes the procedure you follow to determine which COBOL statement was executing when an abend occurred. To do that, you need the program entry point and the interrupt address. To find the program entry point, you must turn to the CICS module map that appears near the end of the transaction dump, shown in part 3 of figure 12-6. Here, item 11 shows the entry point for the DFHXXP00A program. Make sure you use the program entry point, not the load point. The interrupt address is found in the second fullword of the PSW printed at the start of the dump. It's marked as item 6 in figure 12-6.

Next, you subtract the entry point from the interrupt address to determine the offset of the instruction that caused the abend, like this:

```
 31867A
-318050
    62A
```

Here, the interrupt occurred at the instruction whose offset is 62A. Finally, you use the Condensed Procedure Listing from the compiler output to determine the source statement that caused the abend, just as when you use EDF.

How to locate a field in working storage

The procedure you use to locate a particular working-storage field is summarized in figure 12-9. You begin by gathering some basic information from the source listing: (1) the BLW cell (that is, the base locator for working storage), (2) the offset of the field indicated in the Data Division Map, and (3) the offset of the BLW cells within the Task Global Table (TGT), indicated in the TGT Memory Map. These items are highlighted in parts 6 and 8 of figure 12-4. As you can see, PACKED-FIELD-2 uses BLW 0 and its offset is 005, and the offset of the BLW cells within the TGT is 12C.

Next, you must locate the BLW cell within the transaction dump. Because the BLW cell is contained within the TGT, you must first locate the TGT. To do that, scan the TRANSACTION STORAGE -USER storage sections until you find the TGT *signature*: the string constant 'C2TGT+48.' (This search is easy if you're viewing the transaction dump on-line; just use a FIND command or its equivalent to find the string C2TGT+48.) The TGT signature is highlighted as item 7 in part 2 of figure 12-6. Here, the signature starts at location 1087D8.

The TGT signature is 48 (hex) bytes from the start of the TGT, so you must subtract 48 to determine the beginning of the TGT:

```
 1087D8
-    48
 108790
```

So the TGT starts at address 108790. (Although I didn't highlight it in figure 12-6, if you'll look at that address you'll see that it contains the hex value 00108001. This value always appears at the start of a VS COBOL II TGT.)

To find a working-storage field

1. Note the following items from the compiler output:

   • The BLW cell for the field in question, from the Data Division Map.

   • The offset for the field in question, also from the Data Division Map.

   • The offset of the base locators for working storage, from the TGT Memory Map.

2. In the transaction dump, locate the appropriate BLW cell.

   • Find the TGT by searching for the signature, C2TGT+48.

   • Determine the address of the first byte of the signature.

   • Subtract 48 (hex) from the address of the signature to determine the address of the TGT.

   • Add the offset of the base locators for working storage to the address of the TGT to determine the address of the BLW cells.

   • The fullword at this address is the first BLW cell for working storage (BLW=0).

   • If the BLW is greater than zero, count over one fullword for each BLW cell.

3. Locate the field in question.

   • Note the address contained in the BLW.

   • Add the offset of the field in question to it.

   • Find the field's address in Transaction Storage, and note the contents of the field.

Figure 12-9   The procedure for locating a working-storage field

Once you've determined the start of the TGT, you calculate the location of the base locator by adding the offset (in this case, 12C) to it:

```
  108790
+     12C
  1088BC
```

Thus, the base locator for the field we're looking for is at location 1088BC.

If your Working-Storage Section occupies more than 4096 bytes, the TGT will contain more than one BLW cell. In that case, you'll have to count over an appropriate number of fullwords to find the BLW cell that references the field you're looking for. For example, if the Data Division Map indicates that the field uses BLW 002, you'll have to count over two fullwords from the first BLW to find the correct BLW.

Item 8 in part 2 of figure 12-6 shows the BLW cell at address 1088BC, the base locator for the field we're looking for. Here, you can see that the contents of the base locator is 00108960. To determine the address of the field, you add the contents of the base locator to the field's displacement (from the Data Division Map), like this:

```
  108960
+      5
  108965
```

So, PACKED-FIELD-2 will be found at address 108965.

Item 9 in part 2 of figure 12-6 shows the start of working storage addressed by base locator 0 (108960). Counting five bytes over from this address, item 10 shows the contents of the field at address 108965. Once again, you can see that this numeric field contained spaces when it was used in a MULTIPLY statement.

If you're using the OS/VS COBOL compiler, you don't have to use the TGT to determine the base locator. That's because OS/VS COBOL always keeps the base locators in registers. So all you have to do is scan the compiler output to find the register assignments, which tell you which register is assigned to each base locator. For example, the compiler might print a message like this:

```
REGISTER ASSIGNMENT
  REG 6    BL =1
```

Thus, base locator 1 will be stored in register 6. To find a working-storage field that uses BL 1, you simply locate register 6 on the first page of the transaction dump and add its contents to the field's offset.

The trace table

CICS maintains a listing of all its operations in a special trace table that is printed as a part of a transaction dump when a task is terminated. The trace table can be helpful when you're debugging a complex problem. Figure 12-10 shows one page from a trace table.

CICS maintains its trace table in an area of main storage whose size is specified by the systems programmer when CICS is started. As a result, the number of trace entries that can be held in the trace table is fixed. When the table becomes full, CICS simply overwrites the entries at the start of the table. Thus, a trace table that's large enough to hold 500 trace entries will contain only the most recent 500 entries. In the transaction dump, the trace table is formatted so that the most recent trace entry is shown at the bottom of the table. In most cases, the entries near the bottom of the trace table are the ones that will help you identify the problem that led to the abend.

I won't review the details of the trace table because its format is complex, and you won't need to use most of the information it contains anyway. Briefly, the column I've labelled "1" indicates the task that issued the trace entry. Keep in mind that there's only one trace table for an entire system, so all active tasks write to the same table. You're only interested in the table entries generated by your task. (In figure 12-10, all of the entries were made by the same task.)

The column I've labelled "2" indicates the trace entry type, which includes the CICS component that generated the trace entry and the CICS operation that was performed. For example, an entry like this:

```
SCP GETMAIN
```

means that the Storage Control Program (SCP) attempted to acquire main storage. If the storage was acquired successfully, the GETMAIN entry will be followed with an entry like this:

```
SCP ACQUIRED USER STORAGE
```

Trace entries are often made in pairs like this, one when an operation is initiated, the other when the operation is completed.

In figure 12-10, the DFXXP001 program abended before it issued any CICS commands. If it had issued CICS commands, the trace table would include entries generated by the Execute Interface Program (EIP). Each CICS command generates two trace entries: one *before* the command is executed, the other *after* the command has completed. These trace entries look something like this in the trace table:

```
EIP RECEIVE-MAP ENTRY
EIP RECEIVE-MAP RESPONSE
```

Between the Entry and Response trace entries, you usually find several other trace entries that were generated by various CICS subcomponents used to process the command. For example, trace entries are generated when a RECEIVE MAP command retrieves a mapset, acquires and releases terminal storage, and so on.

The column labelled "3" in figure 12-10 identifies the resource associated with a trace entry. Just what this resource represents depends on the type of trace entry. For a BMS operation like RECEIVE MAP, the resource column would indicate the map name. For a program control operation, the resource column would indicate the program name. And for a file control operation, the resource column would indicate the file name.

If a trace table doesn't appear in your transaction dump, it's because tracing wasn't specified during CICS startup. Although you can activate and deactivate tracing with the master terminal transaction (CEMT), it's unlikely that you'll need to. After all, the benefit of the trace table is for diagnosing CICS abends after they've occurred. For testing purposes, you're better off using EDF to trace the execution of a CICS program.

Discussion   Quite frankly, CICS debugging is complex, and I've covered it only briefly here. Fortunately, you can solve most CICS abends using the

CICSTEST   --- CICS TRANSACTION DUMP ---   CODE=ASRA   TASK=DFXX   DATE=04/27/92   TIME=14:26:40   PAGE   6

TIME OF DAY	ID	REG 14	REQD	TASK	FIELD A	FIELD B	CHARS	RESOURCE	TRACE TYPE	INTERVAL
14:26:40.032032	F1	408117A0	CC04	00283	00000280	01176A74	....		SCP GETMAIN INITIMG	00.000000
14:26:40.032608	C8	50D9AC7E	0004	00283	001A2280	8C000288	....		SCP ACQUIRED USER STORAGE	00.000576
14:26:40.032608	FC	0508C6B8	0503	00283	001A0000	0176A74	....	DFHCICSR	ZCP ZSUP START UP TASK	00.000000
14:26:40.032704	FO	4008D9FC	2C04	00283	01000000	0008E258	....		KCP LOCATE-PROFILE	00.000096
14:26:40.032736	EA	4008E67C	0003	00283	01000400	000C33C0	....S.		TMP PFT LOCATE	00.000032
14:26:40.032768	EA	40D9A2C	0C03	00283	0019E6C8	00000000	.WH....	DFXX	TMP RETN NORMAL	00.000032
14:26:40.032800	E5	5008CD98	0C03	00283	00000000	00000000	....		XSP SECURITY CHECK	00.000064
14:26:40.032864	EA	40089C1E	0903	00283	0B010000	0176A74	....		XSP SECURITY RETN	00.000096
14:26:40.032960	FC	7008C87C	0203	00283	01130000	C8D8C3F0	....HQC0		ZCP ZTSP TERMINAL SHARING ATTACH	00.000032
14:26:40.032992	EA	40DBOF14	0203	00283	02020900	0019E9D0	......Z.		ZCP ZLOC LOC REQ UNIQUE REMOTE	00.000032
14:26:40.033024	EA	40DAD97E	0003	00283	01000800	0019E9D8	......ZQ		TMP TCTS GETNEXT	00.000032
14:26:40.033088	FC	40DA9A2C	0003	00283	01000800	0017AAC4	.....D		TMP RETN NORMAL	00.000064
14:26:40.033120	EA	40DADE6B	0205	00283	01130000	01176A74	....	TEST	TMP TCTN LOCATE	00.000032
14:26:40.033120	EA	40A9A2C	0005	00283	01000800	00179294	....		TMP RETN NORMAL	00.000096
14:26:40.033216	F1	40DB1SAC	D304	00283	00178C30	9300071C	....		ZCP RETN ZLOC NORMAL	00.000032
14:26:40.033248	C8	50D9AC7E	D304	00283	00178340	9300000	....		SCP GETMAIN INITIMG	00.000032
14:26:40.033280	C8	50D9AC7E	C304	00283	00173320	850000000	....H..		SCP ACQUIRED SHARED STORAGE	00.000032
14:26:40.033312	F1	50DB1292	C304	00283	00173320	850001008	....		SCP GETMAIN INITIMG	00.000032
14:26:40.033344	DB	50DB12B6	0003	00283	0219E850	40178C30	..Y&..		SCP ACQUIRED SHARED STORAGE	00.000032
14:26:40.033408	F1	40D9A31A	2403	00283	0019EA7C	0176A74	....		SCP GETMAIN INITIMG	00.000064
14:26:40.033408	C8	50089B8	D404	00283	00171A90	01176A74	....		SCP ACQUIRED TERMINAL STORAGE	00.000000
14:26:40.033472	C8	50D9AC7E	0004	00283	00171A90	94000040	....		XTP XFORM2	00.000064
14:26:40.033472	F1	40DAF98	9304	00283	00170019	93170020	....		XSP SECURITY BUILD SNTTE	00.000032
14:26:40.033504	C8	50D9AC7E	0005	00283	0219E850	00178C34	....		SCP GETMAIN INITIMG	00.000032
14:26:40.033536	DB	50DB13B6	2004	00283	0219E850	00178C34	..Y&..		SCP ACQUIRED CONTROL STORAGE	00.000032
14:26:40.033536	FC	50B0A42	0905	00283	0019E6C8	00170020	....H..		XSP SECURITY RETN	00.000096
14:26:40.033632	E7	0008DBE4	8004	00283	00171A90	00178C34	....		SCP GETMAIN INITIMG	00.000000
14:26:40.033632	C9	50089C1E	C804	00283	00171A90	94000040	....		SCP ACQUIRED SHARED STORAGE	00.000000
14:26:40.033696	E5	5008CD98	0C03	00283	00170000	00170020	....	DFXX	ZCP RETN ZTSP TERMINAL SHARING ATTACH	00.000032
14:26:40.033696	EA	40089C1E	0005	00283	00170000	00178C34	.WH...		XSP SECURITY DELETE SNTTE	00.000096
14:26:40.033792	E7	0008DBEC	0004	00283	00170040	00178C34	....		SCP FREEMAIN	00.000000
14:26:40.033824	F2	4008D964	8004	00283	00000000	000000FF	.WH...		SCP RELEASED CONTROL STORAGE	00.000096
14:26:40.033888	EA	400C6D1A	0C03	00283	0019E6C8	0019E218	....		XSP SECURITY CHECK	00.000032
14:26:40.033984	EA	40A9A2C	0005	00283	01000300	0019E9EC	....S.		XSP SECURITY RETN	00.000064
14:26:40.034176	C8	6005ECO	8C04	00283	01000300	01178C34	....		ERM ENTRY	00.000096
14:26:40.034176	F2	8012C5FC	6004	00283	001A2290	8C170908	....		ERM RESPONSE	00.000128
14:26:40.037280	C8	50D9AC7E	0C04	00283	01000000	01178C34	......	DFXXPO0A	PCP XCTL-CONDITIONAL	00.000064
14:26:40.037376	EA	4008D9FC	FE04	00283	0019EDC0	C1E2D9C1	...S.	DFXXPO0A	TMP PPT LOCATE	00.000096
14:26:40.077376	C8	500C4122	4004	00283	0019EDC0	C1E2D9C1	.ASRA.		TMP RETN NORMAL	00.043104
14:26:40.100960	F4	50D9AC7E		00283	00000000	8C0000A8	.ASRA		SCP GETMAIN INITIMG	00.000064
14:26:40.303616	FO	40122F4E	4000	00283	80000000	007EDD80	.=..		PCP ABEND	00.023584
									SCP ACQUIRED USER STORAGE	00.202656
									DCP TRANSACTION	
									KCP WAIT DCI=SINGLE	

Figure 12-10 A portion of a CICS trace table

Execution Diagnostics Facility, and EDF is easy to learn. If your shop has a more sophisticated debugging tool, such as Intertest, by all means learn how to use it. You should resort to analyzing a transaction dump only when absolutely necessary.

Terms

abnormal termination
abend
abnormal termination message
abend message
abend code
program check
data exception
Condensed Procedure Listing
Data Division Map
TGT Memory Map
base locator
displacement
offset
Task Global Table
TGT
Execution Diagnostics Facility
EDF
same-terminal checkout
two-terminal checkout
transaction dump
dump data set
storage class
trace table
module map
signature

Objectives

1. Use EDF to trace the execution of a CICS program and locate the contents of a working-storage field.

2. Given a CICS transaction dump and complete compiler output, locate the statement that caused the abend and the contents of any relevant working-storage fields.

Appendix A

CICS command summary

This appendix summarizes the CICS commands presented in this book. For each command, you'll find the syntax of the command's options that are covered in the text, as well as a figure and page reference that will help you find more detailed information for the command. You can use this summary as a quick refresher on how to code a particular command or option.

The ABEND command   Figure 6-19 on page 133

```
EXEC CICS
    ABEND [ ABCODE(name) ]
END-EXEC
```

The ADDRESS command   Figure 8-41 on page 214

```
EXEC CICS
    ADDRESS [ CWA(pointer) ]
            [ CSA(pointer) ]
            [ TWA(pointer) ]
            [ TCTUA(pointer) ]
END-EXEC
```

The ASSIGN command   Figure 8-20 on page 184

```
EXEC CICS
    ASSIGN [ COLOR(data-area) ]
           [ HILIGHT(data-area) ]
           [ SCRNHT(data-area) ]
           [ SCRNWD(data-area) ]
END-EXEC
```

The DELETE command   Figure 8-7 on page 162

```
EXEC CICS
    DELETE  DATASET(filename)
            RIDFLD(data-area)
          [ RRN | RBA ]
END-EXEC
```

The HANDLE AID command   Figure 8-30 on page 196

```
EXEC CICS
    HANDLE AID
        option(procedure-name)...
END-EXEC
```

The HANDLE CONDITION command   Figure 8-33 on page 201

```
EXEC CICS
    HANDLE CONDITION condition-name(procedure-name)...
END-EXEC
```

The LINK command   Figure 8-14 on page 171

```
EXEC CICS
    LINK  [ PROGRAM(name) ]
          [ COMMAREA(data-area) ]
          [ LENGTH(data-value) ]
END-EXEC
```

The READ command

Figure 6-18 on page 132
Figure 8-1 on page 157

```
EXEC CICS
    READ  DATASET(filename)
          INTO(data-area)
          RIDFLD(data-area)
        [ RRN | RBA ]
        [ LENGTH(data-area) ]
        [ UPDATE ]
END-EXEC
```

The RECEIVE MAP command

Figure 6-17 on page131

```
EXEC CICS
    RECEIVE MAP(name)
            MAPSET(name)
            INTO(data-area)
END-EXEC
```

The RETURN command

Figure 6-14 on page 127
Figure 8-11 on page 168

```
EXEC CICS
    RETURN  [ TRANSID(name) ]
            [ COMMAREA(data-area) ]
            [ LENGTH(data-value) ]
END-EXEC
```

The REWRITE command

Figure 8-5 on page 161

```
EXEC CICS
    REWRITE  DATASET(filename)
             FROM(data-area)
           [ LENGTH(data-value) ]
END-EXEC
```

The SEND MAP command

Figure 6-16 on page 129

```
EXEC CICS
    SEND   MAP(name) ]
         [ MAPSET(name) ]
         [ FROM(data-area) ]
         [ MAPONLY | DATAONLY ]
         [ ERASE | ERASEAUP ]
         [ CURSOR [(data-value)] ]
END-EXEC
```

The SEND TEXT command

Figure 8-28 on page 194

```
EXEC CICS
    SEND TEXT FROM(data-area)
             [LENGTH(data-value)]
             [ERASE]
             [FREEKB]
END-EXEC
```

The UNLOCK command

Figure 8-9 on page 164

```
EXEC CICS
    UNLOCK  DATASET(filename)
END-EXEC
```

The WRITE command

Figure 8-3 on page 159

```
EXEC CICS
    WRITE  DATASET(filename)
           FROM(data-area)
           RIDFLD(data-area)
        [ RRN | RBA ]
        [ LENGTH(data-value) ]
END-EXEC
```

The XCTL command

Figure 6-15 on page 128
Figure 8-16 on page 173

```
EXEC CICS
    XCTL  [ PROGRAM(name) ]
          [ COMMAREA(data-area) ]
          [ LENGTH(data-value) ]
END-EXEC
```

BMS macro summary

This appendix summarizes the BMS macros presented in this book. For each macro instruction, you'll find the syntax of the macro's options that are covered in the text, as well as a figure and page reference that will help you find more detailed information for the macro. You can use this summary as a quick refresher on how to code a particular macro.

The DFHMSD macro

Figure 5-8 on pages 73-74

Format 1

```
name     DFHMSD     TYPE=  {&SYSPARM}
                           {DSECT   },
                           {MAP     }

                   LANG=  {COBOL}
                          {ASM  },
                          {PLI  }

                   MODE=  {IN   }
                          {OUT  },
                          {INOUT}

                   TERM=terminal-type,

                   CTRL=(option,option...),

                   STORAGE=AUTO,

                   MAPATTS=(COLOR,HILIGHT),

                   DSATTS=(COLOR,HILIGHT),

                   EXTATT=  {YES    }
                            {NO     },
                            {MAPONLY}

                   TIOAPFX= {YES}
                            {NO }
```

Format 2

```
         DFHMSD     TYPE=FINAL
```

Terminal types

ALL
3270
3270-1
3270-2

CTRL options

FREEKB
ALARM

The DFHMDI macro

Figure 5-9 on page 77

```
name        DFHMDI    SIZE=(lines,columns),

                      LINE=line-number,

                      COLUMN=column-number,

                      CTRL=(option,option...)
```

CTRL options

FREEKB
ALARM

The DFHMDF macro

Figure 5-10 on pages 79-80

```
name     DFHMDF    POS=(line,column),

                   LENGTH=field-length,

                         ⎧BRT ⎫ ⎧PROT  ⎫
                   ATTRB=(⎨NORM⎬,⎨ASKIP ⎬,NUM,IC,FSET),
                         ⎩DRK ⎭ ⎩UNPROT⎭

                   INITIAL='literal',

                   COLOR=color,

                   HILIGHT=highlight,

                   PICIN='picture-string',

                   PICOUT='picture-string'
```

COLOR values

BLUE	RED
PINK	GREEN
TURQUOISE	YELLOW
NEUTRAL (white)	DEFAULT

HILIGHT values

BLINK
REVERSE
UNDERLINE
OFF

CICS program development procedures for MVS and VSE

This appendix presents JCL procedures for CICS program development tasks under MVS and VSE. Keep in mind that the procedures presented here are intended to be models. You'll have to adapt them to the unique requirements of your system.

MVS Procedures

An MVS job to prepare a BMS mapset

```
//MMA2BMS   JOB  (job accounting information)
//          EXEC DFHMAPS,MAPNAME=INQSET1
//COPY.SYSUT1        DD DSN=MMA2.CICS.ASM(INQSET1),DISP=SHR
//ASMDSECT.SYSPUNCH DD DSN=MMA2.COPYLIB(INQSET1),DISP=SHR
//
```

An MVS job to prepare a command-level COBOL program

```
//MMA2TRAN JOB  (job accounting information)
//          EXEC DFHEITCL
//TRN.SYSIN    DD DSN=MMA2.CICS.COBOL(CUSTINQ1),DISP=SHR
//COB.SYSLIB   DD
//             DD DSN=MMA2.COPYLIB,DISP=SHR
//LKED.SYSLMOD DD DSN=MMA2.CICS.LOADLIB(CUSTINQ1),DISP=SHR
//
```

VSE Procedures

A VSE job to prepare a BMS mapset

```
// JOB MAPSET
// OPTION CATAL,NODECK,ALIGN,SYSPARM='MAP'
   PHASE INQSET1,*
// EXEC ASSEMBLY
/INCLUDE INQSET1
/*
// LIBDEF CL,TO=USRCL2
// EXEC LNKEDT
// DLBL IJSYSPH,'CICS.MAPSET.PUNCH',0,SD
// EXTENT SYSPCH,SYSWK1,1,0,111770,1000
   ASSGN SYSPCH,DISK,VOL=SYSWK1,SHR
// OPTION DECK,SYSPARM='DSECT'
// EXEC ASSEMBLY
   PUNCH ' CATALS C.INQSET1'
/INCLUDE INQSET1
/*
   CLOSE SYSPCH,PUNCH
// DLBL IJSYSIN,'CICS.MAPSET.PUNCH',0,SD
// EXTENT SYSIPT
   ASSGN SYSIPT,DISK,VOL=SYSWK1,SHR
// LIBDEF SL,TO=USRSL2
// EXEC MAINT
// EXEC SSERV
   DSPLY A.INQSET1
/*
   CLOSE SYSIPT,SYSRDR
/&
```

A VSE job to prepare a command-level COBOL program

```
// JOB CICSTRAN
// LIBDEF SL,SEARCH=(USRSL2,USRSL1,PRDSLA,PRDSLB)
// DLBL IJSYSPH,'CICS.TRANSL.PUNCH',0,SD
// EXTENT SYSPCH,SYSWK1,1,0,111770,1000
   ASSGN SYSPCH,DISK,VOL=SYSWK1,SHR
// EXEC DFHECP1$
 CBL LIB,APOST,LANGLVL(2),NOTRUNC
/INCLUDE CUSTINQ1
/*
   CLOSE SYSPCH,02D
// DLBL IJSYSIN,'CICS.TRANSL.PUNCH',0,SD
// EXTENT SYSIPT
   ASSGN SYSIPT,DISK,VOL=SYSWK1,SHR
// OPTION SYM,ERRS,NODECK,CATAL
   PHASE CUSTINQ1
   INCLUDE DFHECI
// EXEC FCOBOL
   CLOSE SYSIPT,SYSRDR
// LIBDEF CL,TO=USRCL2
// EXEC LNKEDT
/&
```

Appendix D

OS/VS COBOL Programs

This appendix contains source listings for OS/VS COBOL versions of the model programs presented in this book. Figure D-1 presents the OS/VS COBOL version of the inquiry program I presented in chapter 6. Then, figures D-2 through D-4 present the OS/VS COBOL versions of the menu program, the maintenance program, and the order entry program I presented in chapter 10.

Because the GETINV subprogram used by the ORDRENT program to obtain an invoice number doesn't contain any non-OS/VS COBOL elements, I didn't include it here. However, I did include two new subprograms: ULSTRIP and ULPAD. These subprograms are used by the maintenance and order entry programs to replace the INSPECT statements used by the VS COBOL II versions to handle underscore characters. ULSTRIP, presented in figure D-5, replaces underscore characters with spaces. ULPAD, presented in figure D-6, does just the opposite: It replaces spaces with underscores. To use either of these subprograms, you code a CALL statement, listing the data area to be processed and the area's length as parameters.

I hope that you see the benefits of VS COBOL II when you examine the OS/VS COBOL listings in this appendix. In particular, the use of the EVALUATE statement, scope terminators (such as END-IF), and in-line PERFORM statements often results in simpler code. So I recommend you use OS/VS COBOL only to maintain existing applications.

```
IDENTIFICATION DIVISION.
*
PROGRAM-ID.  OSINQ1.
*            OS/VS COBOL VERSION.
*
ENVIRONMENT DIVISION.
*
DATA DIVISION.
*
WORKING-STORAGE SECTION.
*
01  SWITCHES.
*
    05  VALID-DATA-SW            PIC X      VALUE 'Y'.
        88 VALID-DATA                       VALUE 'Y'.
*
01  FLAGS.
*
    05  SEND-FLAG                PIC X.
        88  SEND-ERASE                       VALUE '1'.
        88  SEND-DATAONLY                    VALUE '2'.
        88  SEND-DATAONLY-ALARM              VALUE '3'.
*
01  COMMUNICATION-AREA           PIC X.
*
01  RESPONSE-CODE                PIC S9(8)  COMP.
*
COPY CUSTMAS.
*
COPY INQSET1.
*
COPY DFHAID.
*
LINKAGE SECTION.
*
01  DFHCOMMAREA                  PIC X.
*
PROCEDURE DIVISION.
*
0000-PROCESS-CUSTOMER-INQUIRY.
*
    IF EIBCALEN = ZERO
        MOVE LOW-VALUE TO INQMAP1O
        MOVE '1' TO SEND-FLAG
        PERFORM 1400-SEND-CUSTOMER-MAP

    ELSE IF EIBAID = DFHCLEAR
        MOVE LOW-VALUE TO INQMAP1O
        MOVE '1' TO SEND-FLAG
        PERFORM 1400-SEND-CUSTOMER-MAP

    ELSE IF EIBAID = DFHPA1 OR DFHPA2 OR DFHPA3
        NEXT SENTENCE

    ELSE IF EIBAID = DFHPF3 OR DFHPF12
        EXEC CICS
            XCTL PROGRAM('OSMENU')
        END-EXEC

    ELSE IF EIBAID = DFHENTER
        PERFORM 1000-PROCESS-CUSTOMER-MAP

    ELSE
        MOVE LOW-VALUE TO INQMAP1O
        MOVE 'Invalid key pressed.' TO MESSAGEO
        MOVE '3' TO SEND-FLAG
        PERFORM 1400-SEND-CUSTOMER-MAP.

    EXEC CICS
        RETURN TRANSID('OIN1')
               COMMAREA(COMMUNICATION-AREA)
               LENGTH(1)
    END-EXEC.
```

Figure D-1   The OS/VS version of the inquiry program (part 1 of 3)

```
/
 1000-PROCESS-CUSTOMER-MAP.
*
     PERFORM 1100-RECEIVE-CUSTOMER-MAP.
     PERFORM 1200-EDIT-CUSTOMER-DATA.
     IF VALID-DATA
         PERFORM 1300-GET-CUSTOMER-RECORD.
     IF VALID-DATA
         MOVE '2' TO SEND-FLAG
         PERFORM 1400-SEND-CUSTOMER-MAP
     ELSE
         MOVE '3' TO SEND-FLAG
         PERFORM 1400-SEND-CUSTOMER-MAP.
*
 1100-RECEIVE-CUSTOMER-MAP.
*
     EXEC CICS
         RECEIVE MAP('INQMAP1')
                 MAPSET('INQSET1')
                 INTO(INQMAP1I)
     END-EXEC.
*
 1200-EDIT-CUSTOMER-DATA.
*
     IF        CUSTNOL = ZERO
         OR CUSTNOI = SPACE
         MOVE 'N' TO VALID-DATA-SW
         MOVE 'You must enter a customer number.' TO MESSAGEO.
*
 1300-GET-CUSTOMER-RECORD.
*
     EXEC CICS
         READ DATASET('CUSTMAS')
              INTO(CUSTOMER-MASTER-RECORD)
              RIDFLD(CUSTNOI)
              RESP(RESPONSE-CODE)
     END-EXEC.
     IF RESPONSE-CODE = DFHRESP(NORMAL)
         MOVE SPACE          TO MESSAGEO
         MOVE CM-LAST-NAME  TO LNAMEO
         MOVE CM-FIRST-NAME TO FNAMEO
         MOVE CM-ADDRESS    TO ADDRO
         MOVE CM-CITY       TO CITYO
         MOVE CM-STATE      TO STATEO
         MOVE CM-ZIP-CODE   TO ZIPCODEO
     ELSE IF RESPONSE-CODE = DFHRESP(NOTFND)
         MOVE 'N' TO VALID-DATA-SW
         MOVE 'That customer does not exist.' TO MESSAGEO
         MOVE SPACE TO LNAMEO
                       FNAMEO
                       ADDRO
                       CITYO
                       STATEO
                       ZIPCODEO
     ELSE
         EXEC CICS
             ABEND
         END-EXEC.
```

Figure D-1   The OS/VS version of the inquiry program (part 2 of 3)

```
/
1400-SEND-CUSTOMER-MAP.
*
    IF SEND-ERASE
        EXEC CICS
            SEND MAP('INQMAP1')
                 MAPSET('INQSET1')
                 FROM(INQMAP10)
                 ERASE
        END-EXEC
    ELSE IF SEND-DATAONLY
        EXEC CICS
            SEND MAP('INQMAP1')
                 MAPSET('INQSET1')
                 FROM(INQMAP10)
                 DATAONLY
        END-EXEC
    ELSE IF SEND-DATAONLY-ALARM
        EXEC CICS
            SEND MAP('INQMAP1')
                 MAPSET('INQSET1')
                 FROM(INQMAP10)
                 DATAONLY
                 ALARM
        END-EXEC.
```

Figure D-1   The OS/VS version of the inquiry program (part 3 of 3)

```
IDENTIFICATION  DIVISION.
*
PROGRAM-ID.  OSMENU.
*           OS/VS VERSION.
*
ENVIRONMENT DIVISION.
*
DATA DIVISION.
*
WORKING-STORAGE SECTION.
*
01   SWITCHES.
*
    05  VALID-DATA-SW          PIC X        VALUE 'Y'.
        88  VALID-DATA                      VALUE 'Y'.
*
01   FLAGS.
*
    05  SEND-FLAG              PIC X.
        88  SEND-ERASE                      VALUE '1'.
        88  SEND-DATAONLY                   VALUE '2'.
        88  SEND-DATAONLY-ALARM             VALUE '3'.
*
01   PROGRAM-TABLE.
*
    05  PROGRAM-LIST.
        10  PROGRAM-1          PIC X(8)   VALUE 'OSINQ1  '.
        10  PROGRAM-2          PIC X(8)   VALUE 'OSMNT1  '.
        10  PROGRAM-3          PIC X(8)   VALUE 'OSORD1  '.
    05  PROGRAM-NAME           REDEFINES PROGRAM-LIST
                               OCCURS 3
                               PIC X(8).
*
01   ACTION-ALPHA.
*
    05  ACTION-NUM             PIC 9.
*
01   END-OF-SESSION-MESSAGE    PIC X(13) VALUE 'Session ended'.
*
01   RESPONSE-CODE             PIC S9(8) COMP.
*
01   COMMUNICATION-AREA        PIC X.
*
COPY MENSET1.
*
COPY DFHAID.
*
COPY ATTR.
*
LINKAGE SECTION.
*
01   DFHCOMMAREA               PIC X.
*
PROCEDURE DIVISION.
*
0000-PROCESS-MASTER-MENU.
*
    IF EIBCALEN = ZERO
        MOVE LOW-VALUE TO MENMAP1O
        MOVE -1  TO ACTIONL
        MOVE '1' TO SEND-FLAG
        PERFORM 1400-SEND-MENU-MAP

    ELSE IF EIBAID = DFHCLEAR
        MOVE LOW-VALUE TO MENMAP1O
        MOVE -1  TO ACTIONL
        MOVE '1' TO SEND-FLAG
        PERFORM 1400-SEND-MENU-MAP

    ELSE IF EIBAID = DFHPA1 OR DFHPA2 OR DFHPA3
        NEXT SENTENCE
```

Figure D-2   The OS/VS version of the menu program (part 1 of 3)

```
/
        ELSE IF EIBAID = DFHPF3 OR DFHPF12
            PERFORM 2000-SEND-TERMINATION-MESSAGE
            EXEC CICS
                RETURN
            END-EXEC

        ELSE IF EIBAID = DFHENTER
            PERFORM 1000-PROCESS-MENU-MAP
        ELSE
            MOVE 'Invalid key pressed.' TO MESSAGEO
            MOVE -1  TO ACTIONL
            MOVE '3' TO SEND-FLAG
            PERFORM 1400-SEND-MENU-MAP.

        EXEC CICS
            RETURN TRANSID('OMEN')
                   COMMAREA(COMMUNICATION-AREA)
                   LENGTH(1)
        END-EXEC.
*
  1000-PROCESS-MENU-MAP.
*
        PERFORM 1100-RECEIVE-MENU-MAP.
        PERFORM 1200-EDIT-MENU-DATA.
        IF VALID-DATA
            PERFORM 1300-BRANCH-TO-PROGRAM.
        MOVE '3' TO SEND-FLAG.
        PERFORM 1400-SEND-MENU-MAP.
*
  1100-RECEIVE-MENU-MAP.
*
        EXEC CICS
            RECEIVE MAP('MENMAP1')
                    MAPSET('MENSET1')
                    INTO(MENMAP1I)
        END-EXEC.
*
  1200-EDIT-MENU-DATA.
*
        IF ACTIONI NOT = '1' AND '2' AND '3'
            MOVE ATTR-REVERSE TO ACTIONH
            MOVE 'You must enter 1, 2, or 3.' TO MESSAGEO
            MOVE 'N' TO VALID-DATA-SW
        ELSE
            MOVE ACTIONI TO ACTION-ALPHA.
*
  1300-BRANCH-TO-PROGRAM.
*
        EXEC CICS
            XCTL PROGRAM(PROGRAM-NAME(ACTION-NUM))
                 RESP(RESPONSE-CODE)
        END-EXEC.
        MOVE 'That program is not available.' TO MESSAGEO.
```

Figure D-2   The OS/VS version of the menu program (part 2 of 3)

```
/
  1400-SEND-MENU-MAP.
*
      IF SEND-ERASE
          EXEC CICS
              SEND  MAP('MENMAP1')
                    MAPSET('MENSET1')
                    FROM(MENMAP10)
                    ERASE
                    CURSOR
          END-EXEC
      ELSE IF SEND-DATAONLY
          EXEC CICS
              SEND  MAP('MENMAP1')
                    MAPSET('MENSET1')
                    FROM(MENMAP10)
                    DATAONLY
                    CURSOR
          END-EXEC
      ELSE IF SEND-DATAONLY-ALARM
          EXEC CICS
              SEND  MAP('MENMAP1')
                    MAPSET('MENSET1')
                    FROM(MENMAP10)
                    DATAONLY
                    CURSOR
                    ALARM
          END-EXEC.
*
  2000-SEND-TERMINATION-MESSAGE.
*
      EXEC CICS
          SEND TEXT  FROM(END-OF-SESSION-MESSAGE)
                     ERASE
                     FREEKB
      END-EXEC.
```

Figure D-2   The OS/VS version of the menu program (part 3 of 3)

```
 IDENTIFICATION DIVISION.
*
 PROGRAM-ID.  OSMNT1.
*             OS/VS COBOL VERSION.
*
 ENVIRONMENT DIVISION.
*
 DATA DIVISION.
*
 WORKING-STORAGE SECTION.
*
 01   SWITCHES.
*
     05   VALID-DATA-SW                PIC X    VALUE 'Y'.
          88   VALID-DATA                       VALUE 'Y'.
*
 01   FLAGS.
*
     05   SEND-FLAG                    PIC X.
          88   SEND-ERASE                       VALUE '1'.
          88   SEND-ERASE-ALARM                 VALUE '2'.
          88   SEND-DATAONLY                    VALUE '3'.
          88   SEND-DATAONLY-ALARM              VALUE '4'.
*
 01   WORK-FIELDS.
*
     05   RESPONSE-CODE                PIC S9(8) COMP.
*
 01   PARAMETER-LENGTH                 PIC S9(8) COMP.
*
 01   COMMUNICATION-AREA.
*
     05   CA-CONTEXT-FLAG              PIC X.
          88   PROCESS-KEY-MAP                  VALUE '1'.
          88   PROCESS-ADD-CUSTOMER             VALUE '2'.
          88   PROCESS-CHANGE-CUSTOMER          VALUE '3'.
          88   PROCESS-DELETE-CUSTOMER          VALUE '4'.
     05   CA-CUSTOMER-RECORD.
          10   CA-CUSTOMER-NUMBER      PIC X(6).
          10   FILLER                  PIC X(112).
*
 COPY CUSTMAS.
*
 COPY MNTSET1.
*
 COPY DFHAID.
*
 COPY ATTR.
*
 COPY ERRPARM.
*
 LINKAGE SECTION.
*
 01   DFHCOMMAREA                      PIC X(119).
*
 PROCEDURE DIVISION.
*
 0000-PROCESS-CUSTOMER-MAINT.
*
     MOVE DFHCOMMAREA TO COMMUNICATION-AREA.

     IF EIBCALEN = ZERO
         MOVE LOW-VALUE TO MNTMAP1O
         MOVE -1  TO CUSTNO1L
         MOVE '1' TO SEND-FLAG
         PERFORM 1500-SEND-KEY-MAP
         MOVE '1' TO CA-CONTEXT-FLAG
```

Figure D-3   The OS/VS version of the maintenance program (part 1 of 7)

/

```
    ELSE IF EIBAID = DFHPF3
        EXEC CICS
            XCTL PROGRAM('OSMENU')
        END-EXEC

    ELSE IF EIBAID = DFHPF12
        IF PROCESS-KEY-MAP
            EXEC CICS
                XCTL PROGRAM('OSMENU')
            END-EXEC
        ELSE
            MOVE LOW-VALUE TO MNTMAP10
            MOVE -1   TO CUSTNO1L
            MOVE '1' TO SEND-FLAG
            PERFORM 1500-SEND-KEY-MAP
            MOVE '1' TO CA-CONTEXT-FLAG

    ELSE IF EIBAID = DFHCLEAR
        IF PROCESS-KEY-MAP
            MOVE LOW-VALUE TO MNTMAP10
            MOVE -1   TO CUSTNO1L
            MOVE '1' TO SEND-FLAG
            PERFORM 1500-SEND-KEY-MAP
        ELSE
            MOVE LOW-VALUE TO MNTMAP20
            MOVE -1   TO CUSTNO2L
            MOVE '1' TO SEND-FLAG
            PERFORM 1400-SEND-CUSTOMER-MAP

    ELSE IF  EIBAID = DFHPA1 OR DFHPA2 OR DFHPA3
        NEXT SENTENCE

    ELSE IF EIBAID = DFHENTER
        IF PROCESS-KEY-MAP
            PERFORM 1000-PROCESS-KEY-MAP
        ELSE IF PROCESS-ADD-CUSTOMER
            PERFORM 2000-PROCESS-ADD-CUSTOMER
        ELSE IF PROCESS-CHANGE-CUSTOMER
            PERFORM 3000-PROCESS-CHANGE-CUSTOMER
        ELSE IF PROCESS-DELETE-CUSTOMER
            PERFORM 4000-PROCESS-DELETE-CUSTOMER
        ELSE
            NEXT SENTENCE

    ELSE
        IF PROCESS-KEY-MAP
            MOVE LOW-VALUE TO MNTMAP10
            MOVE -1 TO CUSTNO1L
            MOVE 'That key is unassigned.' TO MSG10
            MOVE '4' TO SEND-FLAG
            PERFORM 1500-SEND-KEY-MAP
        ELSE
            MOVE LOW-VALUE TO MNTMAP20
            MOVE -1 TO CUSTNO2L
            MOVE 'That key is unassigned.' TO MSG20
            MOVE '4' TO SEND-FLAG
            PERFORM 1400-SEND-CUSTOMER-MAP.

    EXEC CICS
        RETURN TRANSID('OMN1')
                COMMAREA(COMMUNICATION-AREA)
                LENGTH(119)
    END-EXEC.
```

Figure D-3   The OS/VS version of the maintenance program (part 2 of 7)

```
/
 1000-PROCESS-KEY-MAP.
*
     PERFORM 1100-RECEIVE-KEY-MAP.
     PERFORM 1200-EDIT-KEY-DATA.
     IF VALID-DATA
         MOVE 118 TO PARAMETER-LENGTH
         CALL 'ULPAD' USING CUSTOMER-MASTER-RECORD
                            PARAMETER-LENGTH
         MOVE CUSTNO1I       TO CUSTNO2O
         MOVE CM-LAST-NAME   TO LNAMEO
         MOVE CM-FIRST-NAME  TO FNAMEO
         MOVE CM-ADDRESS     TO ADDRO
         MOVE CM-CITY        TO CITYO
         MOVE CM-STATE       TO STATEO
         MOVE CM-ZIP-CODE    TO ZIPCODEO
         MOVE -1             TO LNAMEL
         MOVE '1'            TO SEND-FLAG
         PERFORM 1400-SEND-CUSTOMER-MAP
     ELSE
         MOVE LOW-VALUE TO CUSTNO1O
                           ACTIONO
         MOVE '4'       TO SEND-FLAG
         PERFORM 1500-SEND-KEY-MAP.
*
 1100-RECEIVE-KEY-MAP.
*
     EXEC CICS
         RECEIVE MAP('MNTMAP1')
                 MAPSET('MNTSET1')
                 INTO(MNTMAP1I)
     END-EXEC.
     MOVE 119 TO PARAMETER-LENGTH.
     CALL 'ULSTRIP' USING MNTMAP1I
                          PARAMETER-LENGTH.
*
 1200-EDIT-KEY-DATA.
*
     MOVE ATTR-NO-HIGHLIGHT TO ACTIONH
                              CUSTNO1H.

     IF ACTIONI NOT = '1' AND '2' AND '3'
         MOVE ATTR-REVERSE TO ACTIONH
         MOVE -1 TO ACTIONL
         MOVE 'Action must be 1, 2, or 3.' TO MSG1O
         MOVE 'N' TO VALID-DATA-SW.

     IF       CUSTNO1L = ZERO
         OR CUSTNO1I = SPACE
         MOVE ATTR-REVERSE TO CUSTNO1H
         MOVE -1 TO CUSTNO1L
         MOVE 'You must enter a customer number.' TO MSG1O
         MOVE 'N' TO VALID-DATA-SW.

     IF VALID-DATA AND ACTIONI = '1'
         PERFORM 1300-READ-CUSTOMER-RECORD
         IF RESPONSE-CODE = DFHRESP(NOTFND)
             MOVE 'Type information for new customer.  Then Press
-                 'Enter.' TO INSTR2O
             MOVE '2'       TO CA-CONTEXT-FLAG
             MOVE SPACE     TO CUSTOMER-MASTER-RECORD
         ELSE
             MOVE 'That customer already exists.' TO MSG1O
             MOVE 'N' TO VALID-DATA-SW.

     IF VALID-DATA AND ACTIONI = '2'
         PERFORM 1300-READ-CUSTOMER-RECORD
         IF RESPONSE-CODE = DFHRESP(NORMAL)
             MOVE 'Type changes.  Then press Enter.' TO INSTR2O
             MOVE '3' TO CA-CONTEXT-FLAG
         ELSE
             MOVE 'That customer does not exist.' TO MSG1O
             MOVE 'N' TO VALID-DATA-SW.
```

Figure D-3   The OS/VS version of the maintenance program (part 3 of 7)

```
/
          IF VALID-DATA AND ACTIONI = '3'
              PERFORM 1300-READ-CUSTOMER-RECORD
              IF RESPONSE-CODE = DFHRESP(NORMAL)
                  MOVE 'Press Enter to delete this customer or press PF
-                       '2 to cancel.' TO INSTR20
                  MOVE '4' TO CA-CONTEXT-FLAG
                  MOVE ATTR-PROT TO LNAMEA
                                   FNAMEA
                                   ADDRA
                                   CITYA
                                   STATEA
                                   ZIPCODEA
              ELSE
                  MOVE 'That customer does not exist.' TO MSG10
                  MOVE 'N' TO VALID-DATA-SW.
*
 1300-READ-CUSTOMER-RECORD.
*
      EXEC CICS
          READ DATASET('CUSTMAS')
               INTO(CUSTOMER-MASTER-RECORD)
               RIDFLD(CUSTNO1I)
               RESP(RESPONSE-CODE)
      END-EXEC.
      IF        RESPONSE-CODE NOT = DFHRESP(NORMAL)
          AND RESPONSE-CODE NOT = DFHRESP(NOTFND)
              GO TO 9999-TERMINATE-PROGRAM.
      MOVE CUSTOMER-MASTER-RECORD TO CA-CUSTOMER-RECORD.
*
 1400-SEND-CUSTOMER-MAP.
*
      IF SEND-ERASE
          EXEC CICS
              SEND MAP('MNTMAP2')
                   MAPSET('MNTSET1')
                   FROM(MNTMAP2O)
                   ERASE
                   CURSOR
          END-EXEC
      ELSE IF SEND-DATAONLY-ALARM
          EXEC CICS
              SEND MAP('MNTMAP2')
                   MAPSET('MNTSET1')
                   FROM(MNTMAP2O)
                   DATAONLY
                   ALARM
                   CURSOR
          END-EXEC.
*
 1500-SEND-KEY-MAP.
*
      IF SEND-ERASE
          EXEC CICS
              SEND MAP('MNTMAP1')
                   MAPSET('MNTSET1')
                   FROM(MNTMAP1O)
                   ERASE
                   CURSOR
          END-EXEC
      ELSE IF SEND-ERASE-ALARM
          EXEC CICS
              SEND MAP('MNTMAP1')
                   MAPSET('MNTSET1')
                   FROM(MNTMAP1O)
                   ERASE
                   ALARM
                   CURSOR
          END-EXEC
      ELSE IF SEND-DATAONLY-ALARM
          EXEC CICS
              SEND MAP('MNTMAP1')
                   MAPSET('MNTSET1')
                   FROM(MNTMAP1O)
                   DATAONLY
                   ALARM
                   CURSOR
          END-EXEC.
```

Figure D-3   The OS/VS version of the maintenance program (part 4 of 7)

```
/
 2000-PROCESS-ADD-CUSTOMER.
*
     PERFORM 2100-RECEIVE-CUSTOMER-MAP.
     PERFORM 2200-EDIT-CUSTOMER-DATA.
     IF VALID-DATA
         PERFORM 2300-WRITE-CUSTOMER-RECORD
         IF RESPONSE-CODE = DFHRESP(NORMAL)
             MOVE 'Customer record added.' TO MSG10
             MOVE '1' TO SEND-FLAG
         ELSE
             MOVE 'Another user has added a record with that custo
-                'mer number.' TO MSG10
             MOVE '2' TO SEND-FLAG.
     IF VALID-DATA
         PERFORM 1500-SEND-KEY-MAP
         MOVE '1' TO CA-CONTEXT-FLAG
     ELSE
         MOVE LOW-VALUE TO LNAMEO
                           FNAMEO
                           ADDRO
                           CITYO
                           STATEO
                           ZIPCODEO
         MOVE '4' TO SEND-FLAG
         PERFORM 1400-SEND-CUSTOMER-MAP.
*
 2100-RECEIVE-CUSTOMER-MAP.
*
     EXEC CICS
         RECEIVE MAP('MNTMAP2')
                 MAPSET('MNTSET1')
                 INTO(MNTMAP2I)
     END-EXEC.
     MOVE 339 TO PARAMETER-LENGTH.
     CALL 'ULSTRIP' USING MNTMAP2I
                          PARAMETER-LENGTH.
*
 2200-EDIT-CUSTOMER-DATA.
*
     MOVE ATTR-NO-HIGHLIGHT TO ZIPCODEH
                               STATEH
                               CITYH
                               ADDRH
                               FNAMEH
                               LNAMEH.

     IF        ZIPCODEI = SPACE
         OR ZIPCODEL = ZERO
         MOVE ATTR-REVERSE TO ZIPCODEH
         MOVE -1 TO ZIPCODEL
         MOVE 'You must enter a zip code.' TO MSG20
         MOVE 'N' TO VALID-DATA-SW.

     IF        STATEI = SPACE
         OR STATEL = ZERO
         MOVE ATTR-REVERSE TO STATEH
         MOVE -1 TO STATEL
         MOVE 'You must enter a state.' TO MSG20
         MOVE 'N' TO VALID-DATA-SW.

     IF        CITYI = SPACE
         OR CITYL = ZERO
         MOVE ATTR-REVERSE TO CITYH
         MOVE -1 TO CITYL
         MOVE 'You must enter a city.' TO MSG20
         MOVE 'N' TO VALID-DATA-SW.

     IF        ADDRI = SPACE
         OR ADDRL = ZERO
         MOVE ATTR-REVERSE TO ADDRH
         MOVE -1 TO ADDRL
         MOVE 'You must enter an address.' TO MSG20
         MOVE 'N' TO VALID-DATA-SW.
```

Figure D-3   The OS/VS version of the maintenance program (part 5 of 7)

/
```
        IF          FNAMEI = SPACE
            OR FNAMEL = ZERO
            MOVE ATTR-REVERSE TO FNAMEH
            MOVE -1 TO FNAMEL
            MOVE 'You must enter a first name.' TO MSG20
            MOVE 'N' TO VALID-DATA-SW.

        IF          LNAMEI = SPACE
            OR LNAMEL = ZERO
            MOVE ATTR-REVERSE TO LNAMEH
            MOVE -1 TO LNAMEL
            MOVE 'You must enter a last name.' TO MSG20
            MOVE 'N' TO VALID-DATA-SW.
*
    2300-WRITE-CUSTOMER-RECORD.
*
        MOVE CUSTNO2I TO CM-CUSTOMER-NUMBER.
        MOVE LNAMEI   TO CM-LAST-NAME.
        MOVE FNAMEI   TO CM-FIRST-NAME.
        MOVE ADDRI    TO CM-ADDRESS.
        MOVE CITYI    TO CM-CITY.
        MOVE STATEI   TO CM-STATE.
        MOVE ZIPCODEI TO CM-ZIP-CODE.
        EXEC CICS
            WRITE DATASET('CUSTMAS')
                  FROM(CUSTOMER-MASTER-RECORD)
                  RIDFLD(CM-CUSTOMER-NUMBER)
                  RESP(RESPONSE-CODE)
        END-EXEC.
        IF          RESPONSE-CODE NOT = DFHRESP(NORMAL)
            AND RESPONSE-CODE NOT = DFHRESP(DUPREC)
            GO TO 9999-TERMINATE-PROGRAM.
*
    3000-PROCESS-CHANGE-CUSTOMER.
*
        PERFORM 2100-RECEIVE-CUSTOMER-MAP.
        PERFORM 2200-EDIT-CUSTOMER-DATA.
        IF VALID-DATA
            MOVE CUSTNO2I TO CM-CUSTOMER-NUMBER
            PERFORM 3100-READ-CUSTOMER-FOR-UPDATE
            IF RESPONSE-CODE = DFHRESP(NORMAL)
                IF CUSTOMER-MASTER-RECORD = CA-CUSTOMER-RECORD
                    PERFORM 3200-REWRITE-CUSTOMER-RECORD
                    MOVE 'Customer record updated.' TO MSG10
                    MOVE '1' TO SEND-FLAG
                ELSE
                    MOVE 'Another user has updated the record.  Try a
-                         'gain.' TO MSG10
                    MOVE '2' TO SEND-FLAG
            ELSE
                MOVE 'Another user has deleted the record.' TO MSG10
                MOVE '2' TO SEND-FLAG.
        IF VALID-DATA
            PERFORM 1500-SEND-KEY-MAP
            MOVE '1' TO CA-CONTEXT-FLAG
        ELSE
            MOVE '4' TO SEND-FLAG
            PERFORM 1400-SEND-CUSTOMER-MAP.
*
    3100-READ-CUSTOMER-FOR-UPDATE.
*
        EXEC CICS
            READ DATASET('CUSTMAS')
                 INTO(CUSTOMER-MASTER-RECORD)
                 RIDFLD(CM-CUSTOMER-NUMBER)
                 UPDATE
                 RESP(RESPONSE-CODE)
        END-EXEC.
        IF          RESPONSE-CODE NOT = DFHRESP(NORMAL)
            AND RESPONSE-CODE NOT = DFHRESP(NOTFND)
            GO TO 9999-TERMINATE-PROGRAM.
```

Figure D-3   The OS/VS version of the maintenance program (part 6 of 7)

```
/
 3200-REWRITE-CUSTOMER-RECORD.
*
     MOVE LNAMEI    TO CM-LAST-NAME.
     MOVE FNAMEI    TO CM-FIRST-NAME.
     MOVE ADDRI     TO CM-ADDRESS.
     MOVE CITYI     TO CM-CITY.
     MOVE STATEI    TO CM-STATE.
     MOVE ZIPCODEI TO CM-ZIP-CODE.
     EXEC CICS
         REWRITE DATASET('CUSTMAS')
                 FROM(CUSTOMER-MASTER-RECORD)
                 RESP(RESPONSE-CODE)
     END-EXEC.
     IF RESPONSE-CODE NOT = DFHRESP(NORMAL)
         GO TO 9999-TERMINATE-PROGRAM.
*
 4000-PROCESS-DELETE-CUSTOMER.
*
     MOVE CA-CUSTOMER-NUMBER TO CM-CUSTOMER-NUMBER.
     PERFORM 3100-READ-CUSTOMER-FOR-UPDATE.
     IF RESPONSE-CODE = DFHRESP(NORMAL)
         IF CUSTOMER-MASTER-RECORD = CA-CUSTOMER-RECORD
             PERFORM 4100-DELETE-CUSTOMER-RECORD
             MOVE 'Customer deleted.' TO MSG10
             MOVE '1' TO SEND-FLAG
         ELSE
             MOVE 'Another user has updated the record.  Try again
-                 '.' TO MSG10
             MOVE '2' TO SEND-FLAG
     ELSE
         MOVE 'Another user has deleted the record.' TO MSG10
         MOVE '2' TO SEND-FLAG.
     PERFORM 1500-SEND-KEY-MAP.
     MOVE '1' TO CA-CONTEXT-FLAG.
*
 4100-DELETE-CUSTOMER-RECORD.
*
     EXEC CICS
         DELETE DATASET('CUSTMAS')
                RESP(RESPONSE-CODE)
     END-EXEC.
     IF         RESPONSE-CODE NOT = DFHRESP(NORMAL)
         GO TO 9999-TERMINATE-PROGRAM.
*
 9999-TERMINATE-PROGRAM.
*
     MOVE EIBRESP   TO ERR-RESP.
     MOVE EIBRESP2 TO ERR-RESP2.
     MOVE EIBTRNID TO ERR-TRNID.
     MOVE EIBRSRCE TO ERR-RSRCE.
     EXEC CICS
         XCTL PROGRAM('SYSERR')
              COMMAREA(ERROR-PARAMETERS)
              LENGTH(20)
     END-EXEC.
```

Figure D-3 The OS/VS version of the maintenance program (part 7 of 7)

```
       IDENTIFICATION DIVISION.
*
       PROGRAM-ID.  OSORD1.
*                   OS/VS VERSION.
*
       ENVIRONMENT DIVISION.
*
       DATA DIVISION.
*
       WORKING-STORAGE SECTION.
*
       01  SWITCHES.
*
           05  VALID-DATA-SW                 PIC X    VALUE 'Y'.
               88  VALID-DATA                         VALUE 'Y'.
           05  CUSTOMER-FOUND-SW             PIC X    VALUE 'Y'.
               88  CUSTOMER-FOUND                     VALUE 'Y'.
           05  PRODUCT-FOUND-SW              PIC X    VALUE 'Y'.
               88  PRODUCT-FOUND                      VALUE 'Y'.
           05  VALID-QUANTITY-SW             PIC X    VALUE 'Y'.
               88  VALID-QUANTITY                     VALUE 'Y'.
           05  VALID-NET-SW                  PIC X    VALUE 'Y'.
               88  VALID-NET                          VALUE 'Y'.
*
       01  FLAGS.
*
           05  SEND-FLAG                     PIC X.
               88  SEND-ERASE                         VALUE '1'.
               88  SEND-DATAONLY                      VALUE '2'.
               88  SEND-DATAONLY-ALARM                VALUE '3'.
           05  ATTRIBUTE-SET-FLAG            PIC X.
               88  SET-ATTRIBUTES                     VALUE '1'.
               88  RESET-ATTRIBUTES                   VALUE '2'.
*
       01  WORK-FIELDS.
*
           05  ITEM-SUB          PIC S9(3)   COMP-3   VALUE ZERO.
           05  LINE-ITEM-COUNT   PIC S9(3)   COMP-3   VALUE ZERO.
           05  NET-NUMERIC       PIC 9(7)V99.
           05  QTY-NUMERIC       PIC 9(5).
*
       01  RESPONSE-CODE         PIC S9(8)   COMP.
*
       01  PARAMETER-LENGTH      PIC S9(8)   COMP.
*
       01  COMMUNICATION-AREA.
*
           05  CA-CONTEXT-FLAG               PIC X.
               88  PROCESS-ENTRY                      VALUE '1'.
               88  PROCESS-VERIFY                     VALUE '2'.
           05  CA-TOTAL-ORDERS              PIC S9(3) COMP-3.
           05  CA-INVOICE-RECORD            PIC X(318).
           05  CA-FIELDS-ENTERED.
               10  CA-PO-ENTERED-SW         PIC X.
                   88  CA-PO-ENTERED                  VALUE 'Y'.
               10  CA-LINE-ITEM             OCCURS 10.
                   15  CA-PCODE-ENTERED-SW  PIC X.
                       88  CA-PCODE-ENTERED           VALUE 'Y'.
                   15  CA-QTY-ENTERED-SW    PIC X.
                       88  CA-QTY-ENTERED             VALUE 'Y'.
                   15  CA-NET-ENTERED-SW    PIC X.
                       88  CA-NET-ENTERED             VALUE 'Y'.
*
       01  TOTAL-LINE.
*
           05  TL-TOTAL-ORDERS   PIC ZZ9.
           05  FILLER            PIC X(20) VALUE ' Orders entered.  Pr'.
           05  FILLER            PIC X(20) VALUE 'ess Enter to continu'.
           05  FILLER            PIC X(2)  VALUE 'e.'.
*
       COPY INVOICE.
*
       COPY CUSTMAS.
*
       COPY PRODUCT.
*
       COPY INVCTL.
```

Figure D-4   The OS/VS version of the order entry program (part 1 of 8)

```
/
 COPY ORDSET1.
*
 COPY DFHAID.
*
 COPY ATTR.
*
 COPY ERRPARM.
*
 LINKAGE SECTION.
*
 01  DFHCOMMAREA              PIC X(352).
*
 01  BLL-CELLS.
*
     05  FILLER               PIC S9(8)    COMP.
     05  BLL-CWA              PIC S9(8)    COMP.
*
 01  COMMON-WORK-AREA.
*
     05  CWA-DATE             PIC X(6).
     05  CWA-COMPANY-NAME     PIC X(40).
*
 PROCEDURE DIVISION.
*
 0000-PROCESS-ORDER-ENTRY.
*
     MOVE DFHCOMMAREA TO COMMUNICATION-AREA.

     IF EIBCALEN = ZERO
         MOVE LOW-VALUE TO ORDMAP1
         MOVE LOW-VALUE TO COMMUNICATION-AREA
         MOVE ZERO         TO CA-TOTAL-ORDERS
         MOVE 'Type order details.  Then press Enter.'
             TO ORD-D-INSTR
         MOVE 'F3=Exit    F12=Cancel' TO ORD-D-FKEY
         MOVE -1  TO ORD-L-CUSTNO
         MOVE '1' TO SEND-FLAG
         PERFORM 1400-SEND-ORDER-MAP
         MOVE '1' TO CA-CONTEXT-FLAG

     ELSE IF EIBAID = DFHCLEAR
         MOVE LOW-VALUE TO ORDMAP1
         MOVE LOW-VALUE TO CA-INVOICE-RECORD
                           CA-FIELDS-ENTERED
         MOVE 'Type order details.  Then press Enter.'
             TO ORD-D-INSTR
         MOVE 'F3=Exit    F12=Cancel' TO ORD-D-FKEY
         MOVE -1  TO ORD-L-CUSTNO
         MOVE '1' TO SEND-FLAG
         PERFORM 1400-SEND-ORDER-MAP
         MOVE '1' TO CA-CONTEXT-FLAG

     ELSE IF EIBAID = DFHPA1 OR DFHPA2 OR DFHPA3
         NEXT SENTENCE

     ELSE IF EIBAID = DFHPF3
         PERFORM 3000-SEND-TOTAL-LINE
         EXEC CICS
             RETURN TRANSID('OMEN')
         END-EXEC

     ELSE IF EIBAID = DFHPF12
         IF PROCESS-VERIFY
             MOVE LOW-VALUE TO ORDMAP1
             MOVE LOW-VALUE TO CA-INVOICE-RECORD
                               CA-FIELDS-ENTERED
             MOVE 'Type order details.  Then press Enter.'
                 TO ORD-D-INSTR
             MOVE 'F3=Exit    F12=Cancel' TO ORD-D-FKEY
             MOVE -1  TO ORD-L-CUSTNO
             MOVE '1' TO SEND-FLAG
             PERFORM 1400-SEND-ORDER-MAP
             MOVE '1' TO CA-CONTEXT-FLAG
         ELSE
             PERFORM 3000-SEND-TOTAL-LINE
             EXEC CICS
                 RETURN TRANSID('OSMEMU')
             END-EXEC
```

Figure D-4   The OS/VS version of the order entry program (part 2 of 8)

```
/
          ELSE IF EIBAID = DFHENTER
              IF PROCESS-ENTRY
                  PERFORM 1000-PROCESS-ORDER-MAP
              ELSE
                  PERFORM 2000-PROCESS-POST-ORDER
                  MOVE '1' TO CA-CONTEXT-FLAG

          ELSE IF EIBAID = DFHPF4
              IF PROCESS-VERIFY
                  MOVE LOW-VALUE TO ORDMAP1
                  MOVE 'Type corrections.  Then press Enter.'
                      TO ORD-D-INSTR
                  MOVE 'F3=Exit   F12=Cancel' TO ORD-D-FKEY
                  MOVE -1  TO ORD-L-CUSTNO
                  MOVE '2' TO ATTRIBUTE-SET-FLAG
                  MOVE '2' TO SEND-FLAG
                  PERFORM 1400-SEND-ORDER-MAP
                  MOVE '1' TO CA-CONTEXT-FLAG
              ELSE
                  MOVE LOW-VALUE TO ORDMAP1
                  MOVE 'Invalid key pressed.' TO ORD-D-MESSAGE
                  MOVE -1  TO ORD-L-CUSTNO
                  MOVE '3' TO SEND-FLAG
                  PERFORM 1400-SEND-ORDER-MAP

          ELSE
              MOVE LOW-VALUE TO ORDMAP1
              MOVE 'Invalid key pressed.' TO ORD-D-MESSAGE
              MOVE -1  TO ORD-L-CUSTNO
              MOVE '3' TO SEND-FLAG
              PERFORM 1400-SEND-ORDER-MAP.

          EXEC CICS
              RETURN TRANSID('OOR1')
                     COMMAREA(COMMUNICATION-AREA)
                     LENGTH(352)
          END-EXEC.
*
  1000-PROCESS-ORDER-MAP.
*
      PERFORM 1100-RECEIVE-ORDER-MAP.
      PERFORM 1200-EDIT-ORDER-DATA.
      IF VALID-DATA
          PERFORM 1300-FORMAT-INVOICE-RECORD
          MOVE 'Press Enter to post this order.  Or press F4 to ent
-         'er corrections.' TO ORD-D-INSTR
          MOVE 'F3=Exit   F4=Change   F12=Cancel' TO ORD-D-FKEY
          MOVE SPACE TO ORD-D-MESSAGE
          MOVE '2'   TO SEND-FLAG
          MOVE '1'   TO ATTRIBUTE-SET-FLAG
          PERFORM 1400-SEND-ORDER-MAP
          MOVE '2'   TO CA-CONTEXT-FLAG
      ELSE
          MOVE 'Type corrections.  Then press Enter.'
              TO ORD-D-INSTR
          MOVE 'F3=Exit   F12=Cancel' TO ORD-D-FKEY
          MOVE '3' TO SEND-FLAG
          PERFORM 1400-SEND-ORDER-MAP.
*
  1100-RECEIVE-ORDER-MAP.
*
      EXEC CICS
          RECEIVE MAP('ORDMAP1')
                  MAPSET('ORDSET1')
                  INTO(ORDMAP1)
      END-EXEC.
      MOVE 1406 TO PARAMETER-LENGTH.
      CALL 'ULSTRIP' USING ORDMAP1
                           PARAMETER-LENGTH.
```

Figure D-4   The OS/VS version of the order entry program (part 3 of 8)

```
/
 1200-EDIT-ORDER-DATA.
*
     MOVE ATTR-NO-HIGHLIGHT TO ORD-H-CUSTNO
                              ORD-H-PO.
     MOVE ZERO TO LINE-ITEM-COUNT
                  INV-INVOICE-TOTAL.
     PERFORM 1220-EDIT-LINE-ITEM
         VARYING ITEM-SUB FROM 10 BY -1
             UNTIL ITEM-SUB < 1.
     MOVE INV-INVOICE-TOTAL TO ORD-D-TOTAL.
     IF       LINE-ITEM-COUNT = ZERO
         AND VALID-DATA
         MOVE ATTR-REVERSE TO ORD-H-PCODE(1)
         MOVE -1 TO ORD-L-PCODE(1)
         MOVE 'You must enter at least one line item'
             TO ORD-D-MESSAGE
         MOVE 'N' TO VALID-DATA-SW.

     IF        ORD-L-PO = ZERO
         OR ORD-D-PO = SPACE
         MOVE 'N' TO CA-PO-ENTERED-SW
     ELSE
         MOVE 'Y' TO CA-PO-ENTERED-SW.

     IF        ORD-L-CUSTNO = ZERO
         OR ORD-D-CUSTNO = SPACE
         MOVE ATTR-REVERSE TO ORD-H-CUSTNO
         MOVE -1 TO ORD-L-CUSTNO
         MOVE 'You must enter a customer number'
             TO ORD-D-MESSAGE
         MOVE 'N' TO VALID-DATA-SW
     ELSE
         PERFORM 1210-READ-CUSTOMER-RECORD
         IF CUSTOMER-FOUND
             MOVE CM-LAST-NAME   TO ORD-D-LNAME
             MOVE CM-FIRST-NAME  TO ORD-D-FNAME
             MOVE CM-ADDRESS     TO ORD-D-ADDR
             MOVE CM-CITY        TO ORD-D-CITY
             MOVE CM-STATE       TO ORD-D-STATE
             MOVE CM-ZIP-CODE    TO ORD-D-ZIPCODE
         ELSE
             MOVE SPACE TO ORD-D-LNAME
                           ORD-D-FNAME
                           ORD-D-ADDR
                           ORD-D-CITY
                           ORD-D-STATE
                           ORD-D-ZIPCODE
             MOVE ATTR-REVERSE TO ORD-H-CUSTNO
             MOVE -1 TO ORD-L-CUSTNO
             MOVE 'That customer does not exist'
                 TO ORD-D-MESSAGE
             MOVE 'N' TO VALID-DATA-SW.
     IF VALID-DATA
         MOVE -1 TO ORD-L-CUSTNO.
*
 1210-READ-CUSTOMER-RECORD.
*
     EXEC CICS
         READ DATASET('CUSTMAS')
             INTO(CUSTOMER-MASTER-RECORD)
             RIDFLD(ORD-D-CUSTNO)
             RESP(RESPONSE-CODE)
     END-EXEC.
     IF RESPONSE-CODE = DFHRESP(NORMAL)
         MOVE 'Y' TO CUSTOMER-FOUND-SW
     ELSE IF RESPONSE-CODE = DFHRESP(NOTFND)
         MOVE 'N' TO CUSTOMER-FOUND-SW
     ELSE
         PERFORM 9999-TERMINATE-PROGRAM.
```

Figure D-4   The OS/VS version of the order entry program (part 4 of 8)

```
/
 1220-EDIT-LINE-ITEM.
*
     MOVE ATTR-NO-HIGHLIGHT TO ORD-H-PCODE(ITEM-SUB)
                              ORD-H-QTY(ITEM-SUB)
                              ORD-H-NET(ITEM-SUB).

     MOVE 'N' TO PRODUCT-FOUND-SW.

     IF       ORD-L-PCODE(ITEM-SUB) > ZERO
          AND ORD-D-PCODE(ITEM-SUB) NOT = SPACE
         MOVE 'Y' TO CA-PCODE-ENTERED-SW(ITEM-SUB)
     ELSE
         MOVE 'N' TO CA-PCODE-ENTERED-SW(ITEM-SUB).
     IF       ORD-L-QTY(ITEM-SUB) > ZERO
          AND ORD-D-QTY-ALPHA(ITEM-SUB) NOT = SPACE
         MOVE 'Y' TO CA-QTY-ENTERED-SW(ITEM-SUB)
     ELSE
         MOVE 'N' TO CA-QTY-ENTERED-SW(ITEM-SUB).
     IF       ORD-L-NET(ITEM-SUB) > ZERO
          AND ORD-D-NET-ALPHA(ITEM-SUB) NOT = SPACE
         MOVE 'Y' TO CA-NET-ENTERED-SW(ITEM-SUB)
     ELSE
         MOVE 'N' TO CA-NET-ENTERED-SW(ITEM-SUB).

     IF           CA-NET-ENTERED(ITEM-SUB)
          AND NOT CA-PCODE-ENTERED(ITEM-SUB)
         MOVE ATTR-REVERSE TO ORD-H-PCODE(ITEM-SUB)
         MOVE -1 TO ORD-L-PCODE(ITEM-SUB)
         MOVE 'You cannot enter a net price without a product code
-        '.' TO ORD-D-MESSAGE
         MOVE 'N' TO VALID-DATA-SW.

     IF CA-NET-ENTERED(ITEM-SUB)
         CALL 'NUMEDIT' USING ORD-D-NET-ALPHA(ITEM-SUB)
                              NET-NUMERIC
                              VALID-NET-SW
         IF VALID-NET
             MOVE NET-NUMERIC TO ORD-D-NET(ITEM-SUB)
         ELSE
             MOVE ATTR-REVERSE TO ORD-H-NET(ITEM-SUB)
             MOVE -1 TO ORD-L-NET(ITEM-SUB)
             MOVE 'Net price must be numeric' TO ORD-D-MESSAGE
             MOVE 'N' TO VALID-DATA-SW
             MOVE 'N' TO VALID-QUANTITY-SW.

     IF           CA-QTY-ENTERED(ITEM-SUB)
          AND NOT CA-PCODE-ENTERED(ITEM-SUB)
         MOVE ATTR-REVERSE TO ORD-H-PCODE(ITEM-SUB)
         MOVE -1 TO ORD-L-PCODE(ITEM-SUB)
         MOVE 'You cannot enter a quantity without a product code'
             TO ORD-D-MESSAGE
         MOVE 'N' TO VALID-DATA-SW.

     IF CA-QTY-ENTERED(ITEM-SUB)
         CALL 'INTEDIT' USING ORD-D-QTY-ALPHA(ITEM-SUB)
                              QTY-NUMERIC
                              VALID-QUANTITY-SW
         IF VALID-QUANTITY
             IF QTY-NUMERIC > ZERO
                 MOVE QTY-NUMERIC TO ORD-D-QTY(ITEM-SUB)
             ELSE
                 MOVE ATTR-REVERSE TO ORD-H-QTY(ITEM-SUB)
                 MOVE -1 TO ORD-L-QTY(ITEM-SUB)
                 MOVE 'Quantity must be greater than zero'
                     TO ORD-D-MESSAGE
                 MOVE 'N' TO VALID-DATA-SW
                 MOVE 'N' TO VALID-QUANTITY-SW
         ELSE
             MOVE ATTR-REVERSE TO ORD-H-QTY(ITEM-SUB)
             MOVE -1 TO ORD-L-QTY(ITEM-SUB)
             MOVE 'Quantity must be numeric' TO ORD-D-MESSAGE
             MOVE 'N' TO VALID-DATA-SW
             MOVE 'N' TO VALID-QUANTITY-SW.

     IF           CA-PCODE-ENTERED(ITEM-SUB)
          AND NOT CA-QTY-ENTERED(ITEM-SUB)
         MOVE ATTR-REVERSE TO ORD-H-QTY(ITEM-SUB)
         MOVE -1 TO ORD-L-QTY(ITEM-SUB)
         MOVE 'You must enter a quantity' TO ORD-D-MESSAGE
         MOVE 'N' TO VALID-DATA-SW.
```

Figure D-4   The OS/VS version of the order entry program (part 5 of 8)

```
/          IF NOT CA-PCODE-ENTERED(ITEM-SUB)
               MOVE SPACE TO ORD-D-DESC(ITEM-SUB)
               MOVE ZERO  TO ORD-D-LIST(ITEM-SUB)
                             ORD-D-AMOUNT(ITEM-SUB)
           ELSE
               ADD 1 TO LINE-ITEM-COUNT
               PERFORM 1230-READ-PRODUCT-RECORD
               IF PRODUCT-FOUND
                   MOVE PRM-PRODUCT-DESCRIPTION
                                   TO ORD-D-DESC(ITEM-SUB)
                   MOVE PRM-UNIT-PRICE TO ORD-D-LIST(ITEM-SUB)
                   IF NOT CA-NET-ENTERED(ITEM-SUB)
                       MOVE PRM-UNIT-PRICE TO ORD-D-NET(ITEM-SUB)
                                               NET-NUMERIC.
           IF CA-PCODE-ENTERED(ITEM-SUB) AND PRODUCT-FOUND
               IF VALID-QUANTITY AND VALID-NET
                   MULTIPLY NET-NUMERIC BY QTY-NUMERIC
                       GIVING ORD-D-AMOUNT(ITEM-SUB)
                               INV-AMOUNT(ITEM-SUB)
                       ON SIZE ERROR
                           MOVE ATTR-REVERSE TO ORD-H-QTY(ITEM-SUB)
                           MOVE -1 TO ORD-L-QTY(ITEM-SUB)
                           MOVE 'Line item amount is too large'
                                   TO ORD-D-MESSAGE
                           MOVE 'N' TO VALID-DATA-SW
                           MOVE ZERO TO ORD-D-AMOUNT(ITEM-SUB)
                                         INV-AMOUNT(ITEM-SUB).
           IF CA-PCODE-ENTERED(ITEM-SUB) AND PRODUCT-FOUND
               IF VALID-QUANTITY AND VALID-NET AND VALID-DATA
                   ADD INV-AMOUNT(ITEM-SUB) TO INV-INVOICE-TOTAL
                       ON SIZE ERROR
                           MOVE ATTR-REVERSE TO ORD-H-QTY(ITEM-SUB)
                           MOVE -1 TO ORD-L-QTY(ITEM-SUB)
                           MOVE 'Invoice total is too large'
                                   TO ORD-D-MESSAGE
                           MOVE 'N' TO VALID-DATA-SW
                           MOVE ZERO TO INV-INVOICE-TOTAL.
           IF CA-PCODE-ENTERED(ITEM-SUB) AND NOT PRODUCT-FOUND
               MOVE SPACE TO ORD-D-DESC(ITEM-SUB)
               MOVE ZERO  TO ORD-D-LIST(ITEM-SUB)
                             ORD-D-AMOUNT(ITEM-SUB)
               MOVE ATTR-REVERSE TO ORD-H-PCODE(ITEM-SUB)
               MOVE -1    TO ORD-L-PCODE(ITEM-SUB)
               MOVE 'That product does not exist' TO ORD-D-MESSAGE
               MOVE 'N'   TO VALID-DATA-SW.
       *
        1230-READ-PRODUCT-RECORD.
       *
           EXEC CICS
               READ DATASET('PRODUCT')
                       INTO(PRODUCT-MASTER-RECORD)
                       RIDFLD(ORD-D-PCODE(ITEM-SUB))
                       RESP(RESPONSE-CODE)
           END-EXEC.
           IF RESPONSE-CODE = DFHRESP(NORMAL)
               MOVE 'Y' TO PRODUCT-FOUND-SW
           ELSE IF RESPONSE-CODE = DFHRESP(NOTFND)
               MOVE 'N' TO PRODUCT-FOUND-SW
           ELSE
               PERFORM 9999-TERMINATE-PROGRAM.
       *
        1300-FORMAT-INVOICE-RECORD.
       *
           EXEC CICS
               ADDRESS CWA(BLL-CWA)
           END-EXEC.
           SERVICE RELOAD BLL-CWA.
           MOVE CWA-DATE    TO INV-INVOICE-DATE.
           MOVE ORD-D-CUSTNO TO INV-CUSTOMER-NUMBER.
           MOVE ORD-D-PO    TO INV-PO-NUMBER.
           PERFORM 1310-FORMAT-LINE-ITEM
               VARYING ITEM-SUB FROM 1 BY 1
               UNTIL ITEM-SUB > 10.
           MOVE INVOICE-RECORD TO CA-INVOICE-RECORD.
```

Figure D-4   The OS/VS version of the order entry program (part 6 of 8)

```
/
 1310-FORMAT-LINE-ITEM.
*
     IF CA-PCODE-ENTERED(ITEM-SUB)
         MOVE ORD-D-PCODE(ITEM-SUB)
             TO INV-PRODUCT-CODE(ITEM-SUB)
         MOVE ORD-D-QTY(ITEM-SUB)
             TO INV-QUANTITY(ITEM-SUB)
         MOVE ORD-D-NET(ITEM-SUB)
             TO INV-UNIT-PRICE(ITEM-SUB)
     ELSE
         MOVE SPACE TO INV-PRODUCT-CODE(ITEM-SUB)
         MOVE ZERO  TO INV-QUANTITY(ITEM-SUB)
                       INV-UNIT-PRICE(ITEM-SUB)
                       INV-AMOUNT(ITEM-SUB).
*
 1400-SEND-ORDER-MAP.
*
     IF SET-ATTRIBUTES
         PERFORM 1410-SET-ATTRIBUTES
     ELSE IF RESET-ATTRIBUTES
         PERFORM 1420-RESET-ATTRIBUTES.

     IF SEND-ERASE
         EXEC CICS
             SEND MAP('ORDMAP1')
                  MAPSET('ORDSET1')
                  FROM(ORDMAP1)
                  CURSOR
                  ERASE
         END-EXEC
     ELSE IF SEND-DATAONLY
         EXEC CICS
             SEND MAP('ORDMAP1')
                  MAPSET('ORDSET1')
                  FROM(ORDMAP1)
                  CURSOR
                  DATAONLY
         END-EXEC
     ELSE IF SEND-DATAONLY-ALARM
         EXEC CICS
             SEND MAP('ORDMAP1')
                  MAPSET('ORDSET1')
                  FROM(ORDMAP1)
                  CURSOR
                  DATAONLY
                  ALARM
         END-EXEC.
*
 1410-SET-ATTRIBUTES.
*
     MOVE ATTR-PROT TO ORD-A-CUSTNO.
     IF CA-PO-ENTERED
         MOVE ATTR-PROT TO ORD-A-PO
     ELSE
         MOVE ATTR-PROT-DARK TO ORD-A-PO.
     PERFORM 1415-SET-LINE-ATTRIBUTES
         VARYING ITEM-SUB FROM 1 BY 1
         UNTIL ITEM-SUB > 10.
*
 1415-SET-LINE-ATTRIBUTES.
*
     IF CA-PCODE-ENTERED(ITEM-SUB)
         MOVE ATTR-PROT TO ORD-A-PCODE(ITEM-SUB)
     ELSE
         MOVE ATTR-PROT-DARK TO ORD-A-PCODE(ITEM-SUB).
     IF CA-QTY-ENTERED(ITEM-SUB)
         MOVE ATTR-PROT TO ORD-A-QTY(ITEM-SUB)
     ELSE
         MOVE ATTR-PROT-DARK TO ORD-A-QTY(ITEM-SUB).
     IF      CA-NET-ENTERED(ITEM-SUB)
         OR CA-PCODE-ENTERED(ITEM-SUB)
         MOVE ATTR-PROT TO ORD-A-NET(ITEM-SUB)
     ELSE
         MOVE ATTR-PROT-DARK TO ORD-A-NET(ITEM-SUB).
```

Figure D-4   The OS/VS version of the order entry program (part 7 of 8)

```
/
 1420-RESET-ATTRIBUTES.
*
     MOVE ATTR-UNPROT-MDT TO ORD-A-CUSTNO.
     IF CA-PO-ENTERED
         MOVE ATTR-UNPROT-MDT TO ORD-A-PO
     ELSE
         MOVE ATTR-UNPROT       TO ORD-A-PO.
     PERFORM 1425-RESET-LINE-ATTRIBUTES
         VARYING ITEM-SUB FROM 1 BY 1
             UNTIL ITEM-SUB > 10.
*
 1425-RESET-LINE-ATTRIBUTES.
*
     IF CA-PCODE-ENTERED(ITEM-SUB)
         MOVE ATTR-UNPROT-MDT TO ORD-A-PCODE(ITEM-SUB)
     ELSE
         MOVE ATTR-UNPROT       TO ORD-A-PCODE(ITEM-SUB).
     IF CA-QTY-ENTERED(ITEM-SUB)
         MOVE ATTR-UNPROT-MDT TO ORD-A-QTY(ITEM-SUB)
     ELSE
         MOVE ATTR-UNPROT       TO ORD-A-QTY(ITEM-SUB).
     IF CA-NET-ENTERED(ITEM-SUB)
         MOVE ATTR-UNPROT-MDT TO ORD-A-NET(ITEM-SUB)
     ELSE
         MOVE ATTR-UNPROT       TO ORD-A-NET(ITEM-SUB).
*
 2000-PROCESS-POST-ORDER.
*
     MOVE CA-INVOICE-RECORD TO INVOICE-RECORD.
     EXEC CICS
         LINK PROGRAM('GETINV')
              COMMAREA(INV-INVOICE-NUMBER)
     END-EXEC.
     PERFORM 2100-WRITE-INVOICE-RECORD.
     ADD 1 TO CA-TOTAL-ORDERS.
     MOVE 'Type order details.   Then press Enter.'
         TO ORD-D-INSTR.
     MOVE 'Order posted.' TO ORD-D-MESSAGE.
     MOVE 'F3=Exit    F12=Cancel' TO ORD-D-FKEY.
     MOVE -1 TO ORD-L-CUSTNO.
     MOVE '1' TO SEND-FLAG.
     PERFORM 1400-SEND-ORDER-MAP.
*
 2100-WRITE-INVOICE-RECORD.
*
     EXEC CICS
         WRITE DATASET('INVOICE')
               FROM(INVOICE-RECORD)
               RIDFLD(INV-INVOICE-NUMBER)
     END-EXEC.
*
 3000-SEND-TOTAL-LINE.
*
     MOVE CA-TOTAL-ORDERS TO TL-TOTAL-ORDERS.
     EXEC CICS
         SEND TEXT FROM(TOTAL-LINE)
                   ERASE
                   FREEKB
     END-EXEC.

 9999-TERMINATE-PROGRAM.
*
     MOVE EIBRESP  TO ERR-RESP.
     MOVE EIBRESP2 TO ERR-RESP2.
     MOVE EIBTRNID TO ERR-TRNID.
     MOVE EIBRSRCE TO ERR-RSRCE.
     EXEC CICS
         XCTL PROGRAM('SYSERR')
              COMMAREA(ERROR-PARAMETERS)
     END-EXEC.
```

Figure D-4   The OS/VS version of the order entry program (part 8 of 8)

```
 IDENTIFICATION DIVISION.
*
 PROGRAM-ID. ULSTRIP.
*
 ENVIRONMENT DIVISION.
*
 DATA DIVISION.
*
 WORKING-STORAGE SECTION.
*
 LINKAGE SECTION.
*
 01   DATA-AREA              PIC X
                             OCCURS 32767
                             DEPENDING ON DATA-LENGTH
                             INDEXED BY DATA-INDEX.
*
 01   DATA-LENGTH           PIC S9(8) COMP.
*
 PROCEDURE DIVISION USING DATA-AREA
                          DATA-LENGTH.
*
 0000-STRIP-UNDERLINES.
*
     PERFORM 1000-REMOVE-UNDERLINE
         VARYING DATA-INDEX FROM 1 BY 1
         UNTIL DATA-INDEX > DATA-LENGTH.
     GOBACK.
*
 1000-REMOVE-UNDERLINE.
*
     IF DATA-AREA(DATA-INDEX) = '_'
         MOVE SPACE TO DATA-AREA(DATA-INDEX).
```

Figure D-5 The ULSTRIP program

```
 IDENTIFICATION DIVISION.
*
 PROGRAM-ID. ULPAD.
*
 ENVIRONMENT DIVISION.
*
 DATA DIVISION.
*
 WORKING-STORAGE SECTION.
*
 LINKAGE SECTION.
*
 01  DATA-AREA            PIC X
                          OCCURS 32767
                          DEPENDING ON DATA-LENGTH
                          INDEXED BY DATA-INDEX.
*
 01  DATA-LENGTH          PIC S9(8) COMP.
*
 PROCEDURE DIVISION USING DATA-AREA
                          DATA-LENGTH.
*
 0000-PAD-UNDERLINES.
*
     PERFORM 1000-INSERT-UNDERLINE
         VARYING DATA-INDEX FROM 1 BY 1
         UNTIL DATA-INDEX > DATA-LENGTH.
     GOBACK.
*
 1000-INSERT-UNDERLINE.
*
     IF DATA-AREA(DATA-INDEX) = SPACE
         MOVE '_' TO DATA-AREA(DATA-INDEX).
```

Figure D-6   The ULPAD program

Index

CICS for the COBOL Programmer

Part 2: An Advanced Course / Second Edition   **Doug Lowe**

This book takes up where *CICS, Part 1* leaves off. It covers all the advanced CICS features you'll use regularly, though you won't need all of them for every program. You'll learn about:

- browse commands
- temporary storage
- transient data
- data tables (including the shared data table feature of CICS 3.3)
- DB2 and DL/I processing considerations
- distributed processing features

- interval control commands
- BMS page building
- and more!

In addition, *Part 2* teaches you which features do similar things and when to use each one. So you won't just learn how to code new functions...you'll also learn how to choose the best CICS solution for each programming problem you face.

CICS, Part 2, 12 chapters, 352 pages, **$36.50**
ISBN 0-911625-67-4

The CICS Programmer's Desk Reference

Second Edition   **Doug Lowe**

Ever feel buried by IBM manuals?

It seems like you need stacks of them, close at hand, if you want to be an effective CICS programmer. Because frankly, there's just too much you have to know to do your job well; you can't keep it all in your head.

That's why Doug Lowe decided to write *The CICS Programmer's Desk Reference*. In it, he's collected all the information you need to have at your fingertips, and organized it into 12 sections that make it easy for you to find what you're looking for. So there are sections on:

- BMS macro instructions—their formats (with an explanation of each parameter) and coding examples
- CICS commands—their syntax (with an explanation of each parameter), coding examples, and suggestions on how and when to use each one most effectively

- MVS and DOS/VSE JCL for CICS applications
- AMS commands for handling VSAM files
- details for MVS users on how to use ISPF
- complete model programs, including specs, design, and code
- a summary of CICS program design techniques that lead to simple, maintainable, and efficient programs
- guidelines for testing and debugging CICS applications
- and more!

So clear the IBM manuals off your terminal table. Let the *Desk Reference* be your everyday guide to CICS instead.

CICS Desk Reference, 12 sections, 507 pages, **$42.50**
ISBN 0-911625-68-2

IMS for the COBOL Programmer

Part 1: DL/I Data Base Processing   **Steve Eckols**

This how-to book will have you writing batch DL/I programs in a minimum of time—whether you're working on a VSE or an MVS system. But it doesn't neglect the conceptual background you must have to create programs that work. So you'll learn:

- what a DL/I data base is and how its data elements are organized into a hierarchical structure

- the COBOL elements for creating, accessing, and updating DL/I data bases...including logical data bases and data bases with secondary indexing

- how to use DL/I recovery and restart features

- the basic DL/I considerations for coding interactive programs using IMS/DC or CICS

- how data bases with the 4 common types of DL/I data base organizations are stored (this material will help you program more logically and efficiently for the type of data base you're using)

- and more!

7 complete COBOL programs show you how to process DL/I data bases in various ways. Use them as models for production work in your shop, and you'll save hours of development time.

IMS, Part 1, 16 chapters, 333 pages, **$36.50**
ISBN 0-911625-29-1

IMS for the COBOL Programmer

Part 2: Data Communications and Message Format Service   **Steve Eckols**

The second part of *IMS for the COBOL Programmer* is for MVS programmers only. It teaches how to develop online programs that access IMS data bases and run under the data communications (DC) component of IMS. So you'll learn:

- why you code message processing programs (MPPs) the way you do (DC programs are called MPPs because they process messages sent from and to user terminals)

- what COBOL elements you use for MPPs

- how to use Message Format Service (MFS), a facility for formatting complex terminal displays so you can enhance the look and operation of your DC programs

- how to develop applications that use more than one screen format or that use physical and logical paging

- how to develop batch message processing (BMP) programs to update IMS data bases in batch even while they're being used by other programs

- how to use Batch Terminal Simulator (BTS) to test DC applications using IMS resources, but without disrupting the everyday IMS processing that's going on

- and more!

8 complete programs—including MFS format sets, program design, and COBOL code—show you how to handle various DC and MFS applications. Use them as models to save yourself hours of coding and debugging.

IMS, Part 2, 16 chapters, 398 pages, **$36.50**
ISBN 0-911625-30-5

VS COBOL II: A Guide for Programmers and Managers

Second Edition   **Anne Prince**

This book builds on your COBOL knowledge to quickly teach you everything you need to know about VS COBOL II, the IBM 1985 COBOL compiler for MVS shops: how to code the language elements that are new in the compiler (and what language elements you can't use any more)...CICS considerations...how to use the debugger...how the compiler's features can make your programs compile and run more efficiently...plus, guidelines for converting to VS COBOL II (that includes coverage of the conversion aids IBM supplies).

So if you're in a shop that's already converted to VS COBOL II, you'll learn how to benefit from the language elements and features the compiler has to offer. If you aren't yet working in VS COBOL II, you'll learn how to write programs now that will be easy to convert later on. And if you're a manager, you'll get some practical ideas on when to convert and how to do it as painlessly as possible.

VS COBOL II, 7 chapters, 271 pages, **$27.50**
ISBN 0-911625-54-2

Structured ANS COBOL

A 2-part course in 1974 and 1985 ANS COBOL   **Mike Murach and Paul Noll**

This 2-part course teaches you how to use standard COBOL the way the top professionals do.

Part 1: A Course for Novices teaches people with no programming experience how to design and code COBOL programs that prepare reports. Because report programs often call subprograms, use COPY members, handle one-level tables, and read indexed files, it covers these subjects too. But the real emphasis in this book is on the structure and logic of report programs, because most beginning programmers have more trouble with structure and logic than they do with COBOL itself.

Part 2: An Advanced Course also emphasizes program structure and logic, focusing on edit, update, and maintenance programs. But beyond that, it's a

complete guide to the language elements that all COBOL programmers should know how to use (though many don't). So it covers: sequential, indexed, and relative file handling...alternate indexing and dynamic processing...internal sorts and merges...the COPY library...subprograms...multi-level table handling using indexes as well as subscripts...character manipulation...and more! In fact, no matter how much COBOL experience you've had, you'll value *Part 2* as a handy reference to all the COBOL elements you'll ever want to use.

COBOL, Part 1, 13 chapters, 438 pages, **$32.50**
ISBN 0-911625-37-2

COBOL, Part 2, 12 chapters, 498 pages, **$32.50**
ISBN 0-911625-38-0

Structured COBOL Methods

Practical guidelines and model programs   **Paul Noll**

Unlike other books with "structured" in the title, this little book presents ideas on COBOL program development that are simple, cost-effective, time-tested, and yet revolutionary in many shops. It doesn't teach the COBOL language itself; instead, it teaches you how to design, code, and test your COBOL programs so they're easier to debug, document, and maintain.

Just open up to any page, take a look at the concepts or the sample design and code, and picture what a difference these methods can make in the program you're working on right now. Then, go to work and start experimenting. You'll be delighted at the results!

Structured COBOL Methods, 6 chapters + 5 model programs, 208 pages, **$25.00**
ISBN 0-911625-94-1

VSAM

Access Method Services and Application Programming **Doug Lowe**

As its title suggests, *VSAM: Access Method Services and Application Programming* has two main purposes: (1) to teach you how to use the Access Method Services (AMS) utility to define and manipulate VSAM files; and (2) to teach you how to process VSAM files using various programming languages. To be specific, you'll learn:

• how VSAM data sets and catalogs are organized and used

• how to use AMS commands to define VSAM catalogs, space, clusters, alternate indexes, and paths

• how to set AMS performance options so you make the best possible use of your system's resources

• what recovery and security considerations are important when you use AMS

• how to code MVS and DOS/VSE JCL for VSAM files, and how to allocate VSAM files under TSO and VM/CMS

• how to process VSAM files in COBOL, CICS, and assembler language

You'll find the answers to questions like these

• How much primary and secondary space should I allocate to my VSAM files?

• What's an appropriate free space allocation for a KSDS?

• What's the best control interval size for VSAM files that are accessed both sequentially and directly?

• Do I always need to use VERIFY to check the integrity of my files?

• What's the difference between regular VSAM catalogs and the ICF catalog structure?

• When should I...and shouldn't I...use the IMBED and REPLICATE options to improve performance?

• It's easy to find out how many records are in a file's index component. But how do I find out how many of those records are in the sequence set?

• How do I determine the best buffer allocation for my files?

• What's the best way to back up my VSAM files— REPRO, EXPORT, or something else?

So why wait any longer to sharpen your VSAM skills? Get your copy of *VSAM: AMS and Application Programming* TODAY!

VSAM: AMS & Application Programming,
12 chapters, 260 pages, **$27.50**
ISBN 0-911625-33-X

VSAM for the COBOL Programmer

Second Edition **Doug Lowe**

If you're looking for a no-frills approach to VSAM that teaches you only what you need to know to code COBOL programs, this is the book for you. You'll learn: the meanings of the critical terms and concepts that apply to VSAM files; the COBOL elements for handling VSAM files; how to handle alternate indexes and dynamic access; why error processing is a must; how to use the Access Method Services utility (AMS) to create,

print, copy, and rename VSAM files; how to code the MVS and VSE JCL to run programs that use VSAM files; and how your COBOL code is affected if you're working under VS COBOL II.

VSAM for COBOL, 6 chapters, 187 pages, **$22.50**
ISBN 0-911625-45-3

MVS TSO

Part 1: Concepts and ISPF   **Doug Lowe**

Now you can quickly master ISPF with this practical book.

Chapter 1 introduces you to MVS (both MVS/XA and MVS/ESA)...good background no matter how much MVS experience you've had. It also shows you how TSO/ISPF relates to MVS, so you'll understand how to use ISPF to control the operating system functions.

The remaining 7 chapters teach you all the specifics of using ISPF for everyday programming tasks. You'll learn how to:

- edit and browse data sets
- use the ISPF utilities to manage your data sets and libraries
- compile, link, and execute programs interactively

- use the VS COBOL II or OS COBOL interactive debugger
- process batch jobs in a background region
- manage your background jobs more easily using the Spool Display & Search Facility (SDSF)
- use member parts lists to track the use of subprograms and COPY members within program libraries
- use two library management systems that support hierarchical libraries—the Library Management Facility (LMF) and the Software Configuration and Library Manager (SCLM)
- and more!

MVS TSO, Part 1, 8 chapters, 467 pages, **$36.50**
ISBN 0-911625-56-9

MVS TSO

Part 2: Commands and Procedures (CLIST and REXX)   **Doug Lowe**

If you're ready to expand your skills beyond ISPF and become a TSO user who can write complex CLIST and REXX procedures with ease, this is the book for you. It starts by teaching you how to use TSO commands for common programming tasks like managing data sets and libraries, running programs in foreground mode, and submitting jobs for background execution. Then, it

shows you how to combine those commands into CLIST or REXX procedures for the jobs you do most often...including procedures that you can use as edit macros under the ISPF editor and procedures that use ISPF dialog functions to display full-screen panels.

MVS TSO, Part 2, 10 chapters, 450 pages, **$36.50**
ISBN 0-911625-57-7

OS Utilities

                                                            Doug Lowe

This short book quickly teaches you how to use OS utility programs to: create, print, rename, reformat, scratch, sort, and merge various types of data sets...create large test files with just a few statements... use the AMS utility for VSAM files...and more!

If you've ever written a program in a high-level language because you couldn't figure out how to use the utility for that function, this is the book for you.

Covers: IEBGENER, IEBPTPCH, IEBISAM, IEBCOPY, IEBUPDTE, IEBDG, IEBCOMPR, IEHLIST, IEHMOVE, IEHPROGM, IEFBR14, Sort/Merge, AMS

Note: All these utilities except IEBISAM and IEFBR14 are also covered briefly in our *MVS JCL* book.

OS Utilities, 14 chapters, 185 pages, **$17.50**
ISBN 0-911625-11-9

 Call toll-free 1-800-221-5528 • Weekdays, 8-5 Pacific Time • Fax 1-209-275-9035

MVS JCL

MVS/ESA • MVS/XA • MVS/370   **Doug Lowe**

Anyone who's worked in an MVS shop knows that JCL is tough to master. You learn enough to get by...but then you stick to that. It's just too frustrating to try to put together a job using the IBM manuals. And too time-consuming to keep asking your co-workers for help...especially since they're often limping along with the JCL they know, too.

That's why you need a copy of *MVS JCL*. It zeroes in on the JCL you need for everyday jobs...so you can learn to code significant job streams in a hurry.

You'll learn how to compile, link-edit, load, and execute programs. Process all types of data sets. Code JES2/JES3 control statements to manage job and program execution, data set allocation, and SYSOUT processing. Create and use JCL procedures. Execute general-purpose utility programs. And much more.

But that's not all this book does. Beyond teaching you JCL, it explains the basics of how MVS works so you can apply that understanding as you code JCL. You'll learn about the unique interrelationship between virtual storage and multiprogramming under MVS. You'll learn about data management: what data sets are and how data sets, volumes, and units are allocated. You'll learn about job management, including the crucial role played by JES2/JES3 as MVS processes jobs. And you'll learn about the components of a complete MVS system, including the role of system generation and initialization in tying the components together. That's the kind of perspective that's missing in other books and courses about MVS, even though it's background you must have if you want to bring MVS under your control.

MVS JCL, 17 chapters, 496 pages, **$42.50**
ISBN 0-911625-85-2

DOS/VSE JCL

Second Edition   **Steve Eckols**

The job control language for a DOS/VSE system can be overwhelming. There are more parameters than you would ever want to know about. And those parameters let you do more things than you would ever want to do. Of course, all those parameters are described in the IBM manuals...somewhere. But who has time to wade through pages and pages of details that don't seem to apply to your situation (although you can't ever be sure because the manuals are so confusing).

Certainly *you* don't. That's why you need *DOS/VSE JCL*. It doesn't try to teach every nuance of every parameter. Instead, it teaches you how to code the JCL for the applications that occur every day in a VSE shop. You'll learn how to manage job and program execution, how to identify the files a program needs to use, and how to use cataloged procedures. You'll learn how to code POWER JECL statements to manage job scheduling and output processing and how to use ICCF to manage POWER job processing. You'll learn how to process tape and DASD files. And you'll learn how to use language translators and the linkage-editor, maintain VSE libraries, and use three utility programs: sort/merge, DITTO, and AMS.

Whether you're a novice or an expert, this book will help you use your DOS/VSE system more effectively. If you're new to VSE, this book will get you started right, giving you the confidence you need to take charge of your system. If you're an experienced VSE user, this book will help you understand *why* you've been doing what you've been doing so you can do it better in the future.

DOS/VSE JCL, 18 chapters, 448 pages, **$34.50**
ISBN 0-911625-50-X

 Call toll-free 1-800-221-5528 • Weekdays, 8-5 Pacific Time • Fax: 1-209-275-9035

Comment Form

Your opinions count

If you have any comments, criticisms, or suggestions for us, I'm eager to hear from you. Your opinions today will affect our products of tomorrow. And if you find any errors in this book, typographical or otherwise, please point them out so we can correct them in the next printing.

Thanks for your help.

Mike Murach

Book title: CICS for the COBOL Programmer, Part 1 (Second Edition)

Dear Mike: _____

_____

_____

_____

_____

_____

_____

_____

_____

_____

_____

_____

_____

_____

_____

_____

_____

_____

Name _____

Company (if company address) _____

Address _____

City, State, Zip _____

Fold where indicated and tape closed.

No postage needed if mailed in the U.S.

NO POSTAGE
NECESSARY
IF MAILED
IN THE
UNITED STATES

BUSINESS REPLY MAIL

FIRST-CLASS MAIL   PERMIT NO. 3063   FRESNO, CA

POSTAGE WILL BE PAID BY ADDRESSEE

Mike Murach & Associates, Inc.

2560 W SHAW LN STE 101
FRESNO CA 93711-9866

Order Form

Our Unlimited Guarantee

To our customers who order directly from us: You must be satisfied. Our books must work for you, or you can send them back for a full refund...no questions asked.

Name & Title _____

Company (if company address) _____

Street Address _____

City, State, Zip _____

Phone number (including area code) _____

Fax number (if you fax your order to us) _____

Qty	Product code and title	*Price
CICS		
___ CC1R	CICS for the COBOL Programmer Part 1 (Second Edition)	$36.50
___ CC2R	CICS for the COBOL Programmer Part 2 (Second Edition)	36.50
___ CRFR	The CICS Programmer's Desk Reference (Second Edition)	42.50
VSAM		
___ VSMX	VSAM: Access Method Services and Application Programming	$27.50
___ VSMR	VSAM for the COBOL Programmer (Second Edition)	22.50
MVS		
___ MJLR	MVS JCL (Second Edition)	$42.50
___ TSO1	MVS TSO, Part 1: Concepts and ISPF	36.50
___ TSO2	MVS TSO, Part 2: Commands and Procedures (CLIST and REXX)	36.50
___ MBAL	MVS Assembler Language	36.50
___ OSUT	OS Utilities	17.50

Qty	Product code and title	*Price
Data Base		
___ DB21	DB2 for the COBOL Programmer Part 1: An Introductory Course	$36.50
___ DB22	DB2 for the COBOL Programmer Part 2: An Advanced Course	36.50
___ IMS1	IMS for the COBOL Programmer Part 1: DL/I Data Base Processing	36.50
___ IMS2	IMS for the COBOL Programmer Part 2: Data Communications and MFS	36.50
COBOL		
___ SCMD	Structured COBOL Methods	$25.00
___ VC2R	VS COBOL II (Second Edition)	27.50
___ SC1R	Structured ANS COBOL, Part 1	32.50
___ SC2R	Structured ANS COBOL, Part 2	32.50
DOS/VSE		
___ VJLR	DOS/VSE JCL (Second Edition)	$34.50
___ ICCF	DOS/VSE ICCF	31.00
___ VBAL	DOS/VSE Assembler Language	36.50

❑ Bill my company for the books plus UPS shipping and handling (and sales tax within California).
P.O.# _____

❑ I want to **SAVE 10%** by paying in advance. Charge to my
___Visa ___MasterCard ___American Express:

Card number _____

Valid thru (mo/yr) _____

Cardowner's signature _____

❑ I want to **SAVE 10% plus shipping and handling.** Here's my check or money order for the books minus 10% ($_____). California residents, please add sales tax to your total. (Offer valid in U.S.)

***Prices are subject to change. Please call for current prices.**

To order now,

Call toll-free 1-800-221-5528
(Weekdays, 8 am to 5 pm Pacific Time)

or Fax us at: 1-209-440-0963

Mike Murach & Associates, Inc.
2560 West Shaw Lane, Suite 101
Fresno, California 93711-2765
(209) 440-9071

BUSINESS REPLY MAIL

FIRST-CLASS MAIL   PERMIT NO. 3063   FRESNO, CA

POSTAGE WILL BE PAID BY ADDRESSEE

Mike Murach & Associates, Inc.

2560 W SHAW LN STE 101
FRESNO CA 93711-9866

Order Form

Our Unlimited Guarantee

To our customers who order directly from us: You must be satisfied. Our books must work for you, or you can send them back for a full refund...no questions asked.

Name & Title _____

Company (if company address) _____

Street Address _____

City, State, Zip _____

Phone number (including area code) _____

Fax number (if you fax your order to us) _____

Qty	Product code and title	*Price
CICS		
___ CC1R	CICS for the COBOL Programmer Part 1 (Second Edition)	$36.50
___ CC2R	CICS for the COBOL Programmer Part 2 (Second Edition)	36.50
___ CRFR	The CICS Programmer's Desk Reference (Second Edition)	42.50
VSAM		
___ VSMX	VSAM: Access Method Services and Application Programming	$27.50
___ VSMR	VSAM for the COBOL Programmer (Second Edition)	22.50
MVS		
___ MJLR	MVS JCL (Second Edition)	$42.50
___ TSO1	MVS TSO, Part 1: Concepts and ISPF	36.50
___ TSO2	MVS TSO, Part 2: Commands and Procedures (CLIST and REXX)	36.50
___ MBAL	MVS Assembler Language	36.50
___ OSUT	OS Utilities	17.50

Qty	Product code and title	*Price
Data Base		
___ DB21	DB2 for the COBOL Programmer Part 1: An Introductory Course	$36.50
___ DB22	DB2 for the COBOL Programmer Part 2: An Advanced Course	36.50
___ IMS1	IMS for the COBOL Programmer Part 1: DL/I Data Base Processing	36.50
___ IMS2	IMS for the COBOL Programmer Part 2: Data Communications and MFS	36.50
COBOL		
___ SCMD	Structured COBOL Methods	$25.00
___ VC2R	VS COBOL II (Second Edition)	27.50
___ SC1R	Structured ANS COBOL, Part 1	32.50
___ SC2R	Structured ANS COBOL, Part 2	32.50
DOS/VSE		
___ VJLR	DOS/VSE JCL (Second Edition)	$34.50
___ ICCF	DOS/VSE ICCF	31.00
___ VBAL	DOS/VSE Assembler Language	36.50

☐ Bill my company for the books plus UPS shipping and handling (and sales tax within California).
P.O.# _____

☐ I want to **SAVE 10%** by paying in advance. Charge to my
___Visa ___MasterCard ___American Express:

Card number _____

Valid thru (mo/yr) _____

Cardowner's signature _____

☐ I want to **SAVE 10% plus shipping and handling.**
Here's my check or money order for the books minus 10% ($_____). California residents, please add sales tax to your total. (Offer valid in U.S.)

*Prices are subject to change. Please call for current prices.

To order now,

Call toll-free 1-800-221-5528
(Weekdays, 8 am to 5 pm Pacific Time)

or Fax us at: 1-209-440-0963

Mike Murach & Associates, Inc.
2560 West Shaw Lane, Suite 101
Fresno, California 93711-2765
(209) 440-9071

NO POSTAGE
NECESSARY
IF MAILED
IN THE
UNITED STATES

BUSINESS REPLY MAIL

FIRST-CLASS MAIL   PERMIT NO. 3063   FRESNO, CA

POSTAGE WILL BE PAID BY ADDRESSEE

Mike Murach & Associates, Inc.

2560 W SHAW LN STE 101
FRESNO CA 93711-9866

Order Form

Our Unlimited Guarantee

To our customers who order directly from us: You must be satisfied. Our books must work for you, or you can send them back for a full refund...no questions asked.

Name & Title _____

Company (if company address) _____

Street Address _____

City, State, Zip _____

Phone number (including area code) _____

Fax number (if you fax your order to us) _____

Qty	Product code and title	*Price
CICS		
___ CC1R	CICS for the COBOL Programmer Part 1 (Second Edition)	$36.50
___ CC2R	CICS for the COBOL Programmer Part 2 (Second Edition)	36.50
___ CRFR	The CICS Programmer's Desk Reference (Second Edition)	42.50
VSAM		
___ VSMX	VSAM: Access Method Services and Application Programming	$27.50
___ VSMR	VSAM for the COBOL Programmer (Second Edition)	22.50
MVS		
___ MJLR	MVS JCL (Second Edition)	$42.50
___ TSO1	MVS TSO, Part 1: Concepts and ISPF	36.50
___ TSO2	MVS TSO, Part 2: Commands and Procedures (CLIST and REXX)	36.50
___ MBAL	MVS Assembler Language	36.50
___ OSUT	OS Utilities	17.50

Qty	Product code and title	*Price
Data Base		
___ DB21	DB2 for the COBOL Programmer Part 1: An Introductory Course	$36.50
___ DB22	DB2 for the COBOL Programmer Part 2: An Advanced Course	36.50
___ IMS1	IMS for the COBOL Programmer Part 1: DL/I Data Base Processing	36.50
___ IMS2	IMS for the COBOL Programmer Part 2: Data Communications and MFS	36.50
COBOL		
___ SCMD	Structured COBOL Methods	$25.00
___ VC2R	VS COBOL II (Second Edition)	27.50
___ SC1R	Structured ANS COBOL, Part 1	32.50
___ SC2R	Structured ANS COBOL, Part 2	32.50
DOS/VSE		
___ VJLR	DOS/VSE JCL (Second Edition)	$34.50
___ ICCF	DOS/VSE ICCF	31.00
___ VBAL	DOS/VSE Assembler Language	36.50

❑ Bill my company for the books plus UPS shipping and handling (and sales tax within California).
P.O.# _____

❑ I want to **SAVE 10%** by paying in advance. Charge to my
___Visa ___MasterCard ___American Express:

Card number _____

Valid thru (mo/yr) _____

Cardowner's signature _____

❑ I want to **SAVE 10% plus shipping and handling.**
Here's my check or money order for the books minus 10% ($_____). California residents, please add sales tax to your total. (Offer valid in U.S.)

*Prices are subject to change. Please call for current prices.

To order now,

Call toll-free 1-800-221-5528
(Weekdays, 8 am to 5 pm Pacific Time)

or Fax us at: 1-209-440-0963

Mike Murach & Associates, Inc.
2560 West Shaw Lane, Suite 101
Fresno, California 93711-2765
(209) 440-9071

BUSINESS REPLY MAIL

FIRST-CLASS MAIL   PERMIT NO. 3063   FRESNO, CA

POSTAGE WILL BE PAID BY ADDRESSEE

Mike Murach & Associates, Inc.

2560 W SHAW LN STE 101
FRESNO CA 93711-9866